About the author

Mick Collins has had an interesting career, including working as a builder's labourer, infantryman, heavy goods truck driver, and living in a Buddhist Monastery. He currently works as a Lecturer in Occupational Therapy and is a Director of Admissions within the Faculty of Medicine and Health Sciences, University of East Anglia, Norwich, UK. Mick has also worked as a therapist in an acute mental health setting and a specialist psychological therapies team. He incorporated humanistic and transpersonal methods into his therapeutic practice. A qualified Holistic Life Coach, Mick works with individuals, groups and organisations to facilitate transpersonal awareness, growth and transformation.

Mick's personal transformative journey includes working through an experience known as *spiritual emergency*. This deep encounter eventually inspired his academic publications on the subject of spirituality and his doctoral thesis. His Ph.D. explored the relationship between individual recoveries from spiritual crises, through new ways of doing, knowing and being, and how these may inform collective transformation. Mick is using his knowledge and experience to explore how humanity can face up to the impact of a burgeoning global crisis, particularly new vistas of awareness and action for the co-creation of an improved future. He lives in Norwich, Norfolk, UK with his wife Hannah. Mick's web address is: www.epiczoetic.co.uk

This book is a treasure to be returned to again and again to gather insight, wisdom and inspiration for one's own life journey and to understand and engage with the radical and painful process of transformation that is affecting all our lives. Beautifully and clearly written, with helpful questions to ask oneself at the end of each chapter, it draws on the insights of an extensive library of authors to emphasise and clarify the unfolding and connected themes addressed. However, endorsing them all is the author's own moving story of his awakening and transformative life experience.

A profound, enlightening and healing book that challenges us to wake up from our technological trance, address the global predicament we have created and discover the unlived potential of our long-neglected soul. If we were able to accomplish this, we would not only embark on an epic mythic journey, dying to our old ways of doing, being and knowing, but initiate a spiritual renaissance which would integrate insight with informed and effective action in the world. A brilliant, inspirational and moving manual for self-transformation and deeper communion with our long-suffering planet.

Anne Baring
Author of *The Dream of the Cosmos: a Quest for the Soul*

Dr Mick Collins has crafted a thought provoking, profound look at the nature of personal and global Spiritual Emergency, and how meaningful occupation (doing), use of archetypes, self-reflection, and dream work can help us to heal ourselves and the planet holistically. I highly recommend this book for physical health and mental health professionals, spiritual seekers, and activists wishing to make a positive difference in the trajectory of the human race and planet Earth.

Dr Emily Schulz OTR/L, CFLE
Occupational Therapist and Associate Professor
at A.T. Still University-Arizona School of Health Sciences
Author of articles on spirituality and health

The Unselfish Spirit *is a tour de force. The book addresses the multiple crises of our time with a holistic perspective. The environmental emergency is in fact a spiritual emergency. To build a sustainable world we need a spiritual awakening. Mick Collins makes this case with courage and clarity, with vigour and vision. The book is an indispensable tool to achieve a better future for all.*

Satish Kumar
Editor-in-Chief, *Resurgence & Ecologist*

Mick Collins is seeking a larger self awareness so that both individual spirituality and day-to-day behaviour resonate with resilience and empathy. This is not a text about the self. It is a text about planetary actuality and communal realisation.

Tim O'Riordan, OBE, FBA
Emeritus Professor, School of Environmental Sciences,
University of East Anglia, Norwich

This is a gem of a book, a book that should be read slowly and deeply. Mick Collins encourages us to both deepen our being but to also deepen our doing. He invites us into a more ecological, sacred and numinous relationship with the whole of creation. This book is a challenging, timely and sometimes disturbing read – with a surprising thread of optimism running through. If you want to glimpse the best possible future for humankind then read this book.

Professor William West
Reader in Counselling Studies, University of Manchester
Author of *Exploring Therapy, Spirituality and Healing*

Today's post-secular societies and global emergencies provide both a real opportunity and a crucial need for a new, transformative spiritual narrative. Drawing from a rich seam of human wisdom, including mysticism, depth psychology, biological sciences, and archaeology, as well as from autobiographical insights, Mick Collins offers a vital spirituality for today's world, based not just in contemplation, but in realisable action. This is a wonderful book which offers the reader wisdom and practical steps for action in this brave new world.

Dr Jacqueline Watson
Director of the Centre for Spirituality and
Religion in Education, University of East Anglia
Author of *Global Perspectives on Spirituality and Education*

This book shows us how the pathway to a sustainable future begins right now with a deep reappraisal of the quality of consciousness and the sense of the sacred that we bring to our everyday doings at work and at home. It provides a passionate re-visioning of how addressing the damaging material impacts of our industrial-consumer society is ultimately a collective voyage of discovery that calls upon each one of us to re-awaken to our common heritage as the story of the human race.

Dr Alex Haxeltine
Senior Researcher, School of Environmental Science, University of East Anglia

The future of living sustainably in the world is dependent on developing awareness of our interconnectedness and transformative potential. Mick Collins provides a novel response to our planetary crisis by examining the human potential embedded within spiritual experience and emergence. Building on the work of scientists, spiritual teachers, and psychological practitioners in the fields of Jungian, Humanistic, Transpersonal, and Process Oriented Psychology, his book provides an inspirational guide for discovering the creative and spiritual potential within everyday life and the subsequent movement toward a more co-creative and sustainable world.

Dr Amy Mindell
Process Oriented Psychologist
Author of *Metaskills: The Spiritual Art of Therapy*

This is the book I wish I had with me when teaching wannabe Members of the Royal College of Psychiatrists. It is a delight to read a cohesive guide, beginning with an occupational vision for a transpersonal future and ending with co-creating an improved future. Opening the Channels between Head and Heart is a lifetime's work. Working through this guide book will shine a light. This is a field book to treasure.

Dr William Hughes
Fellow Royal College of Psychiatrists, MBPF
Analytical Psychologist, Training Analyst Guild of Analytical Psychology

The Unselfish Spirit

Human Evolution
in a Time of Global Crisis

Mick Collins Ph.D.

Permanent
Publications

Published by
Permanent Publications
Hyden House Ltd
The Sustainability Centre
East Meon
Hampshire GU32 1HR
United Kingdom
Tel: 0844 846 846 4824 (local rate UK only)
         or +44 (0)1730 823 311
Fax: 01730 823 322
Email: enquiries@permaculture.co.uk
Web: www.permanentpublications.co.uk

Distributed in the USA by
Chelsea Green Publishing Company, PO Box 428, White River Junction, VT 05001
www.chelseagreen.com

Front cover painting, 'Earth Dream' by Mick Collins, 1987

Front cover model's face and digital enhancement by Andi Sapey, www.andisapey.co.uk

'Preparing humanity for a damaged planet' © Tim O'Riordan, 2014

Designed by Two Plus George Limited, wwwTwoPlusGeorge.co.uk

Index by Amit Prasad, 009amit@gmail.com

Printed in the UK by Cambrian Printers, Aberystwyth

All paper from FSC certified mixed sources

The Forest Stewardship Council (FSC) is a non-profit
international organisation established to promote the responsible
management of the world's forests. Products carrying the FSC
label are independently certified to assure consumers that they
come from forests that are managed to meet the social, economic
and ecological needs of present and future generations.

British Library Cataloguing-in-Publication Data
A catalogue record for this book is available from the British Library

ISBN 978 1 85623 193 0

Author's Note

The information outlined in this book is educational in nature. The exercises at the end of each chapter are experiential, and should not be used or relied upon as means of self-healing. Professional advice or support should be sought from a qualified health practitioner for any medical or mental health matters. In addition, the illustrative stories conveyed throughout the book are real-life examples of people's experiences of change and transformation. These vignettes do not predict or offer any warranty or guarantee of the reader's experience. The author and publisher accept no responsibility or liability for the use or misuse of the information in this book.

Beauty in the natural world can lift our spirits and nourish our souls.
Without it we are lost and destitute.

Dedication

This book is dedicated to my wife Hannah, and daughter, Rosie.

The book is also dedicated to planet Earth and the
numinous spirit that helps us to see her glory.

The following chapters are written in the hope that humanity
can find ways to live more deeply, both inwardly and
outwardly to actualise our full human potential. If we make
the effort to explore how we are all interconnected, we are
more than capable of co-creating an improved future for all,
and for future generations.

Like day follows night, a new sense of action and participation can follow the dawning of our transpersonal awareness.

Contents

We live in a cosmos of interconnections.
Where would we be without the world and each other?

Acknowledgements

There are many people I would like to acknowledge for their inspiration in my life, which in various ways strengthened my resolve to write this book. First, I would like to say a special thank you to Arvind Patel, who in 1986 was a life-line. He had the wisdom to realise that I was going through a spiritual emergency and encouraged me to stay with the process. I am indebted to him. I would like to express my gratitude to all the people who contributed their stories to the book. These accounts bring the theories alive in creative ways. Sincere thanks go to Dr Campbell Purton, Dr Judy Moore, Dr William West and Dr Emily Schulz for encouraging me to write this book. I would also like to acknowledge Professor Fiona Poland for her inspiration, encouragement and always affirming a 'can-do' approach to any task or challenge. I would like to thank Dr Rod Lambert for reviewing the introduction and chapter one of the book and for providing thoughtful comments on the text, with particular reference to the section on doing, biology and evolution. Big thanks go to Helen Wells, Dr Alex Haxeltine and Dr William Hughes for our many thought-provoking and heart-warming conversations over the years. Sincere thanks to Tim O'Riordan, Emeritus Professor, School of Environmental Science, University of East Anglia, who offered very helpful advice on content and style after reading the penultimate draft of the book, as well as writing the Preface.

The evolution and development of my ideas have been greatly influenced by the work of Professor Carl Gustav Jung, Dr Stanislav Grof, and Drs Arnold and Amy Mindell (the co-founders of process-oriented psychology, or process work). Arny and Amy (along with other trainers and friends in the process work community) taught me that the path of individuation is a task to take seriously and also to enjoy. The exercises throughout this book are inspired by my training in process-oriented psychology. In addition, the use of terms such as *consensus* and *non-consensus reality*, *growing edge*, and *channels* are used in accordance with the work of Arny Mindell. The development of my work has been greatly influenced by many occupational scientists; particularly Professor Elizabeth Yerxa, Professor Ann A. Wilcock and Dr Loretta do Rozario. Sincere thanks also go to transpersonal psychotherapist Richard Austin and process-oriented psychologist Mark O'Connell for inspiring me all those years ago – in different ways – to consider the important links between ecology and humanity. I would like to say what a pleasure and privilege it has been engaging with students and colleagues in the Faculty of Medicine and Health Sciences, University of

East Anglia, Norwich on the subject of spirituality. Also, collaborations with colleagues in the Centre for Spirituality and Religion, University of East Anglia have resulted in the development of interdisciplinary approaches that have worked to promote the integration of spirituality into professional practice.

A special thank you goes to Bernie Sheehan, who has worked as an editorial consultant on my doctoral thesis and the original drafts of this book. I can honestly say that my writing has improved because of her editorial support. Her genuine interest in the subject has enabled me to tell the story in the following chapters to the best of my ability. Sincere thanks to Maddy and Tim Harland, as well as Peter Ellington and the team at Permanent Publications, for their creative spirit in bringing this book into the world. It pleases me no end that this book has been published by a team who are sensitive to the connections between ecology and spirituality. My gratitude also goes to all the publishing organisations that gave me permission to adapt the content of my journal articles for this book. Many thanks, too, to Marion Catlin at 'Shift Norwich' for her generous support. I would also like to acknowledge Anne Francis of Carnival Coaching for our open and creative coaching sessions, where we explored what this book means to my evolving journey in the world. A very special mention goes to my dear friend Russ Thornton from Waiheke Island, Auckland, New Zealand for being an awesome example of someone who puts spirituality into action. Over the last four decades Russ has been a deep inspiration to me, and he always makes me smile.

I would like to acknowledge deep and heartfelt thanks to my wife, Hannah, who despite having radical surgery, chemotherapy and radiotherapy during the time that I was writing this book, always encouraged me to keep writing it. Not only did Hannah want to hear how the ideas were evolving, she often provided insights and observations that added something new to what I was writing. I am a firm believer that people grow and develop in loving environments, and Hannah's presence in my life is love personified. Also, deep thanks to all our family and friends for their love and support during Hannah's recovery.

Finally, and hopefully with some humility, I would like to acknowledge the spirit. Writing this book has been a creative venture, and there have been count-less times when the right people, conversations, books or articles have arrived, in meaningful and coincidental ways. This has been particularly evident in the way people's stories have manifested as synchronicities and found their way into the book. There have been other times when during the writing process I have been touched by a moment of grace or a feeling of connection. These have often led to deep reflections and a felt presence that I can only describe as spiritual inspiration.

We are living in a time of emergence and renewal.
The greatest task facing humanity today is to bring forth healing relationships
in all facets of our daily lives, including self, other and the planet.

PREFACE

Preparing humanity for a damaged planet

We live in a conundrum. Humans occupy a planet whose resilience over billions of years is being tested. The planet, of course, will accommodate and live on, as it had done at least six times before. The geological and biological record contains evidence of massive convulsions in the temperature and chemical compositions of seas and air which caused large scale species die-offs in relatively short periods of time.[1] The loser will be us humans. The conundrum is that humans have the capacity to remove the liveability of at least half of their future population. They also have the capacity not to do so. The crisis of the Anthropocene, this new era of human dominance on planetary life support processes, is a moral crisis. It is not a crisis of resource scarcity. Nor is it a crisis of ecosystems damage and debilitation. It is a crisis of greed, selfishness, short-term gratification and a failure to learn from the most dispossessed, those who are best adapted to survive. Sustainability is examining our humanness, the subject of this impassioned book.

The emerging debate lies over how to handle planetary boundaries.[2] The line here is that there is a diminishing arena of liveability caused by the overrunning of planetary chemically and ecologically based life support functions. These boundaries resemble the inside of a shark's mouth. The roof of the mouth is the limit of planetary tolerance. The top teeth are the very different tolerances across the globe of these boundaries. For example while cod numbers are improving in the North Sea due to conservation and under-fishing, hake and whiting stocks, for the time being, are high. The Amazon rainforest is subject to drying out which could just possibly tip it into savannah (which has been its biome before). But the West African rainforest shows no signs of water stress. Nitrogen cycling throughout the planet takes place nowadays at a scale which is much greater than its 'natural cycle'. This is because nitrogen is artificially created in the manufacture of plastics and chemical fertiliser and then cycled all over the planet through the use and disposal of these products.

But there are plenty of locations where fertiliser use could be more effectively applied (mostly where food production is too limited) just as there are plenty of places where fertiliser is grossly overused. Thus the boundaries are uneven, jagged and dispersed.

The bottom of the mouth is the social dignity of decent living and wellbeing for all human inhabitants. This is the floor of the so-called 'planetary safe operating space' which is left for humanity to use. This floor refers to adequate access to healthy soils' sufficient water and diet, shelter, education, gender and class relations and justice and fairness. Again the base teeth are jagged, for social dignity is by no means evenly spread. The well-heeled and safeguarded minorities are holding onto their advantages of prosperity while many of the coming generation are experiencing increasing hardship. So the floor of the operating space of planet Earth is as jagged as the roof. Yet somehow we have to get to a point where we accommodate to socially and environmentally "just" planetary boundaries (where to complete the metaphor, both the roof and the floor are set in a more even plane and prove to be much more resilient. And we have to do this so that the poor and disadvantaged get a slice of this operating space, while the rich tolerate the redistribution. This is a mighty moral conundrum. We have no governing means and no political leadership capable of delivering such a transformation. Nor, arguably, is there sufficient moral compass inside each of us to permit such a distributional revolution.

What Mick Collins offers in the well-crafted text is the basis for shaping our outlooks and behaviour so that living in this transformational world can be seen as right and even joyous. He examines the fundamentals of human 'being' and 'spirituality' to see how far this can be achieved. He explores the best of Jungian and transpersonal psychology to survey the scope for betterment of the soul. He bravely tackles the subtle topic of inner sensitivity of self and selflessness in order to test for the extension of the ego to the worlds of betterment for future generations. He muses on the meaning of ecological altruism for personal and communal survival. This is a noble process and a courageous challenge for the therapist and the reformer.

This text deals primarily with the self. But the message is for the extension of the self to encompass the whole of lived experience, including the joys and suffering of survival. Mick Collins is seeking a larger self-awareness so that both individual spirituality and day-to-day behaviour resonate with resilience and empathy. This is not a text about the self. It is a text about planetary actuality and communal realisation.

This is a very timely call. We are experiencing the deepest and most prolonged recession of the modern era. The economic slowdown is spreading across the globe. And it is being artificially pumped up by 'false money' opaquely termed 'quantitative easing'. Yet investment funds are shrinking, and unemployment amongst young people in particular is stubbornly high. The future of the next generation of school leavers depends on their acquiring skills over accelerating technology and rapidly changing business management styles which at present few are trained to master. So the prospects for prosperity amongst the majority of the coming generation of the labour force worldwide could be bleak if we do not enable them to find skills and motivation for their self-esteem and community building. We are in danger of creating a 'lost generation' out of step with preparing for a sustainable age.

The disturbing report by the Federation of the Red Cross and Red Crescent entitled *Think Differently: Humanitarian Impacts of the Economic Crisis in Europe* (October 2013)[3] paints a sombre picture of increased poverty, of a new impoverished middle class, of losing hope and of despair across the whole of Europe. The report documents how the member charities of the Federation in over 42 respondent countries are facing increased demands from a wide range of individuals and families for food, for shelter, and for counselling, especially amongst the young, but also for the 45 to 55 year olds. It reveals many families having to share very limited accommodation with their offspring who have nowhere else to go. The Federation claims we face a deepening social crisis of poverty, xenophobia, discrimination, social exclusion, violence and abuse.

A recent report by the Organisation for Economic Cooperation and Development entitled *Survey of Adult Skills* (October 2013)[4] found that in England young people were falling behind the rest of Europe in the basic skills of literary, numeracy and computer-based problem solving. Indeed these young people were less equipped for the modern workplace than their parents. This suggests that many of the coming working population could never be appropriately skilled for the employment opportunities that a successful modern economy should deliver. Indeed it offers the prospect of a deepening skills shortage, throttling growth, whilst creating in its wake an unemployable underclass. Again this widening inequality of success and failure breeds the antithesis of any successful transition to sustainability.

We face a renewed need for investing in our young social capital. One logical outcome of wellbeing is the current interest in social investment. This is of two kinds. One is essentially charitable giving where investors place funds in schemes which are designed to better people and societies who are otherwise disadvantaged. The other is to offer schemes of incentives and support to those who are a cost to themselves and to society more generally, so that they take on responsibility and creative community based value, thereby avoiding future financial burdens to the public purse and suffering to themselves and loved ones.

These two disturbing reports do not tackle what Mick Collins is seeking to achieve in us all. Yet it is precisely because a social crisis is in the offing, even more potent than the ecological crisis already in place, which provides the backdrop for this text. Mick Collins' analysis and call to arms are appealing. What we are facing is no less than a transformation of outlook and behaviour. Yet to get there will involve a massive shift in governance, regulation and community togetherness just at a time when these qualities are escaping.

We need to create a culture of saving and a joy in reducing all waste including energy, carbon, water, food and consumables and in showing that this is the 'new culture of the household'. What is being sought is an 'everywhere household' which is comprehensively embarked on sustainable consumption. To get to this means leadership by government and by the faith communities, in the schools and colleges, and in the streets and fields of joint living, in offering moral approval to those experiencing the 'pain' of cutting back and the 'joy' of providing more goods and water and energy and lower carbon for others to use and for future generations to savour. Governments at all scales of action need to set the pace and show the way. This has to be followed by leadership in business. And finally there should be leadership in auditing and regulation so that decent measures of the costs of over consumption and the benefits of sustainable consumption are measured and placed in a robust regulatory framework.

Household embracing experiences are far better for achieving this than individual targeting. And even better still is the focus on streets, on villages, on small communities and on a sense of 'being in this together'. So setting the case for a sustainability identity and a sustainability citizenship should be the central core of this decade. It cannot and must not be ignored or regarded as peripheral if even present day youngsters are to reach their rightful old age with happiness and liberty.

Tim O'Riordan, OBE, FBA
Emeritus Professor, School of Environmental Sciences
University of East Anglia, Norwich

The meaning of adaptation at this time in human history has to be concerned with co-creating a new focus for living. Adaptation is the basis for fluid engagement of our evolutionary potential.

FOREWORD BY THE AUTHOR

Change is not an option, it's a necessity

At the time of writing this foreword the Intergovernmental Panel on Climate Change (IPCC) had just published its 2,000-plus page report, which cites 9,200 scientific publications outlining the consequences of rising carbon dioxide levels (CO_2). This 2013 report explicitly states the risk of catastrophic temperature rises and global surface warming. Fiona Harvey, reporting on the impact of the IPCC findings, quotes the succinct reaction from UN Secretary General Ban Ki-Moon: "The heat is on. Now we must act".[1]

The world is reaching crisis point, and it's clear that human behaviours have contributed to many of the global problems we are facing. Yet there is still time for us to adapt and create an improved future together. In this book I propose that this shift begins with the choices we make today and what we do to live to our full potential now. I argue that 'doing' is not only pivotal for any meaningful engagement in life, but also that connecting to a deeper transpersonal purpose makes profound levels of change possible.

Throughout this book, I will be exploring how we cultivate this shift in our consciousness. The following is the account of a transformational dream in a recent book on sustainability, science and spirituality:

> Deep in the night she dreamt that her consciousness had merged with the life-force of all things. She was for a time transported to an infinite dimension that held all that she knew in miniscule. This was a vast level of being, so different that it holds no reference in our temporal world. For that time she had direct experience of the interconnected Oneness of all things. She knew that in this place of awareness all actions would flow from a centre that was completely at peace, suffused with love, fearless yet harmless to all beings. There was no need of 'morals' or striving for 'right action', as these values arise naturally from unified consciousness. This is the deep secret of peace. We cannot commit self-harm or harm others when we are in love with Life; we cannot damage the web of Life when we are the web of Life itself. From our consciousness our actions arise (p. xiii).[2]

This dream is a beautiful reflection of our deepest human potential. For every such awakening in consciousness we are inspired to co-create a better world, because at heart human beings are cooperative, adaptable, innovative and creative.

The dream also raises two important and interconnected ideas that underpin what I am trying to convey in this book. The first is that at the most subtle level we are deeply enmeshed and embedded within the universe as a whole, yet we behave in the world today as if we were separate from nature. The second point is that we are capable of having deep experiences in consciousness that reveal *experientially* our interconnection with all life. These types of experiences affect our consciousness and identity in such a way that people who are open to them are often profoundly changed. The ability to experience a deeper connection to life may well act as a catalyst to help us reframe our relationship to the world, including other people and species, as well as all nature. Such transpersonal experiences challenge us to think differently about what we do in life and who we are as a species. In this way, *The Unselfish Spirit: Human Evolution in a Time of Global Crisis* is an invitation for people to consider new ways of participating in life's interconnectedness, in everyday contexts. The book draws on diverse areas of knowledge such as ecology, mysticism, anthropology, depth psychology, occupational science and biology. I've included real-life stories that illustrate the deep changes that individuals have made in difficult circumstances. I've also provided reflective exercises that support the reader to gain experience of the ideas expressed in the book.

Each of us alive today has the resources and inner potential to make a profound contribution to solving the global difficulties that lie ahead. Indeed, it is our innate ability to adapt creatively and intelligently, and respond to life events meaningfully, that is the greatest legacy of human evolution to the present time.

Just think, for a moment, about the long process of evolution and how the human journey has unfolded up to the present time. Human beings have survived because our ancestors evolved a range of capacities that enabled them to innovate and create new ways of living. The importance of human occupation (doing) in this evolutionary journey is embodied in the tools and technologies created and used by our ancestors, which helped shape their ideas and abilities as they adapted to meet environmental challenges. We only have to think about the dynamic shifts in the ways humans have lived through the ages, leading to major changes in human occupation: for example, hunter gatherers made quite sophisticated tools such as flint axes. Then there were the innovations and adaptations that helped to usher in the agrarian age, when our ancestors developed new tools for planting and harvesting crops. This era also saw the emergence of settlements for the storage of surplus grain. Much later, there was the monumental technological and scientific shift that led to the Industrial Revolution over 200 years ago, when increased mechanisation resulted in profound changes in our ways of working and living. Our current era, the information or digital age, is again altering the way we work and engage in daily life. History reveals that the hallmark of human beings' capacity for survival is our ability to meet and overcome complex challenges. Yet, our success as a species has created an unprecedented new challenge, as noted by Stephen Emmott[3] who identifies the impact of human innovation, technology and enterprise all over the world. Yet, he wisely points out that our apparent smartness has also been the cause of many of the planetary problems we are facing today. We are living in a time of great adaptation. Our future survival may well depend upon it.

The exponential growth in human population will put further pressure on the world's increasingly scarce resources, exacerbated by climate change. Emmott[3] reminds us that in 1960 the world's population was 3 billion, but is set to explode from its current level of 7 billion to 9 billion by 2050. Emmott rightly terms it an *unprecedented planetary emergency*, which is fuelled by our unceasing appetite for products like cotton, meat, coffee, chocolate and technological gadgets, all of which need vast amounts of water to produce. Yet underground water levels are falling rapidly in countries throughout the Middle East, as well as in China, India and the USA. Intensive agriculture in these regions is over reliant on irrigation, leading to a *peak water* scenario.[4] Consequently, there has been a knock-on effect, where water tables have not had the time to replenish, which has led to smaller yields at harvest times. Essentially, we are sucking the earth dry.

New technologies such as fracking to extract shale gas exacerbate the crisis. Michael Brooks has reported how fracking has been viewed optimistically as a way of extracting a vital source of fuel while we seek to establish more sustainable and renewable energy sources.[5] Yet, Brooks also notes the prediction of the 'World Energy Outlook' report that there will be more than a million shale gas wells worldwide by 2035.[5] Currently there are no guarantees that toxic chemicals for fracking will not pollute underground water reservoirs.

Fracking also impacts on water supplies. *The Guardian* newspaper[6] recently reported the plight of a small Texas town, Barnhart, already hit by drought, which actually ran out of water due to fracking. Suzanne Goldenberg wrote in the article: "In Texas alone, about 30 communities may run out of water by the end of the year [2013]".[6] The people of Barnhart had always used the water from their wells to grow cotton or raise livestock. However, one resident decided to sell the water from the well on their land to the fracking company, which could fill on average 20-30 water trucks a day for a monthly return of $36,000. One of the residents, Beverly McGuire, said at first no one in the community said much when she mentioned that the well on her land was starting to run dry: "Everyone just said 'too bad'. Well, now it's all going dry." Beverly said the first thought that came into her mind when it was apparent that she was running out of water was, "Dear God, help us".[6] The sad experience of Barnhart reveals the human divisions in a community, where some are seeking maximum profit at the expense of all. The misuse of water reservoirs is an example of our commoditised relationship with this precious resource. It shows how we are moving further and further away from old, sacred associations to water, which are connected to myths and spiritual traditions from the earliest of times. Indeed, Ian Bradley[7] reminds us that in Proverbs (Hebrew Bible), people were encouraged to have their fountains blessed. In those days water was considered to be sacred because it was seen as life giving. Perhaps we also need to rediscover this sacred connection to the natural world.

A key question that we have to ask ourselves today is: how will we adapt to the ever-growing challenges of climate change, food and water shortages, as well as the increasing depletion of the planet's finite resources through energy exploitation, deforestation, desertification, and over-population? What will we *do* to meet these challenges? One thing appears certain: we cannot sit back and only expect a political solution to this crisis. Encouragingly, the UK Government published a National Adaptation Programme for climate change in July 2013.[8] The report focuses on resilience, yet it fails to acknowledge the mobilisation of UK citizens to act as a powerful resource for change and innovation. Worryingly, the UK Government forecasts that energy and climate change expenditure is due to shrink from £3.5 billion to £2.9 billion by 2015-16.[9]

An occupational vision for a transpersonal future

In contrast, a meaningful and realistic response to the growing climate crisis is for enough world citizens to act and connect with like-minded people to begin to make a difference. Currently, there are 7 billion people living on the planet and it would only take a small percentage of that number to start a revolution in the way that we live to ensure we safeguard this wonderful planet. At this time of great transition, we need to believe that *what we do* on this Earth can help to meet the environmental challenges facing all of us.

In essence, humans are doers. This may sound like a simple starting point. However, when considered more deeply, *doing* is a key function in the creation of life and underpins the meaning found in most of our human endeavours. Let us reflect for a moment on the human activities we are involved in as free agents, such as learning, inventing, creating, maintaining or relating. We only do what we do if it has some functional, purposeful or meaningful benefit to our life. Occupational engagement reflects a powerful force for creative living, enabling change and shaping new developments and directions in life.

I believe that if we engage change in our social networks and live our full potential through transformative occupations, we are more likely to inspire one another to act in ways that will improve our future collectively. Such networks of transformation would encourage shifts in consciousness, enacted through collaborative efforts and directed towards creating new priorities in everyday life that consider the wellbeing of all. The joy of these kinds of transformations is that they can happen in the here and now. We can all ask ourselves the following questions: *Why* I am doing what I do? *What* am I currently doing that brings meaning and purpose to my life? *How* do my current actions benefit others and the planet? *What* might I consider doing differently with my life? *How* might I join with others to do things differently? *What, where, when* and *how* could I start to do things differently today?

Exactly how we direct our occupational interests for change collectively will soon become more pressing, as we realise the scale of human adaptation needed to address the environmental challenges ahead. But, before we turn to our collective 'response-ability' for change, we need first to consider how we are individually orientated in the living of our daily lives and occupations: physically, psychologically, socially and spiritually. When we appreciate the power of our actions and the scope of our human potential, we can see the exciting possibilities for evolving our consciousness and living more deeply.

I once heard someone say rather dismissively that we are "human beings, not human doings", as if *doing* is merely a consequence or by-product of *being*. I wish to turn that perception around and encourage people to look more deeply at the dynamism, meaning and sense of empowerment that comes with doing. But, even more than that, I would like to explore in this book how *doing* is the movement of life from which *being* emerges. I believe that, collectively, we have lost a deep understanding of what it means 'to do', both symbolically and actually.

The critical question is: what do we need to do today to catalyse the level of transformation that is needed to create a sustainable future? In this book I will be making connections between different theories to address this question, including new biology, quantum physics, cosmology, archaeology, anthropology, depth psychology, mythology, ecology, spirituality, mysticism and the science of human occupation. My intention is to make explicit the important links between our ways of doing, as occupational beings, and the impetus to co-evolve and co-create an improved future.

Getting personal about the transpersonal

I have a deep respect for science; however, I hold the view that science alone will not solve the current global ecological crisis. The collective challenge will undoubtedly inspire new technologies, but to survive we will also need a deeper awareness of the power of our human potential expressed through our occupational lives. The greatest adaptation that we will have to make is to shift from our overly self-centred actions to greater levels of ecological awareness and participation. In this book I discuss how the construction of personal meaning and purpose cannot be separated from a wider ecological imperative, which considers the impact of our occupational behaviours on one another, other species, the planet, and life as a whole. It is here that both mysticism and modern science reveal that we live in an interconnected world, which could act as a clarion call for more cooperative living. The challenge is to find ways of engaging radical shifts in consciousness and behaviours towards greater transpersonal awareness (beyond our individual egos). The stark reality is that our current over-emphasis on individualism will do nothing to secure the future of life on the planet.

We are now entering an era where the only way out of the mess we have created is to face up to the task, work through the challenges, and be transformed by our collective efforts. One thing is for sure: once we start this journey, life will never be the same again, and it is only through our collective appreciation of wholeness, augmented by shifts in our consciousness, that we will be able to renew and co-create our relationship to the world. The journey starts with the realisation that we exist in life as an interconnected whole, and that we have the power to change the habitual things we do in our daily lives to benefit self, others and all nature. However, says David Tacey,[10] modern humans have lost a vital connection to values that articulate a shared vocabulary for the sacred. Rediscovering this vital connection to the sacred could help us to understand the transformational potential between our ego-consciousness and a greater level of Self-realisation. Our task is to embark on that transformative journey of discovery, both individually and collectively.

In the process of writing this book I came to realise that the themes I have developed in each chapter are deeply interconnected, and so I continually return to ideas about consciousness, evolution, human potential, spiritual emergence, living in an interconnected world, cooperation and co-creativity. Rather than exploring these ideas in a linear fashion, I reiterate and go deeper into them as each chapter unfolds. I have added an experiential exercise at the end of each chapter, designed to complement the theme of that chapter. The exercises are optional, and have been developed to aid further reflection if you choose to use them. I have added a list of useful web addresses and a brief glossary of terms at the back of the book, in case some of the terminology in the book is new to you. In addition, there are many books and articles listed in the reference section that may be useful for your ongoing reading and studies.

The great challenge for us all

At the time of this book going to the publishers, a United Nations[11] report on climate change: *Impact, Adaptation and Vulnerability* was announced by scientists from the Intergovernmental Panel on Climate Change (IPCC). The report underlines previous warnings of the growing ecological devastation that will unfold as a result of our failure to act. It states that as climate problems worsen, the hardest hit areas in the world will initially be many low-level coastal regions in Asia. However, it warns that the rest of the world will also become more affected over time. The message is that climate change will impact on all of us; it predicts a dramatic increase in global health problems, as well as a significant decline in global food productivity – decade on decade – at a time when the world's population is rising. Robert McKie says: "The report makes grim reading" (p. 9).[11] For example, between 2000-09 the rise in climate change related natural disasters saw a 300% increase compared to the 1980s.[12] Taking action to manage this ecological catastrophe is not an option, it is essential, we need to do all that we can to prevent things getting worse. Our long-term survival depends upon it, but the question is where do we begin to adapt?

The process of behaviour change starts with our emotional reactions to what we have done to the Earth and how we reflect on the damage we have done. George Monbiot, writing a column in *The Guardian* newspaper, sums up what many people may be thinking and feeling after reading about the global impact of climate change in the latest IPCC report: "As the scale of the loss to which we must adjust becomes clearer, grief and anger are sometimes overwhelming".[13] These words reveal the sort of emotional reactions that will undoubtedly reflect a growing crisis in our collective consciousness, as we witness the unfolding and worsening conditions linked to a global state of emergency. The meaning of human adaptation at this critical time begins with facing our emotional reactions, beginning to transform our attitudes, and then taking action to stop wreaking havoc in the world. Only then will we be able to start building an improved future.

We are on the threshold of an evolutionary shift and it will take a critical mass of people to make such a global transformation happen. Yet, significant change can happen when each of us decides to act for the greater good, when we have a shared sense of world we inhabit. The process of collective change can begin with understanding how *doing* has the potential to connect with a sense of *belonging*, as noted by occupational scientist, Michael Iwama.[14] Citizens of the world need to recognise how we all belong to *One World* and that we must all do something radical in our ways of living, if we are to turn this global crisis into an opportunity. The significance of our occupational engagement for creating sustainable responses to the current global state of emergency cannot be underestimated, as noted by Ben Whittaker[15] and Petra Wagman.[16] It is up to all of us to do what it takes to secure a more sustainable relationship for all life on planet Earth.

Malcolm Hollick has suggested that spirituality for the 21st century will be a discovery of transformative action.[17] The way such transformative processes unfold will be a matter of recognising the scope of human potential linked to renewed ways of doing, knowing, being, becoming and belonging. William West[18] offers a persuasive viewpoint that brings a spiritual focus to the dynamics of human relationships and flourishing, without which we are left with a compromised and damaged relationship to life, including self, others and the Earth. Transformative action is the spiritual task of the age. The key principle within this book is: *I do, therefore I evolve,* and the underlying meaning in this statement is concerned with putting spirit into action, not only words.

MICK COLLINS
Norwich, 2014

*The journey of awakening begins with the recognition that
we are capable of living holistically. Indeed, we exist first and foremost
within a universe that is interconnected and whole.*

INTRODUCTION

*Brave new world –
brave new human*

Evolution in an era of global crisis

The title of this book is *The Unselfish Spirit: Human Evolution in a Time of Global Crisis*, and throughout it I pose questions about humanity's ability to face the challenge of the current planetary crisis. My intention in writing the book is to explore creative ways of adapting to worsening global conditions. The vision that inspires it has two strands. First, I champion the importance of doing as an evolutionary force in nature, from our biological origins to our more meaningful and transcendent expressions in the world as free agents. Second, I contextualise the movement of human potential in relation to doing, linking to the schools of humanistic and transpersonal psychology, which recognise and explore the full spectrum of human development. The research, ideas and exercises presented in this book offer a unique, cross-disciplinary resource that can contribute to the renewal of human meaning and purpose in everyday life. That is, bringing forth insights from mystical states of consciousness, and grounding these in our everyday life experiences, can enliven our transformational potential.

The book covers four major areas that are central to human flourishing and transformation: biological, psychological, social and spiritual. Yet, the main thread that weaves them together is *doing*. A key premise of the book is: 'I do, therefore I evolve'. It is a call to action for the co-creation of an improved future. The evolutionary propensity I emphasise in this book is not exclusively allied to the traditional Darwinian understanding of surviving and thriving (survival of the fittest). Rather, I explore an unorthodox approach to the evolution of human potential, which hitherto has been marginalised in our modern mainstream collective development.

The research, ideas and exercises I share in this book resonate deeply with my own personal journey. In chapter 13, I share an experience that happened to me in the mid-1980s, when I had a mystical awakening that changed the course of my life. It catalysed a transformative process that continues today. Indeed, this book is a continuation of my creative engagement with life as an unfolding mystery. My mystical experience all those years ago was not straightforward, in fact it was debilitating. I was fortunate enough to meet people who understood that the experience was potentially purposeful. But, as is the case with such transformative processes, nobody could tell me *how* such an encounter could be meaningful. I had to find my own way through the complexities it uncovered. It has taken me three decades of inner work, outer work and research to be in a position where I am able to articulate the value of such encounters for personal and collective growth. My journey has included studying spirituality and mysticism, becoming an occupational therapist, training in process-oriented psychology, writing peer-reviewed academic articles on the subject of spirituality, and working as a therapist in acute and outpatient mental health settings.

The subject of this book was also central to my doctoral thesis, which focused on spiritual emergency and the interface between doing and being as complementary functions in the journey of self and spiritual renewal. I have learned that human beings have great capacity for awakening spiritually, which promotes an evolutionary trajectory for finding and engaging deeper meaning in daily life. Such transformative shifts involve the potential for evolving our consciousness, which can then be expressed through purposeful actions. I now realise that such renewed engagement of our human potential and purpose is profoundly useful in our responses to the global crisis we are all facing. The question that interests me is, how do we view the global crisis: as a catastrophe or an opportunity? Let us be clear about one thing, we stand at the threshold of a new evolutionary epoch. What we do as a collective response to this crisis will reveal much about who we are as a species.

Darwin's vision re-appraised

As environmental conditions on the planet worsen, how will we adapt to survive and thrive in the coming decades? This introduction sets the scene for exploring the transformational possibilities and creating a new era in our evolutionary development. It proposes that to meet the global challenges we face, our collective efforts for change will need to be based on a significant reappraisal of what it is to be human. The first question we must ask is: what alternative ways of doing, knowing and being are available to us at this time of evolutionary change? This question underpins the main direction of the book and is based on the notion: *I do, therefore I evolve.*

Human beings are predisposed to evolve biologically, psychologically, socially and spiritually. For example, archaeology and biological science reveal an evidenced-based understanding of life's origins.[1] But, how will human evolution unfold next? Charles Darwin[2] believed that in the future human beings would become more perfected than the people of his time. Darwin did not elaborate further, but he was clearly speculating that humanity would develop in ways that were unknown to him at the time. If we replace Darwin's vague concept of perfection with the word 'potential', it helps us see the part we may play in our evolutionary unfolding. Psychologist David Loye has analysed Darwin's work and suggests that our evolutionary potential has already started, for example in the work of Abraham Maslow and the schools of humanistic and transpersonal psychology.[3] From the 1950s onwards these schools of thought have researched the spectrum of human development from a holistic perspective: body, mind and spirit. In this book I discuss how a transpersonal perspective is central to our next stage of human evolution.

It is vital at this time of global emergency that we understand and embrace our evolutionary potential, for example through developing our capabilities for love and wholeness. David Loye[4] provides a compelling thesis, outlining the evolution of human capacities that have hitherto been collectively neglected, and which we have yet to fully develop. For example, Loye notes that Darwin only wrote about survival of the fittest twice in his book *The Descent of Man*. Yet Loye informs us that in the same book Darwin wrote about *love* 95 times and *moral sense* 92 times. Loye's penetrating insight into Darwin's work intimates the direction of our next evolutionary stage. Cultivating awareness of our connections to one another and all life could inspire our actions to become more moral and loving. Furthermore, Loye points out that of the 141 times that natural selection is mentioned in *The Descent of Man*, Darwin actually questions its applicability to humans 20 times and only affirms its positive attribution to humans 23 times. The point being made by Loye[5] is striking, when he reveals that Darwin restricted natural selection to earlier times of human evolution. Furthermore, he notes that for Darwin natural selection becomes less of an evolutionary driver for humanity as civilisation becomes more developed.

Loye makes a persuasive argument that humanistic and transpersonal psychology could provide a rich new seam for engaging our evolutionary potential collectively. If we draw on the right type of evidence, we find human beings have enormous capacities for developing and transforming in everyday life. The question then becomes: how are we inspired to choose a direction for collective change in this time of growing crisis, and what can we do? The focus of my research over the past two decades has been to make explicit the productive links between human occupations (doing) and our transpersonal potential (being). In this way the book offers an alternative approach for the evolution of our natural human capacities.

Where change can begin

This book does not provide any simple answers to the question: 'What can we do to improve the future?' However, the book does highlight the importance of finding a new story or myth that can galvanise our deepest purpose and meaning to find cooperative ways of living in the world. It sets the scene for how the current global state of emergency can impact on human consciousness, and conversely how we need to be prepared collectively to face the challenges before us. Questions about meaning and human potential will rise up the agenda as we lurch ever closer to a global state of emergency. Thomas Berry[6] even suggests that to be viable, humans need to be in an intimate relationship with the earth's resources. Yet, the current state of the world suggests we have a compromised relationship with it. The first point in awakening our collective consciousness is concerned with the development of awareness about the perilous state of the world. Because many of today's problems are the direct result of human behaviour, we are obliged as a species to consider changing our ways of living. I agree with David Loye,[3,4,5] that in order to evolve our human capacities fully, we have to consider new horizons for our collective development. In this book I explore the meaning of engaging our full human potential from the perspective of expanded states of consciousness, and how these can lead to profound changes in our behaviours and actions. I reveal how doing is central to evolution and the co-creation of an improved future. The key idea in this book, *I do, therefore I evolve*, is based on a deep understanding of how human beings can connect to a universal sense of belonging, as inspired by schools of mysticism and transpersonal psychology. Yet, our insights need to be grounded in daily life as reflected in the discipline of occupational science.

The transpersonal approach is found in the pioneering work of people such as William James and Carl Jung, as well as Abraham Maslow, Stanislav and Christina Grof, Stanley Krippner, Frances Vaughan, Jean Houston, Ken Wilber, Arnold and Amy Mindell, Richard Tarnas and Jorge Ferrer, among many others. All have made important contributions to our understanding of engaging human potential fully. A transpersonal understanding of our evolutionary development values the mystery of life, the development of consciousness, and in particular the evolution of our spiritual potential, as described by the mystics of the world's various spiritual lineages. Robert May[7] even suggests that mystics are at the forefront of humanity's future evolution. However, before we consider the validity or applicability of mysticism to our global predicament, we need to establish what such awareness could mean to our human development and potential. Psychologist William James[8] notes the way mystical states of consciousness enable us to forge new connections and relationships to life.

William James outlines a potential evolutionary trajectory where the integration of mystical states of awareness could catalyse deep changes in consciousness, and impact positively in terms of engaging our transformative potential. It is through our ways of doing, knowing and being, based on the mystical axiom that all life is interconnected, that we find resonances between mystical experiences and a universal consciousness.[7] The premise I put forward in this book is that to produce an improved future, we will need to take both personal and collective responsibility for engaging and evolving our transpersonal potential in our everyday actions. Indeed, it may well take a crisis in the modern world to arrive at what Paul Brunton referred to in the mid-20th century as a turning point for humanity to evolve spiritually.[9] In a similar vein, Thomas Berry[6] believes that we are more than capable of renewing our acquaintance with the numinous dimension of life, thereby bringing forth a new vision and order for humanity's relationship to the planet. In order to turn Berry's vision for humanity into reality, we need to discover and embrace a new myth: one that situates humans in a meaningful relationship to nature and the cosmos.

Embracing a new myth

The discovery of a new myth is part of the process of galvanising our relationship to one another, other species and nature as a whole, which is so important at this time of great change. Throughout the book I reflect on the idea that we are interconnected with all life, and how a new myth must help humanity connect to the realisation that we belong to *One World*.

Cosmologist Brian Swimme[10] has discussed the notion of developing a new mythical perspective that recognises our transpersonal connection to life as a whole. Swimme notes how the universe is both a mystery and continually manifesting in its creative unfolding. He provides a thought-provoking analysis of Edwin Hubble's ground-breaking discovery, that we are all located in the centre of the cosmos. Swimme points out that whilst the universe extends billions of years from our current position in the cosmos, each of us is also at the centre of the cosmos. The suggestion is that the universe is centred at each point in *its* existence. In other words, our consciousness is a point of origin in terms of the universe and its continual unfolding. It is here that a transpersonal perspective is highly instructive in terms of our ways of knowing, in that it reveals how our consciousness is both local and non-local. Swimme elaborates on this *omni-centric* model of reality by asking us to imagine a raisin loaf being baked in an oven. As the raisin loaf expands, each individual raisin gradually moves away from the other raisins. He points out that whilst each raisin is situated centrally in its own existence, all the raisins are connected to a greater whole. Similarly, our experience of consciousness is a point of creative unfolding, which is both individual and universal.

When our everyday ego-consciousness awakens to the notion that we are part of a universal co-creative force in life, it has the potential to bring about a 'death' of our *fixed* ideas of identity, and at the same time can lead to a 'birth' of a transpersonal-Self that is connected to a whole, *fluid* and unfolding universe. Science tells us that the atoms that make up our bodies, such as hydrogen, carbon and oxygen, are billions of years old, and so in essence, the atomic structures which make up the very foundations of our bodies are literally *stardust*. It is this dynamic connection to a wider cosmos that is providing us with ways of inspiring our awareness and how we live in a productive relationship to the whole.

There is now compelling evidence that the universe is interconnected at a sub-atomic level. We know this from quantum experiments where spinning paired particles respond to each other instantaneously, reacting faster than the speed of light, as well as defying the limits of space and time. Such quantum entanglement reveals that no object is on its own.[11] These sub-atomic actions suggest a law of the whole – holonomy – as conceptualised by physicist David Bohm[12]. In such a field there is an *implicate order* of enfolding to the whole as well as an *explicate order* of unfolding from the whole. We live in an interconnected world and yet we still have problems when we try to discuss the meaning of experiences that reveal our intimate connections to a greater cosmos. For example, a common problem in traditional scientific studies is when we attempt to use objective methods to research people's interconnected and subjective experiences.

Dutch cardiologist Pim Van Lommel[13] found that 62 participants in a research study of people who had been successfully resuscitated after cardiac arrest had encountered transpersonal experiences. Van Lommel talks about the complexities of validating people's non-local experiences of consciousness using traditional scientific methods, yet he also reveals the qualities and credentials of a good scientific researcher, in that he is willing to take his research participants' experiences seriously. In doing so, he and other enlightened researchers are not seeking to reinforce outdated ideas of consciousness, but rather are willing to address important questions about what consciousness could mean in light of people's transpersonal experiences. How we explore, understand and integrate the meaning of such transpersonal phenomena into our daily lives may be an important point in catalysing our evolutionary development, as we seek to co-create an improved future.

Evolution and wholeness

We are fast arriving at a point in human history where we need to be more creative in how we view consciousness and the world we co-habit,[14] particularly how we connect to non-local experiences. Stuart Hameroff, Director of the Centre for Consciousness Studies at the University of Arizona in Tucson, USA, has discussed with Susan Blackmore[15] how some scientists used to be vilified for believing that there was a life force or *élan vital*. Hameroff cites developments in new biology, revealing how cells behave in interconnected ways, where cellular communications remain a mystery. But, he notes that research into quantum phenomena, such as *entanglement* and *coherence*, may help to explain how nature operates subtly and in interconnected ways. Hameroff notes the extraordinary impact that biological functions of cellular awareness and interconnectivity have had on his perceptions of life. He now refers to himself as a *quantum vitalist*.

The significance of how 'living cells' operate in profoundly mysterious ways is where we start the journey of transformation outlined in this book.

A brief summary of the content of each chapter is provided below.

Chapter one explores how nature is in a constant process of creation and destruction. The chapter examines how doing is instrumental in the co-creation of life, which is both revelatory and mysterious. The research and ideas in this chapter help to contextualise the magnificent dynamism and subtle vitalism of our existence at a biological level. It sets the scene for a deeper examination of *who we are* as living beings, revealing a vibrant propensity for how we are predisposed to grow and flourish to our full potential.

Chapter two considers how our ego self-identity is an important feature in our human development. The chapter explores the impact of modern industrialism and bureaucracy on our everyday experiences of consciousness. It charts the rise and importance of philosophical ideas linked to the schools of humanistic and transpersonal psychology, and how they initiated new perspectives for understanding human potential, inspiring new opportunities for growth. The ideas examined in this chapter underpin the next evolutionary step of human development advocated in this book.

Chapter three outlines the importance of understanding unconscious processes, as initially proposed by Sigmund Freud. However, the chapter is more aligned to the work of Carl Jung, whose ideas and work on the collective dimensions of the unconscious are central for understanding how we are part of an interconnected world. The chapter also discusses Jung's ideas of the archetypes and how these can connect people to a greater sense of mystery in life, as exemplified through dreams and myths. This chapter reveals the depth of human functioning, which is pivotal for embracing the evolutionary changes I suggest.

Chapter four explores the numinous, which refers to a direct encounter with the mystery in life. The numinous can have a significant impact on the consciousness of people who experience it. This chapter examines literature revealing the luminous and ominous dimensions of numinous experiences. Examples of people's numinous encounters are provided, and how such experiences are found in the world's mythical traditions and religious systems. I propose that humanity will need to develop a greater relationship to the numinous to evolve a greater connection with the sacred dimension.

Chapter five provides an overview of humanity's mystical heritage and how we have evolved technologies of transcendence from ancient times to the present. The chapter examines the need for greater connection to holistic consciousness, which is contrasted against the current consumer-based one-sidedness, so prevalent in the modern world. There is a discussion of the need for a more productive relationship to life as a transpersonal mystery. The ideas in this chapter provide the foundations for cultivating a renewed sacred and holistic relationship to life.

Chapter six considers how human beings can connect their lived experiences with the transpersonal dimension. The chapter affirms the value of everyday activities of daily living, productivity and functioning, but also advocates the need for a greater connection to living with depth. I introduce the idea of archetypal occupations to engage a deeper connection to human potential through daily actions. In this way the chapter provides a foundation for developing an understanding of our connection to the numinous, as grounded spirituality and active participation.

Chapter seven provides a discussion about the complexities of engaging transformations in consciousness. It highlights the work of transpersonal luminaries such as Carl Jung, Stanislav Grof and others, who have been influential in helping humanity to recognise the processes involved when the ego is threatened or (at times) eclipsed when encountering the transpersonal dimension. This chapter highlights how crises can provide opportunities for change, but the critical point is to know how to work with a *crisis as an opportunity*. This is the collective predicament of humanity at this critical time on the planet.

Chapter eight outlines how human potential and the depth approaches discussed in previous chapters are key elements for inspiring a new myth, which could support a shift in collective consciousness. The chapter suggests six areas for deep engagement of collective transformation. It draws on Carl Jung's transformative biography to illustrate the engagement of reflection and action in the service of individuation and wholeness. The chapter identifies that if humanity aspires to co-create an improved future, it will have to engage with a deeper purpose of inner work and outer work.

Chapter nine starts to draw together key themes in the book. It proposes that within this era of change, humanity will need to reflect and act in new ways. I propose two ideas. First, we will have to wake up to the political and commercial binds that ensnare our imaginations and tether them to limiting ideas of lived potential. Second, there needs to be a collective change in our ways of doing, knowing and being in the world, if we wish to co-create an improved future that is not bound to overly self-centred behaviours.

Chapter ten explores the alchemy of occupational engagement. I put forward the premise that alchemy in action is a process of doing, knowing and being, which informs our ways of becoming and belonging as spiritual emancipation. Everyday activities and doing are viewed as ways of connecting to the transpersonal. Yet the chapter also outlines how the global predicament is challenging human beings to find a balance between individual interests and collective responsibilities. It highlights the importance of intelligent appraisal of our human potential in this time of great change.

Chapter eleven outlines three areas of intelligence that humanity will need to consider as part of a greater process of integration for interconnected living: occupational, spiritual and Akashic. These intelligences provide a way of understanding the discrete and overlapping areas of influence for furthering our human potential. I explore our lived qualities of experience and participation, and how these are guided by intelligences that develop our conscious engagement in the world to actively realise our transpersonal potential.

Chapter twelve draws on ancient and contemporary traditions that have focused on dreams as being instrumental within the process of healing. Dreams are also revealed as inspiration for change, as well as guiding deeper engagement of our transpersonal potential in daily life. The chapter illustrates how the spirit of dreaming coheres with a co-creative approach to harnessing our transformative potential. Dreams are viewed in the context of furthering our spiritual development. This chapter reveals the subtle and deep power of dreams to initiate profound transformations in consciousness, leading to changes in our actions and sense of identity.

Chapter thirteen is an autobiographical account of my journey of spiritual crisis and renewal. The chapter pulls together all the themes discussed previously, revealing the significance of such transpersonal encounters for inspiring personal and collective change. It illustrates how doing is central to the journey of recovery, as I discovered through my transformative crisis. The chapter also illustrates how humanity needs to remain open to experiences that are complex, while learning to trust the unfolding nature of transformative processes at this time of global crisis.

Chapter fourteen explores the need for humanity to break through the one-dimensional consciousness that is dominating the world. It advocates the value of connecting with life as a mystery. Moreover, the chapter outlines the need for humanity to develop further its capacities for love and creativity, and to become warriors of the soul (including the soul of the world, the *anima mundi*). It includes inspirational stories of ordinary people who have faced adversity with a deep sense of spirit. These stories reflect what it means to become a warrior of the soul and to co-create an improved future at this time of global crisis.

Beginning the 'Great Work'

We stand at a threshold for engaging our transformative potential, ready for what Joanna Macy and Chris Johnstone have referred to as *The Great Turning*.[16] Such a transformative approach to life begins with the recognition that the *self* is a mystery[17] and it involves a deep process of engagement, as noted by Thomas Berry[18] who speaks about the sacred and numinous mystery that resides in the depths of every living being.

If we accept that each person has the capacity for connecting to a deep sense of universal mystery, it could influence our co-creative abilities to cultivate our transpersonal potential. I argue that we will need to develop a greater connection to the transpersonal in order to survive, thrive and arrive at a new experience of emancipation for living in this time of global crisis. Our transformative journey to a greater sense of wholeness is supported by the knowledge, that at a deep biological, microscopic level – through to a broad cosmological, macroscopic level – we are interconnected throughout. The research outlined in this book reveals that we are more than capable of making a transitional shift, from an overly self-referential locus of being, to greater realisation for interconnected and cooperative ways of living. Transformative change is not only about who we are as a species, it also includes what we do collectively to engage our evolutionary potential to take responsibility for the planet.[19]

Throughout the book I explore the centrality of 'doing' in the process of self and spiritual renewal. Interestingly, David Lukoff, professor of transpersonal psychology, has noted an increase in the number of people reporting intense mystical and spiritual experiences over the last three decades,[20] giving some indication that our human consciousness is attempting to wake up to the mystery of wholeness, of which we are a part. Yet, we must ensure that once our consciousness has been stirred by spiritual or mystical reflections and encounters they are integrated into our ways of doing and processes of co-creative action. If enough people focused and actualised their human potential, the meaning of 'I do, therefore I evolve' could encourage greater participation in the realisation of an improved future. I hope this book inspires you to do just that.

The shift towards a new evolutionary human will not only happen through reading, reflecting or sharing ideas about transformation. It will only occur when we act and interact intimately with life's wholeness. The very essence of who we are.

CHAPTER ONE

The evolution and mystery of human existence

Overview

This chapter discusses our biological evolution, which is powered by doing. It outlines how at a cellular level, biological processes co-evolve to produce tissue, organs and our bodies as a whole. Not only are we self-created as human beings, through nature's way of doing at a cellular level, we are capable of reconnecting with nature through our own conscious acts of doing. Indeed, doing is the movement of life. As part of the process of self-creation we face the challenge of exploring the parameters of our experiences in consciousness.

Programmed cell death, evolution and life

When we understand the incredible biological processes that occur in the human body it helps us appreciate the wonder of being alive. The existence of life on earth is believed to have started with cellular interactions, which eventually evolved to the majestic construction of a human being, consisting of tens of trillions of cells. Yet, every human alive today continues this evolutionary process and goes through an incredible journey of being formed and transformed on a daily basis. Within each human body myriad cells are being created daily, while around 30 billion cells die during the same period. The biological term for programmed cell death is *apoptosis*, a Greek word that refers to leaves or petals falling off a tree or plant.[1] It means that after an approximate seven-year cycle, there is nothing left of the physical entity that *we were* at the start of this cycle. We could say that we are living alchemy, morphing mysteriously, day after day, revealing that at a subtle level we are deeply transformational beings.

Awareness of this phenomenon could inspire a renewed sense of wonder and reflection on this continuous biological transformation. Yet, some people might find it disturbing, says Deepak Chopra[2] when he points out our natural instinct for self-preservation. He notes that few people choose to understand what it means to die as a daily experience. However, if cellular death is a vital link to life's ongoing creation,[2] it raises interesting questions about what it is to be alive, and how we reflect on who we are and what we do in life. Indeed, it has been suggested that a key purpose in our life journeys is to learn how to face death, which can become a profoundly healing experience.[3] How much more so, if we truly realised that we are constantly being formed and reformed in each and every moment. We may find that looking more closely at the dynamic foundations of our biological existence; we can start to cultivate a richer and deeper sense of appreciation and meaning for this wonderful gift of life.

Biologist Bruce Lipton[4] has emphasised the dynamic functions of cellular existence. He notes that our genetic make-up reflects molecular templates that read and act upon information stored in genetic codes, our DNA, that go on to produce cells, tissues and organs. However, the most fascinating process occurs in cellular interactions that lead to the unfolding of life. Lipton goes on to explain that:

> You may consider yourself an individual, but as a cell biologist I can tell you that you are in truth a cooperative community of approximately 50 trillion single-celled citizens. Almost all of the cells that make up your body are amoeba-like, individual organisms that have evolved a cooperative strategy for their mutual survival. Reduced to basic terms, human beings are simply the consequence of collective amoebic consciousness (p. 27).[4]

For example, cells produced for specific neurological functions, such as memory or vision, follow distinct patterns of behaviour, revealing how, at an organisational level, they are forming and functioning as though they are acting with awareness or intelligence.[5] The work of Bruce Lipton[4] helps us to understand the dynamic actions of protein membranes that surround DNA. The genetic information held within the cellular wall cannot be read until the protein carrier enables the cell to make contact with another cell. Regulatory proteins not only make up the cell's membrane, they are also responsible for generating cellular motion. The movement and interactions between cells occur through electromagnetic properties (switches) that operate in every protein within the cell membrane. Lipton goes on to explain:

> To exhibit intelligent behaviour, cells need a functioning membrane with both receptor (awareness) and effecter (action) proteins [...] the behaviour of a cell cannot be determined by examining any individual switch. The behaviour of a cell can only be understood by considering the activities of *all* the switches at any given time. That is a holistic – not reductionist – approach (p. 87).[4]

The two features that stand out in Lipton's description of cellular behaviour are that awareness and action are key factors in the movement of life. Thus, cellular interactions occur in environmental contexts that are based on networks and interconnections. The evolutionary trajectory of life at a cellular level, according to Lipton, actually reflects a process of "ascension to higher awareness" (p. 197).[4] Lipton makes a fascinating observation that the cellular activity which creates our tissues and organs is also a movement in consciousness and awareness. In essence, our cellular activity is consciously *doing* the foundation work that forms all the component parts of our existence into a unitary whole. As fully formed (and functioning) human beings, it is wondrous to reflect on the biological processes linked to nature's ways of doing, which are central to our ongoing journey of self-creation.

It is here that the work of Chilean biologist Humberto Maturana[6] becomes significant. Maturana discovered a phenomenon known as *autopoiesis*, which in Greek means self-creation. During his research into the neurophysiology of visual perception, he asked the question: What is involved in the process of seeing? His investigations led him to explore how biological processes occurring in the nervous system functioned in relation to the act of observation. Maturana realised that he needed to focus on the act of observation without the additional commentary of an observer (himself), and his research question was refined to exploring the functions of seeing, through the direct act of seeing.[6] Maturana was interested in how we create life as we live it, that is, through our immediate engagement in whatever we are doing. It is through direct and active engagement in life that our neural feedback systems underpin these autopoietic (self-created) functions. In turn, our perceptual worlds are constructed and strengthened, and so instead of saying that to *see is to believe,* we could say that *seeing is doing*. Whilst Maturana excluded inner commentaries in his work, the significance of first-person narratives will be discussed later in the chapter.

Evolution and self-creation

The concept of autopoiesis (self-creation) helps us to appreciate the dynamic interface between biological processes and lived experiences. Maturana and Varela[7] ask us to consider what are the qualities found in all living systems, by which we know them to be alive? As we have seen, Bruce Lipton[4] has revealed a cellular intelligence at work in the biological imperative to self-create (*through nature's ways of doing*). It emphasises the interconnections between infrastructures in nature at the most fundamental level.

The hallmark of living systems, then, is that they function through establishing effective networks between their various components. Each component contributes to the overall ability of a system to transform and continually *make itself.*[8] Maturana's[6] research led him to the following conclusion, that our lived experience of *doing* within everyday life contexts, provides a sense of coherence that helps us explain our ways of living. In essence, doing is the mechanism of life's ongoing self-creation. For example, physicist and systems theorist

Fritjof Capra[9] has illustrated how processes of change in an autopoietic system bring about self-renewal in living organisms in two ways. First, the interactions occurring within living systems create changes whilst also maintaining established patterns of organisation. Second, living systems have the potential to create new structures and connections (as developmental processes) through internal dynamics or environmental influences. Hence, systems like the human brain, for example, have established structures and functions that allow for complex operations and interactions, yet they are also dynamic. That is, our brains are responsive to new information, because they have the capacity for plasticity, or fluidity. It means that our brains continue to operate coherently as an integral system, whilst our ongoing neurological development remains open to new environmental stimulus.

There is scientific evidence to support the autopoietic (self-creating) imperative in a phenomenon aptly known as 'mirror neurons'. In the 1990s researchers at the University of Parma, Italy, were studying the area in the brains of monkeys that is linked to planning and executing movements. The brain activity predictably lit up on the monitor when the monkey performed a specific action. However, at one point when the monkey was watching one of the researchers perform a similar action, the same area of the monkey's brain lit up on the monitor.[10] This is a powerful example of *seeing is doing*, as noted above. These mirror neurons are known to exist in the pre-motor cortex area of the brain that deals with pain, empathy and language.[11] Yet, the real fascination with mirror neurons is not that such actions occur, but *why*. Archaeology tells us that human brain size stabilised its phenomenal growth around 200,000 years ago, which suggests that the rise of human culture about 50,000 years ago may have played a significant part in the evolution of mirror neurons, as noted by Dobbs[11] who explains that the mirroring capability of neurons was the result of past genetic adaptations, which enabled humans to develop in terms of learning and communication.

So, not only is doing pivotal to self-creation, our neurological responses also have the potential to be activated when observing others doing. Maturana and Varela have proposed that doing and knowing are intimately connected.[12] The relationship between our capacity to *do*, our ways of *knowing*, and who we are in terms of our *being*, presents us with tantalising opportunities to consider and engage our human potential. If we think about how a baby primarily engages in the world, it is through doing. A baby does not have any notion of a self-referential identity until this starts to develop around the age of two years. However, this does not mean that the baby is not aware and engaged in meaningful activities, far from it. We could say that from the outset, a baby is engaged in the world to such an extent that they are stimulated physically, neuro-developmentally, cognitively, linguistically and socially, which then paves the way for their self-referential sense of *being* to emerge. Here, it is important to stress that *doing* is an essential precursor to *being*, based on the biological infrastructure within us that *acts aware* and which connects to an autopoietic process of self-creation.

The dynamic processes involved in self-creation have important implications for how human beings orientate themselves to living meaningful and purposeful lives. The reality is that we are all connected to a biological transformative potential, brought into existence through nature's way of doing, which can be seen as a primary force in life's creation and ongoing unfolding. It also puts into context the power of human volition and action, which is intimately connected to this life force. How much consideration do we give to the realisation, that each of us lives at the forefront of a universal, self-creative process of unfolding, where life is manifesting at the growing edge of existence? What an incredible point in human awareness, when we co-create with life's unfolding in such a way. Such is the power of doing.

Living systems and self-creation

Maturana and Varela[12] highlight the enormous complexity and pliancy of evolutionary biological processes. For example, the earliest cell formations to evolve as living systems had to be sufficiently stable to maintain a protective cellular membrane, yet, these cells had to be malleable enough (plasticity) to allow changes to occur. Essentially, the organisation and structure of a living system is based on a set of relations between its various component parts, whether a bacterium or the human brain.[8] It is through a dynamic interplay between the system's specificity (boundaries) and plasticity (fluidity) that the system forms a developmental trajectory.[13] That is, we all have the innate biological infrastructure to evolve, but it is our engagement with, and receptivity to, environmental influences that add a dynamic quality to life's unfolding.

The significance of autopoiesis to science is that it radically challenges the duality of subject and object that underpins much of traditional scientific reductionism. Biologist Steven Rose[13] describes scientific reductionism as an attempt to freeze life in moments of time in order to capture its *being*. Yet, Rose[13] notes that this can lead to an 'either-or' reality, which seeks to resolve material determinism from non-material free will and – in attempting to do so – loses sight of life's momentum, emergence and becoming. By way of contrast, the science of autopoiesis or self-creation reflects a living organism that is both determined by its own structure and dynamics, as well as being free.[9] These autopoietic revelations take us beyond the ideas of the 17th-century French philosopher, René Descartes, who proclaimed in 1644 the now famous statement, *I think, therefore I am*. We are now entering a post-Cartesian world, beyond reductionist ideologies into an era of deeper and non-mechanistic understanding of life.[8] The autopoietic revolution asserts that whilst we are bound to inherited biological forms, we are also connected to an emergent process in life. In other words, the reality that is created emerges through doing.[6] A post-Cartesian axiom could be: *I do, therefore I evolve.* This assertion has radical implications for how our understanding of human potential unfolds in terms of how we live with renewed meaning and purpose, physically, psychologically, socially, spiritually and ecologically.

The awesome function of our biological origins, i.e., life creating itself from moment to moment, is exemplified in the evolutionary story of humanity. Human evolution – from its beginning around 3.7 million years ago to the present time – has been an extraordinary process of facing challenges, being adaptable and overcoming obstacles to become more and more creative and innovative.[14] Elizabeth Yerxa[15] has discussed the complex interaction of doing and being, linked to a scientific understanding of human occupations (our ways of doing). She has reflected on the roots of human occupation in terms of how we have evolved skills through the process of adapting to environmental challenges over millions of years. Yerxa[15] noted that the Latin root for the word occupation, *occupacio*, means to seize or take possession. Hence, the 'occupational human' – *Homo occupacio* – is driven by her or his ability to take possession of their world.[15] Indeed, humans are endowed with a great ability to shape and direct the flow of their lives as co-creators, and in so *doing*, have evolved biologically, psychologically, socio-culturally, environmentally and spiritually. It is true to say that as a species we have evolved a level of mastery in the way we have harnessed our skills for adapting and living. However, we are entering an era where a greater understanding of our evolutionary potential is needed, where we comprehend that we live at the frontier of our conscious engagement with life, as co-creators. We have a rich occupational heritage that can lead us into this new epoch of enlightened action.

In terms of the occupational legacy of our human ancestors we can trace an incredible array of innovations and adaptations that have enabled us to reach this point in our evolution. *Australopithecus Afrensis* (southern ape) lived around 3.7 million years ago and was bi-pedal, and their ability to stand on two legs freed up the use of their hands. This early hominid was highly innovative, using rudimentary tools, such as pebbles for chopping. *Homo habilis* (tool maker) lived around 2.4 million years ago and was able to start developing technical mastery by making more sophisticated tools, such as flint axes. These tools enabled a more creative engagement with the environment, which gave *Homo habilis* greater capability to meet challenges. The emergence of *Homo erectus* 1.8 million years ago saw the evolution of humans with longer legs, which gave them the ability to move faster and more efficiently, which would have been advantageous for hunting. The appearance of *Homo neanderthalensis* 350,000 years ago is associated with the first burials.

Our direct ancestors, *Homo sapiens* (wise humans), first emerged approximately 200,000 years ago.[16] However, it was only 35,000 years ago that *Homo sapiens* began producing art in cave dwellings, often depicting animals that the hunters encountered, as well as collections of hand prints on the cave walls. These early humans were very adaptable and innovative. *Homo sapiens* went on to develop weaving looms and hot metal work 6,000 years ago, as well as making the first clay maps (showing the river Euphrates) and inventing wheels for transport 5,000 years ago. The social development of *Homo sapiens* was enhanced by their ability to cooperate through working together and to connect to something greater beyond themselves. The use of ritualistic activities helped our early ancestors to evolve and engage their capacities for transcendence.[17] It is here that we make links to evidence of early shamanic rites, revealing the widespread engagement of spiritual activities,[18] that led to the naming of this phase of human development as *Homo religiousus*.

A good example of the spiritual imperative of our early ancestors is the anthropological discovery of a figure carved from mammoth ivory about 26,000 years ago.[19] This object was buried beside the body of a male aged about 40 years old, but what is of particular interest is the sophistication of the carved figure, which had joints that could be articulated, and would have taken many months to make. McKie[19] asks the question: why would these early humans have invested so much time producing a figure whose only function was to be buried? The suggestion is that the figure had a religious value and purpose, which has led to the hypothesis that the person buried with the ivory figure may well have been a shaman, that is, a person who in life mediated contact with the spiritual realm, and would have been a highly ranked individual in the collective.[19] These fragments of evidence give us a sense of how our ancestors were occupied. The objects made by our forebears reflect the importance of survival (through the evidence of tools) and deeper meaning (through the making of symbolic objects) in their lives.

When we look at the achievements of our evolutionary ancestors it is hard not to be impressed by the scale of innovations and adaptations they developed to meet challenges and overcome environmental obstacles for survival. It was Bronowski[14] who popularised the incredible scope of achievement throughout the evolutionary trajectory of humanity, as outlined above, and he noted the pivotal role of human imagination and innovation in this development. History reveals that when the imagination is combined with creative skills and expressed through human hands, the lived potential is extraordinary. Raymond Tallis[20] explains the role and function of hand tools in the dawning of humanity's collective awareness, which progressed slowly over millions of years from the use of pebble choppers to the incredible feats of the current technological era. In terms of a historical time-line, human evolutionary developments have happened over a relatively short period. Our embodied evolutionary progress has led to a dawning in consciousness. That is, we developed the capacity for self-reflective awareness which allowed our early ancestors to lay the foundations for what we often (and mostly do) take for granted today, which Tallis identifies as a dawning realisation: *I am doing.*[20]

───────────── **Mummy, what is under my skin?** ─────────────

Take a moment and think about all of the elements that are contributing to our abilities to learn and be occupied — we can see, hear, touch, smell, taste, feel and move. As long as these multi-sensory faculties are operating without any problems, we do not think about them very much. In fact, we soon take them for granted as we become skilled in everyday functions. Little children do not. I remember a friend's child once staring intensely at her hand and then in mid-contemplation asking her mother, "Mummy, what's under my skin?" I thought that it was a great question, and as I continued to drink my cup of tea, sitting comfortably, I eagerly awaited Mum's response. To be fair to Mum, she was very busy, and she tried to answer her daughter's question as best she could with a few — well-stated — anatomical facts. I continued to watch the child, who carried on staring at her hand, still contemplating her human form very deeply. I suspect the facts provided by Mum did provide a satisfactory answer to her question at one level, but the dynamic reality of what lay beneath her skin continued to engross the child as she watched the movements of her hand, wiggling her fingers. It was very refreshing to witness this incredible moment of discovery. Due to familiarity we probably do not give the actions that our hands perform a second thought. The dexterity and skills that are honed throughout a lifetime give us the ability to use our hands in everyday tasks with increasing mastery, which helps to give shape to the meaning and purpose we experience in our ways of doing-in-the-world. How often do we stop and reflect on the awesome nature of our human condition?

Gregory Bateson,[21] an anthropologist, once said that we should all take a good look at our hands and see them as an aggregate of relationships. Indeed, from this perspective the hands reflect both form and expression of embodied awareness, where self-agency is represented through our actions.[20] Here, the form and function of human hands play a part in meaningful expressions of freedom,[20] that is, they represent a tangible way of representing self-determination, which is the experience and freedom to act and to create. Thus, the biological form and function of the hands have the potential to express human free will through the way that they purposefully engage practical or creative intentions and aspirations. I am drawing attention to the hands, but we could use other parts of the body to draw similar parallels. For example, people who have no hands have shown that detailed and sophisticated activities such as fine painting can be accomplished with the feet. This is also another incredible reminder of the ways that humans can adapt.

Take a moment right now and reflect on what you do with your hands (or feet). How do they help you shape your present reality and express future aspirations? The child that I referred to above was alive to the questions about herself, and she was probing below the surface of her existence. How many of us have pondered or been troubled by the bigger questions of life at some point, and how often do we drift along in life, functioning on automatic pilot in terms of *what we do* and *who we are*? Remember, that from an autopoietic perspective humans are self-created, dynamic and open systems, forever changing. I referred earlier to how our biological existence also connects us to a mystery, and how this sense of mystery could be valuable by keeping us awake to meaning in life, inclusive of, and beyond our familiar daily routines. Next time you are aware of yourself doing something in your everyday life, look a bit more deeply into the incredible forms and functions that have enabled you to do what you are doing. Also, take a moment to consider the mystery of who you are as you express yourself in your meaningful actions. In addition you might consider how you are connected to an incredible evolutionary heritage, without which you would not be doing what you are doing today. I would like to share a personal connection to our shared evolutionary journey, which was awakened through two dreams.

—— Dreaming of bread, and appreciating the mystery in life ——

In 2006 I had two dreams on consecutive nights, which both involved bread. These dreams led to me experiencing a profound connection to the past, where I felt close to our evolutionary heritage. In the first dream I went into a modern artisan bakery and asked for a round-style country loaf. The baker was very animated and wanted to talk about his speciality breads. In the dream I was impressed with the baker's skill, but I was also getting very irritated and frustrated, as all I wanted was a simple loaf of bread, not a lecture. When I woke up I was quite perplexed about why I had dreamt about wanting to buy a loaf of bread. My initial reflections on the dream highlighted associations with the origins of growing wheat and the connections to the first walled towns in the Middle East, such as Jericho, where humans evolved the ability to grow crops and make settlements, which radically changed our ways of doing and human habitation (this is a subject that I teach to undergraduates). I thought about how wheat has been a staple for humans over the past 10,000 years, but I also reflected on what we have lost in terms of connection to the land. The artisan baker in the dream represented a quality of being-in-the-world that was dissociated, ungrounded or not-earthed; rather he symbolised an extravagance that was not necessary. I contemplated how this dream figure might symbolise or represent something similar in my own life.

The next night I dreamt of being on an archaeological dig, where I was carefully excavating the soil from a deep channel that I was exploring. I felt a round object and carefully released the object from the earth to reveal a perfectly preserved country loaf of bread. In the dream I was quite surprised and awestruck to find such an ancient perishable object in such pristine condition. Upon awakening I worked on the possible meanings and connections that were being revealed in the dream. There were many associations that linked to both dreams, but they shared an overall meaning. Dream one reflected the everyday uses of bread, which sustains us and keeps us alive, but which has become such a familiar commodity that we barely give a second thought to the earthly connection it serves in our lives. The dream was about the celebration of the human as artisan, but not in a humble way. The second dream was very much buried in the earth, and the excavation of the loaf revealed its connection to the actions of human hands from the past. This was ancient bread, and I reflected on its revelatory symbolism and meaning, which honoured our ancestors' ingenuity to recognise how to work with nature, grow and harvest wheat. Interestingly, the symbol of bread reflects an important quality in human relations, as noted by Sam Mickey and Kimberly Carefore[22] who tell us that the translation of the Latin words *cum panis* into English are *with bread*, meaning someone with whom you share food. I also associated the ancient bread as a symbol for connecting (in companionship) to celebrate the mystery of life and the spirit, such as when it is used in its Eucharistic form, as the body of Christ. We also find spiritual connections to the term *bread of heaven*, which symbolises a sense of sacred connection and nourishment.

These two dreams had a profound effect on my life, in that they prompted me to continue looking beyond the surface manifestations of daily life, the roles that are taken, and the objects and symbols we use every day. It was an unexpected connection with our human ancestors. For example, one morning I awoke and went into the kitchen to make some toast for breakfast. I was cutting a round loaf, when a great sense of reverence came over me, which brought about an emotional connection of deep gratitude for the gift of bread, the evolutionary heritage that created it, as well as the tools that were designed to cut the bread. As I carried on slicing the loaf of bread with the knife I experienced a deep sense of our human heritage in action, in the thousands of years of tool use being given full expression through my hands. It was in this deep moment of connection that tears rolled down my cheeks; it was an incredibly humbling moment. For me the links between the dreams and my occupational engagement in the waking state were connected to expressing my appreciation of human capacities and human potential, as well as how we are all linked to life as an unfolding mystery. Such encounters help us not to take doing for granted. They also highlight the parameters for our conscious engagement in life.

Consciousness and autopoiesis

It is beyond the scope of this book to delve into the various theories that attempt to explain the origins of consciousness, that is, if anyone really knows the origins of consciousness at all. One thing does seem certain: consciousness presents us with one of the real mysteries of human existence that we may never fully understand. Yet, each of us has our own subjective experience of consciousness. Ruth Zemke[23] has suggested that a good starting point for discussing consciousness is to seek an alternative to the reductionism of the mind/body duality. Citing the work of neuroscientist Gerald Edelman, Zemke[23] discusses the relational nature of consciousness and how neural processes form cortical groups or maps that are then strengthened by an individual's actions in the environment, which correspondingly reinforces the importance of doing. Zemke[23] states that cognitive processes form the functional patterning for categorising perceptions, memory, learning and other higher level functions, such as the ability to formulate concepts. Each of us experiences consciousness in a highly personal way, and Francesco Varela has discussed the importance of including a qualitative dimension when attempting to understand mind-brain interactions. He has highlighted the importance of *neuro-phenomenology*, where the working of the brain (neurological) is connected to the first-person accounts (phenomenology) of subjective experiences.[24] In short, the autopoietic function of self-creation has evolved our bodies and minds – through nature's ways of doing – and then in life, we act in meaningful ways, which leads to the emergence of a sense of being-in-the-world and the ongoing construction of self-identity. Our personal actions, stories and narratives reflect how we make sense of our conscious existence.

Neuroscience will undoubtedly become more sophisticated as it explores the complexity of the brain's neural relations and networks. However, first-person accounts of experience are an important part of investigations into the phenomenology of self-expression, particularly as the very questioning of the self can change what is known about it. Interestingly, modern psychological science[25] is moving closer to the position of Buddhism,[26] albeit using different methods and for different reasons. Both note that there is no fixed or ultimate sense of self. For example, neuroscience researcher Susan Blackmore[24] has reflected on the question of self-representation and notes that the process of asking questions about consciousness, such as reflecting on what life may mean and *who am I* can be life changing. Of course, it is important to note that a relative, everyday sense of ego-self is necessary in terms of our daily functioning, but it is also important that we ask bigger questions about the meaning of our lives. Some people take opportunities to consciously explore the scope and boundaries of their human potential linked to their psycho-spiritual development.

Edelman and Tononi[27] have suggested that consciousness is not an object, but rather a process, which is underpinned by neural mechanisms and subjective states of consciousness (quale). They highlight the importance of being fully engaged in the process of living, and they draw attention to the difference between being imprisoned by taking a descriptive approach to life, as distinct from gaining a sense of mastery in terms of living with meaning. The suggestion is that, depending on the quality of our conscious engagement in life, we all have the potential to master our human capacities, including meaningful occupational engagement in all that we do. Hence, *doing* is important for cultivating meaning and how we gain a sense of 'mastery' in various aspects of life. Zemke[23] has called for the science of human occupation (the study of doing) to take a holistic view of the mind-body question, and to explore the relationships between consciousness and human functioning from biological understandings through to transcendent perspectives. Because our reductionist tendencies often view the body, mind and spirit as separate entities, we need a more holistic orientation that will support our understanding for expressing our full potential. We have to consider not only the complexities of human existence, but also our subjective experiences of how we engage in life. In terms of developing such awareness, Maurice Nicoll[28] has suggested that we often take consciousness for granted in the same way that we take the material world around us for granted.

We can break our habitual ways of taking life for granted if we become aware of the depth of our biological existence, for example, through the dynamic processes of apoptosis (programmed cell death) and autopoiesis (self-creation). We can then reconsider the unfolding nature of human existence as a form of living alchemy, full of conscious potential, where we are active co-creators in life. We have a biological form that enables us to function creatively in the world, but how conscious are we of engaging our human potential and acting as co-creators in the life we are living? To understand such a proposition requires deeper modes of reflection and action. It also means considering the interactions between the conscious and unconscious processes that inform our direct experiences. In this way we can live with a deep connection to our life trajectories, full of unmet potential and mystery, where we are able to make life choices and take opportunities that determine *what we do* with our life, *who we are,* and *what we become.*

Bronowski[14] refers to human beings as a blend of angel and animal, which is a rather beautiful way of framing our earthly and spiritual potential. Yet, what choices do we make as human beings? What are the parameters of our conscious experience? And what do we do with this incredible human potential that we possess? Vaughan Lee[29] notes that our increasing investment in a materially-orientated existence makes our endeavours self-limiting. He talks about the need for a return to unity. Here, the notion of living alchemy reflects possibilities for discovering and living our life at depth, including transforming consciousness through our ways of doing, knowing and being. When we question the nature of the self and consider the value of *dying* to old and redundant ways of being, we are simultaneously opened up to new possibilities in life. This type of symbolic death is sacramental[30] and offers the chance of self-renewal. The following story is a touching and deep reflection of a person at the threshold of life and death.

—————— Finding a vocation at the edge of life and death——————

I was told this story by a colleague at work who is a neurophysiologist, a scientist. She recounted a powerful experience she had as a 14 year old girl, whilst being treated for a brain tumour. During the three months that she spent in hospital she endured three bouts of neurosurgery. However, the last operation resulted in severe complications resulting in loss of speech and movement, as well as drifting in and out of consciousness. She was admitted to intensive care in a critical condition and the medical team advised the family to prepare for the worst. The internal dynamics within the family ranged from "we need to prepare for the worst outcome", whilst also hoping, praying and "preparing for the best outcome". In the background there were also concerns: if she did survive, what would her quality of life be. There were many unknowns at this time.

The family are practising Catholics and it so happened that her uncle is a Catholic priest (the father's brother). On the day of the third surgery her uncle was driving in the opposite direction to the hospital on church business when he had an overwhelming impulse to turn around and go to his niece. His arrival at the hospital coincided with the medical emergency team doing all they could to stabilise his niece, attempting to tackle the complexities resulting from the operation. As he entered the ward he met the girl's mother who was in floods of tears, and her distress was further amplified because she had been asked to leave the room so the medical team could concentrate on saving her daughter's life. The dramatic twists and turns at this time included the girl's uncle eventually administering the 'last rites', the sacrament of the sick.

Later that day, while her family were discussing the limited medical options available to them, the young girl was left alone. She recalls an experience that happened to her: "I had been drifting in and out of consciousness in the days leading up to the event I am about to describe. It is interesting that I have no clear memories about those early days after the operation. However, I do remember the feeling of great pain due to the surgery, which had left me with 6 bore holes and 86 stitches in my head. I remember feeling frustration and fear. Yet, there was one incident that stood out on this particular day. I remember in vivid detail, awaking to find a man sitting by my bed. He did not speak, but I experienced an overwhelming sense of calm and peace wash over me, as well as an indescribable feeling that I was going to be ok. I had a profound feeling that I will get better." From this point on, her medical condition improved dramatically and stabilised, the doctors were shocked at the speed and level of her recovery to such an extent that it was written up for a medical journal. The doctors wrote about this case, because the level of complexity and unexpected recovery – without any residual disability or complications – is rare.

Against the odds this young girl made a full recovery and went on to complete her academic studies at school and university, completing a doctorate in neuroscience. She now works in a neurological rehabilitation team. During the past 15 years since she has often reflected on her unusual encounter with the figure at the end of her bed: "As a scientist I have tried to rationalise this many times, I have tried to account for this experience both psychologically and biologically but I cannot. Some might say that I was hallucinating, but the scientist in me knows there is no logical explanation to account for this experience. The feeling of calm and optimism that I felt that day catalysed something in me that knew I would get through this terrible event; it drove my motivation and determination for a full recovery."

Before her life-changing experience she was a religious person, but would not have described herself as particularly spiritual. Yet, she strongly believes that her guardian angel came to her in her greatest hour of need, which gave her the strength and confidence to get through the ordeal. She strongly affirms how this life-threatening illness has had a profound and positive impact on her life. Her family witnessed a change in her attitude – post-recovery – noting her frequent use of the mantra "don't sweat the small stuff", which captured the new found positivity she was bringing into her life.

There is a deeply touching quality in this story, in that a young girl found her vocation in such an extraordinary way: "I am glad that I had this experience, it is part of my identity. It made me realise the importance of compassion in the way that I live my life." The skill, dedication and care of the medical team left a lasting impression on her young mind, as did the hundreds of cards from well-wishers, which gave her a heightened sense of the importance of connecting to others, particularly when they are in need. Her recovery led to a deep desire to help others: "The experience has made me aware of my own mortality and the importance of making the most of what I do with my life."

When my colleague told me her story, I was captivated by her encounter with her guardian angel, which coincided with a process of rapid healing, and inspiration to follow a vocation in neuro-rehabilitation. Yet, the most fitting conclusion to this vignette was when she told me that her uncle, the Catholic priest, had baptised her as a baby, given her the last rites as a young girl, and as a grown woman, is due to officiate at her wedding in 2014.

This story reveals the interplay between the temporal and the spiritual. It presents us with a graphic demonstration of forces that are at work in our lives. Yet, the acknowledgement of such events is only one part of the process; the most important realisation is what we do with such encounters in life.

Two key ideas presented in this chapter help us to shift our consciousness away from an overly self-referential or individualised focus. First, the interconnected reality of cellular biology, as discussed by Bruce Lipton, reveals how nature works at a microscopic level, yet it also suggests that humans are part of a greater interconnected whole at a macroscopic level. Second, the function of autopoiesis not only reflects nature's capability for self-creation, but when understood in the context of an interconnected world, it presents us with opportunities to function co-creatively, as nature does. We are challenged to consider our relationship to a greater transpersonal perspective. In the next chapter we will explore how individualist ideas of consciousness are tethered to outmoded beliefs from previous generations, and that a reappraisal of our fixation on ego-identity is long overdue. As Anne Marie Kidder[31] notes, we need to cultivate a willingness to face death and in particular the death of false ideas about *who* we are. In doing so, she suggests that we enter into a richer relationship with nature and unity in the cosmos.

Exercise

- Take some time out to reflect on who you are and the direction you have been taking in life to date.

- Consider what old patterns, habits or beliefs need to die in order for you to take the next step in the changes you would like to make.

- Imagine those old patterns, habits or beliefs dying right now, and open up to the wisdom within. Notice what happens to you, including any dreams, waking fantasies, feelings, images or inner dialogues.

- Let a message come to you about your life from deep within. It could be a message in words, images, movements, feelings or sounds.

- Notice how this message could encourage your growth. For example, if it is supportive, how does it spur you on? If it is cautious, how does it help you to take care about managing change? Or, if it is inhibiting, how does it make you determined to change any self-criticism, or respond to any criticism from others?

- If the above reflections make you feel 'on edge', try and notice the quality of your reaction, e.g., are you a bit disorientated, frightened or even angry?

- Is the reaction above a familiar response or pattern when you meet a situation that you find edgy?

- Is there anything that you can learn from being at this edge? For example, if your reaction above is fear, might this be an old pattern that you are ready to drop? The most important thing is that you take care of yourself and only engage with change at a rate and pace that feels right for you.

- If you need professional support from a therapist to engage with the processes of change, then find one who is trained and open to working on issues at this level. For example, Jungian and transpersonal therapists.

Being true to ourselves and others, as we embark on the journey of
awakening our hearts and souls, is an important life task.

CHAPTER TWO

Authenticity and the courage to do and be

Overview

In this chapter I explore the nature of the self, initially from the perspective of ego-orientation, and then go on to examine the meaning and significance of human potential. I discuss the ideas of key psychological theoreticians, and contextualise some of the existential and humanistic questions that inspired the human potential movement. This provides a basis for understanding the dynamics of consciousness and how doing and being are pivotal for actualising our human potential. The chapter also reveals the impossibility of avoiding processes linked to the unconscious if we are to engage our potential fully.

From self-creation to self-identity

So far we have seen that nature has evolved through complex and dynamic systems, where cellular life is a constant process of dying and creation. Bruce Lipton is quoted in the previous chapter, challenging the overly simplistic interpretations of what it is to be a human being:

> [A]s a cell biologist I can tell you that you are in truth a cooperative community of approximately 50 trillion single-celled citizens (p. 27).[1]

Whilst this is true at a deep biological level, every person alive, to a lesser or greater extent, has some sense of personhood, embedded in a socio-cultural context, with all of its rules, roles and responsibilities. In the western world, for example, the idea of individuality permeates most psychological theories. However, even in non-western societies people still experience a sense of 'I', although their cultural perspectives may place greater emphasis on collectivist and cooperative values. For example, in many indigenous cultures people feel a deep connection and sense of belonging to the land and nature as a whole. Part of the problem in the modern world is its dissociation from a wider ecological perspective, which was crystallised by René Descartes' notion that egocentric thinking is the essential hub of existence. Transpersonal philosopher

Michael Washburn[2] notes that Descartes situated the ego at the centre of our understanding of consciousness. And herein lays one of the main problems we have to deal with in the modern world today. It is our rampant and unchecked pursuit of individualism and material desires, without reflecting on the collective consequences of our actions, which has contributed to the global mess we are in. In the following section we will explore the notion of ego-consciousness, its role in human functioning, and its place within a wider spectrum of consciousness.

In the west, Erik Erikson[3] highlighted the importance of developing individual identity as part of ego-functioning, which he viewed as a key psycho-social task in life.[4] The function of the ego is to maintain a coherent sense of self-identity through the cultivation of routines and habits that lead to self-familiarity.[5] The executive functions of the ego are involved in tasks such as information processing, cognitive aspects of memory, intelligence and self-reflection.[5] This leads Erikson[3] to refer to identity as persistent sameness with oneself, focusing on those characteristics that are known and familiar that can also be shared with others. Erikson[3] was mindful that people can experience crises in personal identity, which he saw as productive for ongoing identity formation.[5] It is through the experience of personal crisis that the ego — as executor — facilitates adjustments and adaptations to life's transitions.[6] In this way the ego develops both awareness and continuity of a sense of self-identity, and is able to reflect that it is an 'I', as noted by most personality theorists.[5]

According to Erikson,[3] emergent self-identity undergoes ongoing development and synthesis in relation to life experiences through processes that are linked to self-renewal. The idea of self-coherence also emerges through self-narrative, where our inner story[7] produces a composite sense of self-sameness. In this way, self-reflections (to do with the past) and projections (to do with the future) also create opportunities for new ways of self-knowing.[8] For example, we may have a spiritual encounter that challenges our fixed notions of self and identity, and this experience could expand the parameters of our existing state of ego-consciousness. Such experiences — that go beyond our previously held notions of ego — offer greater possibilities for the fluid engagement of identity, because they prompt deeper reflections about who we are.[8] These transpersonal experiences help us open up to questions concerning *Who am I?*[9] Recognition of these psycho-spiritual developments challenges the notion that the self is fixed, providing greater understanding for how our self-concepts are constructed. That is, our experiences of self are developed through processes where we transcend or evolve[10] throughout life, which means that we are capable of constructing new self-perspectives as we live. For example, it is through our ability to negotiate transcendent experiences (beyond the ego) that we can develop psycho-spiritually.[11] Such transpersonal encounters can re-align the function of the ego in relation to more holistic experience of consciousness, which give us greater scope for living to our full potential.

Developing our psycho-spiritual potential occurs through engaging our consciousness[12] in constructive ways.[13] There is still much debate about the strength and impact of prior conditioning in terms of how the self develops, based on an individual's past and cultural influences.[14] However, the importance of constructivist narratives, which describe people's meaningful experiences of self and world, cannot be underestimated.[15] If we go back to the idea of fluidity and self-construction, we can understand the importance of transformative processes and how transpersonal states of consciousness enable people to evolve their potential beyond the limits of their established ego-identity.[16]

Crisis and the transforming self

We have established that constructivist self-development supports us to participate (consciously) in the process of engaging our potential, which psychiatrist and analytical psychologist Carl Jung[17] referred to as individuation. The dynamic journey of individuation reflects psycho-spiritual processes, where our self-development involves encounters between the *self* (ego-bound, in terms of personal experiences) and a greater sense of *Self* belonging in the world/cosmos (beyond ego, in terms of transpersonal experiences). This expanded sense of Self-reference[18] highlights the importance of including a transpersonal perspective[19] in the spectrum of human development.[20] For example, recent discussions about the dynamic nature of transpersonal perspectives in relation to the self, have emphasised the participatory nature of humans as co-creators in an unfolding and dynamic mystery.[21,22] This means that we are capable of engaging with our experiences of consciousness, as a continuum between personal and transpersonal dimensions.

I have already mentioned that mystical encounters in consciousness can open us up to wider and deeper experiences in life. Therefore, it must be remembered that as human beings, we are incredibly resourceful and resilient in the ways that we recover a renewed sense of self from situations that have challenged our existing identity.[23] Such transitions (even from the threat of identity dissolution) can result in a greater sense of renewal and transformation,[24,25] which can be harnessed as part of a journey towards individuation and wholeness.[26] Abraham Maslow[27] discussed how dynamic shifts in self-identity, like those found in 'peak experiences', for example, help humans grow psychologically and spiritually through experiences of humility, awe, surrender and reverence. Through such psycho-spiritual experiences we can consciously engage in processes of self-actualisation and transcendence.[28] Scharfstein[29] echoes this point, commenting that the effects of mystical encounters can have a significant impact on people's self-boundaries, providing opportunities for self-renewal and experiences of unity. However, it is important to point out that such deep transformational experiences can also become catalysts for spiritual crises.[30] Rather like the mythical

Phoenix, a bird that arose from the ashes after it was burnt, a transformational crisis can be a productive part of an individual's psycho-spiritual development.

It is the dynamic interface between the experiences of the personal-self (ego-orientated) and encounters with a greater transpersonal-Self (beyond ego) that holds great potential for integrating a renewed sense of self following a spiritual crisis.[31] Clearly, encounters with transcendent states of consciousness can have a profound impact on the experience of everyday self-identity,[32] revealing that at a deeper level there is ultimately no fixed sense of self,[33] and that we are all connected to a more expanded sense of universal belonging. Wallace[34] has referred to these dynamic transformational encounters between the ego and the Self as a process of dying and rebirth, which can be scary. For example, Burnham[35] describes one person's account of the transformational impact of mystical experiences on the ego-self as having the potential to be disorientating and a feeling of disconnectedness, like having no foundation beneath the feet. Yet, such experiences also bring forth new ideas and information for living. It begs the question, what we *do* with the new knowledge gained.

Transpersonal philosopher Ken Wilber[36] talks about the lack of any sense of boundary when we experience moments of transcendence. What he means by this is that we are opened up to a life that goes beyond distinctions or dualities such as subjective and objective viewpoints.[37] So, the development of a productive relationship between ego-consciousness and transpersonal consciousness is pivotal if we are to actualise our psycho-spiritual potential. In order to explain the full impact (and potential) of non-ordinary states of consciousness, Christopher Bache[38] has suggested that humanity will need to expand its individual frame of reference in the context of understanding the fuller dynamics of transformative living. Bache[38] has emphasised that there needs to be a shift away from ego-driven individualism, warning that the current global crisis may well plunge us into a situation where we will have to transform collectively. Indeed, our consumer-based societies will be forced to reappraise the favouring of individualistic appetites at the expense of the collective, particularly as the global and environmental crisis worsens. The most productive outcome would be if the impact of our current environmental degradation spurred humanity to reflect more deeply on ecological issues, and that we started to consider how the environment and the earth's natural resources are worthy of the same regard we afford ourselves.[39] Moreover, David Korten[40] has revealed that such a process of change involves the development of new awareness, which can begin through understanding the stories that have shaped our ways of living and behaviours, as well as our future directions and choices we make as a species.

Not only do we have to evaluate the stories that define who we are and what we have become, we also have to consider how our narratives for change connect to our understanding of human potential, linked to our reflections and actions. Discussing human development and transformation, linked to spirituality and transcendence,[41] Marsha Sinetar[42] insists that any new insights and awareness must be translated into action. The first step is to recognise that we are capable of developing transpersonal awareness. Living and functioning in an interconnected world (what the Greeks called *holos*) has to include a wider and deeper transpersonal-ecological perspective, as noted by Ervin Laszlo.[43] He makes the distinction between people who *know* they are connected to a greater sense of wholeness in life, from those who believe they are separate. I would like to pose two questions from Lazlo's important observations. First, how will humanity cultivate greater recognition of our connection to life as a whole? Second, what does it mean to be an authentic human being who acts responsibly and who is motivated to co-create an improved future?

Honouring authentic human experience

Humanity owes a debt of gratitude to the pioneers who inspired the development of humanistic and transpersonal psychology. They challenged the limitations of scientific reductionism, and promoted the lived reality of the whole person, particularly in terms of psycho-spiritual development. At the start of the 20th century the two major forces in psychology were behaviouristic theory (first force), and psychoanalytic theory (second force),[44] which both viewed and researched human beings from a reductive stance.[45] Running against these mainstream attitudes in psychology were early pioneers such as William James and Carl Gustav Jung, who understood the value, meaning and depth of psycho-spiritual potential in humanity. Indeed, Rene Papadopoulus[46] noted that Jung was discussing the idea of Self-realisation 50 years before humanistic psychologists, revealing the extent to which his ideas were ahead of his time. However, in the early 1950s the advent of humanistic psychology started to galvanise the idea of human potential in the collective mind-set, which reflected the zeitgeist, as ideas of radical change began to stir. The cultural shift in values reflected a new understanding of psychological development, including the exploration of new parameters for living and expressing human meaning and potential. This new approach was described as a third force in psychology,[44] and encompassed more expansive ways of understanding human experience, such as existentialism, phenomenology[47] and self-psychologies.[48]

The mainstream criticisms levied against third force psychologies centred on concerns that empirical research into areas such as human meaning, purpose and potential would not stand up to legitimate scientific investigation and scrutiny.[49] In summarising the issue Westland[48] reported that if psychologists cannot gather valid evidence, then there is nothing to discuss, yet he recognised that the problem remains a human one. The idea that human beings had to be objectified and studied from a reductive stance was at odds with the values of humanistic psychology. It was supported by the ever-growing discontent and dissatisfaction in society about the impact of industrialisation on people. Humanistic psychology was part of a movement that set in motion a more penetrating analysis of the scope of human potential, in the context of an increasingly mechanised existence. Erich Fromm[50] articulated the dehumanising effect of mechanisation, both on individuals and societies. Indeed, third force psychology was subsumed in the 1960s counter-cultural movement,[51] which arose in response to the worst effects of industrialised ways of living. Thus, existential and humanistic psychology's contribution to this revolution in society was summed up as a response to the *unheard cry*[52] and *search for meaning*.[53] We only have to look at the state of the world today to find evidence of the need for a better balance between our technologically-driven values and our human potential. The legacy of these early forward-thinking psychologists remains highly relevant today.

The guiding ethos of humanistic ideologies was to value the authenticity of people's subjective experiences,[54] which connected to a wider counter-cultural movement.[55] This movement challenged the widespread conformity in society and politics[56] and highlighted the one-dimensional mind-set that was symptomatic of over-administered lives.[57] The spirit of these times is reflected in the words of Paul Tillich,[58] who asserted the right of every human being to have courage and be oneself. Moreover, the work of Alan Watts[59] identified and questioned the taboo against self-knowledge, where he encouraged people to become who and what they are. Humanistic psychology acted as an antidote to the patriarchal attitudes and values of mid-20th century consensus reality. For example, the person-centred approach of Carl Rogers[60] was representative of this new movement in psychology. Rogers focused on authentic self-representation, advocating that each individual has the right to be true to themselves. That is, he honoured the authentic representations of *being* in the process of *becoming* a person who is capable of engaging their human potential.[60]

Carl Rogers embodied his philosophy to living authentically, noting that he was always reflecting on and studying his personal experiences of life.[61] Such a self-reflective stance places great value and trust in human experience, and emphasises the deep importance of phenomenological perspectives that guide authentic lived experiences.[54] Rogers summed up an important thread of this humanistic-orientated development, recognising that people have incredible resources to make changes, to construct and live authentic lives.[62] Such third force developments influenced the emergence of a new paradigm of human inquiry,[63] which contributed to new methods of research that valued authentic human experiences. This approach addressed dichotomies such as humanism vs. mechanism, holism vs. reductionism, courage vs. fear.[64] Each one of us today stands at a threshold of choice, with possibilities to break free of the political and mainstream influences underpinning our established notions of consensus

Such a proposition is not a mandate for anarchy: rather it concerns the exploration about who we are as human beings in our full potential.

Having the courage to do and be

The theoretical perspectives of Carl Rogers influenced Abraham Maslow, one of the key theoreticians and proponents of humanistic psychology. Rogers – the first American psychologist to challenge the dominant theories linked to European psychoanalysis – was interested in getting to know the mystery of what it is to be human.[65] Maslow went on to research the lives of what he described as the mentally healthy, which gave rise to his interest in not only understanding people's deficiencies, but also what makes them develop and grow.[55] Maslow began investigating the experiences of individuals who were considered to be engaging their self-actualising potential.[66] However, the implication that self-actualisation was some kind of predetermined end-point in human development was rejected by Victor Frankl,[67] who pointed out that engaging human potential is complex and requires reflection on the types and qualities of potentialities to be actualised. Maslow[68] also recognised that people not only had tendencies towards growth, development and being fully human, but that they also experienced fear, death wishes and defensiveness. Humanistic (and existential) psychologists realised that the journey of self-actualisation demanded both the willingness of people to honestly appraise the meaning of their existence, as well as the courage to explore the parameters of their human potential. For many of us today the legacy of humanistic psychology has given us permission to discover and live our full potential. Such an endeavour still takes courage and resolve, despite the plethora of supportive workshops and written material now available.

Maslow's research was based on the notion that individuals will consider their higher needs, like self-actualisation, once they have established other needs, such as security and self-esteem.[69] In addition, he noted that self-actualising individuals have tendencies towards mystical experiences, a term he later revised to the more neutral-sounding 'peak' experiences.[66] This shift in terminology reflected Maslow's interest in human experiences that went beyond conventional representations of identity and personality. These humanistic perspectives (allied to the exploration of human potentials and experiences) acknowledged that human development had to transcend the limitations imposed by the narrow executive functions of ego-identity. Moving beyond the ego represented a shift in focus that opened up new opportunities for people to share their human experiences, authentically and deeply.[70] Moreover, there was the recognition that a humanistic conscience is more likely to develop naturally and spontaneously, once the conditions for more productive ways of living are engaged. For example, we may experience greater solidarity and cooperation with others when we consider our existential needs, which include opportunities for self-actualisation. [71]

It is this potential for collective growth and development that could still be one of the defining characteristics of the modern era. Humanistic psychology not only emphasised change and transformation, but by identifying the challenge of exploring and actualising new ways of *being* in order to live authentic lives, it also highlighted self-transcendence as part of the creation of a new direction in human spirituality.[68] Yet, the key emphasis in these developments was on the role and function of *being* in relation to the constraints of mid-20th century consensus reality. In his book *A Way of Being*, Carl Rogers[72] wrote about humans having the potential to move away from the destructive habits and behaviours that are the hallmark of our modern existence, suggesting a propensity towards the development of new modes of awareness and consciousness. It is my contention that this new trajectory in consciousness will have to include shifts in our ways of doing, knowing, being, becoming and belonging (see the work of Occupational Scientist, Ann A. Wilcock).

The cultivation of new levels of awareness, linked to *doing* is ripe for development today. Elizabeth Yerxa[73], one of the founders of an academic discipline known as occupational science, was right to challenge the way human occupations have been trivialised in the modern world, particularly in regard to occupations being essential for survival and health (body, mind and spirit). Indeed, if humanity is to shift towards the actualisation of a new type of consciousness, people will need to differentiate between superficial acts of doing and those that are directed towards greater depths of occupational engagement. I suggest that our habitual modes of doing in daily life can provide a great source of purpose and meaning, and when connected to transpersonal states of consciousness, they tap into a vast potential for radical transformation. The following case study (adapted from a previous publication) [74] is illustrative of the shift that I am writing about in this book:

——————— **Life crisis and a dream of winning the lottery** ———————

I once worked with a client in the UK National Health Service in an out-patient mental health service, as part of the psychological therapies team. The client told me the story of his life and I soon appreciated how hopeless he felt about everything. He had grown up in a minority community and had experienced hatred from people; moreover, his parents were extremely harsh and he endured a childhood of emotional neglect and physical hardship.

In adult life the client was admitted into an acute psychiatric unit, following a crisis. A divorce followed and he also experienced financial hardship. He managed to get through this very difficult period and carried on with life. He eventually met a woman and they got married, in addition he found a job that he enjoyed and they settled down. It appeared as if everything was going well, until one day he started to develop physical symptoms, which had a profound effect upon him psychologically. Eventually he was referred to the mental health services again.

The client was referred to me for psychotherapy. When we met I was struck by how furious he was, which left him drained of energy. The only way that he could make sense of all the crazy events from his past was to say, "I must have been Adolph Hitler in a previous life." He experienced violent nightmares on a regular basis. Yet, in our work together he spoke about things that he liked to do, for example, he loved to talk about cars and was a handy mechanic. In one of our sessions I said, "Why don't you get a cheap second hand car to work on?" I was quite surprised to find out some weeks later that he had managed to locate and buy a cheap, classical, and very powerful car that needed a lot of work doing to it. My surprise was based on the fact that this person had no money, and yet he had managed to scrape enough cash together to buy an old wreck to restore. He worked on the car whenever he could; it wore him out at times and he often wanted to smash the car to pieces out of frustration.

In our therapy sessions, we would talk about past events as well how the work on the car was coming along. We came to the conclusion that working on the car was akin to him working on his *self*, and I was reminded of the book *Zen and the Art of Motorcycle Maintenance* by Robert M Pirsig. Working on the car infuriated my client, yet he could recognise that he was making slow progress on the repairs as well as his own sense of recovery and renewal. Eventually he finished the car and it was then that he had a night-time dream that he had won the lottery. He said that he had never had such a dream before and his associations to the dream were about hope, and that his fortunes would change.

Following the completion of the car and the dream described above, the client began to look more at peace with himself, and indeed, he became more appreciative of his life. He and his wife took regular journeys in the car to places of natural beauty. One day he told me about a stunning sunset that he had seen on one of his evening outings. He had tears streaming down his face as he spoke: "I used to cry for all the suffering that I have experienced, but these are tears for something special." After 18 months of weekly therapy we ended our work. I reflected on his dream of winning the lottery and in our final session he said to me: "You cannot turn your head without witnessing a miracle."

Actualising human potential through doing and being

The illustration above provides a glimpse of the human potential that can be activated when we engage 'doing' as well as 'being' in the journey of self-discovery and self-renewal. Psychologist David Loye[75] has considered the question of how to engage an *action-orientated* perspective that takes account of human potential. Loye discusses the need for an active alliance between humanistic and transpersonal psychology as an important step in human evolution in the 21st century. You can see a clear example of Loye's[75] recommendations in the connections between self-actualisation and spiritual awakening, which reflect a continuum in the spectrum of our human potential and development.[76] Such a proposition has much currency in today's world, because it provides new possibilities for a holistic philosophy in life. For example, Mack[77] has noted that new theories in biology, physics, transpersonal psychology and consciousness studies etc., are revealing the limitations of a dominant materialistic philosophy for understanding life, which is having a catastrophic impact on politics, economics and ecology. As a species, we are ripe for change and a radical reappraisal about what it means to be alive. But, we need to prepare ourselves for such an undertaking as change is not always straightforward. But what alternatives do we have?

There is a need to trust the process of transformation when engaging and integrating psycho-spiritual insights into our lives, particularly as the actualisation of our human potential can arise from complex and painful experiences, as well as more positive states of change.[69] This means that we are challenged to face the human condition, as it is, without becoming overly attached to a preferred outcome. Growth in our awareness means that we work with *what is*. Abraham Maslow's[65] original research provides us with insights for cultivating transcendent awareness, which takes us into a process of engaging our relationship to life as a sacred whole, both within and without. It means that we are receptive and willing to undertake a radical examination of what brings us meaning and purpose in life.

It is the negotiation of the transitional boundaries between self-actualisation and self-transcendence that reveals the complexities of what human beings *will do* as well as what they *will be*.[67] This dynamic tension between the functions of doing and being could enable a more complementary and fuller expression of our human potential, with spiritual and transpersonal significance. It is important to note here that processes connected to self-transcendence are not only mediated by reflection, but also by action.[78] Such an occupational focus for change and transformation could lead to new opportunities for a reinvigorated sense of meaning, purpose and renewal in our ways of living.[79]

Appreciating how our potential could connect to a renewed sense of engagement in life to help tackle the emerging crisis in the modern world,[80] could reinstate our sacred connection to life. The destructive nature of human behaviours suggests a deep loss of meaning – individually and collectively – that may be reflecting a lack of spiritual connection.[80] Put another way, a loss of spiritual meaning could also be indicative of the collective under-development of our psycho-spiritual potential. In this context, an emerging sense of spiritual crisis in humanity could be seen as a natural reaction in consciousness against the reductionist and consumer-based attitudes that have contributed to the current global state of emergency. Connecting our occupational engagement and our transpersonal development[41,81] could affect how we direct our actions in purposeful ways to address the crisis we have created.

The current world situation challenges us to engage our full human potential in terms of personal, transpersonal and collective levels of transformation. Since we are inextricably connected to all life as an integral whole, any such notions have to be considered and embedded within a collective context, and we will have to address the tensions between the global ecological crisis and how we manage a growing crisis in human consciousness. This critical situation challenges us all to change what we are doing with our lives, and as the global crisis worsens, it may even lead to an escalation of psycho-spiritual crises for many people. This is the consequence of neglecting our relationship to a wider interconnected cosmos.

Crises and opportunities for growth

The contemporary focus on the links between spiritual emergence and processes that are activated through spiritual emergencies[82] is concerned with understanding the productive value of transformational crises. That is, spiritual crises are not necessarily bad, but they may be significantly uncomfortable or even distressing experiences in the short to medium term. Emma Bragdon[83] neatly sums up the dynamic differences of these transformational potentials, suggesting that spiritual emergence is a natural process of transformational development, leading people to be creative, compassionate and engaging in acts of service. Whereas spiritual emergencies are experiences that result in chaotic and unpredictable behaviours, often the result of a sudden awakening or shift in consciousness which most people in the modern world are ill-prepared to face.

Such a process of transformation naturally leads people to ask questions such as "Who am I?" and "What am I?", revealing the importance of spirituality, particularly in relation to having a sense of purpose and meaning in life.[84] Spiritual crises also contribute towards processes of self-renewal,[85] as these powerful transitions in consciousness[86] can reflect an uncompromising shift into a transpersonal reality.[87] Such transitions are often complex, and when people experience them it is often difficult for them to appreciate that the crisis is potentially transformational, meaningful and purposeful. It is the ignorance or denial of such transformative potential in the modern world that has had serious consequences for us all. That is, because individuals who have experienced spiritual emergencies are at the forefront of a new synthesis in consciousness, revealing new frontiers and parameters for understanding life, self and human potential.

Spiritual crises are a natural part of human development, since interruptions in identity can provide deep opportunities for transformation.[88] Yet, the process of engaging spirituality carries risks, due to the fragile nature of our psyches at times,[89] and this is particularly true when experiences of crisis go beyond a well-adjusted, productive, conventional sense of ego-self.[90] Indeed, the fact that spiritual emergencies are transpersonal means they have the potential to reveal a consciousness of unity and interconnectedness to all life.[91] This holistic perspective holds possibilities for catalysing, awakening and integrating experiences of consciousness in daily life.[92] Laszlo, Grof and Russell[93] have called for a radical shift in the ways we engage doing, being and learning, suggesting that we need to be inspired and encouraged to take a more innovative stance to further our evolutionary development. They believe that for humans to be able to face the challenges of the modern world, a major re-orientation is needed to develop a deeper appreciation of life's interconnectedness. This has major implications for how individuals consider their identity and everyday behaviours.

The key question remains: how will we make such a radical shift from the shallow dominance of the personal-ego, which is so prevalent in the modern world? The problem is that our personal-ego invests time and energy in activities that shore up a limited self-referential worldview. Benedictine monk Bede Griffiths[94] has stated that one of the great illusions of the ego is that it considers itself to be free, and behaves as if it were a law unto itself. Griffiths believes that when the ego is no longer the centre of our actions, it makes space for higher operations to act, involving the spiritual dimension of the Self. Although human beings are capable of engaging their spiritual potential, Griffiths[94] proposes that a quantum leap is needed from the ways most of us are behaving in the world today. However, he is not suggesting that the ego must be sacrificed. The role and function of the ego needs putting into context, says David Tacey,[95] particularly as the ego plays a pivotal role in facilitating our contact with others and in the world. Tacey is right to point out that the ego should not be seen as a problem in terms of spiritual development, but, the fact that it is viewed in such a way, may have much to do with popular misunderstandings about the ego. It is evident that we need an ego, but how do we facilitate a greater connection to our wholeness in consciousness? In the modern world, the ego has come to dominate, rather than serve. We need to develop a more productive relationship between the personal-ego and the transpersonal-Self, including an understanding of how our relationship to unconscious processes can influence our lives.

Jungian analyst Erich Neumann[96] was discussing the problems of ego-dominance in the 1950s, when he declared that modern humans have yet to cultivate new vistas of conscious awareness between the personal (ego-self) and the transpersonal (spiritual-Self). The integration of the spiritual is essentially a re-alignment of the ego-self relationship, where the ego is in balance and operates in the service of wholeness. However, developing such a relationship to the spiritual-Self is difficult in societies where we have over-invested in consumer-based pursuits and under-invested in realising our human potential. The irony is that whilst consumer-based economies are crumbling in a mire of fiscal deficits, the real problem lies in what Neumann[96] has referred to as a bankruptcy within modern consciousness. Such neglect of our human potential led him to declare that our whole psychic system is fragmented. This is a shocking realisation; it underlines the wholesale waste of our human talent (and potential) for co-creating societies that are based on deep values.

If we are serious about transforming our consciousness, any deep reflections about change will not only have to include the precarious state of our personal egos, but will also have to examine the collective values and morals that have led to the current state of affairs in the modern world. For example, the 2008 global banking crisis has had a catastrophic impact, both morally and ethically in the world. Yet, this crisis was not simply about the actions of a few greedy capitalists, it also revealed our complete adherence to a system dominated by shallow economics and material gain, where we are all complicit somewhere in maintaining such a system: directly as shareholders, or indirectly through national or corporation pension fund investments, and so on. There are no easy answers for how we evolve new ways of learning, doing and being, but thanks to the pioneering work of psychological and spiritual innovators, such as William James, Carl Gustav Jung, Rudolph Otto, Abraham Maslow, Frances Vaughan, Christina and Stanislav Grof, Amy and Arnold Mindell, Jean Houston and Joanna Macey, among many others, we have a deeper understanding of how human potential can be considered. Indeed, anyone concerned with enabling transpersonal change will find the formula put forward by Henryk Skolimowski[97] encouraging. He notes that for spirituality to be reborn, consciousness will need to be reborn. It is through the cultivation of a reciprocal relationship between spirituality and consciousness that transformative potential can be actualised. Deepak Chopra[98] expresses the process of engaging in a transformational relationship with consciousness, as one that provides us with more potential to create.

How we engage our self-development is set to become an important factor in our ability to adapt to fast changing ecological conditions on planet Earth. We have incredible capacities as human beings, yet in the western world we have overlooked the importance of developing our transpersonal potential. The following experience occurred at one of the early process work seminars I attended in 1997 on body symptoms with Drs Max Schupbach and Jytte Vikkelsoe. The experience opened my mind and heart to take my deeper experiences more seriously:

————————————— **Seeds of change** —————————————

When I arrived at the seminar I did not know many of the 30-plus people attending the event. The atmosphere was welcoming and I was keen to experience the methods developed by Arnold Mindell and his colleagues. The first session started on a Friday afternoon and we had some instruction followed by a dream work exercise. That night I dreamt of two people in the seminar who I had not spoken to. In the dream the man and the woman were identified as healers and the woman had a giant seed (bigger than a coconut, including its outer layer of covering). Upon awakening, I thought it might be nice to get to know these people over the course of the weekend and share the dream I had about them. However, at the start of the seminar that morning the facilitators asked if anyone had a dream they wanted to share from the night before. I volunteered to talk about the dream I had, mentioning the couple and the giant seed. As I concluded the dream the woman reached into her bag and pulled out a giant Coco de Mer seed from the Seychelles, just like the one in the dream. I was speechless.

It transpired that the couple were both involved in healing work. The woman in the story is process-oriented psychologist Iona Fredenburgh, who became a good friend over the many years we studied process work together. She recounts the story from her perspective: "We were staying for the weekend with my dearly beloved friend Sherrell from South Africa, whose father had been a pastor in the Seychelles for a time. Sherrell had regaled us with tales of the Coco de Mer, which apparently grows in one particular place, and has a mysterious and very erotic mating pattern. Sherrell showed me her magnificent Coco de Mer (the heaviest seed in the vegetable kingdom), and she allowed me to bring it to the seminar the next morning. I was eager to introduce the seed to the group. Max began the seminar in the morning asking people about their dreams. Then Mick shared his dream, and that was so magical! I then took the seed from my bag and passed it round the circle, so people could appreciate the truly delicious shape."

This experience had a profound impact on me, it made me take my dreams more seriously, which helped me deepen my purpose connected to what I do in life. In chapter twelve I discuss the power of dreams as catalysts of transformation in more detail. In the next chapter I will outline the complexity and dynamism of our transpersonal potential and how such knowledge and experience can profoundly change the ways that we live.

Exercise

- Take a moment to reflect on your life to date. Find a few key words that summarise what your life journey means to you.

- Using the words from the question above, create a working title that could be used for the biography of your everyday self.

- Now take a moment to consider life from the perspective of your soul. What deep dreams, passions, connections and invitations have you neglected to follow or have yet been unable to fulfil?

- Take a moment to be still, and try to connect with how your soul has been calling you: for example, through different ways of doing or being. Try and get some sense of what this *calling* might be referring to.

- Spend some time getting to know the quality of your calling from a multi-sensory perspective:

  o What does the message say to you and how does it sound, e.g., is it accompanied by soft tones or is it a sharp direct message?
  o What is the quality of the feelings connected to this calling?
  o Does this calling inspire movement, gestures or stillness?
  o Is there a fragrance or smell that you would associate this calling with?
  o Are relationships involved? If so, what is important about the way this calling relates to others?
  o How does the world look or appear to you from this perspective?

- Find a few key words that connect to the reflections above.

- Using the inspiration of these key words, try to create a title for your hidden biography.

- How does the *biography of your everyday self* compare and contrast with your *hidden biography*? Really explore the richness between these two realities.

- What current/future direction – action – occupation – vocation does your hidden biography suggest?

There is a delightful twist in the process of becoming 'more' conscious and aware.
First, we have to turn to the living unconscious where we find
'more' than we bargained for.

CHAPTER THREE

The depth and dynamism of human potential

Overview

The discussion in this chapter is centred on the importance of engaging the unconscious in terms of our human potential. I will provide a brief history of developments that led modern psychotherapists to understand and incorporate the unconscious into their work. The theories of Carl Jung are highlighted for their importance in terms of understanding how we exist in an interconnected field, known as the collective unconscious. Jung's theories of the archetypes and the numinous are also considered. I explore how the deep and dynamic experiences connected to unconscious processes can also reveal a mystical dimension. I discuss such transpersonal encounters in terms of engaging our human potential, doing and evolving.

Going deeper

It is evident that there has been a destructive split in the modern human psyche, which has manifested as a crisis in the modern world. This crisis has two important and interrelated antecedents, as Neumann[1] suggests. The first is humanity's elevation and resultant dissociation from nature and the second is the divorce of ego-consciousness from the unconscious. Our ongoing objectification of life has resulted in us not only becoming cut off from the natural world, but also dissociated from a deeper relationship with our unconscious or psychic nature. While industrialisation has produced material benefits that have enabled many people to experience more comfortable lives, a negative consequence has been a widening gap in people's spiritual and mystical connections with life. It is no coincidence that the poet and artist William Blake (and others) reacted so strongly to the grim reality of the 'dark satanic mills', referring to the type of oppressive working environments where people were increasingly forced to work as the Industrial Revolution took hold. Philosopher Herbert Marcuse[2] argued that the mechanisation of modern life had created a one-dimensional existence, in which we neglect the cultivation of our potential as human beings. One of the tasks for us today is to reconnect with the depth of experience in consciousness, as suggested by Barbara Marx Hubbard,[3] who discusses the need to bridge the gap between our unconsciousness and connect to a greater evolution of consciousness. The first step in this process is to understand our relationship to the unconscious and its impact in our lives before we can consider the evolutionary development of our conscious potential. It may well be that we have got ourselves into such a mess because we have not paid attention to the wisdom in the unconscious.

Understanding the unconscious involves facing a host of submerged and unexplored experiences or impulses,[4] including repressed memories (as noted by Freud). It also includes making connections to our transpersonal heritage and spiritual potential (as originally described by William James and Carl Jung). Bede Griffiths[5] describes the relationship between the unconscious and spirituality as a way of enabling us to break out of the prison of individualism and learn to be at *one* with all life, including the divine Spirit. Cultivating a relationship to the unconscious involves meeting the archetypes: symbols, figures or images that have formed in the psyche, which we share collectively. For example, the archetype of the divine feminine is embodied in figures such as Inanna of Sumeria, Athena of Crete, Isis of Egypt, Kwan Yin or Tara in Asia, and Mary in the west.[6]

The archetypes in the collective unconscious provide human beings with opportunities to connect with a numinous or mystical dimension of consciousness, which Caroline Myss[7] notes is communicated through the experiences such as dreams and symbolic experiences. Yet, working with the unconscious is not a quick fix to our current problems in consciousness. Rather, it is about deepening our journey into life, where we meet challenges and complexities, as well as new connections that can lead to emancipation. The work of re-aligning the ego (as an executive function in everyday conscious experience) into the service of Self-realisation involves the integration of psychological and spiritual insights, whilst simultaneously living in the everyday world. Such an undertaking requires a willingness to trust our experiences, as well as cultivating an attitude of acceptance. Understanding the significance of the personal and the collective unconscious is a pivotal first step in connecting with the deeper layers of existence, in particular the meaning that resides in the unconscious.

The historical developments of the unconscious in the west have their roots in the work of Pierre Janet, who practised under the medical supervision of Jean-Martin Charcot in Paris and was a precursor to and rival of Sigmund Freud.[8] Charcot and Janet had already determined – via hypnosis – that certain action systems (such as involuntary twitches) have an autonomous function, and these actions remain outside of a person's conscious, or voluntary control. Freud's eventual discovery of the talking cure was in effect a way of accessing repressed experiences in the personal unconscious through conversation, revealing that unprocessed traumatic experiences are incompatible with a censuring ego. Freud discovered that individuals may develop defence mechanisms to protect them from experiencing the effects of repressed traumas. Keeping traumatic memories in the personal unconscious in this way eventually leads to symptom formation.[9] Sigmund Freud's therapeutic focus was primarily on the personal unconscious, whereas Carl Jung's conception of the unconscious included both *personal* and *collective* representations.

Jung was already a well-established psychiatrist prior to his professional relationship with Freud, which was initially a productive and collaborative alliance. However, their relationship fractured when Jung began to pursue his own theories that extended far beyond the Freudian worldview.[10] Jung was interested in exploring the meanings of primordial images and symbols in the psyche, noting the dynamic and often numinous effects that are produced when these symbols and images are encountered. Jung noted how such experiences are overpowering to the ego.[9] It is interesting to note that it was Jung's split from Freud that actually produced a breakthrough in Jung's understanding of the collective unconscious via his own transformational crisis – when he thought that he would become lost in the depths of the unconscious.[11] Between 1913 and 1916, Jung passed through a deep crisis and he came close to experiencing a psychosis, fearing that he would lose his mind. Rosen[11] has described how Jung came close to the edge of madness, yet he was committed to working through the crisis, which eventually resulted in him becoming free to explore and develop his own ideas. Jung placed great trust in the process of transformation, saying that he was its servant.[12] Jung's productive relationship with the unconscious enabled him to evolve his understanding of the ego-Self axis and progress his ideas about integration and individuation in the psyche.

Jung's theory of the collective unconscious

Jung[12] went beyond Freud's model of the personal unconscious and he faithfully recorded his encounters with the collective dimensions of the unconscious in his *Red Book* in the years 1914-30. *The Red Book* provides penetrating insights into the beginnings of Jung's journey of individuation. It reveals the deep significance of his archetypal encounters, which helped him understand the nature of his transformative process as he passed through the crisis. Jung realised that there were no maps in the modern world to guide him on his journey into the psyche. However, as Jung formulated his ideas, his studies in alchemy were invaluable. Haule[13] explains that the process of transformation in the psyche begins with the dissolution of established structures, such as the dominance of the ego. In his own case, Jung realised the limitations of trying to deal with material from the collective unconscious via Freud's model of the relationship between the personal unconscious and ego. Jung saw the importance of establishing a relationship between the personal-ego and the transpersonal-Self. His experiences show that such a journey of individuation is a continuous process across the life-span, with some stages in life resulting in smaller or greater psycho-spiritual crises.[14] For Jung, his discovery of the collective unconscious and the process of individuation revealed the need for greater awareness of archetypal symbols, which he viewed as resources for spiritual development.[15] Interestingly, Jung took a creative approach to his transformative experiences of consciousness.[16] He called it *active imagination,* which enabled him to work with the archetypal symbols arising from the collective unconscious.[17] His pioneering and transformational healing journey, from crisis to renewal, forged a new understanding of the link between the personal and transpersonal levels of experience,[18] which connects human beings to a collective dimension.[19]

The value of understanding collective representations of consciousness is put into perspective by Greenwood,[20] who has discussed the links between Jung's psychology of *collective unconscious* and Émile Durkheim's sociology of *collective representations.* Greenwood says that the use of the term *transpersonal* could represent a new *enlightened* understanding that reflects the psychological and sociological aspects of both collective consciousness and collective unconsciousness.[20]

Deeper connections between the sociological and psychological spheres of collective functioning could offer new opportunities for understanding transformations in consciousness, which are likely to become highly significant in the coming years. The challenge of tackling problems in the world, especially linked to the current global and spiritual crises, will require management of our resources for survival. This will need to include the ability to develop shared responses to our collective difficulties for the wellbeing of all life on the planet. The work of Christopher Bache[21] develops this idea, suggesting that the current global crisis could tip human consciousness into a far-from equilibrium state where our experiences of collective unconsciousness could manifest into our experiences of collective consciousness. However, for such a possibility to become reality, we need to become more deeply reflective and actively engaged with our human potential. For example, we become more open to moments of synchronicity and synergy. Indeed, our psycho-spiritual intent and development is capable of catalysing meaningful change in the modern world. It is here that our conscious engagement in bringing forth a new relationship to life is part of a collective *rite of passage,* one that has never happened before (on such a scale) in human history.

Jung advocated that people should develop a relationship with the unconscious processes that surface in their lives. For example, he reflected in his *Red Book* that his patients should prepare their own journals to support their journey of transformation, stating that it will reveal a spiritual connection to a process of renewal.[12] In 1971 David Lukoff, who is now a professor of transpersonal psychology, revealed how his own spiritual emergency led him to read books by Carl Jung and Joseph Campbell in order to try and understand his non-ordinary encounter. Six years after his own transformational crisis, Lukoff entered Jungian analysis, recounting that he had a dream of a big red book.[22] In his reflections, Lukoff did not mention knowing the existence of Jung's *Red Book* (which was not published at this time), and neither did he report if his analyst made any reference to it (who undoubtedly would have been aware of its existence). The connection between having a spiritual crisis and then dreaming about a red book at the start of analysis shows how the unconscious provides relevant symbolic (and wise) guidance for the journey being undertaken. Marie Louise Von Franz[23] highlights the importance of Jung's work in this area. She speaks about how Jung recognised the need to face the irrationality within the unconscious, but she also noted how he believed the unconscious contained a new emergent potential for humans in the form of *Anthropos*, which is a synthesis of the inner individual Self, connected to the whole Self of humankind. It is fascinating to reflect on the synchronous emergence of Jung's *Red Book* being published just at a time when humanity is at the edge of a collective spiritual crisis (linked to a global state of emergency).

We cannot underestimate Jung's contribution for how we evolve our relationship to consciousness, particularly in the way that we need to wake up and work with the collective dissociation to the natural world. Central to Jung's legacy is his theory of the archetypes of the collective unconscious, containing those images, symbols and processes that have collective meaning for our psycho-spiritual growth. It is crucial that we begin to understand the symbolic language of transformation. It is here that we can turn to a source of collective wisdom.

The archetypes

Richard Tarnas[24] informs us that the concept of archetypes dates back to early Greek philosophy. Plato evolved the ideas of his teacher Socrates, suggesting that archetypes can manifest as transcendent ideas or forms that provide us with meaning. Tarnas[24] explains Plato's concept with the example of a person contemplating an object of beauty who – at the same time – is also participating in an archetypal process aroused by that beauty. Furthermore, he tells us that the archetypes take various philosophical and psychological forms, such as the Freudian view of instinctual life, or from a Jungian perspective, where the archetypes are considered original patterns, principles or possibilities within the human psyche, revealing modes of expression that reside in the collective unconscious, which connects us to a world of wholeness.[24]

Jung's theory of the archetypes reflects an attempt to explore the psychological impact of forces from the collective unconscious upon the personal-ego, and how these encounters can help to evolve human awareness of the transpersonal-Self. Yet, one of the problems for Jung was his insistence on trying to explain these ideas within the constraints of empiricism. His ideas are hard to prove. For example, Jung's work went beyond clear delineations of subject and object, especially in his later reflections on the phenomena of synchronicity, where his theories explored the place of human consciousness in a wider context of unitary existence.[25]

An example of a synchronistic event is presented from my own experience, where I dreamt about being in a seminar run by Carlos Castaneda on the 3rd July 1998:

A connected reality

In the dream a small group of us were sitting in a circle with Castaneda awaiting instruction about spiritual matters. Frustratingly, Castaneda was about to teach the group when someone said something to me in the dream, which interrupted the expectant atmosphere. Upon awakening I could not recall what was said. Three days later on the morning of the 6th July 1998, I went to buy *The Guardian* newspaper, and as I sat down to eat my breakfast and read the news, I turned a page to find an article about Carlos Castaneda, who unbeknown to me, had passed away a month or so earlier. I was struck by such a meaningful coincidence. I was aware of the work of Carlos Castaneda, although I cannot profess to have studied his ideas in earnest; moreover, I had not been thinking about him or discussing him with anyone. To have such a vivid dream about Castaneda a few days before reading about his death reinforced the idea that we live in a reality that can reveal meaningful coincidences. Yet, whilst such events enhance our experience and understanding of an interconnected world, we cannot prove this. I explored the meaning of the dream to my process of individuation, particularly as at the time I was engaged in a training that valued the shamanic path.

The synchronicity of the above dream and life event was quite incredible, but it is what we do with such experiences that are of equal importance. My reflections on this dream are centred on my meeting an influential person (Carlos Castaneda) who inspired a generation or two about the importance of the spiritual and shamanic dimensions of life. If I put this dream into the context of my own process of individuation it is representing an archetypal meeting between a student and teacher, one that encourages the engagement and integration of the transpersonal into daily life. Such teacher-student relationships throughout antiquity are primarily focused on supporting greater *Self*-awareness as spiritual practice. Moreover, such dreams deepen one's mythical and archetypal engagement in life.

Objections to Jung's formulations about the *archetype of the Self* were centred on criticisms that it was a poorly disguised alternative for God.[26] However, it is important to consider the spiritual element of Jung's theories, whose roots are found in the work of religious scholars Mircea Eliade and Heinrich Zimmer, and which were elaborated further by Joseph Campbell.[27,28] These world mythologies revealed the symbolic language of individuation, and Campbell's work coheres with the ideas conceptualised by Jung. Taylor[29] discusses the progression of these religious and mythological ideas, suggesting that they have been translated into a valuable psychotherapeutic tool (Jungian analysis), which connects depth psychology and spirituality into a path of Self-realisation (individuation).

Functioning as patterns of instinctive behaviours or propensities,[30] the archetypes also have neuro-psychic properties.[31] This suggests that recognition of the archetypes emerged as part of the evolution of the human brain and consciousness. In short, the archetypes are independent of cultural traditions, and yet around the world they can be found as symbolic representations of typical life encounters[32] with socio-cultural significance,[20,33] that are also linked to dreams,[34] myths and fairy tales.[27,28,34] Jung identified how these deeply symbolic, archetypal representations in human consciousness[35] are empowered by the numinous (spiritual/mystical) experience that often accompanies them.[36,37] To illustrate the relationship between the archetypes and the numinous, imagine having a dream where a person meets an influential figure, who has spiritual (archetypal) significance or gravitas. Let's say that in the dream this figure gives the dreamer a message about the way they are living their life, and in particular how they are squandering their human potential. Then, upon awakening the person experiences a deep sense of awe and mystery linked to that dream. We can see how the archetypal image of a spiritual figure activates a numinous response in the dreamer that goes beyond their everyday ego-identity.

Because the archetypes bring people into contact with unconscious processes that have a numinous dimension[37] they have the power to influence the potential for deep transformation,[38] as noted in Jung's own transformative experiences. Such numinous encounters can link people's experience of consciousness to the transpersonal dimension of the psyche.[39] For example, Stanislav Grof's[40] observations in his studies into non-ordinary states of consciousness cohered with Jung's insights about the archetypes, stating that they may possess a quality of the numinous, which is sacred and different from mundane life experiences.

The archetypes and transformative potential

Archetypes, as discussed by Jung were considered as forms which held possibilities for certain types of perception or action.[41] Moreover, these archetypal forms were not considered static: rather they are recognised for their ability to change over time in relation to deep interactions throughout life.[42] Also, the way that the archetypes manifest in people's lives require careful interpretation of their possible meanings, where taking an *as-if* approach to the symbolic meaning is deemed more productive than a literal translation.[43] If we return to the example in the previous section, where in a dream, an archetypal spiritual figure challenges the dreamer to stop squandering their human potential, we can then actively imagine this dream figure saying something along the lines of: "You have neglected the spiritual life, but the spirit has not neglected you." The engagement and meaning of the dream encounter, through reflection and active imagination, provides new vistas for our transformational potential. Richard Tarnas[44] has stated that archetypal forces have an important function in the unfolding of our imaginative relationship to spiritual engagement and how we live in connection to the cosmos. Thus, the archetypes have a deep impact on our awareness, as well as informing us about what it means to be alive.

Jung directly experienced the powerful reality of archetypal forces during his own transformational crisis and also saw how they connected to his patients' processes,[45] revealing how both past memories and experiences can form around an archetypal symbol.[46] Because human beings (via the collective unconscious) have access to the archetypes,[47] there are cultural stories that convey the trials of individuation, such as the myth of the hero.[48] In the modern world we have new heroic icons in popular culture, as found in contemporary film. The stories found in modern films are packed full with archaic themes of heroism, facing trials, encountering good and evil, etc. However, the modern focus is often placed on famous actors and directors who talk about their work, rather than using the archetypal themes in films to inspire collective change. The film industry is such a powerful media that it could be more of a hot bed for social change and activism than it is.

There is a discernible lack of cohesion for how a new myth could inspire or harness our collective potential for global transformation. This lack of a collective mythic cohesion could have dire consequences for how we navigate our experiences of consciousness. According to Erich Neumann[1] it is our modern-day arrogance and contempt for the transpersonal dimension that actually puts us in a very vulnerable position. He speaks about the ancient Greeks and how they used myth to further awareness, for example the story of Icarus who tried to fly high with feathered wings which were held together by wax, only to plunge into the sea. These stories often resonate with our human predicament and can be used metaphorically to aid our awareness.

In antiquity, such myths provided narratives of human relationships with the transpersonal dimension and contained wisdom for how humans could encounter challenges or trials, especially when archetypal forces were confronted. In short, they challenged people to grow in transpersonal awareness. It is important here to note that our myths need to convey both the trials of human existence, but also how they have a collective resonance for growth and new beginnings. Neumann[1] has made a clear reference to the limitations of modern-day consciousness in this regard, stating emphatically that an overly individualistic mind-set creates a separation from the archetypes. In other words, the opposite is needed. Our orientation in life has to be bound to the collective dimensions in which we live. Richard Holloway[49] eloquently states the relevance of myths to the human condition, suggesting that there is no point asking if a myth is true or false. He believes the right question to ask is if the myth is alive or dead. Furthermore, perhaps the real issue surrounding a living myth is what we do with it.

A clear example of the hero myth, to illustrate the trials encountered in psycho-spiritual crises, can be found in the work of Paul Rebillot,[50] who has noted how people undergoing intense transformational experiences may also find that it becomes a rite of passage where the only way out of the experience is to go through it. This proposition is the basis for Jungian therapy, and in taking such a journey we find new reference points for living. Within such encounters, the process of individuation brings to the fore challenges that are linked to personal myths.[51] These personal myths reflect the meanings in our individual life trajectories and propensities, including our personal struggles, and how we relate to our talents, personal gifts and potentials that are trying to manifest in our lives. Our work is to try and understand the bigger story within us, to live the potential we possess, and develop a productive relationship to archetypal material from the collective unconscious (dreams, etc.).[52] The deep patterns of growth and development found in symbolic forms and processes (like in the myth of the hero) actually reveal an archetype of individuation.[53] This reflects our human predisposition to develop, as we cultivate an authentic and productive relationship to the healing forces in the unconscious.

Traditions that support the process of individuation such as are found in Jungian and transpersonal psychology enable people to *go beyond* the executive functions of the ego and the everyday mask of the persona in readiness to face the unconscious. Christopher Bache[21] argues that in light of the challenges facing humanity, the idea of the individual hero needs to make way for a collective representation of the heroic. This translates as a call for the collective mobilisation of the archetype of transformation, and it is here that Jung's theories have strong resonances with the work of Stanislav Grof,[54] who found that people's experiences of transpersonal states of consciousness bear striking similarities to Jung's archetypal symbols. It further suggests that a numinous quality can be accessed in the deeper layers of the psyche, when the ego's dominance is eclipsed – revealing that the ego is not the centre of consciousness – and the recognition of this enables us to enter a world full of mystery and potential.

Mystery and meaning

The reality that life is a mystery can be found in philosophical reflections going back to the ancient Greeks. Bede Griffiths[5] quotes the early Greek philosopher, Heraclitus, who stated that reality is in a constant state of flux. Heraclitus contemplated the forms and flow of life, and was inspired to say that the spirit is a source of creative emergence.[55] These reflections are helpful to us when we probe and question the various experiences that form the different contexts of our life, as illustrated by Vickers[56] who speaks about the famous proclamation by Heraclitus, that *we never step in the same river twice.* Yet, Vickers asks us to differentiate the *form* of the river banks from the water that *flows* through it at any given moment. Only then do we appreciate the conundrum set by Heraclitus and how we have to face our assumptions about what constitutes our understanding of the river, the form or the flow?

Heraclitus's observations are helpful to us in the modern world. For example, we probably all get lulled into thinking that the forms of everyday life are solid, fixed and durable, but as we explored in chapter one, even our own bodies are in a constant state of dynamic flow and transformation. The paradoxical statements made by Heraclitus make us think about how we participate in everyday life, and with what level of conscious engagement we approach our experiences. How often do any of us regularly question or examine closely the forms in which we function on a day-to-day basis? I would imagine a few dedicated souls do, but not the vast majority of people. It is here that such reflections have a part to play in how we develop a discerning attitude towards our life experiences. For example, in order to appreciate the meaning of life as a mystery we have to understand that its function is to take our attention away from superficial appearances, to a deeper level of engagement,[4] that is, beyond the executive functions of the ego.

Today we are immersed in and influenced by the technological and consumer-based world of appearances. As a consequence we live in a world that is over-developed in terms of our consumer based ego-orientations, and we have an underdeveloped relationship to the deeper world of the psyche, connected to the collective unconscious, the archetypes and the mystery of the numinous. Jung stood out as a pioneer ahead of his time, especially when he announced in the mid-20th century that there will come a time of confrontation in the human psyche when we will be forced to wake up to what we have become and what we have neglected to develop. This poignant observation is now becoming more pressing as we enter the 21st century and are facing a burgeoning ecological crisis. Jung[57] stated that Heraclitus taught the law of enantiodromia, meaning a process of *conversion into the opposite.* It is becoming increasingly clear that our modern one-sided consumer-orientated consciousness is not sufficiently prepared to face the decades of over-investment in rationality, which has been the growing legacy of the modern technological era until the present time. Indeed, our attempts to divorce ourselves from the natural rhythms of life to dominate and conquer the planet are set to haunt us as we face the consequences of our collective actions.

Jung's concern about the state of modern ego-consciousness in 1945 shows our collective avoidance of the unconscious is longstanding. What would Jung say today about our relentless fixation on consumerism, and our reckless pursuit of economic gain? We have an opportunity to begin to reappraise and understand the significance and meaning of the numinous.[58] However, this means we have to start developing our relationship to a transpersonal dimension of consciousness, and begin to integrate transformational shifts into everyday life. Griffiths[5] explains that it is through engaging our spiritual potential that the executive function of the ego evolves a new relationship to consciousness, as the Self comes more into focus. What this means at a deeper level is we are opened up to new experiences, beyond consensus reality, towards more life-changing and transformative opportunities. The following example (adapted from a previous publication)[59] reveals how a process of psycho-spiritual emergence not only initiated a former client's recovery, but also how it catalysed a meaningful transformation in his spiritual journey in life.

—————————— **The hidden healer** ——————————

During an initial assessment in an outpatient psychological therapy service with a client who had a complex life history, I was struck by a very peaceful presence in the room, and I respectfully asked the person if they had any spiritual interests in life. Within seconds of asking the question the client was raging about a whole series of injustices that had happened in his life. We worked together to understand how his life history was impacting on his mental health difficulties.

About one year after I had discharged the client from my caseload, I was working in another city and received a call from his consultant psychiatrist asking if I would be willing to telephone my ex-client, as he had something important that he wanted to tell me. I agreed, and the ex-client recounted the following story on the phone. He was at a social event with his wife, when a woman he had never met before said to him that she felt a sense of peace in his company and asked him if he was a spiritual person. He said to the woman that she was the second person to have said this to him.

The conversation at the party led him to become curious about spiritual matters, and what this could mean for him. When we spoke on the phone, he said: "It's like all the bits of the jigsaw coming together." The transformation in this man from the time that I had first met him was quite significant. He had started to find his spiritual direction in life, exploring the meaning of new ways of 'doing' in his life through becoming a spiritual healer. From the point of view of our work together, I did nothing except respectfully, and in a non-directive way, mention the subject of spirituality. The main focus of our work together had been on helping him understand the impact of traumatic events in his life. It is my view that putting the trauma into context enabled this client to be attentive to his spiritual potential.

Ursula Le Guin[60] has encapsulated the idea of an unfolding journey of discovery in life, alluding to the idea that there is no purpose in asking questions about what the meaning of life is. She believes that whatever ideas we may have about meaning, are not really questions, they are about how we live our lives, wherein we find that we are the answer. How we encounter a deeper sense of meaning in life is often through numinous experiences, which can touch into the very foundations of our existence. The significance and meaning of the numinous to the journey of transformation we have been discussing so far will be explored more fully in the next chapter.

Exercise

- Write down, in brief notes, the general direction that your life has been taking:

    o In what contexts are you troubled in life?
    o In what contexts are you strengthened in life?
    o In what contexts are you diminished spiritually?
    o In what contexts do you flourish spiritually?

- Go inward and try to connect to the deeper undercurrents in your life – through your dreams or deepest aspirations.

- Recall if you feel (or have previously felt) a connection with a hero or heroine who inspires you. This could be a living or historical figure, or it could be a character from a dream you have had.

- Bring that figure to mind and examine the qualities he or she possesses. Think about qualities that you admire.

- Using your imagination – interact with and speak to the figure – try to find a meaningful connection to this figure that will inspire the direction you are taking in life.

We are blessed when the sacred mystery breaks into our everyday lives.
These blessings can impact on the meticulous plans of our ego-consciousness.

CHAPTER FOUR

The meaning of the numinous

Overview

In this chapter I explore in greater depth the human connection to numinous encounters. These deep experiences have important implications for appreciating the mystery of the self, in terms of who we are and the mystery of life. A central theme of this chapter is the way that the numinous can help us enter into a productive relationship with our transformational potential, which is based on a deep process of renewal in consciousness. I discuss how the numinous is linked to ancient spiritual traditions, such as shamanism, which were found throughout the world and have existed for tens of thousands of years. The numinous is identified as a key variable for facilitating the much-needed shift in consciousness at this present time of global crisis.

The numinous as sacred mystery

The numinous is a type of mystical encounter that transcends the usual reference points of everyday living. Such experiences have a quality of meeting the holy,[1] which can be either overpowering or captivating.[2] Numinous encounters can be triggered spontaneously, when connecting with the natural world for example, or they can be induced by spiritual practices[3] such as fasting, meditation or prayer, as well as taking part in the creative arts, experiencing natural beauty, engaging in physical activities, or through crises in personal relations.[4] These experiences result in people having a feeling connection[5] with the transcendent dimension.[6]

Rudolph Otto's[2] pioneering work on the numinous from a cross-cultural perspective created an awareness of religious experiences,[1] and how spiritual traditions and practices across the globe share an ability to activate a spark of the divine in our lives.[7] Hence, the numinous is often experienced as an encounter involving a sense of revelation or intimation of divine forces,[8] which can have a dramatic impact on an individual's experiential understanding of the sacred dimension. Sir Alistair Hardy[4] has published an extensive array of first-person accounts of numinous encounters, which are consistent in showing how people's direct experiences impact on their consciousness and/or understanding of spirituality. Hardy identified how spiritual experiences affect people's sense of time and space. For example, one person mentioned an experience of time standing still and a feeling of exultation, whereas another reported an experience of *understanding* the meaning of universe accompanied by a sense of lightness, exhilaration and power. Jung[9] emphasised how these mystical/transpersonal experiences can initiate and catalyse major transformations in consciousness. He noted that the way human beings respond to experiences of the numinous was significant, particularly as they can help people become aware of their potential for wholeness and individuation. For example, Hick[5] reports a first-person account of a deep transcendent experience where the respondent spoke about feelings of ecstasy, but they also noted how the encounter led to a deep sense of humility. It reveals how the numinous can be experienced as an affective sacred encounter that impacts on consciousness, underscoring the phenomenological importance of such experiences.[10]

Rudolph Otto[2] noted that contact with the numinous – *mysterium tremundum* (awesome and overpowering mystery) and *mysterium fascinans* (fascinating and captivating mystery) – are active and affective processes that can have a dynamic impact on people, through opening their conscious awareness[11] to the transcendent dimension. Jung's psycho-spiritual understanding of the numinous endorsed the view of the 14th-century mystic, Meister Eckhart, who believed that the sacred must be born, so that it can see through our eyes and consciousness.[12] That is, such mystical experiences are akin to awakening to a new dimension of conscious awareness and experience. Jung's position on the psychological importance of the numinous coheres with Otto's research, in which the theologian noted that the numinous had to be considered in relation to its impact on our direct experiences and our consciousness.

An encounter with the numinous not only takes us directly into a dynamic reality,[13] it can reframe our perceptions of life, where we begin to evolve a new relationship to the transcendent. Elkins[14] describes the development of such capacities like being able to see with sacred eyes. Humans are multi-sensory beings and such transcendent experiences will impact on our sensory world of perception and expression in a variety of ways. Jennifer Elam's[15] research describes a participant whose sensory perceptions were fully engaged and heightened by their mystical experience, which included a sense of being part of everything (wholeness) and beyond ordinary time. Our various multi-sensory modes of perception and expression, such as visual, auditory, touch, smell and movement, should be taken into consideration when reflecting on numinous encounters.[16,17] These modes of perception and expression are mostly involved in our everyday engagement in the world, but they can also mediate our direct experience of the sacred.

According to psychotherapist, author and former monk Thomas Moore,[18] all humans have the ability to be receptive to the numinous. He has suggested that it involves cultivating a new type of awareness and attitude that is open to encounters where we are seized by awe or beauty. However, it also needs to be stated that an experience of the numinous is not always a pleasant mystical experience that enhances our everyday understanding of life. It can also be accompanied by a great surge or force of energy, which may be experienced as intoxicating or terrifying. Jung[19] is quoted as saying that such an experience can upset our ideas and aspirations, even changing the course of our lives for better or worse. Thus, an encounter with the numinous awakens a sense of urgency and vitality. It is also loaded with emotion and is characteristically non-rational.[20] Therefore, the energy that comes with numinous experiences needs to be treated with great respect and approached with a degree of humility, particularly as numinous experiences will always be beyond the control of ego-consciousness. This is why the numinous is a harbinger of transformation, awakening our innate sense of spirit and eclipsing the dominance of the ego. It is when we consciously work to make sense of such experiences, and integrate new insights into the fabric of our everyday lives, that we deepen our connections to life as a mystery.

The meaning of the numinous in everyday life

The power of numinous experiences can often shock us into experiencing a new quality of consciousness, as well as bringing about a change in our relationship to the world.[21] Such encounters with the numinous enable us to engage more fluidly with the inner and outer dimensions of our lived experiences: our ways of doing, knowing and being. These experiences bring new opportunities for cultivating a deeper relationship to the mystery of life. Alan Watts[22] once said that human beings need to have experiences or feelings of a new sense of I. Interestingly, Eric Erikson,[23] who did much work on understanding identity through the life-cycle, incorporated the numinous into his formulation about the types of experiences that inform identity developments. In this way, the presence of the numinous awakens new responses to life that can be expressed in our everyday lives.[18]

It is evident that numinous encounters carry the revitalising power of sacred experiences, described by Larsen[24] as a breakthrough to the numinous, which he terms as either a spiritual illumination or a mythic encounter. An important issue for us today is whether we are able to acknowledge the existence of the numinous, and have the willingness to engage with the mystery that it brings. The numinous is unpredictable, and it is capable of intruding into our lives when and where there is an opportunity,[25] that means that our consciousness is predisposed to experience moments of mystery and a re-awakening of the sacred, which can be revealed and realised through our reflections and actions. Our human response to this important area of transpersonal development cannot be overstated. Maslow[26] noted that we become ill, bored or aggressive when we lose contact with the transcendent. We only have to look at the state of the modern world today and how our relationship to it has become de-sacralised, through our behaviours and attitudes toward one another, other species and nature as a whole. The collective attitudes and activities currently being perpetuated in the world, particularly in terms of environmental destruction, war and the propagation of greed, are very real examples of such dissociative behaviours. We might consider how an appreciation of the sacred dimension in life provides a powerful counter-balance to the consumer-based mind-set that is so prevalent in the modern world today. Allen and Sabini[27] offer a thought-provoking reflection when they ask, where will we find sources of healing the more our rational values, attitudes and behaviours (including institutions to which we belong) are disconnected from the sacred and the healing power of the numinous?

The numinous brings human beings into a direct relationship with the sacred, which reveals a mystical dimension to life that can become a sacrament and a transforming power.[28] Indeed, it is an appreciation of the spiritual dimension in everyday life that Ann Bancroft[29] has described as being inspirational for living a sacramental approach to life. We cannot force the numinous into existence, as it comes *unbidden* – yet, as Jung was keen to point out – it is our conscious response to numinous encounters, which takes us into a deeper connection with life. Eric Erikson[23] also warns that the sacred dimension cannot be manipulated by our ordinary consciousness, noting that the numinous becomes more elusive if it is pursued as an ego-driven acquisition or activity. There is a need to cultivate an orientation in life that acknowledges the depth, mystery, and meaning of life as a sacrament without the expectation that we will regularly experience full-blown mystical encounters: we may, or we may not. However, it is more important that we are awake to life's subtleties and mysteries. It is our responsibility to train our awareness to understand how the sacred dimension permeates the whole of existence. Thomas Moore[30] reminds us that the numinous is experienced as a profound sense of awe, as well as connecting us to nature, others and a mysterious creative power in life. Thus, if we are open to the numinous it can have consequences for our identities, relationships, and actions in the world. In this way the mystery of the numinous infuses our everyday engagements and experiences in life, where it guides, nourishes, challenges and inspires us to value the presence of the sacred.

The numinous and human potential

Rudolph Otto's[2] research into the numinous focused on exploring the sacred in terms of phenomenal experience,[31] and he emphasised the importance of a transcendent dimension of consciousness. Otto[2] believed that in the journey of developing spiritual consciousness, human beings have to evolve their awareness. This evolutionary connection to the sacred has important implications for how humanity considers its spiritual heritage, particularly the interface between spiritual emergence and spiritual emergencies.[11,16]

In a previous publication I explored how the dynamic qualities of numinous encounters bring the transpersonal dimension into direct contact with ego-consciousness, which can either be life-enhancing or existentially challenging.[16] The resulting experiences may connect to processes that enhance spiritual emergence or catalyse spiritual emergencies.[32] Otto[2] illustrated two qualitatively different experiences of the numinous and the impact of such encounters on human consciousness.[11,16] The first coheres with processes linked to spiritual emergence, which reflect *luminous experiences* describing the sacred as beatific, tranquil and resonant. Whereas the second is more indicative of an overwhelming encounter, which is marked by *ominous experiences* that are described as intoxicating, wild and ecstatic. The latter experiences are more connected with spiritual emergencies.[32] Otto's[2] view of the numinous reveals an evolutionary propensity and connection to sacred forces that dates back to ancient history and early human experiences of the transcendent dimension. From this perspective every one of us carries a spark of the sacred in our human heritage.[11,16]

In evolutionary terms, our ancestor's encounters with the numinous are be-lieved to have developed through rituals that resulted in new understandings of transcendent awareness,[33,34] that may have correlated with their capacity to develop new levels of meaning-making. It has been proposed that the evolu-tionary significance of the numinous and its connection to ritualised behav-iours,[11,16] has led to the development of more sophisticated brains that guided the modification of consciousness.[33] This evolutionary (ritualised) trajectory may have caused new connective pathways in the brains of early humans, which laid the biological foundations for the emergence of human consciousness.[33]

The question is, if ritual numinous encounters played a part in the development of early human consciousness[33] through learnt *pre-religious* behaviours,[35] then this hypothesis lends support to the argument that the human brain may be neurologically-wired[36] to experience the sacred.[37,38,39] For example, evolutionary psychologists have considered how art in the Pleistocene period is an expression of spiritual ideas, where the groups that our ancestors belonged to became more unified through the production and use of such artistic symbols, which provided a sense of collective focus.[40] Sir Alistair Hardy[41] has noted how a felt sense of the Holy (an experience of the sacred) could be as ancient as the beginnings of evolution and consciousness. By this he means that early humans appear to have recognised a connection with a mysterious power that was greater than them. Indeed, it has been suggested that early human ritualised behaviours not only provided access to transpersonal states of consciousness,[42] they also present a plausible explanation for the presence and centrality of transformational crises,[16] seen across cultures in ancient spiritual traditions and practices, such as shamanism.[43,44]

The origins of the sacred in human experience are ancient.[16] For example, the evolutionary development of the neuro-anatomical areas involved in religious experiences has been discussed by Joseph,[45] who points out that early humans possessed well-developed areas in the brain, which are implicated in modern humans having the capacity for mystical experiences (inferior temporal lobe and limbic system). Moreover, Joseph[45] viewed these sacred encounters from a (Jungian) archetypal perspective, suggesting that human beings' capacity for having deep (numinous) experiences is connected to collective ideas, including *God, the Great Spirit* and *the Goddess*. However, Professor of transpersonal psychology, Les Lancaster[46] cautions that any presumed links between spiritual experiences and the brain require thorough analysis about the key features of those experiences being researched. Newberg[47] concurs with this perspective, noting that the subjective nature of such encounters adds complexity to the issue.[16] Yet, our spiritual heritage is ancient and whilst it is a difficult subject to research, we should continue to do so. *Homo sapiens* cultivated pre-religious sensibilities and evolved what is referred to today as *Homo religiousus*.[16,35,48] The role of our spiritual heritage in the development of our evolutionary potential is important for our current understanding of mystical and transpersonal states of consciousness. The specialised field of neuro-theology is helping to reveal how mystical encounters, as experienced in the brain, are beginning to shed light on scientific understandings of spiritual phenomena.[49,50,51] If, as Caroline Myss[52] suggests, our biology intrinsically connects to an embodied theology, then it is incumbent upon all of us to consider what this sacred connection means in terms of our lived experiences – our ways of doing, knowing, being, becoming and belonging. The numinous spark in every person can be ignited, and such encounters can illuminate deeper meanings in life.

The numinous and spiritual renewal

Our human capacity to construct meaning[53] and to make sense of the numinous adds a transcendent dimension to living.[16] However, there is a further connection between the evolutionary development of cultural myths[54] and the numinous,[55] which adds greater meaning for understanding our ancestor's early pre-religious behaviours. Anthropological theories support the notion that the cross-cultural prevalence of ancient shamanic practices has contributed to the evolution of consciousness.[56,57,58] Furthermore, Erich Neumann[59] has pointed out that early humans engaged with the transpersonal dimension, and the meaning of these early ritualistic activities led to a greater contact with a sacred *ground of being*, where the spirit could be experienced as *wholly other*, yet can also be experienced as a reality to which they could connect and *belong*. This is where the power of ritual enables the personal dimension to be momentarily transcended.[59]

A key observation of such ritualistic encounters, as found in shamanic initiations, is that spiritual crises are recognised as an integral part of the initiation process.[16] Yet, the potential value of recognising spiritual emergencies for understanding how we engage our transpersonal potential has not yet been considered in neuro-theological investigations.[32] The recent Jungian perspective put forward by Haule,[60] exploring the evolutionary influences of consciousness, archetypes and the numinous, is an encouraging development. However, there needs to be more discussion about the role and function of spiritual emergencies in such evolutionary neurological developments for two reasons. First, if human beings have the capacity to develop their transpersonal potential, then any scientific or cultural avoidance and denial of the numinous and sacred dimension is a wasted opportunity. Second, if the suggestion is correct that the global crisis is reciprocally linked to a spiritual crisis, as originally noted by Jung,[61] then there is an urgent need to understand how such crises could be productive in terms of engaging transformative potential, as recorded in shamanic lineages.[43] This highlights the significance of numinous encounters to modern humans. It suggests that they are highly valuable in terms of their impact on states of being,[62] including their contribution to processes of healing.[63] We find this numinous link to healing in religious traditions like shamanism and in-depth psycho-therapy,[16] particularly the Jungian and transpersonal schools.[8,64,65] It means that they are alive and active in our world today.

Experiences of the numinous – as transpersonal phenomena[66] – will undoubtedly challenge the collective values that inform our understanding of everyday consensus reality,[67] and can also impact on and shape our collective attitudes and behaviours.[68] Indeed, such mystical encounters reveal experiences that reflect a non-consensus reality,[69] where the margins between consensus and non-consensus experiences (connected to mystical/spiritual states of consciousness) also highlight the potential socio-political impact on the psyche.[70] For example, Christopher Bache[71] believes that the numinous could activate a more connected and integral experience of life, as distinct from the political consensus that informs much of everyday reality today. He notes that the work of Carl Jung, Stanislav Grof and Richard Tarnas has already laid foundations for the evolution of unitive states of consciousness, where the numinous leads us into a renewed understanding of our connection to all life and the cosmos. Bache underlines the importance of our experiences of the numinous, which Jung had already said could lead to greater insights on our transformative journeys.[72] Yet, it has to be pointed out that the process of individuation needs more than a numinous encounter alone.[73] Indeed, the numinous can only inspire humans to wake up. From then on, effort is needed for the work of integration and transformation.

─────── **A Jungian analyst's reflections on the numinous** ───────

A friend of mine, a Jungian analyst, spoke to me about a client he once analysed, which led to a powerful numinous experience. The woman he worked with had been a successful business woman and was head of a family with all the hallmarks of success in the world. The woman's husband had long since died, and she spent time in her room, reading, writing her journal and painting. Nobody shared this part of her life with her, not even her husband when he was alive.

The psychotherapy – coming towards the autumn of her life – highlighted the imbalances arising from her powerful masculine role at work and at home. She held the belief that anything a man could do she could do better. The male analyst was not seduced by her stories of meeting and knowing powerful people. Instead he probed the meaning of the dynamics underlying these stories, and gently encouraged her, over and over again, to trust her own psyche. Eventually, a deep sadness welled up within her, which connected to a feeling of betrayal for the lack of any real representation of the feminine in her life: that is, what it means to be a complete woman. It transpired that outwitting all the men in her life had not been enough.

In one of the psychotherapy sessions they both experienced a weary sense of defeat. In humility my friend reflected with his client on the work that they had done together, and how she had reached a place where she now accepted herself as a widow, a mother and grandmother. However, my friend said to his client that in terms of finding and connecting to her deeper nature as an individuating whole woman, such a process would have to come from within her. Shortly after this session their work together came to an end. The woman's family had always been dismissive of her coming to therapy. However, 10 years later my friend had a telephone call from the eldest daughter saying that her mother was going in and out of coma states following a stroke. The daughter said her mother had asked that my friend be contacted and invited to visit her in the hospital.

In recounting the event that follows, my friend said that the hairs on his body stood up. He went on to say: "I arrived at the hospital and upon entering the dimly lit room the family got up and left. I sat in meditation by the side of the woman's bed, as she lay there with her eyes closed, and I remembered the many learning experiences in the analytic encounters we had shared. Then, suddenly she sat bolt upright in the bed, looked at me with her piercing blue eyes and said: 'I just wanted to say thank you.' That was all she said but the atmosphere in the room was electric and in a flash I understood the connection between the analytic work and something far more powerful. It was a moment where time stood still and where a palpable sense of the spirit was present, as it always had been." She died shortly afterwards. He then goes on to say: "This experience deepened my understanding about what it really means to be invited into the *psyche* of another person and to share some of the journey with them. The experience was such a revelation that the use of the word sacred to describe the event does not seem out of place."

When I asked how such numinous encounters affected my friend's work, he went on to say: "In my professional work at that time I was serving on the Board of a National Health Service, Mental Health Trust as Medical Director, providing a consultant-led psychotherapy service and running a private practice in analytical psychology. The realisation that my everyday working life can connect with something far beyond it enabled me to become more comfortable with the idea that a mystical aspect of reality is ever present. I had more confidence that going on retreats was not only about recharging my batteries, but that it energised my work spiritually. The ongoing administrative duties and endless project planning did not diminish my conviction that one by one we can prepare each other to drop our illusions and face reality as it is. The *way* for me became more illuminated. I realised deeply that therapeutic work can be a starting place, indeed it can become a true *Temenos* for transformation, as long as we realise that spiritual development is not only about endless reflection, it must be put into action."

The above illustration is a powerful reflection on the deep, meaningful and numinous nature that such psychological work brings to our lives. Sonu Shamdasani[74] explains Jung's therapeutic outlook as a journey of individuation, where a person confronts their personal experience of hell (the disavowed unconscious) and then returns to integrate new insights into lived reality. This is akin to the process of initiation that is found in shamanic cultures. Encounters with the numinous challenge humanity to enter into the mystery of life, which also provides opportunities for humans to participate in a creative expansion of consciousness.[75] The lack of meaningful recognition of the numinous in modern societies has no doubt contributed to reinforcing a one-dimensional worldview with an overemphasis on consumer-based lifestyles, which has resulted in a progressive and collective loss of contact with the sacred. In addition, the excessive celebration of human achievements in the material world has also cast a shadow, as Mircea Eliade[76] notes, saying that the more humans engage in acts that *desacralize* each other and the world, the more the sacred becomes a barrier to real emancipation.

This is a compelling argument for humanity to start relinquishing the dominance of the rational ego as the only reference for living consciously. Around the world there is ample evidence of historical sacred lineages that have evolved technologies of transcendence, and these are paths to freedom, that is, they require a deeper engagement of consciousness. A theme that I address throughout the book focuses on what can happen when our experience of self is expanded by profound connections to life and the universe. An example of how a profound experience of connecting to the universe can lead to a profound shift in consciousness, is described in the following story adapted from a previous publication.[77]

Opening to the universe

Dr Edward Whitney M.D.,[78] who described himself as a person with a lifelong interest in spirituality, was stopped by police one day as he was wandering along a beach in his underwear and T-shirt. He said that on his walk he was connecting electrons in galaxies far away and seeking God. He spoke about a deep feeling of transformation concerning the meaning of everything that had ever happened in his life. The power of this transpersonal experience was so great that a few days later he was detained in hospital for 72 hours. He told the duty psychiatrist that he was overwhelmed by a sense of angelic presence. In response, the duty psychiatrist told him that his ideas were psychotic and prescribed medication. Deep transformational experiences can appear as, and sometimes overlap with, a psychotic presentation. The important point is to be able to make clear distinctions about what is happening for the person having the experience and to provide the right support.

Reflecting on his experience with the psychiatric services, Dr Whitney said that the mental health professionals and he had different opinions about the experiences he was having. He said the mental health professionals did not know anything about the concept of spiritual emergency, let alone know how to help him. Dr Whitney conveyed the complexities of experiencing such non-ordinary occurrences in the face of conventional medical ideology, which is still not fully prepared to tackle questions of a transpersonal nature. He said that if he had followed the advice of the mental health professionals without questioning, he doubts whether he would have lived to tell his story. The very thought of such an outcome would have led to complete despair. Eventually Dr Whitney met a psychiatrist who understood that he was experiencing a spiritual/transformative crisis, which many people have passed through successfully. Rather than a psychiatric breakdown, Dr Whitney had had an unexpected and deeply connected transpersonal experience, where he felt a profound connection and sense of oneness with the cosmos. We all have the potential for such moments of connectedness, and I share my own experience of spiritual emergency in chapter thirteen.

It is easy to imagine a very different outcome for Dr Whitney had he not had the inner resolve to trust his experience and also the good fortune to meet a psychiatrist who understood the meaning of transformational crisis. Two professional psychiatrists had diametrically opposed opinions on Dr Whitney's experience, with potentially very different consequences for how he moved forward purposefully in his life. If they are to be of any help, professional opinions about what constitutes our identities and ways of doing, knowing and being require a full appreciation of the spectrum of human potential and development, as noted by transpersonal orientated scholars and practitioners. More importantly, as a society we need to acknowledge that there are experiences that go beyond the norm, and which can impact deeply on people's lives. This vignette again illustrates two significant and interrelated points I am trying to convey in this book. The first is that at the most subtle level we are stardust, deeply enmeshed and embedded within the universe as a whole, yet we continue to behave in overly self-referential ways as though we are totally separate from nature. The second point is that we are capable of having deep experiences in our conscious engagement with the world, revealing how we are experientially interconnected with all life. Such encounters widen our experience of consciousness and identity in ways that people who have gone through them are profoundly changed by. The types of changes that people report are often of a deep and mystical nature.

David Tacey[79] puts into context the need for a more expansive frame of reference when considering human development and consciousness in the modern world. He points out that our conceptual understanding of the psyche is restricted, and he raises the alarm about the state of our modern consciousness when he speaks about the neglect of our psychic totality. In short, our one-sided ego-consciousness leaves us open to the forces in the unconscious, which are capable of destroying our wellbeing, as well as the planet. Tacey informs us that this is why Jung was dedicated to understanding the forces that operate in the psyche and particularly the insights from mythological, cosmological and religious ideas that point to a more holistic relationship to life. The mystical heritage of humanity will be explored in the next chapter, where I will identify what this means in terms of cultivating a deeper relationship to the sacred dimension.

Exercise

The experience of the numinous is described as an encounter with an awesome and fascinating mystery.

- Recall a time when you were awestruck or fascinated in the face of life and its deep mysteriousness. Write down the key features of that numinous encounter, including your reactions and feelings.

- Now bring to mind an issue or problem that you are facing in your everyday life. Write a list of the moods and impact that this issue is bringing into your life.

- Take a moment to feel the sense of difficulty, despair or hopelessness that this problem brings.

- Go back to the notes you made about the numinous experience you had. Re-read your words and imagine a helpful apparition or presence that would come before you now (from that numinous experience). It could be a spiritual figure, an angel, a quality or element in the natural world, or an animal.

- Notice something inspirational in this apparition or presence. Consider what meaning this inspirational quality has for your life.

- Find out how this inspirational quality may help you face the problem or issue in point three.

*The emergence of an engaged and dynamic relationship to our
transpersonal potential is a birth into the mystery of who we truly are.
At such times, the spirit is like a wise and ancient midwife.*

CHAPTER FIVE

The mystical heritage

Overview

This chapter discusses the diverse spiritual heritage of mystical traditions
around the world. The deep potential within spiritual practices for transforming
consciousness is contrasted with the modern propensity for over-investing in
a one-sided, consumer-based ego-consciousness. I describe how our mystical
heritage could help us evolve a new relationship to spirituality, based on a re-
sacralised view that engages in life from a more holistic perspective, through our
ways of doing-in-the-world. This would allow us to connect more intimately
with other people, other species, and nature as a whole.

Technologies of transcendence

Since the earliest of times, humanity has evolved religious ideas and practices,
from Stone Age shamanism to the Eleusinian Mysteries of ancient Greece;[1] from
the religions of India, including Hinduism and Buddhism, to the Middle East
traditions of Judaism, Christianity and Islam.[2,3] Humanity's spiritual heritage
reveals a vast spectrum of rituals and practices that underscore the prime importance of humans finding ways to live a sacred life.[4] Karen Armstrong has written
about the inspired and ingenious responses to sacred encounters by human beings,[5] in particular the emergence of religious developments during the Axial Age
(900 to 200BC). Armstrong has pointed out how spiritual traditions developed
practices that integrated compassion, kindness, love and recognition of the impact of the transcendent on human consciousness.[5] Spiritual traditions that have
methods of awakening our conscious relationship to the whole reveal the art of
transpersonal development and the evolution of technologies of transcendence.[6]

Technologies of transcendence[6] include (among many others) shamanic journey-
ing, which involves entering into a mystical process of symbolic death and
resurrection.[7] In Buddhist tantra, we find meditations that connect people to the
subtle body, through channels (nādī) and flow of energy/wind (prajnā), which
are intended to awaken the mind to a direct cognition of emptiness (shūnyatā)[8]

and non-duality.[9] We find in Sufi practices a focus on the inner path of self transformation (from the personal-self of the ego, to the transpersonal-Self of the Spirit),[10] which are designed to connect people to mystical experiences and provide a sense of spiritual renewal.[11] And in Christianity there are practices, such as divine indwelling, which are intended to lead to greater clarity (from illusions)[12] as a way of contemplation and redemption.[13] The quality of the inner spiritual journey[14] is reflected in the mystical perspective of 14th-century German mystic, Meister Eckhart who noted that our eyes and God's eyes are one.[15]

A helpful way of understanding the need for technologies of transcendence[6] is found in Rudolph Otto's[16] analysis of the function of the numinous, describing it as a universal quality of the holy. He stated that the numinous is the core of religious or sacred experience. It must be remembered that the numinous was considered by Otto[16] as pivotal for connecting experiences of the sacred to human consciousness, but he was also careful to point out that the numinous is awakened through spirit. In other words, the mystery of the numinous is revelatory and cannot be manipulated by human will. There are many famous accounts of saints and sages who have encountered the numinous and awakened to the trials that such experiences bring, for example, Saint Teresa of Ávila, Sri Ramana Maharshi, Mother Julian of Norwich, Jiddu Krishnamurti and Saint Francis of Assisi, among many others. These inspirational people exemplify the humility and devotion of those who have encountered the sacred. Yet, such experiences evoke deep (and often) profound challenges.

The writings of Carmelite monk, Saint John of the Cross (who lived in Spain, circa 1542), reveals how the trials of numinous encounters can manifest as a dark night of the soul, leading to an experience of purgation, that is, where a person is opened up to the mystery of the divine.[17] The former Catholic monk, now a psychotherapist, Thomas Moore,[18] has spoken about the dark night of the soul as a process of deep change and transformation. This sense of darkness can be considered more like an eclipse of the ego, where consciousness undergoes a process of awakening. It is crucial that such mystical experiences are recognised as transpersonal developments, otherwise we are capable of labelling such states as mental illness.[19] This is a highly important point, particularly as many well respected spiritual figures have passed through deep transformational crises, which adds credibility and recognition that these processes are an integral part of spiritual development. Yet, these deep and profound transformational experiences reveal that the mystical path is fraught with complexities. It can often take genuine courage to stay with the unfolding nature of a transformative process, especially when encountering life as a deep mystery and journey into the unknown, as intimated in the poetic writings of Saint John of the Cross, who through his mystical encounters alludes to the death of the dominance of his ego-self, but he also mentions the renewed Self that lives on.[20] The beauty of the lives of saints and sages is that they reveal not only their sacred epiphanies and illuminations, but also their struggles and challenges as they opened up to a new dawn in consciousness.

An encounter with the numinous brings great potential for healing as well as growth in awareness of the sacred. Dourley[21] suggests that such encounters with the numinous are powerful enough to convince anyone who experiences them, that they have been touched by the divine. Jung[22] went to great lengths to point out that it is one of our tasks in life to wake up to these important numinous experiences. He said that life will continue with or without our conscious awareness, but he offers a sobering reminder of the futility of trying to ignore a deeper engagement of consciousness. Essentially, if we ignore the meaning of the numinous (and by implication our wholeness), we stagger one-sidedly to our fate. In this way, Jung's work is a testimony to his deep respect for how the sacred is part of our wholeness. The point is that both major and minor events in life can become sacramental, providing opportunities for deepening our process of individuation. The numinous informs and inspires our transformational journeys, particularly since it can bring about significant changes in human behaviour.[23] The following story reveals the inspirational journey of one man who encountered the spirit and how it profoundly changed his life.

The armed robber who became a monk

Each year my wife and I attend a retreat at a Benedictine monastery. During one of our visits some years ago we met a lay member named Ralph who was living and working in the community. I was struck that he always wore white clothes and found out that he had aspirations to become a monk. Ralph lived in the monks' quarters and always stood with the monks during the sacred offices and services. We first met when Ralph was cleaning the kitchen in the men's guest house, and we had a deep discussion about the spiritual path. I asked Ralph questions about how he had ended up in the monastery.

Ralph's story is extraordinary. He did not tell me much about his early life, but I found out that he had spent 15 years in the Royal Navy. After leaving the service, he drifted into a life of crime and was convicted of armed robbery, serving a sentence of 14 years in prison. He spoke about one New Year's Eve in prison and an event that profoundly changed his life. That evening, in his cell, Ralph had an apparition of an angel, which he believed was the Archangel Michael, and he was awe struck and shocked as this numinous encounter unfolded. The cell was full of peace, love and warmth and he felt protected. As the experience gradually faded, Ralph was a changed man (Spanish author, Mariá Vallejo-Nágera[24] has written a novel based on Ralph's story, outlining the events in more detail). In prison Ralph became a Christian and was baptised in the Catholic faith. During his time in prison Ralph was sent two books that he cherished. One was the Jerusalem Bible, and the other was a book on becoming a monk. The change in Ralph was obvious to all in the prison, and he was offered parole at a time when he still had three years of his sentence to serve (following the apparition of the Archangel Michael). He refused to take it, preferring to serve his sentence in full to atone for the crime he had committed.

Naturally, Ralph's deep encounter had a transformational impact upon him, and despite his best efforts to communicate the experience, words could never do justice to the experience. On his eventual release from prison, Ralph contacted 14 religious houses telling them about his apparition, hoping that he would be able to stay in a community where he could reflect, pray, integrate the experience, and start to cultivate his spiritual vocation. However, he found that for some reason these religious communities were not so welcoming of his life story and epiphany. I guess it must have been difficult to respond to a man who describes himself as a former armed robber, who then had an apparition of the Archangel Michael, and now wants to live in a monastery. Yet, Ralph persisted on his pilgrimage and was eventually welcomed to stay at a Benedictine monastery. The community provided sanctuary for Ralph, which helped him to establish some boundaries on his experience of the Archangel Michael and devote his life to spiritual reflection.

In many ways this monastic community helped Ralph to put his experience into a new context. The monks (and the nuns in another part of the community) acknowledged that it had been a powerful catalyst that awakened his spiritual direction. Yet, they also helped Ralph integrate the experience through engaging in the rhythms and routines of religious life in the community. On the occasions that I met Ralph he was a deeply happy man who was just as content participating in the religious offices of the day, as he was cleaning floors and washing dishes in the men's guest house. Ralph made no secret of his longing to become a Benedictine monk. However, the Abbot of the community refused his pleas, and one of the monks told me some years later that Ralph wept with disappointment. Then one day Ralph became unexpectedly ill, and it transpired that he had cancer of the liver. When Ralph eventually came out of hospital the Abbot agreed that Ralph should enter the Order of Saint Benedict (OSB) as a monk. On the day of Ralph's solemn profession (25 August 2002), one of the monks who was present at the ceremony told me Ralph looked radiant. Yet, Ralph's new vocation was to be short lived, as he passed away on 12 September 2002. Brother Ralph OSB (who took the spiritual name Michael) died aged 56 years, and he had lived in the monastery for two and a half years.

Every time I visit the monastery I go to the small garden of remembrance and the commemorative plaque to Brother Ralph (alongside all of the other monks and nuns who have passed away). I am always touched and inspired when I think of his story, for he embodied the commitment to transform his life by humbly trusting the Holy Spirit that guided him.

Brother Ralph's story is a beautiful illustration that no matter how depraved or meaningless our existence has become, we are capable of redemption when we are awoken *by the spirit*. The apparition of the Archangel Michael to Brother Ralph was a powerful catalyst that sustained him, especially when he was seeking to become a monk and encountering rejection from one religious house after another. It helped him to continue on his pilgrimage unbowed. When he eventually found a spiritual home in the Benedictine monastery he embraced his new vocation, which included the menial chores that were part of his working day. In fact, doing the cleaning alongside religious offices provided a deep and structured focus for his daily occupational routines and facilitated his spiritual path and integration, which is a central feature in the Order of Saint Benedict. The story serves as a reminder that whatever fate has befallen us we can be transformed if we have the inner resolve, conviction and ability to recognise that life is more than material existence. However, the modern world has become increasingly one-sided, in terms of materialistic attitudes.

Almost 50 years ago Carl Jung[25] commented on the modern tendency towards a one-sided consciousness, which overwhelmingly favours the rational and mostly dissociates from myth and mystery in everyday life. Jung lamented the loss of focus for the numinous in our understanding of human potential. He noted how modern attitudes had widened the gap between conscious life and the unconscious, and declared that if anyone had a mystical experience today, they would be sure to misinterpret its real meaning, and as a consequence would avoid or repress its numinosity. Jung also said that to the modern mind the holy has little or no value,[25] and he even went as far as to suggest that we are so dissociated from the sacred we are capable of diagnosing numinous experiences as pathologies. Yet, as Jennifer Elam[26] points out, consensus reality is not the only reality; indeed, beyond the norms of our modern consumer-based consciousness there are diverse ways of experiencing and knowing life.

One-sided brains and a life out of balance

Jung appreciated the psychological importance of a religious attitude, based on his understanding of encounters with the numinous that led to an alteration in his consciousness.[27] These transpersonal shifts in consciousness enable the process of individuation to evolve into a path of Self-realisation, which is linked to healing, regeneration and wholeness.[27] That is, the Self in Jung's psychology is linked to transformative states of consciousness that reflect a spiritual attitude.[28] Jung commented on how our modern 'split-off' relationship to the psyche revealed itself in our attitudes and behaviours, which reflect an unbalanced materialist worldview. Morton Kelsey[29] has noted how, following the Enlightenment, the contributions of philosophers such as René Descartes led to more emphasis being placed on reason and an increase in rationalistic and mechanistic ways of understanding life. By the 19th century this materialistic outlook had become quite dogmatic, and subsequently humans became prisoners trapped in a system where the psyche was considered far less important than our dealings with the material world.[29] Thus, the spirit had been reasoned out of our lives with efficiency and precision.

Stephanie de Voogd[30] suggests that the dominant materialist philosophy that has underpinned modern human development has made us all more literal minded.

The sad reality of our over-developed rational and literal mind-sets is that we have lost the deeper meanings associated with the symbolic and mystical. A wonderful example of our modern one-sidedness is found in the book: *The Master and his Emissary*, by Iain McGilchrist[31] who meticulously crafts a compelling argument about the role of the left brain in our over-developed rationality, which represents a functional, technical and utilitarian approach to living. McGilchrist[31] identifies the Industrial Revolution as the cause of a left-brain *assault* on life, which has been a key defining characteristic of the modern world. McGilchrist argues that the right brain has been marginalised, with qualities such as spirituality being devalued, because the dominant left-brain discounts or dismantles all that does not fit its utilitarian and reductive position.[31]

McGilchrist provides powerful evidence for the way that the left brain has eclipsed the sensibilities of the right brain in modern humans. McGilchrist's thesis is a wake-up call to the danger for how our one-sidedness is unleashing chaos in the world. Even sceptics would find it hard to argue against his concluding remarks, when he points out that even if the divided brain is only metaphorically mirroring what is happening in the world – for example the split between reductionists and holists – he notes that metaphors should be highly regarded for the insights that they convey.[31]

McGilchrist should be applauded for tackling our one-sided worldview so systematically. Yet, it has been said that few neuroscientists would support such a clear-cut division of left brain/right brain,[32] based on the brain's capacity for fluidity and plasticity. This does not mean we should overlook the location and function of discrete neural operations. For example, Deepak Chopra discusses an experiment monitoring the neural impact of compassion, which revealed the involvement of a left-brain focus (prefrontal cortex) in Tibetan monks while meditating. Researchers studied the brains of the monks who were experienced meditators. The monks entered a brain scanner (a functional MRI) and were asked to meditate on compassion. The findings revealed high levels of Gamma waves, which are connected with the higher cognitive function of thought, as well as enabling the brain to function holistically.[33] The research shows how we could use the focus of the left brain to direct our awakening, via meditation on compassion. It lends support to McGilchrist's thesis in terms of highlighting the need for a more holistic approach to understanding human functioning and purpose.

McGilchrist's[31] thesis is perhaps most helpful in calling for greater awareness of 'wholeness', by drawing attention to the imbalances in our current ways of living and our modern one-sided consciousness. It helps us appreciate where we have under-invested in our human potential and development. It is here that Jung's deeper connection to life, in relation to the ego-Self axis, is pivotal for a *rebirth* of the spiritual, without which we are capable of destroying all life.[27] Jung was one of the first to understand that the crisis in our material worldview was linked to a spiritual crisis. As De Gruchy has noted, Jung's solution was for individuals and societies to discover the dynamic power of numinous experiences.[27] But the question has to be posed: will such a transformative process take hold in the modern world?

Mass-mindedness and the re-sacralisation of everyday life

A few years ago I wrote a publication with two Jungian analysts, in which we explored the impact of our modern one-sided approach to living.[34] In that article we discussed the observations made by the philosopher Herbert Marcuse,[35] who noted in 1964 how modern people's thoughts and actions in technological societies were passive and bound to a one-dimensional existence. He commented on the need to engage human thoughts and actions in order to fulfil unmet potential, which he believed would involve transcending the societal limitations imposed upon us. Marcuse stated that in the modern world, human agency – masked as freedom – is allied to highly controlled, bureaucratic, administrative structures, and that human productivity is mostly centred on wealth creation, material gain and consumption.[34] We only have to take a look at the way our daily lives are controlled and administered to witness the scale of mass conformity to societal rules and structures. Throughout our lives we are fed values and beliefs in the institutions to which we belong, including education and employment, etc. Here, Marcuse observed that the specific characteristics of conformity include a lack of constructive criticism of the modern structures in which people live, and that this lack of critique curtails people's interest in exploring their full human potential. Marcuse's[35] observations hold true and can be seen in the modern use of mass media, which has been implicated in the political economy of manufacturing consent.[36] Mass media have the power to reinforce norms, expectations and consensus values, leading to what Marcuse[35] described as unchecked conformity. This phenomenon is illustrated by Skolimowski[37] who asks us to consider the enormous power of mass media and advertising in the modern world. He points out that these market-driven forces are able to influence our values, perceptions and behaviours. Skolimowski is correct in his assertion that these forces are not remotely interested in our wholeness or spiritual development.

The potential destructive power of mass-mindedness not only leads to the per-petuation of self and societal deception, but also leads us astray from the challenge of cultivating self-knowledge.[38] Yet, people's occupational interests, in all the diverse ways that humans *do* life, are full of potential for new vistas of reflection and expression, including the exploration of spirituality and consciousness. If we are to explore our human potential and break out of the one-dimensional administrations of the modern world, we need to confront what Marcuse[35] described as the tensions of engaging our potentialities and actualities. This could generate new possibilities for living a life permeated with a deep sense of the sacred and the spiritual. Jungian analyst James Hollis[39] highlights the importance of having meaningful connections with numinous encounters, and further suggests that if a person is linked to a mystery they will somehow be transformed by it. Moreover, Skolimowski[37] notes that such shifts in consciousness can change people's connection to life. For example, if the earth is experienced as a sanctuary, rather than a commodity for our consumer-based appetites, our human actions on this planet are more likely to become 'sacred'. It would encourage us to act with more reverence to the earth and its inhabitants. That is, we are capable of living with an appreciation of life's mystery and wholeness.

As well as the obvious benefits that modern technologies bring to our lives, such as the internet, there are also problems that come with instant communication, such as becoming addicted to surfing, gaming and messaging. There is the very real issue that we gradually become more disconnected with nature and life's mysteries. The word mystery comes from the Greek word *mystikos*, which means 'secret' according to Vesey and Foulkes.[40] Arnold Mindell[41] has suggested that all phenomena are in a constant state of change, and the real revelation of existence is recognition of the fluid and dynamic presence of this mystery in life. Mindell[42] has further suggested that human beings are capable of connecting to this wider secret (mystery) in life. However, life's mystery is not something tangible that is easily found and held on to in some preferred shape or form; in fact, the opposite is true. That is, the world and all its inhabitants are part of this unfolding and dynamic mystery, which creates opportunities to deepen our experience in life. Larsen[43] offers a compelling insight into the effects that encounters with the numinous can bring to the conscious life of human beings. He asserts that the impact on our consciousness enables us to consider new directions in life. When we experience the sacred it enables us to live with a deep sense of reverence in accord with an awe inspiring cosmic mystery. Here, the numinous opens us up to a renewed relationship with the divine, and the secret sacrament that is connected to life's unfolding.

Between the 'I' and the 'Thou'

It is evident from the previous chapters that an encounter with the numinous can excite the divine spark within us.[44] The impact of such deep mystical moments in our lives not only brings great potential for healing and psycho-spiritual growth, but Dourley[21] has even suggested the experience may leave people with a sense that they have encountered the sacred. Depth psychologists such as Carl Jung valued the profound psychological implications of numinous phenomena in the process of healing and individuation. Jung's psycho-spiritual focus situated the numinous in relation to the collective unconscious and the archetypes. However, philosopher Martin Buber put forward a serious criticism of Jung, complaining that Jung's theories reduced the reality of God (or the sacred dimension) to a psychological phenomenon, and in doing so, suggested that God has no reality outside the realm of the human psyche.[45] It is true that Jung used the theological concept of the numinous in his writings, but it must be remembered that this cross-fertilisation of ideas was not only one-way, for the theologian Rudolph Otto[2] also spoke about the psychological impact of the numinous on people's consciousness.

Otto[2] termed the numinous the 'wholly other', and Jung did not dispute or attempt to change this orientation. Indeed, it is the numinous that awakens our human consciousness, and offers possibilities for shifting our awareness from the dominance of the personal-ego to include the influence of the transpersonal-Self. Smith[46] helpfully points out that whilst Jung's work on the numinous reflects our inner experiences of the sacred, it does not mean that humans are being deified, or conversely that working with the numinous devalues the sacred. On the contrary, Jung was clear in his proposal that human beings can cultivate a relationship to the divine; however, he warns that this does not give us licence to be overly identified with the sacred (inflation). Indeed, Tacey[47] notes that Jung used the term *religious attitude* as something distinct from formal religions. Jung wanted to draw attention to the qualities of experience and consciousness for our psycho-spiritual growth and development, helping us to remain open to the sacred as *wholly other*.

It is this awareness of a presence, or a possibility of encountering the numinous, as the *sacred other*, that can inspire religious awe and fascination. It can lead to a spiritual approach to life that explores a deep seam of psycho-spiritual renewal. Jung's therapeutic work advocated developing a religious-spiritual attitude as an essential life task. He believed that life was wasted if we missed this important opportunity. The vignette that follows is a wonderful example of the types of spontaneous events that are infused with numinosity and can inspire our spiritual direction in life.

——— **Illustration: A spiritual mother helps an earthly mother** ———

This story is about a friend of mine who had an inspiring encounter whilst holidaying in a Spanish mountain region. The story begins with Peter's relationship with his mother and sister. Peter is a loyal son who loves his mother very much; however a difficulty has arisen since his mother has been advancing in age and experiencing health problems. The main problem is that Peter lives a long distance from his mother who is now a resident in a care home. He has a very demanding life, juggling work, family and his commitment to supporting new businesses and people. Apart from holidays and visits, it is Peter's sister who calls in on their mother on a more regular basis as she lives closer. His sister often raises the issue of him becoming more involved in their mother's care.

Prior to an extended walking holiday in a mountain region of Spain, a discussion between Peter and his sister questioned the quality of care their mother was receiving in the residential home. They noticed that their mother was becoming quite inactive for long spells, due to limited opportunities for engaging in stimulating activities. They also became concerned that residents were not being encouraged to eat in the communal dining area. These factors were not helpful for tackling the depression their mother had experienced for many years. It was agreed that they would broach the question with their mother about finding another residential home locally, one that would keep her more active and engaged. There were no plans made at this point in time.

It was whilst Peter and his wife were on their five week walking holiday in Northern Spain that Peter's sister messaged him, saying that she had been given the name of a good residential care home. She asked Peter to take the lead in sorting out the arrangements with the new establishment: "You need to sort this out, I've done far too much for mother recently and you haven't been involved." In the shadow of the mountains that surrounded him, Peter recounted his thoughts at the time: "How the heck am I going to do all this from Spain?" He decided to sleep on the problem.

The next day Peter was still unsure what to do, but he and his wife had already planned a walk in the remote region of the Pico de Europa. They had decided to take a pilgrim route to the shrine of our 'Lady of the Light'. It was a hot day and there were no other walkers. It took a few hours of sweat and toil to get to the shrine, and upon arrival they took a well-deserved rest. Peter and his wife relaxed against the wall of the shrine, enjoying the vast and expansive view. They had not seen anyone all day, but they were pleasantly surprised to see small group of people appearing in the distance. It turned out they were an English family and lived in the same region as Peter's mother and sister. Further discussion revealed that the man they spoke to worked in the field of elderly care and knew the residential care home that Peter's sister had recommended the day before. Peter was speechless as the man gave him all the names and contact numbers of the people he needed, including the manager and the activities organiser, as well as information about which rooms had the nicest bathrooms, in fact he told Peter everything he needed to know and said how lovely the residential home was.

Peter and his wife are not religious, but they were deeply touched by this incredible synchronicity. They went into the shrine and thanked 'Our Lady of the Light' and proceeded to walk back down the mountain, not seeing anyone else all day. This story has a huge spiritual quality to it without needing to be religious. The event happened at a shrine dedicated to the spirit of Mother Mary, and this realisation was not lost on Peter as he rested content that his mother's needs would now be more adequately looked after.

Peter's reflections on the above event enabled him to review how he approaches difficulties. He has always had the habit of leaving complex problems and dealing with them at a later date, believing that the universe will provide inspiration or a solution to the situation. Peter has always been open to things being resolved from unexpected sources. The above story is an example of the way that such uncanny occurrences can unfold in life. It confirmed to Peter that something quite wonderful, a force, a spirit, or something is at work in this world, which can be most helpful if we really trust it. He spoke to me about "feeling tuned in" and is always full of gratitude for the unlikely help that he constantly receives throughout his life. Peter is always seeking to be a helpful presence in the world, and such a connection to life means that he trusts there will always be a way through the twists and turns that he encounters. Since his experience at the shrine Peter believes in a greater quality of relationship to life as a whole. This holistic orientation continues to inform and deepen his actions in the world. It also confirms to Peter that his life is on the right track: "If the world can help me in such ways, then I am also committed to being more helpful in the world."

How we evolve our sense of direction in this world and remain open to a spiritual attitude is an important task, otherwise we are liable to objectify the world and all that lives in it. Martin Buber[48] has spoken about the different realities found in the experiential world of *I-It*, compared to the relational world of *I-Thou*, noting that the quality of the *Thou* is also eternal. One of the main points of Buber's[48] analysis was to point out that as soon as a *Thou* becomes *It*, the connection to a greater universal and cosmic perspective is excluded. Buber makes it clear that the objective world of *It* can be transformed by spirit, and this spirit manifests in the transcendent relationship between *I* and *Thou*.[48] Yet Buber has cautioned that if we let the objective and experiential world of *It* have mastery, *It* can take over. I would say that we are caught in the grip of relating to life in a literal or overly rational way that is too objectified; in essence we are collectively caught up in an objectified world of *It*.

A quick look at our treatment of the world is enough to realise that we are not *relating to nature* and other species as *Thou*. Thus, Kelsey's[49] observation that the material world alone cannot satisfy our deep need for transcendence and meaning in life is instructive: people have a deep need to connect with the numinous.[50] However, Buber speaks about the staggering levels of alienation between the sense of *I* and the *world*, and he notes the important relationship that could be developed, between *one and all,* highlighting that we must do something to address the problem.[48] A crucial aspect of recognising the sacrament of daily life is to shift from our current over-investment in consumerism, to a new depth of living that appreciates the mystery in life and the numinous potential that exists in our daily actions – in all the things we do – and could do. It is in relation to the *Thou* that our meaningful occupational engagement can be expressed as spiritual activity. Then an evolutionary shift would be grounded in a collective recognition and understanding that *I am Thou, and Thou art I*.[48] Such reflections have the power to initiate deep transformation through our occupational engagement: 'I do, therefore I evolve'.

The deep and spiritual nature of everyday occupations is framed anew by Bede Griffiths,[51] who has highlighted the importance of karma yoga in Hinduism, where spiritual practice is engaged as a path involving direct action in the world. Here, daily life is considered as spiritual activity, where an individual *doing* their everyday routines and tasks can be as spiritually engaged as a contemplative who sits in meditation. From a sacramental perspective, it reveals a shift in consciousness away from self-centred drives towards ways of engaging in life that are in the service of spiritual expression. Thus, sacred action is expressed both inwardly and outwardly, between our ways of doing, knowing and being,[52] where we engage life as a relational *Thou*, not an objectified *It*. Our daily occupational engagements in life can play a pivotal part in re-aligning our actions as co-creative spiritual expression, enabling deep participation in the world. Such actions place a spiritual view of reality as equal to material existence, and most importantly, where the divine can be revealed through our active participation in life.[37] Barbara Marx Hubbard[53] explains that we can develop our consciousness and wisdom as we engage our ways of doing in the everyday world. Yet, the main focus of the transformational shift that is needed in the world is orientated towards evolving the transpersonal-Self. That is, when our inner and outer modes of consciousness are functioning beyond excessive levels of self-gratification and aggrandisement, becoming more aligned with a transpersonal whole. There are many examples of people who have inspired a more holistic relationship to life.

At the time of writing this book Nelson Mandela passed away. His story of struggling as an activist to bring about equality and civil rights is an inspiration for those seeking to transform themselves and the world into a better place. Mandela was a deeply spiritual person, who said that the reason he managed to endure 27 years of incarceration, was through the strength of his prayer life. We are reminded that eighteen years were spent in the brutal prison on Robben Island, where he endured a life of hard labour. It is evident that his spiritual philosophy was connected to doing and action when he spoke about the differences we can make to the lives of others, which in turn determines the sort of lives we lead. Nelson Mandela became an inspirational *citizen of the world* because his spiritual values were forged in the heat of oppression, yet he radiated love and care for all, even the prison guards who kept him under lock and key. He reflected something great in humanity, because we recognised the goodness in his actions, and how these connected to the goodness in our own lives in terms of our capacities for justice, peace and freedom.[54]

Perhaps Nelson Mandela is more than a role model; maybe he is a catalyst who can help us recognise that *we can do* something more to help each other and the world. In the next chapter we explore spiritual emergence in the context of everyday life.

Exercise

- In the Benedictine monastic tradition they use a form of contemplation called *Lectio Divina*, which roughly translates as "the divine word".

- Find an inspirational poem or a short passage on the spiritual dimension in life. You can use the poem below if you wish – *The Phoenix*.

- Read *(lectio)* out the poem or short passage once, slowly. Sit in silence with the words that you have read. Then re-read the short passage again – open up to the words – and let a single word or short phrase capture your attention.

- Notice how the word impacts on you. Make space for this word in your whole being:

  o Hearing the word – how does it sound? Quiet, loud, direct, or lyrical?
  o Feeling the word – is it calming, inspiring, light, or heavy?
  o Seeing the word – how does the word inspire your vision?
  o Moved by the word – is there a gesture, movement, or sense of stillness?

- Now connect to a quality in this word as it is experienced more deeply in your being, or soul. Be with the word in a meditative way *(meditatio)*.

- Let this word reveal some meaningful connections for you. Notice how the word connects you to the spirit (in whatever way that is meaningful to you). Give thanks *(oratio)* – as a praiseworthy or prayerful response to the spirit.

- Try to connect with the essence of this word. What is it revealing to you? Use this word as a means of further reflection *(contemplatio)*.

- Finally, the Benedictine practice of *Lectio Divina* is deepened through taking action *(actio)* in our daily occupations *(occupatio)*.

The Phoenix

Consumed by fire,
snared in the flames of fate?
This moment, a sacrament, a catalyst –
glowing, opaque with shadowy embers.

The past – *no meaning* – here,
as self-reflections are incinerated.
Yet, alive in an incubating dream;
a cauldron, a labyrinthine myth.

This, a dark night of redemption,
a metamorphic unfurling.
Revealing a seed of renewal; where
the *self* transforms unto it*Self* – reborn.

Mick Collins, 2012

*Our everyday actions and occupations are an unlimited
source of spiritual awakening and emancipation.
Such is the mystical force of doing.*

CHAPTER SIX

*Spiritual emergence
and doing*

Overview

Throughout this chapter I make connections between spirituality and doing.
I explore how our occupational potential, when linked to a transpersonal dimension of consciousness, can enable a deeper understanding of life to emerge.
I discuss how our human ancestors, by virtue of their occupational engagement,
evolved the capacity to have transcendent experiences. And I argue that everyday
occupational participation can result in an archetypal connection, which brings
us into direct contact with the numinous dimension. Such transcendent
encounters need to be integrated into our everyday lives as they help us fulfil our
occupational potential. However, any profound shift in consciousness always
carries a risk to the dominance of our existing ego-functioning.

Spiritual emergence and occupational potential

In the past human activities had a greater relationship to the divine, as noted by
Bede Griffiths,[1] who writes about the role of occupations as integral and natural
activities, such as ploughing, spinning, weaving, dancing and singing. Such
everyday occupations of many people in the past were viewed as connecting
them to a sense of wholeness. Griffiths[1] has also noted that since the Industrial
Revolution, many people's work has not only become mechanistic, but
also destructive for the soul. I believe Griffiths[1] is correct in saying that this
wholesale shift to mechanised ways of living changed something important in
the collective mind-set. As we have adapted to new technological advances, it
has impacted on our experience of consciousness; as Skolimowski[2] notes, our
modern consciousness is mostly a reflection of the mechanised world that we
have created. This staggering observation could have the capability to catalyse
a wake-up call for modern humans. That is, if we are interested in finding out
what lies beyond our mechanised lives? However, because our current states
of consciousness are mostly dissociating from the rich connections to the

unconscious, we are in danger of being completely submerged in a collective rational-mindedness. The status quo is akin to a mass-trance, fuelled by fantasies of relying on technological mastery alone to solve all our problems.

There is no denying the advances and benefits of technology, but it is also difficult to avoid the devastating consequences of a consumer-based consciousness that has plundered the world's natural resources at an alarming rate. We can no longer remain in denial about the disturbing legacy of our technological assault on life, which has led to relatively short-term materialistic gain for some people, and serious deprivation for others. For many, it has also led to the loss of a meaningful connection with the spiritual dimension.[3] However, when our daily actions are connected to cultivating our full human potential, we can engage a deeper relationship to processes of self-renewal,[4] revealing possibilities for new ways of living, inclusive of the spirit.[1] Such experiences highlight possibilities for an interface between personal and transpersonal orientations in life: that is, between *what we do* and *who we are* in all the ways that we live. Caroline Myss[5] has stated that if mystical encounters and experiences of illumination impact in our life, and if the numinous assumes a prominent role that supports an awakening in our consciousness, then it can also help guide our life directions. This illustrates that when we encounter the numinous, we are capable of acknowledging and prioritising the sacred or divine forces in our everyday orientations and actions.

As stated earlier, the concept of self-actualisation, including ego-transcendence,[6] acknowledges that people not only have spiritual needs,[7] but also that the numinous dimension of their peak experiences reflects an important aspect of human development.[8] The transformative processes linked to self-actualisation arise not only through our *states of being*, but also through our *ways of doing*, as expressed by Fidler and Fidler[9] who have noted that 'doing' is linked to processes, such as experimenting, problem solving, creating and living with curiosity. Furthermore, the spiritual links to doing are neatly summarised by Egan and DeLaat,[10] who suggest that it connects us to our truest representations of self, which we can express in all that we do. They go on to emphasise that the unfolding nature of spirituality in our personal lives and stories often conveys a sense of mystery.[11] The idea of human occupation as spiritual activity[12] has also been noted for its importance to cultivating meaning and health,[13,14,15] as well as being linked to experiences of transcendence[16,17] and a sense of connectedness.[18,19] My own investigations into spirituality and human occupations were conceptualised through understanding people's quality of experience in everyday life contexts. It revealed how the interface between doing and being can catalyse deep processes of self and spiritual renewal.[4]

My work as a UK National Health Service occupational therapist in an acute admissions mental health unit, as well as working within a specialist psychological therapies team, enabled me to see first-hand the powerful links between people's occupational engagement and spirituality, which can be hugely beneficial for individuals in the midst of a deep crisis. I focused on recognising the unique ways that people's intentions and expressions in their daily activities could impact on their sense of meaning and being, sometimes with spiritual significance.[4] For example, one of my cases concerned the recovery of a client who was receiving treatment for a major depressive episode and suicidal impulses. I published the work that I did with this client[4] to illustrate the complementary relationship between doing and being in his journey of recovery, which also initiated a process of self and spiritual renewal for him. The following account is adapted from that article.[4]

Thoughts of death, doing and transformation

I once worked with a middle-aged man, Iain (not his real name) who was severely depressed and suicidal. This man was admitted to an acute mental health ward in the hospital where I worked. He was preoccupied with committing suicide to end his despair. I managed to persuade him to attend some occupational therapy (OT) sessions. Initially he was very uncomfortable in the group work, but he gradually began to participate more as time went on. One day he joined a writing group that was exploring the neutral theme of *comfort*. Initially he said that he had nothing to write about, but as he sat in the group he started to think about friends, his pet and music, which had been sources of comfort to him before the onset of his depression. He said that the group made him reflect and that, "My situation was different from how I was seeing it." He went on to say that the group had unexpectedly confronted him with a side of his life that he had put to one side: "I think being forced to look at my situation made me angry and I almost wanted to die because of that."

After the writing group, he was in a reflective mood and ended up having a conversation with a nurse. The talk had a spiritual focus, which included the possibility of finding a purpose for living. He went on to say: "The outcome was to find a reason for living, and that night I did, as a result of earlier in the day at OT ... It didn't make everything right, but it started the process." He said that being in the OT group and talking to the nurse had been "a critical day for me ... a turning point." It is evident that Iain had regained a spiritual focus when he said: "I've always believed in God, I've never rejected that." He went on to say that the OT writing group and the conversation with the nurse hit "an underlying chord". Life was still difficult for Iain, but he persisted with his OT sessions, which led to a gradual transformation and sense of renewal through his occupational engagement, which linked to his quality of lived experience, as follows:

Intention: He attended a variety of groups including art, craft, writing and baking. Initially, his primary intention was "to come to OT just for something to do."

Expression: He spoke about doing activities that he had never tried before. For example, "It was the first time I had done any baking in my life...it made me feel pleased with myself. I got some reward from it."

> **Meaning:** He gradually realised that occupational therapy could offer him more than he had initially considered: "From just going to kill time, I went on to develop the feelings I was having of self-worth and enjoyment ... it was the best time of the day."
>
> **Being:** He said: "Self-worth was beginning to develop. I still have very low self-esteem, but now I have some, and I had none. I do not want to die anymore and that is a big change."
>
> **Spiritual:** He described his experience in the writing group and the conversation with the nurse as being a "special day". He said that it not only "hit a chord", but "we should always be looking out for these critical moments." Indeed, his participation in occupations opened him up to reflect and reconsider the meaning and purpose of his life with spiritual significance.

My work with this client illustrated the dynamic links between human occupation, spiritual emergence and self-renewal. It demonstrates the way that subtle reflections on our actions can profoundly affect our ways of doing and states of being. In this case, a man who was severely depressed and suicidal was able to transform, through engaging in new activities and behaviours in a therapeutic context. Indeed, he went on to make a full recovery and started to change his daily occupations to reflect the journey of transformation and renewal that he initiated in his occupational therapy sessions. It highlights the interactions between 'doing' and 'being', and raises questions about the way we live, through cultivating a deeper relationship between transpersonal states of consciousness and the human potential that can be expressed in our everyday occupations. It also illustrates we need more than just intention alone to make any real changes in life.[5] We have to *dig deep* if we are interested in catalysing our psycho-spiritual development to engage our transpersonal potential, which can bring about our transformative actions in the world. Here, doing and being play complementary roles in the evolution of our conscious engagement in life.

Human occupation and the transpersonal dimension

Renewed interest in the meaning and purpose of doing led to a new academic discipline in the late 1980s known as occupational science,[20] underpinned by humanistic values.[21] It gave greater impetus to exploring the connections between doing, being and human potential inclusive of spiritual considerations. Occupational scientists investigated how *doing* has the potential for engaging personal and social transformation.[22] Indeed, the philosophical underpinnings of occupational science led researchers to consider the centrality of doing to enable people to express their occupational potential.[23,24,25]

Occupational potential resonates with Maslow's[3] original concept of self-actualisation and understanding the nature of "full-humanness". Occupational potential has been described by Asaba and Wicks[23] as a way of bringing together processes of *being* and *becoming*, which are linked to the *doing self.* Asaba and Wicks' provide a focus for considering and harnessing our potential through what we do; however, we also need to take into account the potential of factoring-in transpersonal states of consciousness, and indeed what impact such experiences of the sacred can have on the *doing self.*[23] At the same time that Alison Wicks[24,25] was working on occupational potential, I was exploring the synergy between doing and being in the context of transpersonal states of consciousness. I discussed how deep shifts in identity are an integral part of occupational engagement and potential, linked to the cultivation of self-awareness.[26] I had noted the need for understanding an expansive and dynamic view of occupational potential (as expressed through doing), and for engaging *fluidly* with identity, especially when considering the integration of transpersonal states of consciousness into our daily lives.

The innovative work of occupational scientist and transpersonal psychologist Loretta do Rozario[27] laid the foundations for a paradigm shift in occupational science, having significant implications for how occupational engagement could be understood. Do Rozario[27] proposed explicit links between the humanistic principles of development that underpinned occupational science[21] and a transpersonal dimension of ecology. She initiated a much deeper dialogue about the interface between doing and being, which placed greater accent on the role of consciousness, noting that it can give expression to transcendent experiences, beyond the control of the ego, such as joy and a harmonious connection to all life. These transcendent qualities are significant in the context of lived transpersonal experiences in relation to others, nature and the cosmos.

The integration of a transpersonal perspective within occupational science encouraged new parameters for exploring identity.[27] Such an expanded focus on human occupations went beyond the boundaries of humanistic influences. My own contributions to this academic discipline focused on the reflexive question: "Who is occupied?" This question was designed to consider the interactions between human consciousness and the complementary relationship between doing and being, inclusive of the transpersonal dimension of our lived potential.[28] It highlighted the need for a fluid approach to identity and consciousness, especially when integrating spirituality into our self-exploration and actions.[29] I further emphasised the need to develop links between self-awareness and adaptation, because facilitating shifts in identity has to include both *outer* and *inner* processes of change. This was based on a psychological understanding that people who engage in transformative processes such as self-actualisation need to be adaptable.[30] It also underscores how our engagement in daily occupations provides opportunities to express shifts in self-awareness through our actions.[26]

I continue to be amazed at the *power of doing* in my own life and in the lives of others, as I seek to understand the significance of our transpersonal potential.

It is an incredible privilege to have shared the transpersonal journeys of others, witnessing all the resources people draw upon to adapt, change and grow, whether through working on an inspirational dream or following a new venture in life. Thus, doing in life affords us opportunities to explore and discover our talents and gifts, which provide us with means to engage our unbounded potential in a spirit of discovery. Transformation through doing connects our daily actions, awareness and unfolding process of meaning into a path of service. Here, we enter a co-creative flow with life's wholeness.

The notion that our self-awareness and processes of adaptation can accompany our occupational engagement[31]acknowledges the fluid nature of human identity and engagement in life, and it assumes that self-awareness is never static. We have opportunities to develop self-awareness through our multi-channelled modes of perception and expression, including how we see, hear, think, move and feel, as noted by process-oriented psychologist Arnold Mindell.[32,33] These multiple modes of perception and expression inform our everyday experiences and engagement in life, which can connect to a wider transpersonal understanding of consciousness and identity development.[32,33] Such meaningful engagement of our transpersonal potential underpins the importance of the reflexive question *Who is occupied?* This question emphasises that we have opportunities for deeper engagement in life through a "shift towards synthesising inner reflection and human adaptation in the service of fulfilling the occupational potential of human beings" (p. 30).[26] It further illustrates the relationship to Abraham Maslow's[27] invitation to explore and understand the farther reaches of human nature, particularly self-transcendence.[34] Most importantly, it honours our deep spiritual connection to life, linked to what we do.

My interest in considering transpersonal developments from an occupational perspective includes how we activate and integrate transformations in consciousness into our daily lives and behaviours. If we return to the concept of autopoiesis, discussed in chapter one, we can appreciate that *doing* is a central feature in nature's biological processes of self-creation. However, as fully formed human beings, we become co-creators, and can act as free agents as we explore, engage and express our doing through all our multi-sensory channels of perception and expression. If, as conscious agents living in the world, we are open to the transpersonal, it adds another dimension to our co-creative expression and this extends the scope of our lived potential to transform our consciousness. In this way, the reflexive question: *Who is occupied?*[26] becomes relevant throughout our life as we explore and integrate the meanings associated with the expression of our talents and interests, connected to our lived potential.

The power of doing

The importance of transcendent states of consciousness, as noted above, had long been recognised by the pioneers of humanistic and transpersonal psychology.[35,36,37] It was through people's capacity to experience transcendent states of consciousness, such as mystical encounters,[38] that transpersonal psychology developed a more comprehensive consideration of the wider spectrum of consciousness available to humans.[39,40] It was transpersonal psychology's continued exploration of the boundaries of human potential that took it beyond humanistic psychology's focus on self-actualisation.[41] This development revealed new parameters, meanings and possibilities for what transcendent states of consciousness could mean for understanding and expressing human potential.[40] Transpersonal researchers recognised that human beings have a tendency to be drawn towards experiences of self-transcendence,[34] and this realisation encouraged them to ask questions about the full scope of our psycho-spiritual potential for being all that we are capable of being.[34] These explorations continue to have implications for how we actualise our transformational potential today and most importantly, how we explore the links between transpersonal consciousness and doing.[42]

Exploring our occupational potential, inclusive of a transpersonal perspective,[26] is paramount in the world today. The danger is we may overlook or underestimate our opportunities for human development.[29] The very act of doing, with awareness of the transpersonal, empowers human beings to be co-creators for new perspectives in consciousness and lived existence. In such moments, we can connect to transformative states of flow,[43] which psychologist Mihalyi Csizentmihalyi refers to as an *optimal experience* that brings meaning and purpose to life. Questioning our occupational potential means that we are always evolving connections between reflection and action. Here, the question of *Who is occupied?*[26] is not a semantic puzzle to be solved, but rather an invitation to explore our human identity and potential in all facets of our daily lives. As part of my explorations into transpersonal consciousness and human occupations, I looked at the depth, roles and functions of human occupation in relation to self-actualisation[44] and self-transcendence.[42] There is a rich seam of unexplored human development to be found between our transpersonal potential and what we do in the world.

In my publications[42,44] I explored the importance of doing in relation to Maslow's[6] finding that human beings are at risk of developing pathologies associated from boredom and lack of inspiration if we do not engage our unmet transpersonal potential. In making the links between Maslow's[6] emphasis on the operational meaning of self-actualisation and self-transcendence from an occupational perspective, I developed the concept of *occupational intelligence*. Maslow's[6] original premise was that intelligence is a variable in the process of engaging human potential, which inspired me to explore the occupational links further.[42,44] The concept of occupational intelligence provides a way of understanding how our occupational potential can be recognised and engaged through our multi-sensory modes of being[32,33] and doing,[26] inclusive of transpersonal levels of development. This idea of occupational intelligence finds support in the writings of Deepak Chopra[45] who notes how intelligence is linked to our multi-sensory capabilities, such as sight, sound, smell, touch and taste. Our multi-sensory capacities are a source of intelligence that can be engaged in the world.

I firmly believe that all human beings have talents, waiting to be discovered and developed, which can connect deeply to our dreams and aspirations. The essence of occupational intelligence is to use our multi-sensory capacities to explore our world and express our potential, with spiritual significance. It means that we direct our actions as part of our psycho-spiritual growth and development. The original premise I put forward is that multi-channelled functioning (as noted by Arnold Mindell) and occupational engagement (doing) can facilitate and mediate creative transitions in identity and consciousness, which can, in turn, provide a greater range of opportunities for expressing transpersonal potential in daily life.[26,42] Therefore, *doing* is complementary to deepening our experience of *being*, based on the view that there is always more to be discovered in terms of our human potential.[46] Indeed, an occupational perspective for transpersonal development opens up new relationships for understanding our relationship to life as a whole, that is, belonging to a wider ecology and cosmology, as noted in the introduction of this book. Every action is packed with opportunities for connecting to and expressing our transpersonal potential.

Doing with depth

Jungian analyst Marion Woodman[47] has noted a lack of understanding about the deep and sacred value of human actions in the modern world, suggesting that for many people the act of doing has become an avoidance of being. Transpersonal psychologist John Welwood[48] also argues that, whilst doing and being appear mutually exclusive, they need to be considered together in order to engage spirituality in everyday life. The exciting proposition of bringing doing and being together via our unmet transpersonal potential is that it opens up new opportunities for living beyond our previous ideas of consciousness, identity and action, which may even have seemed unimaginable.[49] The key point being expressed here is to question how our interests and talents are actually used in daily life, and how we explore the farther reaches of our occupational potential,[42] which is grounded and expressed in our everyday actions.[50]

The transpersonal literature emphasises the need to take an integrated approach towards developing our transformative potential in everyday life.[51] Indeed,

Sheena Blair[52] has noted how occupations can assume a pivotal role as we make such transitions in life. I have previously outlined four propositions where occupations interface with the transpersonal dimension[53] (adapted below), which demonstrate the importance of a transformative imperative in the context of our daily lives:

1. A transpersonal orientation considers the whole person in relation to body, mind, emotions, community, culture and spirit.[54] All the actions that are carried out in everyday life: for example eating, washing dishes, socialising and sexual relations, are potentially sacred or spiritual.[55]

2. Transpersonal experiences impact on ways of doing, knowing and being.[56] The transpersonal dimension of human occupations[27] reflects a participatory vision for human spirituality and a multidimensional engagement with life.[26,57,58]

3. Transpersonal states of consciousness can affect the usual boundaries upon which human beings construct personal identities. A transpersonal perspective suggests that everyday identity is relative, and cannot provide a full account of who we are.[59] This viewpoint underpins the reflexive question, *Who is occupied?*[26]

4. Transpersonal identity reflects a spiritual transformation of the personality,[60] and encourages the development of capacities such as wisdom, compassion, intuition, receptivity, creativity and consciousness.[61] Human occupations are important for mediating, grounding and integrating transpersonal experiences and transformations in identity.[26,62,63]

There is an additional element to the four propositions listed above, linked to the engagement of our transformative potential. Such connections to our transpersonal potential also highlight our relationship to the archetypes, which can have a powerful impact on our lives.[64] Archetypal (and often numinous) experiences confront people with the tension between the *known* world (of consensus reality) and an *unknown* world (as mystery).[65] The interface between two poles of experience, between the known and the unknown highlights the importance of Jung's concept of the "transcendent function", described by Miller[66] as a form of mediation between our everyday ego-consciousness and a more expansive experience of consciousness (inclusive of the collective unconscious). Effectively, the transcendent function enables us to connect with a larger transpersonal reality, of which we are already a part. The transcendent function provides us with opportunities to *transcend* the dominance of our ego-orientation and our over-developed self-referential attitudes,[67] and in doing so, can further promote psycho-spiritual development. However, it is evident that such development needs to be integrated in daily life. Shlitz, Vieten and Amorok[68] have noted in their research on *living deeply* that greater balance can be found between body, mind and soul through engaging in transformational practices, which provide greater integration between doing and being. Their research is most inspiring in this time of global crisis because it supports the relationship between our everyday ways of doing and being with depth.

The archetypal dimension of human occupations

In chapter four, I presented an interesting anthropological hypothesis, formulated by Alondra Oubré,[69] that encounters with the numinous were believed to have occurred during rituals in ancient human communities, and which eventually led to the development of transcendent awareness. For example, when our early hunter-gatherer ancestors had to prepare for the dangers of the hunt, the ritual enactments associated with it were designed to mediate collective anxieties. Oubré[69] has referred to the development of this ritual capacity in early humans as *Homo transcendalis,* which means that our ancestors were adept at meeting challenges and employing strategies that enabled them to meet the demands of survival. This ability to adjust and adapt was a hallmark in the evolution of these early wise humans. It revealed how they developed ritualistic practices that connected them to productive and transformative states of consciousness.[70] Anthropologist Michael Winkelman[71,72,73] provides a theoretical perspective that lends support to Oubré's[69] hypothesis, revealing that biological, cultural and spiritual domains are connected in our evolutionary development. His cross-cultural understanding of ritualised shamanic practices has illustrated the importance of altered states of consciousness in early hunter-gatherer societies.[70] These included ritualised practices that involved being deeply occupied in activities such as drumming, dance and chanting.[70] We could say that part of our human and transformational heritage is linked to early ritualised, archetypal developments, which evolved through doing.

Shamanic rituals evoked and mediated physiological arousal through harnessing symbolic representations and actions (dancing and drumming etc.),[70] which engaged our ancestors' sensory perceptions, and in doing so helped to forge neuro-cognitive structures in their brains.[72,73] Indeed, the evolutionary trajectories of shamanic rituals may have played a significant role in stimulating various states of consciousness,[70] through community bonding, enhancing psycho-physiological integration, as well as coordination and coherence across many areas of the brain.[72,73] The connections between early humans' physical, psychological, social, cultural and spiritual behaviours provided a foundation for the deep structuring of our evolutionary and occupational development. Thus, *Homo occupacio*[20] is the embodied evolutionary propensity for humans to innovate, adapt and meet environmental challenges. It would appear that through evolutionary rituals and behaviours, early humans established new patterns in consciousness that catalysed deep levels of occupational engagement. However, because such evolutionary human developments included ritual connections to the numinous, they also reveal the origins of an archetypal dimension of doing, linked to our collective transpersonal heritage. This suggests that our activities of daily living, including self-care, tool use, preparing food, our artistic and creative endeavours have an archetypal root.

Archetypes are symbols[33] that can be reflected in human experiences, or expressed through actions and behaviours in life.[70] These archetypal patterns can be found in the stories and myths of different cultures, yet their underlying content is often very similar.[74] My interest in considering an archetypal level of human occupations is based on two dynamic elements that have probably interacted throughout human history.[75] The first is linked to our ancient capacity to evolve through the engagement of doing, innovation and adaptation in life, such as the *Homo occupacio* noted by Elizabeth Yerxa,[20] and the second concerns our ability to transcend and evolve through meeting challenges, the *Homo transcendalis*, as noted by Alondra Oubré.[69] Here, the foundations for an archetypal dimension of human occupation are based on deep patterns of doing that are connected to evolutionary trajectories in human consciousness, with transpersonal significance.[75] I further suggest that because occupations are connected to an archetypal level, this brings the numinous into the equation (as Jung explained, the numinous is often expressed through the archetypes). This offers a plausible explanation for why our deep occupational engagements in life are experienced as profound spiritual phenomena. The nature of daily occupations highlights their significance for connecting people to transcendent experiences as well as the integration of them in daily life.[75] In addition, Jung noted that it is important for people to remain grounded during their spiritual development,[76] and such a proposition is well catered for from an occupational perspective. Yet, there is still a wealth of untapped potential in the ways that we engage in everyday occupations to connect with the archetypes and the numinous in daily life.[75]

Because archetypal occupations are like portals to the numinous, it means that a transpersonal dimension of consciousness is intimately connected to our everyday human actions.[75] Maxwell and Tschundin[77] provide various examples of people experiencing the numinous whilst carrying out everyday occupations, such as doing a crossword, cooking lunch, sitting at a dressing table, walking, listening to music, digging in a field and other tasks. They have stated that when a person has a transcendent experience that enables them to be more aware, also it can awaken a renewed sense of creativity and responsibility. In turn, such actions become value-led and provide more possibilities for choice, freedom and depth in the ways that we live. The archetypal dimension of lived experience, linked to numinous encounters, is highly productive for activating and fulfilling our human potential. Indeed, it is my view that archetypal occupations may even be the most unexplored aspect of our psycho-spiritual development.

I say this because much of what we already do in life, that which we take for granted, is closer to the numinous than we have collectively acknowledged. As Jean Shinoda Bolen[78] acknowledges, the process of individuation (becoming whole) reflects a patterning in the human psyche, which can be viewed as archetypal. Interestingly, Shinoda Bolen links this innate *universal longing* for individuation and wholeness as an expression of our deepest need to fulfil what we are capable of and inspired to do in this life. The operative word here is to *do*; however, the integration of the archetypes can also challenge the very foundations of who we are in terms of our identity. I recall a rather humbling experience that jolted me to be more authentic in how I was living:

Zen and the art of keeping it real

In the mid-1980s I attended a week-long retreat in a Buddhist Monastery with Vietnamese Zen teacher, Thich Nhat Hanh. I attended the retreat with my good friend Russ Thornton from New Zealand, and typically whenever we meet up we tend to laugh a lot. We managed to engage in the meditation sessions and silent meals, but were prone to occasional bouts of laughter. Thich Nhat Hanh had suggested at the start of the retreat, if we have a sense of the Buddha nature in another person we could stop and bow, and if it felt right, the other person could bow back to the Buddha nature in the other. One morning I left the dormitory a bit early to get to the session, and as I turned the corner to walk the fairly long corridor to the meditation room, I came face to face with Thich Nhat Hanh who was coming from another direction. As we walked slowly to the meditation room, facing one another (for what seemed like an age), I became more awkward and suddenly I bowed to him out of my self-generated internal pressure. I did not really consider the Buddha nature of Thich Nhat Hanh. When I stood upright he did not bow in return. We walked into the meditation room and I then had to sit with the discomfort of my own lack of authenticity and the running commentary of self-criticism. This encounter catalysed a process of reflection that has guided my actions and relationships in the world to the present time. It has made me determined to be as authentic as I can be in whatever I do in life (with varying degrees of success). Yet, it is the intention that matters. This was the perfect Zen teaching from a Zen master (archetype), which made me take greater responsibility for my actions.

The above illustration was a painful lesson, and yet, it deepened my understanding of the need for reflection and action in the transformative process. In the next chapter I explore how engaging in transforming consciousness can challenge our existing notions of identity.

Exercise

- Interpret all the ways that you are occupied in your life as an act of creation. Can you now try and connect to what it is you are creating?

- What have you been creating with your life to date? Are you happy with the processes and products of your creations in life so far?

- Notice where you could give yourself some positive encouragement for what you have done so far with your life.

- Notice where you could give yourself some constructive criticism for the things that you have done so far in your life.

- Imagine having an appraisal with your soul, or guardian angel, or some spiritual figure that has significance for you.

- Find out what the next stage in your journey is and how you can best use your limited time on earth to find greater meaning and purpose.

- How are you challenged by this appraisal in terms of self-awareness, adaptations that may need to be made, or tasks that you would like to undertake?

It is the emergent connection between personal and transpersonal dimensions of consciousness, which act as thresholds for our evolutionary potential. This is where we co-create with life.

CHAPTER SEVEN

The farther reaches of human potential

Overview

In this chapter I make a connection between the deep engagement of our human potential and the possibility of it leading to a transformational crisis. At the moment, an individual who experiences a deep crisis will most likely be treated by mental health services. These services are becoming more recovery-focused and beginning to integrate spirituality into practice. However, there is still a gap in the training and understanding of mental health professionals around the meaning of deep transpersonal experiences. I discuss the role and function of doing in the management of spiritual emergencies, and explore the need for a new myth to understand the importance of transformations in consciousness in this era of global crisis.

Transformational crises and mental health

The previous chapters have shown that human beings are able to experience the transpersonal dimension in everyday life situations and occupations. From the perspective of mainstream consensus views of reality, transpersonal experiences could be seen as odd moments, unusual or anomalous events. For some people, when the numinous enters their consciousness it is a pleasant life-changing experience, for others it will result in troubling encounters that scare them, or they may even repress it. The reality of transpersonal experiences is they cannot be controlled by the ego alone, and it may well take people to the limits of their known world, as noted by White,[1] who speaks about arriving at the edge of what it means to be human, both individually and collectively, as a process of lived exploration and experience. It suggests that when we encounter the numinous, we must work with the limits of our identity, of *who we are*. Depending on the pre-existing state of our psychological and spiritual awareness, the transition through the shifting states of consciousness may be either smooth or tumultuous.

Spiritual awakening and the development of our human potential involves re-orientating our ideas about identity, and such shifts can result in a transformational crisis,[2] otherwise known as a spiritual emergency.[3,4] Such overwhelming spiritual experiences or insights can profoundly affect a person's day-to-day functioning. It may appear to the person having the experience, or others looking on, that they are having mental health problems due to the disorientating nature of such transformational processes. However, in the last three decades, key theoretical developments have started to address spiritual emergencies, and have helped our understanding of psycho-religious and psycho-spiritual problems in the field of mental health.[5,6,7]

Stanislav Grof revealed to Ervin Laszlo and Peter Russell[8] that many people being treated in psychiatric hospitals are actually experiencing transformational crises. My own work as a therapist in the field of mental health included working with people's spiritual needs. I saw how their deep psycho-spiritual potential (and transformation) could be addressed in mainstream mental health settings.[9,10,11] There is no reason why mental health services could not be developed specifically to help people integrate the complex psycho-spiritual processes associated with spiritual emergencies, as non-pathological phenomena.[12] Maxwell and Tschundin[13] provide a very helpful example of the dynamic impact of a spiritual awakening. They discuss a person in their research findings who found that their spiritual experience resulted in a long period of psychological trauma. They were shocked to find hitherto unexplored truths about their self. However, they also described how the spiritual encounter (full of grace) provided opportunities for change and further psycho-spiritual development.

Stanislav and Christina Grof[14] have described the difference between spiritual emergence and spiritual emergency, suggesting that the latter includes feeling unsettled, overwhelmed or threatened by new spiritual insights that may be personally or philosophically challenging to a person's existing view of reality.[15,16] Spiritual emergencies are more likely to occur during times of great physical and emotional stress or crisis. Possible triggers include childbirth, near-death experiences; transitional stages of life, as well as engaging in spiritual practices, all of which can impact on an individual's routines and their ability to carry on functioning in everyday life.[17] In such cases people find that they need help to integrate their experiences. However, this may lead to further difficulties. Research about people's experiences of spiritual emergencies[18] identified that some participants felt inhibited or reluctant to explore their extraordinary or unusual experiences with professionals, because the responses they received were often unhelpful or unsympathetic, and some participants feared being labelled mentally ill. Davis, Lockwood and Wright[19] found that people do not find it easy talking about transcendent encounters, and de Waard[16] suggests that people often avoid clinicians and therapists in times of spiritual crisis, and she recounts that those people who did seek professional support kept very quiet about certain experiences. The fear of misinterpretation of these non-ordinary experiences is a particularly difficult issue. Society could benefit from people sharing their transformative experiences[15] to address the collective silence or avoidance about the existence of such states of consciousness. A lack of any meaningful response to our transformative potential in a collective context increases the possibility of profound isolation for individuals in the midst of such crises.[20] Moreover, we are all impoverished if we neglect our collective opportunities to grow.

Trauma, transitions and transformations

My own work in this area has considered the important links between doing, spirituality and consciousness in order to raise awareness of people's needs in the midst of a transformative crisis,[20] rather than always assuming a pathological perspective of mental ill health.[21,22,23,24] It has been suggested that current developments in this area of research are gradually enabling a *new language* to evolve that reveals the subtleties in people's connections to the cosmos and their own psyches.[25] Over the years a number of authors have contributed to the discussion of the interface between spiritual emergencies and mental health issues.[26,27,28] I believe that this is an area of research that is set to grow, particularly in relation to such experiences resulting in a process of self and spiritual renewal,[20] both individually and collectively. Transpersonal psychiatrist John Nelson[29] writes about a person who had a mystical experience that resulted in a spiritual emergency and a period of psychiatric hospitalisation. The mystical experience provided insights into the person's life meaning and purpose, it helped to put past events into a broader context of a life journey, as well as bringing a sense of renewal, which they described as a birth into a new state of consciousness. We know that the experience of such expanded states of consciousness can affect the boundaries of the self, between the personal-ego and a transpersonal dimension. Yet, this realisation underscores the intricacies of managing transitions in consciousness as people engage their transformative potential in life, wittingly or unwittingly.[20] As a society, we need to appreciate such complexities exist in order to move on in our understanding of how we can all engage our consciousness and human potential.

If we accept that we are co-creators in our ways of doing, knowing and being, and that our experiences of transpersonal consciousness can connect us to a wider cosmos,[29] we can begin to appreciate how the boundaries between self, others, nature and our place in the universe can become blurred and sometimes confused. Such expanded states of consciousness underscore the complex processes of self-adaptation and adjustment that are needed to negotiate the (sometimes) profound impact of transpersonal encounters on identity.[15] Skolimowski[30] makes an often overlooked but important point about consciousness, evolution and human development, when he states that the formative force in the cosmos is *transcendence*. This sharp observation reveals that in nature nothing remains the same, so why should we expect human identity and ego-consciousness to be any different? Gilbert[31] highlights the importance of encounters that connect people to a mystical reality, especially those that impact on our states of consciousness. He notes that such transcendent experiences are ineffable, and can include an altered sense of time, a new sense of emotional engagement and meaning, as well as a quality of renewal.

The work of Stanislav and Christina Grof[a] has been illuminating for many people whose experience of spiritual emergence turns into a spiritual crisis or emergency. Stanislav Grof[32] describes the initial stage of one young woman's spiritual crisis who he helped. Karen had experienced an unexpected crisis that overwhelmed her, and she was so absorbed in the experience that she could no longer care for her son. I explored Grof's story about Karen in a previous publication,[20] and her descriptions about her experience of transformation as a *second birth*, resulting in her process of self-renewal as opening to *life, love and light*.[32] Through her experience Karen found her voice as a singer. The story cohered with my own experience of spiritual emergency, which was profoundly debilitating (see chapter thirteen). Karen's story as told by Grof also supported the research focus I was taking, which explored the significance and meaning of occupational engagement during such encounters, noting their value for establishing balance:

> [B]etween the inner and outer adaptations required to establish routines, activities and the more creative forms of self-expression that support self-renewal (p. 510).[20]

The deeper meaning of spiritual crisis has yet to be embraced in the modern world. Here, humanity has an opportunity to consider the emergence of a new evolutionary trajectory in consciousness at this time in history. We are being confronted with a challenge to adapt and change in the face of a worsening ecological emergency and it is essential that we start to explore in greater depth, our conscious responses to our lived experiences.[33] Indeed, Skolimowski[30] points out that consciousness is a process that is emergent, therefore when we are faced with a need to change and adapt, this also presents opportunities for transformation, between our ways of doing, knowing and being.[20]

The ongoing global crisis confronts us with the stark reality that our lack of care and compassion towards the world, its inhabitants and finite resources will eventually be reflected back in our lives. For example, it is plausible that the dawning realisation about what we have done to the planet, to one another and to other species could itself become a catalyst or tipping point that sparks spiritual change or crisis in people. In the west it would be the mental health systems that would attempt to treat people's presenting crises.[20] Yet, without a clear understanding that the *global crisis* is a *spiritual crisis*, our mental health services will not be able to signpost or support people's transformative potential effectively. As noted above, mental health systems in the west are beginning to integrate spirituality into clinical practice. But more needs to be done so they recognise the special conditions that may lead someone to experience a transpersonal crisis. The challenge at the moment is not to take a superficial approach to change, but to evolve new parameters for living, as noted by Barbara Marx Hubbard,[34] who has suggested that our collective efforts need to be directed towards co-creating and co-evolving a greater connection with nature and spirit.

Spiritual emergencies as major life transitions

As part of our collective response to the public health issue posed by the impact of the growing global crisis, mental health systems potentially offer an important resource for helping transitions to greater transpersonal awareness. It is my view that in the future they could provide public education or awareness-raising events that show how human beings are connected to a wider ecology, inclusive of transpersonal developments. As a former UK National Health Service mental health professional, I have had first-hand opportunities to understand, facilitate and share people's deep engagement with their psycho-spiritual potential.[11] I have seen the possibilities for deep change, as well as the importance of integrating an occupational focus (doing) with spiritual considerations for people's journeys of recovery and self-renewal (being).

I found that integrating spirituality in my work with people experiencing severe and enduring mental health problems led to unexpected and positive outcomes in terms of their recovery, which prompted me to write about how spiritual engagement can unfold naturally,[35] and how healing processes find their own unique paths.[10] My own experience and research into the literature on spirituality also led me to consider the unfolding nature of spirituality in four areas, linked to people's *beliefs*, personal *needs*, relevant *experiences* and particular *journeys* they may have taken in life. I found that transformative experiences are more likely to occur if given time and space to emerge.[16] The following story of self-renewal with deep transpersonal significance has been adapted from a previous publication. It concerns a young teenager (Molly), who had been paralysed from the neck down and was understandably in a state of crisis.[36]

——————— **Crisis and the spirit of transformation** ———————

I first read about Molly's story in a journal article published by Howlett.[37] Molly was a 15-year-old teenager who had been severely injured in a road traffic accident, resulting in damage to her cervical spine, which left her paralysed from the neck down. The impact of Molly's injuries raised difficult questions for her, such as how she can live with such dramatic change. It is clear that her injuries reflected a deep sense of loss and crisis. It was during this period of grief that she had a deep spiritual encounter, where she felt an experience that touched her soul, and took her beyond herself. From that moment on she decided to deal with the anger and unhappiness that was both inside and around her. Molly also prayed and meditated to find a renewed sense of purpose in life.

This reappraisal of her life, via her spiritual experience, helped Molly to transform her circumstances. I have formulated her process of transformation into three categories, which describe the impact of her spiritual encounter on her life experiences,[36] as follows:

Doing: Molly worked towards her goals as a process of guided purpose, where she was in touch with her body, mind and soul as interdependent and related (wholeness).[37] The power of her spiritual encounter enabled Molly to engage in new ways of doing that were infused with spiritual meaning.

Knowing: Molly found a new strength of spirit that was unknown to her before her accident.[37] She was opened up by the spirit into new ways of knowing.

Being: Molly redirected her energies, and in doing so redefined her sense of self and her journey in life.[37] Her spiritual experience went beyond everyday ego-identity, and she saw the value of this transpersonal encounter to her life as a whole.

Molly had a renewed sense of meaning and purpose in her life that inspired her to complete her schoolwork and graduate with her class. She also recognised the needs of other people with spinal cord injuries, and she supported those people as a volunteer to help them find holistic ways of engaging their own healing potential. Despite her own difficulties, Molly was inspired to serve others, and this is typical of the sorts of changed values and behaviours following deep transpersonal encounters. Shortly after her transformative experience, Molly agreed to have a corrective surgical procedure. During the operation her heart stopped and she died. Yet Molly's story lives on as a powerful reminder that human beings can be in deep existential crisis, and still encounter the sacred and be transformed by the depth of the transpersonal experience, leading to new ways of doing, knowing and being.

This illustration shows how Molly was engaged in occupations that provided a transitory function towards her renewed identity, as well as providing structure for the integration of transpersonal experiences in her daily life.[36] Caroline Brett[38] provides another example of the value of occupational engagement in the process of self-renewal, in her study into people's journeys of transformational crisis. One of her research participants noted how she benefited from carrying out everyday chores, such as meal preparation and cleaning (for self and others), which provided routine and structure. An occupational focus can be subtle, but nonetheless pivotal in a process of spiritual transformation. It also reveals how it is important to be responsive to people's levels of vulnerability during times of transition or transformation, as well as ensuring their spiritual well-being.[39] Managing such vulnerable transitions requires helping people engage in meaningful occupations at a level that is tolerable, understanding the potential impact of the experience on self-identity, and adapting to changing circumstances, fluidly.[20] This last point is important, as tasks or activities that are too demanding or too stimulating can be overwhelming. It reinforces the importance of using basic activities to achieve optimum engagement and establishing routines, especially in the early stages of the crisis.[20]

Stanislav Grof[40] has observed that there is often a need to surrender to the process when the experience of a spiritual emergency is very intense. However, surrendering or letting go can itself be a frightening prospect that adds to the distress and confusion already being experienced, and is a considerable adaptation for many people to make.[15,41] Indeed, it is understandable that we attempt to cling to our familiar notions of identity when facing such powerful spiritual encounters, thereby avoiding the opportunity and challenge of engaging our transformative potential.[42] Unsurprisingly, such anxiety, resistance or avoidance only serves to stifle the process of renewal that is trying to emerge.[20] Again, engagement in meaningful occupations can support transitional processes of self-renewal, which are mediated through adapting new ways of doing, as a response to the experience of fluctuating states of consciousness.[20]

Peter Gilbert[43] alludes to the importance of fluid representations of self, linked to people's spiritual experiences, noting that at this time in human history identity is a key issue, in terms of how people form and reform a sense of *who* they are. This notion of fluid identity has resonances in my own life and also in my work with people diagnosed with severe mental health problems. Those people who said spiritual issues were not important to them at the outset of therapeutic engagement often discovered new dimensions during their recovery, linked to their psycho-spiritual potential. The case illustrations found throughout this book provide more examples of people who have made both small and large shifts psycho-spiritually in their lives. The point I am making is that in the context of mental health services, the relevant professionals have the opportunity to add another dimension to their existing knowledge, supporting those people who are in a transformational crisis (if they are capable of working with it) through a deeper process of recovery, inclusive of transpersonal considerations.

If Grof and Grof's[4] non-pathological model was more widely acknowledged in mainstream mental health contexts, it could begin to deepen society's relationship to profound transformational encounters – with the emphasis on health being the operative word. Yet Richard House[44] has observed that as a society, our collective sense of normality may still be binding us and inhibiting us from truly valuing our subjective *exceptional experiences*, e.g., those types of encounters that go beyond the collective norms. This observation helps us understand how societies can become static in terms of the collective context for engaging our human potential.[45] Such a socio-cultural (mainstream) hiatus may hinder the integration of our transpersonal experiences,[46] particularly our collective relationship to the transpersonal, where we are capable of discovering new dimensions of the self[47].

A few years ago I worked with my friend and colleague, art psychotherapist and process worker, Helen Wells in outpatient mental health services, where we provided therapeutic opportunities for people experiencing severe and enduring mental health difficulties to engage in a process of self-discovery. We ran these groups over a four-year period.[11] The feedback from group participants revealed that the issues we worked with tapped into people's deep reservoirs for recovery. One person said: "Imagination and inner visions were worked on and encouraged", and another recounted how: "It surprised me to find something that looks at the person as a whole, in the face of whatever instabilities they may have suffered." People used a variety of words to sum up their experiences of participating in the groups, such as: *expanding, dreaming, creative, exhilarating, scary, powerful, puzzling, insightful, spiritual, self-actualising, liberating, enlightening and humane*. What is particularly interesting is that these people were encouraged to explore themselves in a safe therapeutic environment, and to find ways of supporting their healing journey, as noted by one participant who discovered that: "I have an internalised set of tools for problem solving." My colleague and I still believe that the journey of recovery has to include the process of recovering a sense of wholeness.[11]

Our therapeutic approach was informed by humanistic and transpersonal theories (especially process-oriented psychology). It included being client-centred, accepting of complexity and conflict (internal and external), as well as a receptivity to explore human potential, and most importantly trusting our client's authentic experiences. To this end I have also found the work of John Swinton[48] very helpful when integrating spirituality into a mental health context. He identifies the important interface between intrapersonal and interpersonal approaches, as well as the need to be mindful of the transpersonal dimension. Swinton's holistic perspective is sensitive to the interactions of experiences within and beyond the person. In a similar vein, transpersonal psychiatrist John Nelson[29] has stressed the need to include knowledge about different states of consciousness in mental health practice. For example, he identified that people who have experienced extreme states of consciousness and spiritual emergencies reveal that the experiences are not necessarily harmful. On the contrary, they are certainly helpful for facilitating enriched lives and provide inspiration for transpersonal development. This is certainly true in my case, as I continue on my journey of psycho-spiritual growth three decades after encountering a spiritual emergency (see chapter thirteen).

The political imperative that accompanies such knowledge of altered states is that practitioners in western-orientated mental health systems need more confidence (and training) to engage with transpersonal phenomena, and especially the transformative potential of spiritual emergencies.[20] The publication, *Spirituality in Psychiatry* (Royal College of Psychiatrists, UK),[49] includes a small section on spiritual emergency, which is an enlightened and progressive step towards enabling such a shift.

There has been a marked increase in people reporting intense mystical and spiritual phenomena over the last 30 years,[50] that suggests that these types of experiences need greater recognition in the collective consciousness. I believe that the escalating global crisis will gradually shift people's attention towards a greater spiritual awakening, where the sacred dimension of the earth and all its inhabitants is increasingly recognised. However, my concern is that there will also be fall-out, partly because we have collectively over-invested in materialism and become profoundly cut off from a deep ecological reality, inclusive of the transpersonal. Spiritual emergencies teach us that such shifts in consciousness can have a profound impact on our sense of self, causing a de-adaptation,[51] which means that cultivating an adaptive response in the collective consciousness is essential.[20] Some transpersonal experiences will be close to transitory psychotic episodes,[52] which reflect a radical deconstruction of established ways of being,[53] and we need to be prepared. It calls for an understanding of the factors that contribute to a fluid reconstruction of the self, inclusive of doing.[20,54] Catherine Lucas[55] has rightly stated that if approached in the right way, non-ordinary and altered states of consciousness can lead to healing and growth. The key issue is that people in the midst of spiritual crises need to have their human potential valued as an important part of the process of recovery.[26,56] It is here that *doing* is a critical part of the process of recovery and renewal.[20]

The 'doing self' and the process of renewal

I believe that the healing trajectory from spiritual crisis to self-renewal needs a greater focus on doing, so that the process of recovery includes people's occupational interests, as well as a focus on identity, and valuing the engagement of human potential. The links between occupations, identity, and spirituality[57] can shift perceptions of self, where such transcendent experiences not only exist, but are recognised in terms of a shared understanding of human potential. From this perspective we can use activities in our daily lives to inspire, engage and actualise our transpersonal potential, growth and development.[58] My own research into these phenomena has identified the important role of human occupation in the renewal of identity,[9] which requires people to develop a fluid sense of self to help get them through the transformative dimension of a crisis.[20] This occupational focus is concerned with how people participate in meaningful endeavours, orchestrate new possibilities for living, and in particular reveals how their interests and talents are engaged in relation to cultivating an *evolving* sense of self.[59] Indeed, we are reminded by Nelson[29] that whilst spiritual emergencies temporarily eclipse the ego, the ego is not dissolved. From this perspective human occupations are not only pivotal for the construction of identity,[60,61] but in the case of spiritual emergencies, where transitions in self-identity can be existentially challenging, the emphasis on renewed *ways of doing* are central for creating stability for re-emergent *states of being*.[20] Here, new insights gained are transitional and directed towards experiences of holistic ways of living.[62]

Interestingly, Hamel, Leclerc and Lefrancois[63] have described the process of human beings actualising their transcendent potential, stating that transpersonal growth occurs in daily life when our intentions and actions are connected to goals that include a transcendent dimension. Such a perspective holds new possibilities for people to participate creatively and meaningfully in life.[64,65,66] This transpersonal-occupational imperative is exemplified by self-reflection[67] and how people use their co-creative potential for engaging a deeper meaning, connected to doing, whilst living in a mysterious universe that is continually unfolding.[68] Puhakka[69] also alludes to the importance of an occupational perspective for the integration of our transformational potential. She notes that our ways of knowing are not *state* orientated; rather they are *active* processes that can have a substantial impact on our understanding of transformational experiences, in that they provide a sense of connectivity to our experiences of consciousness. Thus, the ability to facilitate new awakenings in consciousness connects to the integration of our awareness, actions and behaviours. However, the sticking point in collective transformation is the value placed on transformative experiences, like spiritual emergencies, which go beyond social norms. The problem with the modern socio-political status quo is that because of its collective denial or avoidance of transformative potential, people are not incentivised to question the potential value and relevance of such encounters.[12] Yet, these non-ordinary experiences are fertile and are capable of catalysing new ways of knowing, doing and being.

Many commentators have acknowledged that the current planetary crisis may be edging humanity closer to a global state of emergency.[8] This escalating crisis will require a collective reappraisal of consciousness in order to consider alternative actions for the co-creation of a sustainable future.[62] A global state of emergency[70] will have far-reaching implications that will undoubtedly challenge the foundations of our materialist and consumer-based societies and behaviours. The synergy between a global state of emergency and individual experiences of spiritual emergency[8] presents societies with a key challenge for the future, one that requires a more enlightened approach to transpersonal states of consciousness and transformational crises. It is through the engagement of human potential, as outlined in the fields of depth and transpersonal psychology that transformational crises may begin to be recognised for their value to collective change. However, psychiatrist R.D. Laing[71] noted that any consideration of our transformative potential will first require that we confront our collective *psycho-phobia.* By this he means the ways we alienate our self, others and the universe. In doing so, Laing identifies that we become split off and dissociated from life, reinforcing a *schizoid* existence, one that avoids a healthy relationship to life as a whole.

Societies need to understand the meaning, depth of experience and pathways for renewal through these spiritual emergencies.[15,21,41] As we have seen above, a substantial number of people being treated for psychosis in the mental health system are actually experiencing a crisis of transformation.[8] Talking about his work as a transpersonal psychiatrist, Grof recounted that people's orientation shifted when they discovered the numinous dimension of their psyche. This revelation enabled these people in the midst of a transformational crisis to consider new ways of relating to self, other and nature.[8] Here, the numinous is important because of its ability to catalyse or activate processes of spiritual transformation.[72]

Jung (among others) has made an important contribution to the evolution of transpersonal theory,[73,74] and his perspective could be helpful in terms of shifting the focus away from individual consciousness towards more collective representations that tackle the current ecological crisis. Jung's approach highlighted a need to develop a greater relationship between the inner dimensions of the psyche and the outside world of nature.[75] This can lead to deep contact with the numinous dimension,[76] as well as activating processes that lead to ego-transcendence.[77,78] Jung[53] explains the importance of activating our psycho-spiritual potential, linked to the numinous. Indeed, his therapeutic approach is strongly allied to making acquaintance with the numinous, rather than putting the focus on pathology.

Jung sees the numinous as a way to enable human beings to become aware of their potential for wholeness. Furthermore, Jungian analyst Frey-Rohn[79] has noted that when an individual communicates valuable insights, which have been gained from the process of individuation and working with the unconscious, the society in which they live can benefit from that person's struggle and integration of new perspectives in consciousness and lived experience. This viewpoint is particularly evident in the biographical work of Carl Jung whose personal struggles inspired countless people to explore new ways of conceptualising our relationship to psycho-spiritual growth. Yet, there is still work to be done with the integration of insights from people who have encountered spiritual emergencies and the shared understandings for how these spiritual crises can benefit collective consciousness. One of the problems we face collectively is not only how to face up to the disruptive elements of transformational experiences (such as spiritual crises), but also how we are inspired to connect to life beyond the reaches of our ego-identities. At a collective level we can begin to exercise the development of our consciousness through an appreciation of myths and stories that inspire us (like the myths of ancient times), which can begin to stimulate new vistas of meaning.[80] The following dream was an inspirational moment that reflected a turning point in my personal mythic journey and how dreams are pushing us to awaken to the spirit.

The lion and the lamb

During the early years in my psychotherapy training I dreamt of standing in a dusty wilderness at sunset. I was looking into the distant horizon and I noticed an object coming towards me at speed. As the object came closer, I noticed it was a huge single lion pulling a chariot. Eventually the lion and the chariot reached where I was standing and came to a halt. The scene was breathtaking, as I stood looking at this massive ferocious lion, with powerful musculature, enormous sharp teeth and a mane covered in streaks of blood. It was an awesome sight. But it was even more unusual in that this majestic beast was pulling a chariot, like a two-wheeled war chariot used by the Romans.

I was so awestruck by the lion that I barely paid any attention to the man who was driving the chariot. He had the same physical build, and was dressed in almost the same way as the fictional archaeologist adventurer, Indiana Jones; complete with hat, bull whip, and rolled-up shirt sleeves. He looked stern and focused as he stepped of the chariot platform and walked towards me. There were no words spoken between us, but I saw that he was carrying a woolly lamb under his arm. He gave me the lamb and then walked back to his chariot. I looked at the small animal entrusted to me and was completely startled when I noticed that I had been given a lion cub that had grown a coat of lamb's wool. As I remained standing with a young lion-lamb in my hands, in the middle of a desolate place, I awoke.

I have some notion that this dream is pointing to my longer-term process of individuation. Yet, I am also mindful that the dream is somehow connected to something much bigger than me. My initial associations to the dream were focused on the fierce, powerful lion (covered in blood) pulling a war chariot. However, the dream is also full of subtleties and nuances; for example, the lion is harnessed and appears to be working in harmony with the adventurous archaeologist Indiana Jones.

Archaeology helps us understand our relationship to the past and also to the symbolic meanings found in our human heritage and myths. In this way, the dream is full of powerful symbolic references and strong mythical motifs. For example, we find in the myths of Asia Minor the Goddess Kybele,[81] and the Greek Goddess Rhea[82] are both depicted riding sacred chariots that are drawn by strong, ferocious lions. The suggestion is that these Goddesses had harnessed the wildness of lions.[83] Interestingly, Rhea-Kybele share a role of being identified as the Great Goddess in both Asia Minor and ancient Greece. I have thought about this dream often, particularly from the perspective of collective consciousness.

For example, we learn that a lion pulling a chariot is actually an ancient mythical image that is identified as a vehicle of the Great Goddess, but in the dream there is a missing connection to the divine feminine, in that it is a male archaeologist who is driving the chariot, and not the Goddess. What could a dream like this mean to man who has grown up in a patriarchal, overly rational society, which appears to have lost a sense of the sacred and a loss of soul? The dream suggests a journey of an awakening consciousness that is missing an important connection to the sacred feminine.

There is also deep symbolic meaning in the representation of the lion and the lamb. We find references to the images in the Bible (particularly in Isaiah and Revelations), yet whilst the two animals are seldom portrayed together,[84] they are represented as aspects of Christ. They metaphorically connect the courage and gentleness associated with a sacred and divine consciousness. Perhaps the symbol of the young lion and the lamb, made into *one*, is an apt representation of our ability to be courageous and gentle in our spiritual development. Interestingly, I associated the young lion-lamb to a new *sacred consciousness* – which is delivered by a lion pulling a chariot – which represents (mythically) a vehicle for the *sacred feminine*. The emergence of a sacred consciousness connected to the sacred feminine an integral part of our evolutionary potential at this time, yet we have to dig deep (like archaeology) to discover these inspiring and soulful connections in life. For a more in-depth discussion about the depth and richness of our sacred connection to the feminine, the recent publication by Jungian analyst, Anne Baring, *The Dream of the Cosmos*,[85] offers a powerful awakening for our souls.

The above dream provides a powerful way of considering the archetypal forces at work in our consciousness. It shows how symbolic forms can connect to mythic themes, enabling us to be inspired to reflect and act deeply. As human beings we are profound beyond measure, and at this time in human evolution it is our responsibility to connect to myths that can galvanise our bodies, minds, souls and spirits. In doing so, we can be inspired to find ways of stimulating a new relationship to life. In this era of global crisis, a new myth for the transformation of collective consciousness is waiting to emerge. How we work with our dreams and aspirations may be the difference that helps us to catalyse our transpersonal potential.

Exercise

- Bring to mind an aspiration or interest that would enable you to express your full human potential.

- Now imagine creating a bridge between your everyday identity and your full human potential.

- How is your bridge constructed? Imagine the materials that have been used in the construction, its design, any decorations or symbols that have meaning for you.

- Imagine crossing this bridge – what do you experience in your body? How does it feel?

- Notice how you feel, as you are able to cross from the experience of your everyday identity and connect to your full human potential.

- Notice how the bridge connects and mediates your inner experience, between two different parts of your lived experiences.

- Consider the qualities of your bridge, for example, it could be one of the following, or a combination:

  o A bridge of strength?
  o A bridge of resilience?
  o A bridge of love?
  o A bridge of courage?
  o A bridge of healing?
  o A bridge of awareness?
  o A bridge of forgiveness?
  o A bridge of...? (make up your own)

*The purpose of a mythic connection to life is that it awakens our minds and
souls to the eternal. Once these myths are alive and active, they can
live through us in all that we do. That is, if we honour them.*

CHAPTER EIGHT

Towards a new myth for collective consciousness

Overview

In this chapter I explore the basis for a new mythical perspective in modern life.
I examine how our transpersonal potential requires new parameters from which
to engage life more deeply. I build on the knowledge of archetypal occupations
to illustrate how doing is instrumental in the alchemical process of transforming
consciousness and changing human behaviours to create an improved future,
while acknowledging the complexities of engaging such shifts in consciousness.
I also explore the current barriers and resistance to such change.

The mythic, numinous and archetypal dimension of spiritual encounters

The value of myths to the individual or the collective is that they help to guide
our actions and behaviours. Historically mythology has provided us with ways of
relating to the mysterious (and often irrational) encounters with the numinous
dimension of reality in an objective manner.[1] Mythologist Joseph Campbell[2]
relates its function to our psycho-spiritual heritage, suggesting that myths serve
a dynamic purpose in the reconciliation of our everyday consciousness to a
wider mystery in the cosmos. That is, contact with the numinous brings us into
direct relationship with the sacred, and our potential for deep and meaningful
connections to transcendent experiences.[3] It is the stories that we tell each other,
and the interest in those stories that can help us explore a renewed sense of
meaning beyond our dominant material and consumer based worldviews. The
following story is a beautiful illustration that reveals how cultural myths are not
only alive; they can guide our actions in life.

--------------- **Spirits of the sea** ---------------

A few years ago two friends of mine visited the UK from New Zealand. I took
them to the north Norfolk coast, to Holkham beach, which for me is a very

spiritual place. Indeed, a few years earlier an ancient *seahenge* was discovered not far away. The henge comprised a circle of oak stumps and in its centre was a huge upturned base of an oak tree – was it a sacred altar perhaps? My wife and I were lucky enough to see this ancient seahenge before it was removed to be preserved. There is a deep sense of sacredness on this huge expanse of natural coastline. As my friends and I walked along the beach we noticed a young dead dolphin on the shoreline. One of my friends, who is a Māori (and partially sighted) walked up to the dolphin and scooped it up into his arms. He then walked fully clothed into the sea, carrying the young dolphin. He said prayers for it and placed it gently back into the sea.

This event revealed to me a profound moment of reverence for nature, and I learnt that Māori people have a special relationship with these mammals. Dolphins are often described as *taniwha*, which roughly translates as spirits of the water. There are stories in Māori myth and culture where dolphins and other sea mammals have helped human beings. A short while after, I asked my friend if he would lead a Haka on Holkham beach, which was a fitting response to the prayers already said for the young dolphin. I learnt how cultural values come alive and can be lived in connection to myths. The significance of this story is that my friend's actions were deeply inspirational and revealed how myths touch our lives and inspire us to act. Witnessing my friend's actions that day had a profound impact on my understanding about the importance of myths and how they help to guide our ways of living in the world.

Modern societies have few guiding myths for reconciling our waking consciousness to the mystery of the numinous, and Campbell[4] has referred to this sense of alienation from the spirit as a *mythic dissociation*. Noting this dislocation from our deep and ancient mythical heritage, Jungian analyst Edward Edinger[5] argues that western societies need to create a new myth, one that is connected to finding purpose in life through a creative engagement in consciousness. In this era of planetary crisis, we are being called to find ways to reconsider our relationship to life as a whole, and the function of a new myth will help us embrace a wider global perspective.[6] Indeed, we need a new story to help guide our intentions and actions.

Erich Neumann[7] evaluated the importance of re-awakening modern consciousness to the meaning and functions of myths. He noted our modern tendency to *reduce* or marginalise our meaningful connections to the transpersonal dimension, and in doing so, he believes that we have become *reduced* in terms of ability to understand our human potential fully. By way of contrast, he explains that our ancestors took the mystical dimension seriously and so became *illuminated* by their transpersonal encounters. It is evident in these modern times that we have become somewhat divorced from the meanings associated with the myths from the past, and yet, as Skolimowski[8] has rightly noted, we need myths to live by. What stories will guide humanity through the challenges of the current escalating global and spiritual crisis? McGilchrist[9] offers a sobering analysis of our current mythic dissociation when he points out those myths are not an added extra when exploring meaning in life. On the contrary, he notes that the absence of a productive guiding myth means that we fall prey to living with the status quo. In the modern world, a fitting metaphor that sums up the status quo is a mechanistic myth, one that reveals our relationship to the technological machine that is gripping our lives.

Does it undermine technological advances to reinstate the important function of myths as a way of guiding collective values and principles? On the contrary, the modern world is crying out for a new myth that will galvanise our collective efforts to restore and heal ourselves, as well as our relationship to other species and nature as a whole. Such mythic renewal will have to reflect a deeper and more interconnected relationship with all life. Due to the scale of the global crisis, radical change is inevitable and Deepak Chopra[10] quotes Albert Einstein, who said that a definition of insanity is repeatedly doing something the same way, over and over, with an expectation that the result will be different. Chopra wistfully reflects that historically, humanity has often acted in this way. However, our task is to wake up to the world's peril and find a new direction. For example, if there were more understanding of how encountering the ineffable and symbolic qualities of mystical experience leads to self-renewal, it could inspire a new mythic outlook.[11] According to Griffiths,[11] this is where the foundation of myths reveals productive connections for Self-discovery (through the unconscious), which is full of mystery. That is, any guiding myth in this time of crisis has to include a deeper connection to life through a transpersonal dimension of consciousness.

The challenge is to envision and create an inspirational myth that unifies individuals, families, communities, nations and the world,[12] including taking account of other species. It would reflect an archetypal view of reality, one that brings forth the philosophical and spiritual heritage that resides in the collective unconscious.[13] From an integral perspective[14] archetypes are interlaced between psychological, spiritual and ecological dimensions of our relationship to daily life, whilst providing a connection to a transpersonal (numinous) level of consciousness.[15] This puts human beings in a holistic context, connected to all life and nature. Hence, the new myth must reflect the interconnected nature of reality. Corbett[14] stresses that within modern cultures there is a separation between the material and spiritual domains, which is distinct from pre-industrial times, where people related to the Earth as sacred. Corbett notes that Jung placed great emphasis on understanding the meaning and function of the numinous in our modern lives for reconnecting with the sacred dimension in nature. In doing so, he asserts that we are then capable of connecting with a continuity of the Self (whole) as it is experienced both inwardly and outwardly in our relationship to life.

The transpersonal re-aligns human experience – mythically – to a wider and deeper view of consciousness.[16] Moreover, it reconnects humans to our deeper spiritual heritage, based on the realisation that ego-identity is a relatively recent phenomenon in human history.[17] As discussed earlier, one of the key problems of ego-consciousness in relation to modern life is that we have become increasingly one-dimensional.[18] That is, modern humans have cultivated a consciousness that is divorced from the psyche as a whole, yet in reality the human psyche is connected to a wider ecology of life.[19] The problem with our ego-dominated and consumer-based consciousness at the present time is that it is creating a distortion, believing that it is at the centre of consciousness. This limited ego-orientation is contrasted with the indigenous wisdom of shamanic traditions, where humans' connection to the cosmos is understood to be multi-sensory and connected to the whole.[20] It is here that the archetypes provide access to a deep seam of human potential and development, which could inspire a more expansive relationship to life as a whole. Mythically, the archetypes carry the potential for numinous experiences, which increases our opportunity to connect with the transcendent dimension[21] in ways that can inspire a new attitude to life.[22]

Humanity has the potential for engaging in processes of psycho-spiritual change, which Jung referred to as *archetypes of transformation*.[23] These are situations or events that symbolise deep patterns of change. Jung[24] proposed that such archetypal forces are only activated when transformation is called for. In today's context, the current global state of emergency could be indicative of an archetypal level of change.[25] Indeed, our current unsustainable ways of living are gradually confronting us with the consequences of our modern lifestyles, which reflects a much-needed transformation in consciousness.[26,27] And it would appear that to establish a sustainable future, we will have to actualise our transformational potential.[28,29] This trajectory for human development reflects a process of collective awakening and individuation,[30] where life's interconnectedness informs our efforts to adapt and manage the crises we are facing.[31]

Transforming selves for a sustainable world

It is becoming harder to ignore the need for a collective response to the current global and spiritual state of emergency, which I have described previously as the need for "transcendent action in the service of collective transformation"[32]. This means that our individual efforts for change are also aligned to a collective level, as we work for the greater good. From this transformational perspective, human consciousness is reconnected with nature and a wider experience of the cosmos (transpersonal), where we are reacquainted with the numinous dimension of the natural world. No great leap of the imagination is needed to understand how worsening environmental conditions are revealing a numinous power in nature,[33] as found, for example, in extreme weather patterns like hurricanes, earthquakes and floods. There is a direct correlation between global temperature increases and the incidence and severity of hurricanes, as seen in the 2012 storms tearing into the coastline of the USA. Such occurrences should motivate us to deepen the dialogue about engaging transitional and transformative states of consciousness to co-create an improved future.

If we need reminding of the severity of our global crisis, Lord Nicholas Stern, who published a report on climate change in 2006, was reported saying in January 2013 that earlier predictions on climate change were wrong: the reality is much worse. Lord Stern tells us that global temperatures are set to rise significantly higher than he predicted in 2006.[34] In the same report Stewart and Elliott[34] quoted the president of the World Bank, Jim Yong Kim, who predicts that our inability to produce enough food in the near future will result in widespread conflicts for resources, such as food and water. The call for a shift in consciousness is not based on mystical musings, but on an urgent need to wake up to the reality we have created, and to find a new way of living, one that is based on modest appetites and a more sacred view of life as an interconnected whole. It requires that we wake up to the global predicament we have created,[25] for we have been sleep-walking into this collective nightmare for decades. The lack of any meaningful collective reaction to the global state of emergency reveals the extent to which we have become dissociated from these issues. It is time we woke up collectively and prepared ourselves to meet the challenges of a fast changing world.

Jung evolved a psychotherapeutic approach where the development of consciousness is based on a relationship to the unconscious,[35] where we are gradually released from the grip of our one-sided ways of living (ego-consciousness). The key to such a transformation is the recognition that everything in nature eventually flows to its opposite, which is encapsulated in the ancient Greek philosophical term *enantiodromia*.[36] For example, the one-sided attitudes and behaviours that are so evident in the modern world are reaching a tipping point, and the *enantiodromia* of this current era reflects a potential to shift the balance to a new state of consciousness.[25] Jung's[36] work on *enantiodromia* supports the notion that an increase in the number of people experiencing spiritual crises could catalyse shifts in collective consciousness in this time of global crisis.[25] The size of the transformative task is put into context by Yunt,[19] who provides a Jungian-informed viewpoint on the problem. He points out that as our one-sided rational consciousness becomes more separated and alienated from life as a whole, the unconscious becomes more active – in an attempt to restore balance in the psyche – and it does this through projections, dreams, conflicts and disturbances.

Spiritual crises could reflect an *enantiodromia* or potential tipping point in collective consciousness, which, if understood properly, could act as an alarm for humanity.[25] Richard Tarnas[37] explores this idea further, asking if the modern psyche is undergoing a rite of passage. If Tarnas is correct, any transition will need to address those collective processes that have been split off from consciousness, for example, where we have lost the value of myths, or when we assume that individuals in the midst of transformational crises have mental health problems.[25,38] Thus, we need to see the emerging archetypal potential of collective transformation as a solution for inspiring and engaging collective change. However, the shift from personal (individualised) consciousness to a more transpersonal (universal) consciousness in society also requires a level of political awareness and engagement in two ways. First, there needs to be an understanding of the ways that certain political forces (more focused on economic concerns) have served ideologies that are more centred on wealth creation and consumer-based lifestyles, rather than the needs of the whole: people, other species and the planet. Second, there needs to be more political and collective involvement to bring about a more progressive and non-pathological understanding of spiritual crises,[25,31] which values expanded states of consciousness.[39] From this perspective, we need to reframe the deeper meaning of mystical and spiritual encounters, as suggested by Caroline Myss[40] who says that some shifts in life are like *alters* where we are transformed. The questions remain, where, when and how will we start to change our consciousness and behaviours collectively?

Six dimensions for collective transformation

In this book I am proposing that the current global state of emergency is an opportunity to re-align humanity to a re-sacralised socio-political vision,[25] one that takes into account the deep reality of the psyche.[30] It involves encouraging people to engage a deeper and more sacred relationship to life, which can facilitate transformational change in six broad areas: *learning, citizenship, democracy, culture, ecology* and *human occupation.* In an article I co-published with two colleagues, both Jungian analysts, we argued that these six domains could act as focal points for a re-sacralised political vision for the 21st century, which advocates transformative action from crisis to renewal. The following is adapted from that publication:[25]

> **Deep Learning:** This process reflects the great potential of human beings for living creatively, through engaging their imaginations and innovations in daily life.[41] Deep learning involves being interested and motivated in life.[42] It is the depth of learning that connects people's potential for meaningful engagement,[43] and also for having transformative experiences.[44] Interestingly, the Latin word ēducāre means to 'bring out',[45] which identifies that deep learning is both transformative and a lifelong process.[46]
>
> **Deep Citizenship:** Being engaged in life as a citizen naturally cultivates a deep political outlook. Deep citizenship reflects a process of discovery about what it is to be human, as well as having concern for self, others and the

world.[47] Citizenship from this perspective is allied to the politics of everyday life, between the inner life of people's private world, and the outer life of public engagement.[48] Deep citizenship is not a one-dimensional association with a given society,[18] it is a multi-levelled perspective for ways of living and being-in-the-world. In light of the global crisis, it means working for the greater good.

Deep Democracy: This encourages dialogue and interaction between diverse socio-political viewpoints, including consensus and non-consensus experiences.[49] Jung's[50] interest in the psychological dimension of democracy was developed further by Arnold Mindell[51] and his colleagues, who conceptualised 'deep democracy', to include a spiritual attitude that requires the cultivation of awareness.[52] If humanity is serious about creating a just and fair world that is based on diversity and respect for all ways of being, then a deeper understanding of democracy will be needed, one that includes finding a 'voice' for nature.

Deep Culture: Global living provides many challenges and opportunities for understanding and sharing diverse worldviews through cultural dialogues and exchanges. The concept is based on the need to foster cross-cultural competencies in the way that we relate to one another, developing greater appreciation and awareness. Deep culture reflects a desire to explore and understand the variety of meanings in human behaviours, with an emphasis on cross-cultural learning.[53] This viewpoint provides opportunities for developing self-other awareness, about how processes of enculturation are internalised and represented.[54]

Deep Ecology: The perspective of deep ecology, as discussed by Naess,[55] reflects a deeper, wider, and more expansive relationship to the world both within and around us.[56] Deep ecology goes beyond the surface concerns of environmental problems and represents a much more comprehensive philosophical standpoint.[57] It is a perspective that provides opportunities for human beings to reflect on the ways that they are participating in the world, whilst acknowledging the interconnectedness of all life.[58] Thus, human beings are embedded in a deep ecology of life, not separate from it.

Deep Occupations: People's active participation in daily life contains possibilities for evolving their consciousness and awareness, linked to creative adaptations and occupational intelligence.[59,60] Such processes include psycho-spiritual developments[61,62] with transpersonal significance.[63,64] Thus, occupational engagement also includes connections to unconscious processes,[65,66] where dynamic properties such as the archetypes[67] can inform and align our endeavours with deep purpose and meaning.

The six dimensions outlined above highlight key areas where transformative shifts in consciousness could be engaged. For example, *deep learning* reflects our incredible capacity for engaging with new challenges; *deep citizenship* identifies the value we place on a sense of collective belonging; *deep democracy* reveals how we are able to integrate a range of perspectives and appreciate different viewpoints; *deep culture* highlights the diverse and interesting ways that our communities can interact and learn from each other; *deep ecology* connects us to nature and life as a whole, beyond human-centric constructs; *deep occupations* express our personal and transpersonal potentials as participants and co-creators in life. These six dimensions are a starting point that may help to catalyse our transformative reflections and actions.

This recognises the deep potential of our capacity for adaptation as humans. People's spiritual emergence (and emergencies) could act as a potent force for bringing about a wider change in collective consciousness (*enantiodromia*).[25] They set an agenda in collective consciousness, which highlights greater need for reflexivity in relation to the global state of emergency. Such transformative awareness would naturally shift our actions and behaviours to face up to the challenges that lie ahead. Our collective potential needs to be harnessed through an intelligent understanding that we are deeply connected to nature and one another. Theodore Roszak[68] reminds us that at a deep level, the collective unconscious harbours an intelligence that connects us to a wider ecology of life. Recognition of this ecological intelligence is pivotal to us as a species. Indeed, greater communion between humans and nature provides opportunities to engage in a *participation mystique* – as discussed by Jung – revealing how people have the potential for a deep identification and relationship to the natural world.[69] For example, when the archetypes of the natural world are encountered – trees, mountains, rivers, flowers and so on – they may be experienced as part of nature's mystery.[70] Thus, it is our capacity to reflect deeply[71] and engage with the numinous quality of such natural encounters that further highlights their importance for developing a reflexive level of consciousness in the process of transformation.[31] The healing power of nature can inspire and guide deep archetypal connections within everyday life.[67]

From numinous reflections to transformative actions

I have written previously about the need for greater reflexivity when exploring transformative states of consciousness in society,[29] especially those sorts of experiences that are disruptive[72] and frightening, such as spiritual crises. In my estimation there is still a major threat of disruption in our times, linked to the collective avoidance of what spiritual emergencies mean in relation to a burgeoning global state of emergency.[29] If we understand the viewpoint that each of us is connected to the whole, then it takes no great leap of the imagination to awaken to the reality that crises in the outer world can be reflected in the crises of our inner worlds. It is here that an increase in spiritual emergencies reveals a growing edge in collective consciousness to transform. From this perspective, a central question that has to be asked is how we can develop greater reflexivity between our inner and outer worlds? [29,67]

The root of the modern word 'reflexivity' comes from the Graeco-Roman term *parrhesia,* or truth-telling.[73] Here, the act of reflection encourages people to take responsibility for their life stories and actions.[74] I have suggested elsewhere[29,75] that there are two key areas for reflection and transformation in the context of a global and spiritual state of emergency. First is the necessity to reflect honestly on the scale of human destruction in the modern world, and second is the need to acknowledge the parameters of our full human potential, which not only focus on self-responsibility, but also on our attitudes to one another[75] and all forms of life.[29] These two points highlight the value of the transformative narratives of people who have transited spiritual emergencies.[32] Such narratives demonstrate a capacity for reflection and action that could help to inspire trust in engaging collective change.[29] Here, Griffiths[11] illuminates the role of reflection, as a precursor to action. He says that our consciousness has a reflective capability and if we reflect on the Self (transpersonal) and its relationship to the ego, we are able to foster growth in consciousness as a process of *Self-realisation.*

The reflexive value of transformative narratives – i.e. from the personal to the transpersonal – is their ability to convey autobiographical accounts of change[29,32] that go far beyond the self of the author,[76] particularly in relation to exceptional human experiences[77] such as spiritual crises.[29] Gathering biographical evidence of these transformational encounters is important,[32] because they could be used to encourage acceptance in the collective of such states of consciousness. Richard House[78] has identified the centrality of this *trans-biographical* dimension of change in relation to understanding exceptional personal encounters or experiences. Moreover, Jung's autobiographical account of his transformation through a spiritual crisis exemplifies the important role of engaging in a process of individuation and Self-realisation.[67] Jung's inspiring reflections on his own transformative journey (in his *Red Book*) constitute a detailed testimony of the deep transitions in consciousness that he encountered, which could have wider applications for humanity at a collective level.[67] My correspondence with Stanislav Grof highlighted the importance of Jung's crisis encounter with the unconscious, and the influence of his archetypal encounters on the field of transpersonal studies:

> The stormy personal history of C. G. Jung shows the extraordinary creative power that spiritual emergency can have under the best of circumstances: when it happens to a person with an unusual gift for introspection, great intelligence, and impressive educational background. Jung's psycho-spiritual crisis gave birth to a new psychology that in recent decades has had increasing influence on the field. His recently published *Red Book* is an extraordinary travelogue of his own "Night Sea Journey" (p. 464).[67]

Previously I have discussed how people's non-ordinary experiences of consciousness[79] will require the development of a *trans-reflexive* position within consciousness.[32] Trans-reflexivity is recognition of the deep connections that exist between humans, nature, other species and the planet as a whole. A trans-reflexive position is concerned with developing a greater capacity between personal and transpersonal experiences of consciousness, whilst recognising that such encounters are often ineffable and may even transcend the everyday boundaries of the self.[31] Trans-reflexivity means that we consider our conscious connections to life as a whole, inclusive of, and also going beyond, the borders of our executive ego-functioning.

Jung the explorer and Jung the guide

How we engage with information from the unconscious to support our life choices and directions raises compelling questions about how we fulfil our deep potential. Jung was always adamant that people are wise to pay heed to the messages that come from the unconscious. In the mid-1990s I had a dream where I stood before a huge 'Terminator'-like figure, who wore a helmet that completely covered his face and head, except for a small slit across the helmet for the eyes. In the dream I stood as an observer, watching the Terminator figure get on a very powerful motorbike and ride it around sharp mountain bends at break-neck speed. The early part of the dream had lots of references to power and was quite scary.

The dream then switched to me driving a car on a beach road, and I noticed that very large lizards were eating smaller mammals on the beach, which was very unpleasant. I continued driving on the beach road and noticed a white building, which reminded me of a scientific laboratory with a domed roof. In the dream I walked up to the laboratory carrying a pelican skeleton. I reached the entrance, knocked on the door, and stood waiting. A short while later the door was opened by Carl Jung. His face was stern and he looked at me and the pelican skeleton, saying: "Do not waste your time with pelican skeletons, go and find dinosaur bones." He then put some correction fluid on my arms. In the dream I stood at the door speechless.

Upon awakening I was struck by the numinous quality in the dream. I intuitively knew that the dream had meaning for the way that I was living my life. I worked on the dream in my psychotherapy sessions, particularly on issues of power and being empowered. However, about six months after having this dream I was reading a book about Jung's life and came across a dream that Jung had, as discussed by Segaller and Berger.[80] In the dream, Jung was in a dark wood (near the Rhine) and he found a small mound that appeared to look like a burial site. He started to dig and discovered some bones of prehistoric animals, which captured his imagination. In the dream Jung knew intuitively that he needed to study natural phenomena, and learn about the world that surrounded him.

I was struck by the meaningful parallels, where Jung in his dream discovers prehistoric animal bones, and then in my dream Jung instructs me to seek dinosaur bones. I sought to integrate the meaning of this dream into my life and it struck me, by way of analogy, that whilst dinosaurs are extinct, evidence for their existence is found in archaeological excavations. I reflected on the dream, and about what humans have lost since ancient times, particularly in connection with the sacred. My deepest interest personally and professionally has been to explore the links between human beings' occupational lives and the vast potential connected to what Jung referred to as the *ancient human* that exists in everyone. This interest is not only about historical facts, but concerns the evolution of our ancestors' relationship to the spark of the numinous and how they developed and lived in connection to awe and mystery. It is no surprise that I spent nine years training in transpersonal psychotherapy, where the relationship to the archetypes and the numinous are uncovered in our unconscious processes. Yet, my training in occupational science and therapy also enabled me to consider how *doing* holds so much of our unconscious processes and our transpersonal potential. My conceptualisation of archetypal occupations has evolved through many years of excavation, but most importantly, my research led me to understand the importance of trans-reflexivity to help rediscover what has been lost in terms of our transpersonal-occupational connection to life.

Analytical psychologist Barbara Hannah[81] cites a talk given by Jung three years before his death, in which he referred to the 2 million-year-old human that is part of our evolutionary legacy. Similarly, psychologist Timothy Leary[82] describes the deep meaning of a sacrament, as something that connects people to an ancient flow within. This is why human occupations link so powerfully to an archetypal dimension.[67] It is hardly surprising that *doing* has so many healing benefits, particularly as the very modalities for our multi-sensory engagement in the world have evolved for countless millennia from our early ancestors onwards. These reflect a rich inherited predisposition for deep expression: purpose and meaning in lived experience, as part of our evolutionary development.[67] Our occupational lives are full of spiritual potency and mystery, with the potential to express lived experience as a sacrament towards experiences of wholeness and healing. Indeed, it was Jung who viewed human beings as *Homo mysticus*.[83] We have a great opportunity to explore how this mystery – of which we are a part – connects to our process of individuation in everyday lived experiences.[62,67] It is with such intention that our transpersonal potential can connect to our actions in the world: 'I do, therefore I evolve'.

During his transformational crisis Jung worked with images and symbols arising from the collective unconscious that went beyond his usual ego-functioning.[67] Jung's journey of discovery made clear the connections between the archetypal (and numinous) processes involved in spiritual development and the unfolding journey of individuation, linked to processes of self and spiritual renewal.[84] It is interesting to note that in his work on holotropic states of consciousness, Grof found many resonances with the myths that Jung had noted in the formulation of his theories on the archetypes.[79] It was through his own transformational crisis that Jung evolved a new stage of conscious development, which was initiated through archetypal encounters with symbols from the collective unconscious,[67] and – as is often the case – the emergence of these deep processes arrived spontaneously.[85]

At the time of his crisis Jung's involvement in academic pursuits, which had been central to his life, halted abruptly and he did not read much scientific literature for a number of years.[86] This sudden change in his occupational behaviours indicates the disruption of his everyday routines. However, Jung intuitively engaged with the disturbance that he equated symbolically as an experience of being in a desert, and in one inner dialogue with his soul, he asked the question what he should do?[87] He experimented and developed a process known as active imagination, where at a deep level, a soulful response to his inner complexes revealed a direction for him, suggesting that his creative life force needed further connection to his experiences at a soul level. Through a process of engaging active imagination, Jung realised that we remain stunted unless we are prepared to go beyond the limiting intentions of the ego and explore the depth of our inner unconscious responses to life. Jung commented on the predicament of modern humans, pointing out that we are resistant in our commitment to living fully (wholeness).[87] Jung can be credited with pioneering ways to engage the psycho-spiritual dimensions of the unconscious. He worked through many disturbing and illuminating encounters as he incorporated new insights into his process of individuation. Working with symbols arising from the unconscious can inspire both reflection and action, as Kelly[88] suggests, our insights (ways of knowing) need to be put into action in order for meaning to be integrated into our life as a whole.

Archetypal occupations and the alchemy of transformation

Jung[86] described his journey of individuation as a process that preoccupied him intensely, particularly as he dealt with the continual flow of material from the unconscious that held him captive.[67] The publication of his *Red Book*[87] has provided an understanding of how he engaged and transformed his preoccupations into meaningful reflections and actions.[67] The important links between *doing* and *being* in Jung's individuation process were a key focus in his journey of recovery.[67] Yet, his process of individuation was an arduous journey of transformation, as noted in his questions about what we *do* with the unconscious.[86] In wanting to know what we should do with the unconscious, Jung reveals the importance he placed on the need for action. That is, he highlighted the importance of reflections that translated into ways of *doing*, not only what it is to *be* with the unconscious.[67] In Jung's journey of individuation we find an important exchange, between his meaningful occupational engagement that resulted in the production of the *Red Book* (through written and symbolic representation of the material he was encountering from the unconscious), and the construction of his retreat tower at Bollingen (through building and engaging in craftwork as meaningful representations of his individuation process).[67] Jung reflected and acted deeply throughout his transformational encounter with a spiritual crisis.[67]

Jung's process of individuation revealed how encounters with the numinous reflect an archetypal process of initiation[89] which can be experienced through spiritual emergencies, connecting us to an archetype of wholeness.[90] To this end, the revelations in Jung's *Red Book* reflected the depth of the uncharted territory he was exploring from the unconscious.[67] In addition, Jung continued to integrate the process of individuation, through exploring new ways of doing and being at his Bollingen Tower. Yet, the construction of the tower was much more than an act of ego expression for Jung, who tells us that he built it in a kind of *dream*.[86] That is, he was attempting to integrate unconscious processes in his daily life and occupations.[62,67] Here, Jung's archetypal encounters are reflected in new ways of living. The quality of Jung's[86] trans-reflexive experience is expressed in his writings, when he describes feeling connected to nature and having a sense of belonging to trees, clouds and creatures, as well as the ever-changing seasons.

In a previous publication I discussed how transformations in consciousness include the ability to work with archetypal symbols and images (inner work) and to consider how these are encouraging a synergy with the lived potentials that are expressed through everyday occupations and actions (outer work).[67] Jung's[86] own words bear testimony to the possibilities for individuation following a transformational crisis. He speaks about a dual process of experiencing increasing uncertainty about himself, whilst at the same time feeling a growing connection with all life. This underlines why a transpersonal perspective is greatly needed in the world today. It highlights the importance of discovering a new relationship to *doing* and *being* in the process of self and spiritual renewal at an individual and collective level. The expression of our transpersonal potential, through deep reflections and actions, represents a quality of engagement in life that connects the archetypes to our occupational engagement.[67]

The conceptual development of archetypal occupations[67] reflects a theoretical perspective for understanding the centrality of doing in our transpersonal development. It draws on Jung's occupational engagement (via the creation of the *Red Book* and the building of the tower at Bollingen), which emphasises the role of doing in the integration of transpersonal consciousness within everyday lived experiences. The biographical details of Jung's narrative of transformational crisis and renewal reveals that deep transitions in consciousness are possible.[67] The theoretical basis for archetypal occupations is underpinned by Jung's[91] observation of the archetypes as systems that are primed for action, which can spur us on to participate deeply in the world. We are now entering an age where we will have to radically reappraise our ways of doing and, if we are serious about co-creating an improved future, we will need to consider how archetypal occupations enable and express the deeper levels of transformation required for living more sustainably.[67] Indeed, as Caroline Myss[40] points out, when we engage our life at a soul level, it can lead to an experience of *active illumination*. There is a potential synergistic relationship between the active processes that connects to processes of individuation, through active imagination, as a deep form of active engagement, which enables an active illumination of our human potential.

The scale of the current global crisis makes our ways of living on the planet – with increasing populations and finite resources – a political issue. Yet, most political leaders have ignored the need to transform our relationship to the Earth and its finite resources. We have to ask, why are we not preparing or resourcing ourselves for the co-creation of an improved future: for example, in terms of *deep learning, deep citizenship, deep democracy, deep culture, deep ecology and deep occupations.* There appears to be no genuine public acknowledgement or recognition from politicians that our economic models and consumer-based behaviours and lifestyles are unsustainable.[92] Yet, the world's population is predicted to explode to 9 billion in the very near future. Combined with unstable weather patterns due to climate warming and escalating demand for energy and food production, it is clear that urgent change is needed in human actions. Vaughan Lee[93] refers to the spiritual nature of the task when he speaks about the catastrophic impact of our industrialised ways of living, resulting in the devastation of much of the natural world (including many species of animals), along with increased levels of toxicity and pollution. The resultant global imbalance is highlighting an urgent appraisal of how we reconnect to the soul of the world, as our ancestors did.

Doing soul work

Humanity is at a crossroads, and the more the damaging consequences of ecological devastation become evident in our daily lives, through droughts, hurricanes, floods, forest fires and so on, the more likely it is that people will acknowledge their part in the wholesale neglect and destruction of the planet. As humanity awakens to this collective tragedy, we will undoubtedly tap into a deep seam of *collective trauma* for the damage we have done to the world, but also the toxic legacy we have left for future generations. A newspaper article by Anne Karpf[94] revealed her honest struggle about coming to terms with the impact of global warming, admitting that everyday mundane concerns receive greater priority in her life: "I've got a bad dose of all-or-nothingness: if I can't do something big, I do nothing at all". Karpf acknowledges that 'doing' is connected to important practical changes we can all make, such as reducing our carbon footprint. Yet, she also points out how we are all entangled in an economic web that is spun by market forces and commercialism: "Our imagination has been colonised". It is here that Karpf touches on one of the most pressing issues of our time:

> It is going to take a huge cultural change to counter the unbridled narcissism, which demands immediate gratification, and inculcate the idea that we're just trustees of the earth instead (p. 53).[94]

I believe the cultural change Karpf is referring to will not happen with our current ego-orientation: it will only occur through a radical change, by jettisoning our over-reliance on consumerism. It will involve a re-imagining of who we are as a species. Hence, we need a new myth to live by.

Very soon we will have to reconsider what it means to live a meaningful life. We will have to think carefully about the consequences of our reckless misuse of resources. At a collective level, our current conception of what constitutes 'a meaningful life' is mostly focused on an insatiable appetite for all things new or novel. Without reappraisal and reflection to take action, it is evident that we will experience a growing sense of meaninglessness. The bottom line is that our present mode of consciousness is unsustainable. The call to live more deeply is an opportunity to act. If we ignore the call to change, we are likely to slip into an even greater crisis. In essence, the future is ours to co-create or destroy. Skolimowski[8] appeals to us to develop a new awareness based on our highest potential, in order to bring about new ways of living in the world. We need to develop greater concern for what we can all do to make the world a better place. Our reflections and actions need the infusion of a deeper connection to the numinous, with deep transformative potential, as Stephen Larsen[95] suggests. He reminds us not to forget that the sacred is a universal experience that can bring people into meaningful contact with an existence that is full of mystery, which (by implication) can open us up to a greater sense of awe. The last point connects to the next evolutionary step for humanity, which will be discussed in more detail in the next chapter.

Exercise

- Reflect on where you already have talent, creativity, skill/s or knowledge that could be used to engage your deepest vocation in life.

- What else would need to happen to further engage your deepest calling and vocation in life?

- Notice if you get excited – what turns you on about engaging this calling/vocation?

- Notice if you get worried – what freaks you out about it?

- Identify an achievable goal that kick-starts the connection to your calling, and which reflects the expression of your deepest sense of self (vocation). Choose a goal that you are able and/or willing to engage. Goal_____

- Now, imagine the near future. Dream into how you are living your vocation and achieving your goal:

  o How are you looking?
  o What are you saying to yourself or others?
  o How are you feeling?
  o What kind of postures, movements or gestures are you making?
  o How are you relating to others?
  o What is your sense of purpose in the world?

- How are the above points expressing a deep intelligence in your life? Name this intelligence, e.g. gaining self-awareness or understanding how you can use your skills differently in life.

- Now take some time to look around the room or outside the room and find a spot that somehow resonates with the *spirit* of your true vocation. The spot might not make sense to you immediately (it could be a piece of furniture indoors, or a tree outside), just follow your strongest impulse/intuition.

- Walk slowly or mindfully towards this spot, and as you walk notice if you have any connections with your true vocation – notice any feelings, images or ideas.

- When you arrive spend a few minutes in that spot connecting to the qualities that drew you there. For example: beauty, hidden, light/shade, peace, sharpness, and softness – whatever feels right.

- Explore these qualities in the way that suits you best, e.g., silence, dreaming, moving, gesturing, touching or singing. Find out what is right about these qualities. Notice if they connect with you at a meaningful level.

- Look back at the previous spot (where you walked from) and give yourself a message (words/feelings/gestures). Try and connect with the spiritual purpose of the goal you have chosen.

- Create something that reflects the transition you would like to make in the coming year. A short poem, prayer, image, movement/gesture or dance, which affirms this potential in the here and now.

*Transcendent experiences are exalted when they are
integrated into the fabric of our daily lives,
where they become a force for transformation.*

CHAPTER NINE

Transforming self and society through new ways of doing

Overview

This chapter focuses on doing as integral to the deep transformation of self and society, as well as engendering a greater sense of connection to life. I propose that it will take a critical mass of human beings connecting to their occupational potential for collective change to happen. If we fail to act soon through choice, to willingly engage in the transformation of our consciousness and behaviours, we will inevitably be forced into action due to the scale of the crisis before us. The position I take in this chapter is that doing, and collective transformation to fulfil our human potential, is a form of political activism that by default begins to take care of the planet. In this way, every little action matters if enough people decide to act.

Finding an occupational myth

If we subscribe to the notion of 'I do, therefore I evolve', we are challenged to find a deeper story for engaging our transformative potential. We could call this an *occupational myth*. Any astute observer of the sociological, political and ecological state of the world today would quickly appreciate that we are behaving in ways that have not only resulted in us being cut off from the natural world, but more importantly have made us forget that the world is an interconnected whole, and exists as a sacred entity.[1] Bede Griffiths[2] has talked about the impact of modern civilisation on the world and how its technological influence has spread across the globe, which has resulted in the demise of the sacred. It appears that our appreciation or awareness of the transpersonal dimension fades, or sometimes disappears altogether when our technologically-driven consumer-culture flourishes. Jungian analyst John Weir Perry[3] concurs with this view, suggesting that in terms of human and planetary welfare, it is our consciousness that is the problem. He points out that our unbounded aggression and self-aggrandisement is at odds with the eco-system to which we belong. In other

Sorry we could not buy
your item.
OrderNumber:3149660
Reason: Liq
Date: 2024-03-14

00066712996

000667 **2996** 3

words, modern humans are not as smart as we think we are. In our pursuit of material gain we have undermined our relationship to the very resources that we depend on for survival. We fail to see the Earth and all life as sacred.

Finding a way through the deepening global crisis will be considerably challenging, says Barbara Marx Hubbard[4] because there is no human being alive today who has lived through the types of change that are needed to bring about global transformation. Unless we wake up and act, we will continue to sleepwalk into the future, with potentially dire consequences. Throughout this book I have proposed that the potential for change and transformation rests with our ability to engage a transpersonal dimension of awareness, in conjunction with deep occupations to co-create an improved future (through new ways of doing and being). Affirmative action, which fully engages our human potential, requires a radical shift in the ways that we are orientated in life, as Saionji[5] suggests; each person has the capacity to evolve their consciousness, yet the catalyst seems to be linking this potential to a greater life-purpose. Surely there is no greater purpose than our survival? Yet, the reasons for how we begin to wake up and live our potential will be unique for each person.

We will need a new myth collectively to galvanise our efforts to co-create an improved future. However, to make this happen we will need to engage our own occupational myths for how we can use our unique talents and skills to help bring about a better world. Such a proposition means living close to opportunities that awaken our transformative potential. The illustration below reveals how an encounter with a crow led to an incredible rite of passage and life-changing journey for a friend of mine.

An extraordinary encounter with a crow

This story is about a middle-aged male friend, who at the time was experiencing many demands and pressures in his life, which resulted in him feeling depressed and having suicidal thoughts. One weekend he was attending a transpersonal training seminar. After the first day of the seminar he went home and had a heated argument with his partner and in an act of desperation he tipped a glass of water over his own head, accidentally cutting himself with the glass. He said that this unintentional self-harm seemed to express a kind of self-hatred that was always just below the surface of his everyday life. After the weekend seminar had ended he was travelling home contemplating the next stage of his psychotherapy training and he was thinking about the possibilities of starting a practice in his hometown.

Buoyed by the positive experience in the training seminar, he recovered a sense of wonder and the feeling that anything is possible. On the journey home he stopped to withdraw some money from a cash machine, and it was whilst he was walking back to his car that he found a large bird sitting on the roof, just above the driver's door. He said that he was astounded, and had never seen such a big beautiful black bird, a carrion crow, which stopped him in his tracks. He spoke about how they stared at each other for what appeared an age, before the crow unexpectedly flew onto his left shoulder, leaving him stunned and overwhelmed by its apparent friendliness, fearlessness, curiosity and blackness. My friend said that the crow remained perched on his shoulder for quite some time, and he wondered if this wonderful bird would fly off – ordinary time seemed to stop in its tracks (which is typical of such numinous encounters). He turned to walk across a pedestrian road and caught sight of a flower shop that still had a Halloween display in the window, complete with pumpkins and witches. My friend and the crow were facing the colourful floral presentation as people passed behind them. Then the crow hopped across from the left shoulder to the right and started pecking at his glasses, which he described as not in the least bit frightening, rather it amplified the experience of amazement and wonder that he was already feeling. The crow then flew down to his feet and started pecking his shoes repeatedly, as well as turning over wet leaves, whilst intermittently looking up and continuing to make eye contact. There was no sound uttered between my friend and the crow, but then it suddenly flew to a nearby bollard and then a tree. He spoke about a feeling of love and connection with that beautiful bird.

As he walked to his car, he was stunned, and eventually managed to drive home. My friend was reminded of Carlos Castaneda's first book, which described his shamanic transformation into a crow, and how this represented a type of initiatory step on his path. My friend went on to say that since his encounter with the crow, his outlook had changed completely and he had experienced seismic shifts in terms of depth and awareness. He spoke about being in touch with the richness of both his inner and outer life, which had enabled him to be freer in terms of his expressiveness and creativity. In terms of identity, he said that "I see myself as different now – no longer bound by handed-down parental injunctions, intimidated by authority figures, or limited by cultural norms. I also feel less frightened by death, and a greater appreciation of what is important in my life."

Soon after the encounter with the crow, I met my friend and we discussed how the experience had opened him psychically, enabled him to develop a much deeper relationship to the spirit, and how it had brought about a greater sense of prayerfulness in his life. He told me that "it is a longing for something meaningful, a calling, a vocation, a path." He spoke about the importance of being able to talk about his experiences, as for him they acknowledge the mysterious world of the spirit.

Recent contact with my friend prompted a review of the above experience, which happened 10 years ago. He views the encounter with the crow as a remarkable turning point in his life. Two years after the experience he left his career, which he had worked in for 32 years. Then, he and his wife moved to another country, thousands of miles away. He now has another career, and has learnt to speak a new language fluently. In terms of his identity, he says: "I could not have foreseen such a dramatic turn in my life for the better. In a sense I see my old life almost like another incarnation. The way I relate to myself and to life has changed. Of course, I am ascribing some meaning to the event [the encounter with the crow] in the context of how I view my life retrospectively. However, in my subjective experience, it is meaningful to me.

The event remains so vivid, evocative and totally unforgettable to this day. After that experience I remember thinking that I would be open to explore the new and unexpected in my life."

This illustration shows the impact of such numinous encounters on our lives. It is fascinating to recall that the experience with the crow was dramatic, but it also appeared as though this bird was engaging with my friend in unusual ways, for example, pulling at his glasses, pecking at his shoes, and turning over wet leaves, all of which can be reflected on symbolically. It is not my intention to offer any such analysis, which I believe is the privilege of the person who has had such an experience; however, it is evident that my friend's encounter with the crow catalysed a process of transformation for him, where he eventually *turned over a new leaf* to live a completely new life. The meaning that we gain from such events is determined in part by our relationship with the numinous dimension of such encounters or events in our lives, whether it is a spiritual illumination of a mythic encounter.[6] The impact of the numinous may be beatific, mystical or frightening. However, there is one point that we need to be aware of that is, the numinous finds a way into our consciousness when we least expect it.[6] The real question then becomes, what we do with such encounters, and what they mean for how we participate in life and meet our potential? It is in such potent moments of awesome inspiration that we can connect deeply to our evolving inner and outer story, our occupational myth, which can transform our ways of participating in everyday life.

Participation and meaning

The Latin meaning of the word 'participation' is derived from the word *particepts* and *capere*, which refer to part-taking and share in.[7] Fundamentally, participation through occupation covers the fullest possible range of human pursuits, including physical, psychological, social, spiritual/transpersonal and ecological dimensions of experience. In this time of global crisis, deteriorating environmental conditions will impact on how we participate in life. Unless we act soon, the worsening state of the world will lead to increased levels of deprivation that impact on people's opportunities to live productive lives.[8] We cannot underestimate the impact of this global crisis, as environmental damage through floods and drought leads to shortages of food, fresh water and safe habitation. Yet, there is still time to act. You will notice that I use a verb to illustrate the way forward: without direct action our problems will become potentially insurmountable.

The depth of our occupational participation in daily life is reflected in our capacity to actively engage the full spectrum of consciousness available: political, psychological, socio-cultural, or spiritual/transpersonal, ecological influences and so on. Occupational scientist and transpersonal psychologist Loretta do Rozario[9] has discussed the challenge of waking up to the negative impact of reductionism in our lives, where we just do things for the sake of it. Yet, she also suggests that whilst life can be lived with low expectations, there is always the possibility of doing activities that are full of ritual meaning and transpersonal significance. The challenge in these troubled times, I believe, is in our ability as *meaning makers* to reconsider the scope of our participatory potential for how we live. A worsening global crisis is confronting us with the need to adapt, cultivate greater ecological awareness and actualise our human potential in our daily lives.[10] We are entering an age that will be characterised by our ability to develop and work with deep processes of change and new ways of participating in life, where, in a previous publication, I have suggested that:

> The convergence of inner and outer worlds will invariably lead to uncharted territories and will require creative and adaptable solutions (p. 29).[11]

We need to work with our transpersonal and occupational potential to meet the ecological and spiritual challenges that lie ahead.

The participatory turn in transpersonal theory[12,13,14] reflects a vital shift that has created new horizons for considering contemporary spirituality.[15] Jorge Ferrer[16] has discussed transpersonal participation as a need to go beyond any predetermined plan of action, noting that humans already live in a cosmos that is both dynamic and mysterious. The value of Ferrer's[16,17] work is that it has emphasised the notions of embodiment and enacting, which involve the participation of a person at all levels. This underscores the need for an active shift in consciousness to address our arrested development, which has resulted from a collective exclusion of the transpersonal dimension in our understanding of human potential. The scale of the task ahead will require effort and integration to bring about changes in our lived orientations and daily occupational engagements.

It is evident that Jorge Ferrer's[17] notions of transpersonal participation have deep resonances with an occupation-focused approach to living, for example, when he says that meaning needs to be embodied. He further suggests that this deep engagement of living in the presence of a mystery evolves a new sense of knowing, but that such a process is ongoing and is never complete.[15] I would add that the embodiment of a transpersonal participatory vision in our daily occupational engagements not only touches on issues to do with how we find *meaning-in-life*, it also raises questions about how we reflect on the *meaning-of-life* at times. From a transpersonal-occupational perspective, there is a distinction between the two: meaning-in-life can refer to those tangible actions we carry out in life, as co-creators. Meaning-of-life, however, connects to a quality of trans-reflexivity, where we realise we are fully embedded in a wider cosmos, which can also inform our ways of doing, knowing, being, becoming and belonging.

The key point about understanding *meaning* in terms of our consciousness and actions is neatly summed up by Deepak Chopra,[18] who intimates the need for fluidity in our approach to identity and living. He points out that we need to break out of the habit of rigidly compartmentalising meaning into limited understandings of the universe. The idea is for each of us to find what makes our lives meaningful and to consider how this fits with a greater purpose for living, one that considers life as a whole.

I am suggesting that human occupations act as a participatory connection in these unfolding spheres of meaning (personal and transpersonal), linking our reflections and actions. Here, the experience of meaning is a process by which we discover new connections to life, which are revealed through our active participation in all that we do. The quality of our occupational engagement, therefore, enables us to make deeper connections to the wider cosmos, in an ever-unfolding and indeterminate mystery.[15,16]

Our capacity to engage meaningfully in *life as a mystery* connects to a wider and deeper sense of occupational participation, which John Heron[19] has linked to our multi-sensory ways of perceiving and engaging in the world (seeing, hearing, touching etc.). Thus, our ways of living are interactive and relational, in that they are interdependent with the sacred dimension. Heron's approach to the sacred aligns with the multi-sensory transpersonal approach that I have written about from an occupational perspective.[11,20] It fosters awareness between our ways of doing, experiences in consciousness (being), as well as the engagement of our human potential.[21,22,23] Heron[24] helpfully connects his multi-sensory perspective to a *transcendent* spiritual consciousness, which can be linked to an *immanent* spiritual life, in the here and now. In this way, Heron[19] tells us, we transcend experiences of alienation and separateness as we connect to a living mystery in daily life, where we are at *one*, living within an interconnected whole.

Living in an indeterminate mystery, says Jorge Ferrer,[17] we are permeable to moments of awareness that are connected to transcendent processes, which enable us to embody spiritual insights and energies.[15] Transpersonal events occur in everyday experiences and may inspire people to participate more creatively and meaningfully in daily life.[17,25] Indeed, a balanced view of the mystical has to include both the transcendent and the immanent,[26] which brings a sense of universal connection (transpersonal) within everyday life experiences.[27] Jung[28] was clear about the relationship between human potential and the expression of the spiritual in our daily lives, where we have opportunities to live and express the truth of our existence. We are reaching a point in human history where the absence of spirituality in our collective lives will soon be rekindled as we seek a renewed relationship to life's wholeness. This connection is inevitable, because the Earth, from which we have become dissociated, is sacred.

The dynamics of collective transformation

Refinements in our conscious engagement in life have been ongoing and developing since the end of the Second World War. Metzner argues that this has led to a new culture that has sought to bring about an expansion of consciousness,[29] for example, in movements advocating civil rights, ecology, women's liberation, and creative expression through the arts.[29] Coupled with these developments is the more recent growth of interest in justice and reconciliation, while the expansion of spirituality and transpersonal perspectives are also informing our understanding of deep ecology, social ecology, ecofeminism and ecopsychology,[29] and in a growing number of professions.[30] The upsurge of interest in these new perspectives is indicative that it is possible to create a new worldview.[29]

Jorge Ferrer[31] has suggested that engaging in this life involves human intentional participation, emphasising the value of occupational engagement. In addition, Richard Tarnas[32] notes the significance of a participatory approach to engage our spiritual potential is when the spirit is lived through human sensory engagement, emotions, imagination and actions. It is where new meaningful insights emerge as a creative connection between human consciousness and nature. The notion that there is a reciprocal and whole relationship between human consciousness and a wider transpersonal existence underlines our role as co-creators. It brings together meaningful occupational engagement and transpersonal consciousness in ways that can unleash innovative ways of living in the world, full of our unfolding potential. It also suggests that the spiritual dimension of experience conveys deep meaning through our occupational engagement, as an expression of our connection to a transpersonal dimension of consciousness. However, we have yet to recognise the full value of our transpersonal potential to inspire and engage the creation of an improved future.

Humanity's current predicament in the face of a global state of emergency has been described as a collective decline in our awareness,[33] particularly of the negative impact of our actions on the environment. However, when examined in the context of the theories of Carl Jung and transpersonal psychology, it could be argued that modern societies are reflecting a loss of soul or disconnection from our feelings about the lives we inhabit.[34] Essentially, humanity is failing to grasp that all life exists as an interconnected whole,[35] as I have explored previously:

> The transformative value of people making personal changes within everyday activities and relationships at home, in neighbourhoods, towns, and cities, etc. reflects possibilities for developing transpersonal potential collectively. Transpersonal ways of participating in life are based on an understanding that – if all life is connected – what we 'do' in our everyday activities, to one another, and the planet – we also do to ourselves (p. 219).[36]

As the global crisis deepens, Loy and Stanley[33] have asserted that we will eventually have to wake up collectively from our skewed and distorted view of reality. The over-emphasis (particularly in the western worldview) on individualism, rather than a shared sense of a collective 'we',[37] impacts on our relationship to a wider ecology of life and the environment. For example, Roger Walsh[38] has discussed humanity's lack of meaningful response to the global crisis, illustrated by typical avoidant behaviours, such as not wishing to take responsibility, or believing that there is nothing we can do. The paradox here is that *doing* is key to the transformative journey we need to take collectively in order to effect deep change. Therefore the crux of the issue highlighted by Walsh needs to be reframed into a challenging vision that inspires us all to find ways of responding to the crisis we are in. A friend reminded me about the words by Joan Baez, who said words to the effect: *action is the way out of despair*. Yet, we appear to be living in an era of inertia and we need to find the zest for engaging transformative action. We need to know and believe in the emancipatory power that can be found in actively participating in the expression of our full human potential: 'I do therefore I evolve'.

Former US Vice President Al Gore[39] has stated that the current ecological problems are highlighting a crisis in our identity at a collective level, with people now beginning to reflect on questions such as: *Who are we?* and *What is our purpose?* Gore[39] goes on to assert that at the heart of the modern world there is a void that is akin to a spiritual crisis, revealing a deep lack of spiritual meaning and purpose. It puts into context the visionary perspective of Thomas Berry[40] who called for a collective response to the ecological and spiritual crisis, which he termed the *Great Work*. He noted that the inner world and the outer world impact on one another, observing that if the natural world is lost, then so is the emotional and spiritual life of humanity. In essence, we need to co-create the future through *doing*, not sitting passively in a vacuum of despair, contemplating *being* in a mess. Thus, the challenge is to start engaging in meaningful adaptation and participation, through sacred actions.

The age of metanoia *and deep transformation*

The political 'one dimension' that underpins our lives is a reflection of our compromised (collective) relationship to a greater transpersonal representation of reality. Our current ways of living-in-the-world, merely skimming the surface with our consumer-based tendencies, mean that we need to go deeper if we wish to affect a profound and meaningful level of change. As we saw earlier, Richard Tarnas[41] has asked if the modern psyche is undergoing a rite of passage. If so, this transition will need to address those collective processes that have been split off, generating great remorse. Indeed, Tarnas lists some examples where we will have to encounter the grief for all the oppression that has happened in our name, for example, the suppression of women by men, the poor treatment of children and animals etc. Awakening to this collective shadow, that has been disavowed and repressed will take a monumental change and sacrifice, says Tarnas.

Inspired by the words of Tarnas, I worked with two Jungian analyst colleagues.[42] We examined the meaning of deep change in the world at this time of crisis, connecting to the idea of sacrifice, which is linked to the word sacred. It requires that modern consciousness will inevitably have to confront and change its consumer-based appetites, hedonistic lifestyles and nihilistic attitudes if we are to establish a deeper, more meaningful relationship to life as a whole.[42] Such a process could be catalysed by the simple act of noticing and affirming our emotional reactions to what is happening in the world. In doing so, we acknowledge what we have done to one another and the world.[42] Such moments of emotional connection could initiate the start of a deep process of reflection and potential transformation.[43] These types of emotional connectedness are key to facilitating transitions, and according to Tarnas,[44] are like a spiritual birth that initiates a change in our attitudes, behaviours and actions in the world. This is how we can begin to initiate a deeper and more archetypal pattern of transformation.[42]

In this time of crisis, eco-philosopher Joanna Macy[45] is convinced that we are morally strengthened by spiritual practices that enable us to see reality as it is. However, there is still very little acknowledgement at a collective level of the parallels between the global state of emergency[46] and people's experiences of spiritual emergencies.[42,47] Catherine Lucas[48] describes it as a reciprocal relationship, between the spiritual awakening of individuals and the collective awakening of consciousness for humanity. Furthermore, Caroline Myss[49] powerfully iterates how the microcosm of our everyday lives interacts with the macrocosm of a deteriorating world and worsening global conditions. She describes the interconnected and sacred bond that exists between humans and the natural world, and appeals for us to notice the levels of pollution in the world. She suggests that we imagine the assault on the rain forests (the Earth's lungs) and to notice what this does to our own breathing. It is this level of intimacy with the natural world that we need to develop, yet humanity appears to be in denial about the scale of the problem it has created. Activist Susan Murphy[37] harrowingly expresses the collective silence in the world as our planet and endangered species are being systematically destroyed. She gives voice to the fear and anxiety that is yet to be expressed, by asking how each of us is handling the planetary situation. And she asks if we are alarmed at this unfolding ecological catastrophe. In view of the lack of any authentic collective reaction to the scale of the global crisis, the question that has to be asked is *why* are we so silent? Denial and avoidance are certainly factors that need to be considered. However, I believe that it is our one-dimensional consciousness that is the main problem.[42] We need to re-align ourselves to a renewed commitment for engaging collective change if we stand any chance of co-creating an improved future.

The current global crisis could be an antecedent for a spiritual renaissance. Morris Berman[50] has called for a re-enchantment of the world, yet he cautions that transformation will probably happen slowly. Indeed, there is no merit in shocking people or inducing panic in order to deliberately cause a crisis in consciousness; yet we have to get the balance right, for if we let things drift too long, we will undoubtedly slip into a deeper, more unproductive and unmanageable crisis. This tension highlights the need for a gradual and grounded transformation of ego-based consciousness. After all it is not the ego *per se* that is the problem, rather the current lack of relationship between the personal-ego and the transpersonal-Self. We must be aware, says Berman,[50] that a *quick fix* in ego-consciousness will not guarantee improvements in the state of the world. A more productive relationship within the ego-Self axis is needed, and so any sustainable transition in consciousness will require gradual integration.

In his conversations with Carl Jung, anthropologist Laurens Van Der Post[51] noted the psychologist's belief that one of the reasons why modern people have become so impoverished spiritually is that they no longer value the symbolic. The functional implications of living symbolically have deep significance for how human beings relate to one another, other species and the natural world. Because the global crisis can be viewed as a collective spiritual emergency,[52] an archetypal level of transformation is required, and this has major implications for our *ways of doing* and *states of being*.

The politics of doing and beyond

Previous chapters have explicated how the dominant focus on spiritual emergence is through states of *being*. Le Grice[53] has stated that in a time of such transformative potential some people are already attempting to find new ways of living, and new ways of considering the self. We have neglected the transpersonal level of *doing*, and yet we need it to assist in the exploration and integration of human potential.[23] If we recall the humanistic foundations that have encouraged productive links between doing and being,[54] including the development of a transpersonal perspective,[55] it reminds us that there is incredible scope for understanding the deep integration of spiritual experiences in daily life.[56] Clearly, to co-create a sustainable future, we need to break away from the traditional ways of doing and being that have led to the current crisis. Humanity will need to find solutions outside of the reference points that shape current ideologies and practices. As we have seen, philosopher Herbert Marcuse[57] suggested that a one-dimensional, overly conforming and bureaucratic mind-set is limiting, and definitely not conducive for engaging our transformative potential. He is concerned with knowing how we will be emancipated from our complicity with the administrative forces that now dominate our lives. Marcuse notes that we have squandered our liberties and he asks how we will break free from the vicious binds that tether us to the systems we have created. How, he asks, will liberation happen?

The first problem with a one-dimensional mode of consciousness is that it must liberate itself from the self-imposed limitations that it has created.[42] Such a predicament underlines our compromised relationship to a greater transpersonal representation of reality.[47,58] There is a need for a renewed politics of consciousness[59] that gives greater recognition to what are currently termed 'non-ordinary states of consciousness', such as spiritual emergencies,[60] which are predicted to increase as the global crisis worsens.[42] Yet, recognition of the value of such transformative states of consciousness is still beyond the boundaries of mainstream thinking. John Nelson[61] observes that we need to go beyond our everyday states of consciousness and connect with our divine nature to tackle the ecological and societal problems that confront us. In doing so, he suggests that we can be stimulated and inspired in our creative expression, which can lead to a deeper sense of group experience and cohesion.

In noting the need for a transformational response to the current global situation, Emma Bragdon[62] has stated that first we need to do inner work to increase our connection to a global consciousness, and she sees this as a form of collective spiritual emergence. This last point highlights the importance of a critical mass of people doing their inner transformational work (as exemplified by Carl Jung's process of individuation), but also joining with others to co-create transformative shifts through our outer transformational work (as inspired by the participatory philosophy of Jorge Ferrer). Such transformative processes must take into consideration the complementary functions of doing and being in the journey of renewal for both individuals and the wider collective. We urgently need an injection of new levels of inspiration to change our ways of living on this planet:[63] to enliven us and motivate our interest to engage in a process of psycho-spiritual renewal. It is through such new ways of doing and being, that we can activate our collective human potential.[64] The following story reflects such a transformative awakening:

————— When lightning did strike twice —————

I have a friend who has had two close encounters with lightning. The first experience happened when Anne was walking down St Benedict's Street in Norwich during a storm. Anne thought she was safe to keep walking home, when out of the blue, a bolt of lightning hit the pavement just in front her, striking a metal man hole cover. The impact of the lightning hitting the metal caused a flash of light that temporarily blinded her. She had to be helped into a nearby shop to sit down and wait for her sight to recover. This event had been pretty spectacular, but it was only a precursor for the next lightning event, which struck even closer a few years later.

At the time of the next encounter Anne was working as the manager of a play scheme with responsibility for her staff and over 50 children. On the day of the second lightning strike there was a midday storm, which was very loud and Anne had to reassure all the children who were frightened when all the lights in the building went out. Anne went to find the fuse box at the back of the building to turn the lights back on. She had never had reason to go to the electricity cupboard before and due to having no lighting she could not see where the fuses were. Anne remembered there was a nearby door to the outside of the building and she opened this to let in more natural light. Just as she was reaching up to touch the fuse box, a mighty flash of lightning struck the car park and part of the bolt shot through the back door, hitting her bent elbow and travelled up to her index finger. Anne was understandably shocked, yet she mustered all the composure she could, as she knew she had to be calm and reassure the children. The lights came back on and she went back to be with the children and staff and let them know all was well.

The children resumed their play activities and it was then that Anne confided what had happened to another staff member. Anne recalls the experience: "My lower arm was tingling from the inside out and I was in a state of shock, one of my staff members supported me and made a light hearted remark that the story reminded him of Super Ted (a 1990s children's cartoon character who developed super powers after being struck by lightning)." Of course this made Anne laugh and helped her out of the state of shock so that she could return to her supervisory role. But something strange happened when Anne returned home that evening. As she walked into her house she announced to her husband: "You'll never guess what happened to me today?" and without hesitation he replied: "You were struck by lightning at midday." He said to Anne that whilst the storm was raging he had a thought that she had been struck by lightning, but he did not dwell on this, dismissing it as a random idea that had simply popped into his head.

The impact of the lightning strike left Anne's arm tingling for 24 hours, and the hospital reassured her that there was no serious damage. One might think that two close encounters with lightning would have made my friend a little more circumspect, and of course it would be quite understandable if she felt like staying indoors during storms. However, the reverse is true. To this day she holds a fascination with electrical storms, actually loving them and going outside during them whenever she can. She feels no fear whatsoever and connects with an overriding sense of awe for the mighty powers inherent in nature (numinous). She says that these events confirmed her belief that there is a dynamic, tangible connection between all living things, maybe even non-living. This sense of life's interconnectivity was confirmed when her husband had 'known' about her encounter with lightning. The synchronistic experience underlined her belief that there is a collective dimension to consciousness.

Anne also mentioned to me how she no longer feared death, especially after the second lightning experience, which could have killed her. She goes on to say: "We never know when death will take us, we may not have time to say goodbye, to put our things in order, and this is just how it is. Not something to fear, but something to enable us to live openly with the full knowledge that every breath is precious." Anne is someone who lives life to the full, someone who uses every breath as though life is a gift. She embraces new experiences and sees the potential for growth in all life events, including those that are pleasurable and painful. Anne in her personal and professional life is like a beacon for others, and encourages people to do all they can in life to live to their full potential.

Jungian analyst Anne Baring[46] has stated that new frameworks for ethical and moral actions will emerge once life's sacred oneness and interconnectedness are perceived. The key question at this juncture is how to engage such a vision. Ervin Laszlo[64] offers a tantalising glimpse of future possibilities, suggesting societies also need to be connected to a transpersonal consciousness that respects diversity. The perilous state of the world and the arrested development of our transpersonal potential are prime ingredients that could, if integrated into daily life, catalyse a shift in consciousness. Without this shift, we will compromise our relationship to life as a whole.

Exercise

- Try to summarise the meaning of your life to date:
  - What sense of meaning are you deriving from your ways of doing-in-the-world?
  - What sense of meaning are you deriving from your ways of knowing-in-the-world?
  - What sense of meaning are you deriving from your ways of being-in-the-world?
  - What sense of meaning are you deriving from your ways of becoming-in-the-world?
  - What sense of meaning are you deriving from your ways of belonging-in-the-world?

- What are the key points that stand out in the story of your life so far?

- What is your response to the growing global state of emergency?

- What could you do in your life that connects your personal meaning to a greater sense of transpersonal and ecological meaning?

- With this renewed sense of meaning and potential in mind, what is the story that supports you to bring this potential into action? In other words, what is your occupational myth?

*Our multi-sensory engagement in the world is both ancient and emergent.
It is through a soulful connection to our sensory and imaginative worlds that a
process of alchemy comes alive, which is expressed and enacted in our
ways of doing and being.*

CHAPTER TEN

The alchemy of occupational engagement

Overview

In this chapter I discuss further the power of doing in an interconnected world, which impacts on our participation in life. I draw on literature that reveals how the quantum world may reflect subtle connections to a wider field of consciousness. To this end, I consolidate ideas about the complementary functions of doing and being, and how the process of transforming consciousness is alchemy in action. I explore how we can live productively in such an interconnected world, and how we will need to use our intelligences to co-create an improved future.

Alchemy in action

The way doing is viewed in the modern world often reveals a one-sided under-standing of human potential. For example, it has been suggested that people who engage in active processes of transformation have shifted their focus onto *being* as opposed to *doing*.[1] Whilst there is a need to understand the differences between doing and being, it is more important to view them as complementary in the transformative process. This is illustrated by Satish Kumar,[2] who has commented on participation in life, especially in simple activities such as baking bread or cooking food, where spirituality is *discovered* through the interaction between doing and being. One of the central themes in this book is how doing gives deep expression to our transformative potential, which in turn can also ground and integrate any shifts in consciousness. In this way a focus on doing is as necessary as awareness of being on the spiritual path. Indeed, when doing and being are combined in this transformative work, the lived reality of engaging our potential is akin to alchemy in action.

Doing is a vital part of any transformative process, where our human potential is expressed through meaningful engagement in life.[3] Our active participation in everyday daily life contains possibilities for evolving deeper relationships to life as a whole. Indeed, Ram Dass[4] has stated that everything we *do* as human beings reveals the extent to which our consciousness has evolved. This not only acknowledges that psycho-spiritual developments in daily life reflect how awakened our consciousness is, they also reveal the extent of our applied occupational intelligence[5] in the ways that we construct and express meaningful lives. Such intelligence brings about possibilities for a revolution[6] in our daily activities, and the way that we live our lives.[7] Thomas Berry[8] explains this intelligent self-awareness, as one that is open to the mystery of the numinous, and connects with all life in joy and celebration. Yet, with the current ecological crisis associated with a collective sense of spiritual emptiness and disenchantment,[9] the need to engage deeply with the transpersonal through meaningful occupations becomes paramount.

I have explored elsewhere[10] how the interface between doing and being could yet reveal deep and unexpected trajectories on this archetypal and alchemical journey of transforming consciousness.[10] For example, Johnson and Ruhl[11] believe that the way human beings express what they do in life depends on the consciousness they bring forth, whereby our ways of doing are placed in service to our being. James Hollis[12] also stresses the importance of doing to being, when he says that we do not live nouns, but verbs. Dynamic interactions between doing and being can have profound consequences for people's psycho-spiritual development. For example, Thomas Moore[13] considers the work of human hands as a representation of the spiritual dimension in our daily lives, and Matthew Fox[14] says such events are sacramental. Everyday activities create opportunities for encountering the transpersonal dimension, where the relationship between reflection and action helps to bring greater balance to human consciousness through doing and being.[15] Thomas Moore[13] has noted further the important links between doing, being and individuation for living a sacred life. Moore[16] explains that *a life at work* is also spiritual when it helps us connect to a greater reality in the world.

The term *a life at work* sums up our deep covenant with the development of our transpersonal potential through acts of doing, which reveal a transformative and alchemical relationship to life as a whole. Indeed, a life at work reflects the *mystery of doing* at its core, as found in Jung's biography. Jung's process of individuation was punctuated by the creative activities he performed as part of his psycho-spiritual development, for example, from the writing of the *Red Book* to the construction of the tower at Bollingen, which revealed the influence of the archetypes in his daily life and occupational engagement.[10]

Jung and the alchemy of doing and being

Carl Jung[17] had a series of recurrent dreams that revealed the existence of an annex attached to a house. He reflected on his dreams and associated the meaning of the extension to his house as being connected to a hitherto unknown part of his personality.

The 'discovery' of the annex in his dream had strong resonances with the eventual *dreamlike* construction of his tower at Bollingen, which (as Jung alluded to) became an alchemical container for his individuation process. Jung stated that he experienced a profound sense of renewal at the tower from the very beginning.[17] That is, the work in the tower was an expression of his soulful connection to life, both inwardly and outwardly. In doing so, he manifested an aspect of his spiritual life in the world. The tower at Bollingen was a deep response to the undercurrents in Jung's psyche, where his dream life manifested in the world.

Jung's dream life was signposting ways to engage new vistas of his human potential. Jung took the meaning of his dreams as symbolic forms that could be engaged in the individuation process, leading to new forms of action-in-the-world. Indeed, Jung spoke about his work at the tower and his need to work with stone as a form of *confession*.[17] It is interesting that Jung chooses to make his *confession* in his actions and not words. Jung's need to work in stone has resonances with alchemy, where working with stone is associated with releasing divine spirit, and Churton mentions the Gospel of Thomas, which refers to finding the spirit when lifting stone and splitting wood.[18] The depth of Jung's inner and outer work – as an alchemical process of transformation – coheres with the writings of Mircea Eliade,[19] who has identified that spiritual initiations (for example, Jung's spiritual crisis) can lead to illuminations in the material world. Indeed, Jung was wise enough to ground his transformative experiences in everyday activities.

In many ways Jung lived like a wise old sage when he spent time at Bollingen: chopping wood, cooking simple meals on an open fire, tending to repairs, and engaging in crafts, such as carving in stone and painting murals. In essence, Jung's tower at Bollingen was a manifestation of his individuation process in the material world, which not only resonated with his night-time dreams, but was also constructed as if he were in a dream.[17] During Jung's alchemical journey of individuation, his daily occupations became a vehicle for connecting to the mystery through simplicity. As the old Taoist saying is apt to point out: *Before enlightenment, chopping wood and carrying water – after enlightenment, chopping wood and carrying water.* This appears to sum up Jung's quality of lived experience at the tower.[10] For a more in-depth discussion on alchemy see Edward Edinger's book, *Anatomy of the Psyche*.

Jung's work at Bollingen was an expression of his commitment to working at an archetypal level. If we translate the meaning of Jung's pioneering work to this time of collective human crises, such deep reflections and actions could inform the evolution of collective human awareness.[20, 21] In this way the true purpose of individuation and awakening is greater communion with the planet,[22] which means that the process of engaging transpersonal potential is connected to doing and being of service to others and to the world. This offers great potential for engaging what futurologist Barbara Marx-Hubbard[23] has described as *cooperative action* for the evolution of a new global consciousness.[24] Such transformative action will require all our human capacities to actively engage our potential. For example, Michael Daniels[25] has also highlighted the links between deep engagement of our full human potential, which involves awakening to a greater collective experience of consciousness and meaning. He advocates the idea of a whole person involvement (head, heart and hands) in the journey of fulfilling our transpersonal potential, so that we connect with self, others, nature and the world.

Human occupation and spiritual emancipation

Our actions in the world at this time of great transformation mean that processes of co-creation are not only about what each of us does to make a difference in our own lives, but also take into account what we do together – with others – to live with a new understanding of responsibility.[26] The idea of co-creating an improved future will require a new mind-set, where we work deeply on ourselves and also work productively together to bring about transformation. Collectively, we will need to understand the importance of transcending our damaging modes of doing and being in the world. The quality of engagement will be determined by our attitudes and our actions, as Skolimowski[26] notes; if we interact with the Earth in mechanistic ways then we will treat it as a machine, whereas, if we relate to the Earth as sacred, we will treat it as sacred. It is our choice if we act aggressively and with indifference to the planet, or whether we choose to treat the Earth and one another with respect and love. When navigating these deep vectors of transformation collectively, we will falter unless we accept full responsibility for the world that we can co-create collectively, including taking greater responsibility for crises that currently we have chosen to ignore.[27]

The process of transforming consciousness requires an attitude of acceptance, learning and trust, which means having the courage (and support) to accommodate the productive elements of a crisis, in the knowledge that these antecedents for individual change also reflect the potential for collective transpersonal development. To this end, how we deal with spiritual crises may well act as a barometer for how we understand the trials of transformation at a collective level, grounded and integrated through doing. Schlitz[28] has noted the importance of doing in the transformation of being, where living deeply involves changes in the self, giving expression to the sacred, via our actions.[10] It is clear that deep processes of change associated with transformative crisis connect to the complementary nature of doing and being in the journey of spiritual regeneration. Furthermore, this includes understanding the connections between the ego, the Self and processes of collective renewal. Here, *a life at work* is about fostering a greater relationship between our human potential and living in an interconnected whole.[10]

Awakening to the reality of the current global crisis, we will all need to see the earth as an essential life support system, rather than a commodity to be used,[29] continually reminding ourselves that we are not separate from the planet we are currently destroying. The future of humanity may well depend upon individuals working together towards what Wesselman[30] has referred to as communities of transformation. Barbara Marx Hubbard[31] reminds us about the consequences of a failure to act when she says that as a species we are putting ourselves at great risk of extinction. She also notes that the risk has been created by our human actions. Therefore, we need to find collective and culturally competent ways to navigate what Catherine Lucas[32] has recently described as a *global dark night of the soul*. We need no reminding that the earth is not an inanimate object; it is connected to each of us at a soul level, known as the *anima mundi*, or soul of the world. This brings home why we need to develop our transpersonal potential as a way of reconnecting to life as a whole, and recalibrate our awareness to include an understanding of ourselves as belonging to an interconnected cosmos. This requires emancipation from our current debilitating ways of relating to life.

Lajoie and Shapiro[33] remind us that a transpersonal perspective is an experience of consciousness that connects us to the unity in the cosmos. Moreover, transpersonal scholar Ken Wilber[34] has noted how this expansive field-like consideration for psycho-spiritual consciousness connects to new paradigm thinking.[35] This paradigm shift was particularly evident in the early work of forward-thinking physicists,[36,37,38,39] who in turn contributed to the development of a field-like understanding of consciousness, including the spiritual (holistic) dimension.[40,41,42] These psycho-spiritual links to quantum physics are a continuation of the ideas explored originally by physicist Wolfgang Pauli and psychologist Carl Jung.

Jung observed in 1964 that whilst psychology and physics are separate disciplines, in many ways they are converging.[43] For example, when transpersonal experiences impact on people's temporal and spatial awareness, it can also expose individual consciousness to the non-local connections in the universe.[44] The influence of non-locality in human functioning is well represented in Mindell's[45] theory of a reciprocal relationship between individual experiences of being in the world and the world within the individual. The reality is that at a quantum field-level, we exist in an interconnected world. Skolimowski[26] puts the revelations of quantum physics into perspective, when he notes that the Newtonian universe is being confronted with a radical new perspective of life in the cosmos, so much so, that we are unsure how to view it. This is the challenge of participation and co-creation in a new era of living, which will require us to evolve in new and responsible ways of acting as universal beings. These possibilities are connected to human potential in ways that have not been explored in the collective, yet.[10]

Recent developments by systems theorist Ervin Laszlo[46,47] persuasively integrate quantum theory with transpersonal considerations, seeking to galvanise humanity to respond to the current global crisis through a shift in collective consciousness and behaviours.[24] These field-theory representations of consciousness are consistent with Ken Wilber's[48] assertion that humanity has contributed to the ecological crisis through a dissociation with nature and life as a whole, including neglecting to cultivate a deeper relationship with the sacred or divine.[49] Whilst we may entertain the idea that our modern consciousness is progressive, the reality is we are still living in a world that is dominated by Newtonian thinking.[50] That is, we are still tethered to the ideas of an individual-atomistic consciousness, whereas from a quantum, non-local perspective, we have the potential to reappraise how reality appears to us, which is also critically dependent upon the way that we perceive it.[50]

The importance of such a quantum perspective for understanding fluid representations of self[50] and society[51] is that it reflects the subtle, field dynamics of an interconnected universe. It is from this perspective that people are seeking a new worldview, one that gives a more complete understanding of our relationship and unity with all life, which if acknowledged could encourage more sustainable ways of behaving.[51] Indeed, such a quantum perspective indicates that at a subtle level our bodies and minds are in a constant process of flow and entanglement with all beings and life.[52] Ervin Laszlo's[46] theoretical connections between the quantum field and the transpersonal dimension are beginning to contribute ideas about a whole-systems approach to life, which could shape a new vision for humanity, one that embraces a more interconnected worldview. From the perspective of collective transformation in consciousness, the idea of engaging deep change is a monumental undertaking. It will involve the need to accept a deeper/wider sense of transpersonal identity,[53] one that is actualised as part of human growth and development[54] in everyday life contexts.

Human occupation and transpersonal consciousness

We have already discussed how engaging our potential for change will take collective effort, and undoubtedly will only be achievable if we can engage our talents and skills for living together[55,56] and begin to cultivate an attitude of service in the world.[57] Whitmyer[58] has noted the collective importance of transformation, suggesting that the insights gained from depth, humanistic and transpersonal psychology are revealing an important relationship between the needs of the individual and the needs of the collective. However, it must also be remembered that it is through our occupational engagement that we can cultivate and integrate new experiences in daily life, as we reconnect to what it means to be fully human, inclusive of our transpersonal potential. It is fitting that Whitmyer[58] pointed out that it is up to us to create the future, and that the basis of a new world is connected to a new conceptualisation of humanity. This shift will require human beings to develop capacities, such as love and friendship, if we are to cultivate a new alignment for collective consciousness,[59] one that is directed in the service of others.[60] Mary-Jane Rust[61] notes that in the current world situation we are being powerfully challenged to negotiate the tensions between our individual interests and our collective responsibilities, as we grapple with the enormity of the task before us. The hitherto unexplored potential between doing and being in relation to spiritual emergence and the collective global state of emergency could go some way to fulfilling the early aspirations of the founders of humanistic and transpersonal psychology.[10] That is, by its collective efforts, humanity can find ways of fulfilling its transformative potential.

We can find inspiration for change from people like Mahatma Gandhi, who struggled to make sense of the gross inequalities he met in his life, first as a lawyer, politician and then spiritual seeker. He was an advocate for women's emancipation and equality for the untouchable caste. He attempted to help religious groups overcome their differences, particularly Muslims and Hindus. He attempted to make a difference in the world and is quoted as saying that love should be the basis for whatever we do.[62] He developed a philosophy for living called *Satyagraha*, which roughly translates as an *adherence to the truth*; it is a lived expression, a silent, universal force, which is connected to the soul.[63] It suggests a quality of lived experience that acts in harmony with all life. It reveals a willingness to live in service to the individual soul, which also connects to the soul of the world.

So, what can be done today to support a shift in people's consciousness individually and collectively to develop more awareness of our transpersonal potential? The dynamics of such a transformative process is summed up in the words of Sri Ramana Maharshi, who has revealed that the mystical journey starts with each human being exploring the reality beyond the ego-self and embarking on a discovery of the real Self.[64] In Jungian/transpersonal terminology, Lionel Corbett[65] expresses the collective dimension of such an undertaking as the *personal-self* having an archetypal connection to the *transpersonal-Self*, meaning that we live our full potential in all facets of our lives.[66] There is growing recognition that activity and participation as (potentially) numinous phenomena can be engaged through everyday modes of human engagement. For example, Corbett[65] has noted how numinous experiences may occur in innumerable ways in daily life, through activities, such as music, writing, dance, art, craft, play, working in nature and preparing meals. He suggests that when these types of activities lead to numinous encounters, and they are engaged regularly they can become channels for spiritual practice. Indeed, our ways of doing are like portals to the mystery in life, where our abilities to express spirituality through action reflect unique thresholds for our personal and transpersonal participation in the world. Our natural talents, qualities and skills, when expressed fully, can connect us to a sacred sense of wholeness. Deepak Chopra[52] conveys the mystical potential of doing, through the example where a dancer is at one with the dance. Yet, at a collective level we need to connect our movement towards oneness (the dance) with others.

In such a worldview, human beings have the opportunity to wake up to what Michael Washburn[67] has described as the *mystical body*, where we connect to a sense of spiritual belonging. Although transformations in consciousness necessarily start with the individual, it is through the power of human relationships that people can work together and open up to their collective potential. Indeed, Washburn[67] notes the inspirational impact that people can have on one another when he states that people who are awakening and committed to spiritual development become *numinous attractors*. This magnificent proposition underlines the power of our human potential to have a spiritual impact upon one another. The suggestion is that if we make a commitment to engaging spiritually in our ways of doing and being, we can inspire one another in our myriad words and deeds. The mystery of life challenges us to consider living in the presence of awe, sacredness and reverence. The importance of recognising the mystical in the mundane is well stated by Reardson[68] who mentions that everyday life experiences can suddenly open up to a transcendent reality, which shines through our lives and can radically alter our relationship to how we live. The following story is an incredible reflection of a woman's transformative journey.

———————— Stripping away layers of delusion ————————

I attended a play in 2013 called 'The Stripper' directed by former Buddhist nun Pema Clark at the School of Drama, University of East Anglia. The play was part of Pema's MA in drama Studies about the life of her friend, Zangmo Alexander who, now 60 years old, had worked as a stripper in her twenties.

The play was attended by Zangmo, and the production by Pema was engaging and mesmerizing. The story portrayed all the tensions, tenderness and turmoil of family life as Zangmo was growing up, including love, pain and death. The play revealed Zangmo's reflections and questions about life and relationships, which were extracted from her written journals and expressed visually through drawings, paintings, photography and video. The play portrayed the journey of Zangmo's life as she worked at the edges of her existence to find meaning and happiness.

As a young adult, she met Tim, a charismatic shop owner who had connections with strip clubs, and this friendship led to a seismic change in Zangmo's life. It was not long before Zangmo herself became a stripper. She and Tim eventually married. Being a stripper provided financial security and it fulfilled her creative and material needs, yet the false eyelashes, wigs, alluring costumes and baring her body to strangers led to a disillusioning existence, which eventually became more and more empty.

Tim, who was an alcoholic, died in 1984, which opened a new chapter in Zangmo's life. She entered Jungian psychotherapy and it dawned on her that she was stripping away the delusory facade of her previous lifestyle and was learning to bare her soul instead of her body. Zangmo found the introspection and reflection of psychotherapy a powerful way of getting in touch with her feelings and finding deeper meaning in her life. The depth and complexity of the work is put in her own words: "The process was like unblocking the drains." At the same time as her psychotherapy, Zangmo worked as a psychiatric nurse in a hospital, where she revisited her childhood love of painting in a staff art therapy group, exploring ways to express her inner worlds and experiences. She also studied healing and spiritual psychotherapy, which added a new dimension for her creative expression, helping her begin to see how "doing art is a spiritual practice".

The deep expressions Zangmo found through her art and psychotherapy were a combination of creativity, insight and catharsis, opening up new possibilities and ways of engaging in life. During this time Zangmo's dream life and experience of archetypes were awakened, revealing the untapped potentialities percolating within her. One such dream involved a witch eating an erect penis. This dream is full of rich symbolism in terms of powerful characters, which emphasise a dynamic and integrating life force arising in the psyche. In particular, the witch as an archetype represents a figure that is capable of transforming situations (magic). The same dream then led to a peaceful scene, revealing a transcendental vision of a woman sitting in meditation, an image that was to become a future reality for her. The journey through art and psychotherapy had begun to germinate the seeds of self-acceptance and self-actualisation for Zangmo, as she transformed past traumas into creative expressions in her life.

Beginning to feel the need for spiritual depth she embarked on a search through Judaism – the religion of her ancestors, Christianity and Hinduism, while continuing to explore her own spirituality through abstract painting on a BA Painting course, as well as visiting India. In 1993 she found her spiritual home – Tibetan Buddhism, in particular Mahamudra and Dzogchen. In 2003 she started dreaming of being dressed in Buddhist robes and eventually she was ordained as a Buddhist nun in 2007.

Zangmo's inspirational story is rich with symbolic parallels with each phase of her life. First, she becomes a stripper and bares her body to the world. Second, she enters the private world of Jungian psychotherapy and art to bare her soul to herself, witnessed only by the analyst. Third, she discovers as a Buddhist that, "meditation is like peeling away layers of an onion, revealing the naked essence of my mind". Zangmo's life shows how the journey of awakening and cultivating awareness is hard work, but taking such a path holds many possibilities for deep healing and living with more awareness, equanimity, loving-kindness and authenticity. Zangmo's life is a profound journey that shows us how doing and being are intimately connected to the expression of our transformative potential. Since 2007 she has completed a Master's degree in Fine Art, trained as a coach and facilitates meditation and art retreats, meditates regularly and practices as a visual artist.

How we harness our capacities to be receptive and experience awe and wonder will be important variables for motivating and sustaining a long-term journey of transformation in collective consciousness. During this period of transition, we have a great opportunity to be innovative, inspired, adaptable and creative.

We can open ourselves to a journey of discovery as we seek to heal the planet, ourselves and other species. Yet, David Elkins[69] reveals that we have to seek out where to find meaning and purpose that nourishes our lives. Our reflections and explorations need to inspire us to find ways of healing ourselves, one another and the planet. When we fully wake up to what we have done to the world we will undoubtedly feel sadness, shame and sorrow, yet we also need to move forward, as noted by Schlitz[70] who has spoken about crisis also being a positive catalyst for a transformational shift in our belief systems and outlooks. Any shift in our belief systems must cohere with a shift in our actions, and David Tacey is correct, in my view, when he identifies that our approach to the sacred has to be considered in direct proportion with our ability to respond to the sacred.[71] It is my contention that engaging the creative mystery that flows through our lives – inclusive of the transpersonal – requires intelligence to help a deeper connection and meaning to unfold. This intelligence requires a reappraisal for how as humans we consider ourselves to be embedded in life as a whole.

Physicist and process-oriented psychologist Arnold Mindell[72] has discussed a quantum perspective for our everyday functioning, where he notes that our individual actions and the fields that permeate our lives require awareness of how human agency might operate in an interconnected world. Mindell[72] goes on to reveal the point where a shift in awareness is required, between our local and non-local experiences. It suggests that a new view of intelligent action is needed in order to consider the meaning of our full human potential. For example, Zohar and Marshall[73] identify the root meaning of the word intelligence (euphyia), from the Greek to *grow well*. A pressing question in this era of global crisis concerns how we harness our human potential and development intelligently and ecologically. Anne Marie Kidder[74] mentions how the German poet Rainer Maria Rilke would muse on ideas of growth in the outer world, only to find that he was imagining a tree that was growing within. This is an apt example of how the inner and outer worlds can merge. Perhaps the mystical poets can help us break out of our entrenched individualism.

Exercise

- Go outside into the natural world (if you live in a city, then focus on aspects of the natural world, such as trees, grass, flowers, birds, the sky, wind or water).

- Be present to the natural world with all of your senses.

- Let some aspect of nature catch your attention. It could be birdsong or a rustling tree in the wind.

- Let all of your senses come into play:

  o What is it like to see this aspect of the natural world?
  o How does it appear to your sense of hearing?
  o How do you respond to it with your feelings?
  o Do you want to move towards it, move away from it, or does it make you want to stand still?

- Let your mind, body and soul dream or imagine the spiritual connection you have to this aspect of the natural world and connect with its life-world. Consider how it belongs to a greater force in nature – mother earth.

- Imagine if this aspect of nature had a message for you about the needs of the natural world. It could come as an image, symbol, word, or a synchronous message – such as an advertisement on the side of a bus, which catches your attention.

- Reflect on the message that comes to you (in whatever form). Try not to marginalise it if it is a bit unusual (by consensus standards).

- How might the message you have received impact on your relationship with the natural world? Does it prompt you to do something in terms of action or appreciation for nature?

- In what ways are you a co-creator when you embody or act in connection with this deeper resonance with life?

As we transcend the narrow confines of our ego-existence, we become more open to a universal intelligence that is akin to coming home.

CHAPTER ELEVEN

Revolutionary intelligences and interconnected living

Overview

In this chapter I discuss the important role of human intelligence from three diverse, but interconnected perspectives: occupational, spiritual, and Akashic intelligences. I explore how intelligence helps us to engage transformative ways of living, through transpersonal participation in daily life. The uses of our intelligences connect us to a quality of consciousness that not only leads to a deeper relationship to lived experience, but also fosters a healing relationship to our own lives and to nature as a whole.

The evolution of 21st-century intelligences

In a previous publication I explored the use of our intelligences to enable us to grow in ecological awareness.[1] The current global predicament is revealing that we must do something to reverse the worst effects of environmental degradation, for example, reports by the World Federation of United Nations Associations' (WFUNA) State of the Future[2,3] indicate the scale of the challenges facing humanity today. They outline how a large percentage of the world's population are becoming increasingly vulnerable to social instability due to the scarcity of water and food, climate change, desertification, increasing energy prices, as well as deteriorating economic conditions. The WFUNA reports[2,3] also cite other future threats, such as increases in corruption, violence and an escalation of terrorism.[4] However, we must not lose sight of the potential for these crises to become tipping points for transformation, rather than destruction.[1] The main stumbling block appears to be human actions, and according to Lean and Owen we may well "blow it through inequality, violence and environmental degradation" (p. 8).[4] We may already be discussing the collapse of the modern world, but we still have the capacity to make choices and change behaviours.[5,6] For change to become a reality, humanity will have to overcome the weight of history, as there is no escaping the fact that human behaviours in the past have mostly been dominated by issues of power, oppression, exploitation and inequality.

Research psychologist Mihalyi Csikszentmihalyi[7] has suggested that if the third millennium is to be an improvement on its predecessors, more of us will have to develop goals in life that go beyond self-interest, or to use his terminology, transcendent goals.[1] The evolution of such an altruistic perspective is dependent upon people embracing goals that are orientated towards the wellbeing of all life, including families, communities, humanity, other species and the planet.[7] Csikszentmihalyi has further stated that the development of transcendent goals and selves will require the use of intelligence and spirituality.[7,8,9]

There is no doubt that the 21st century will challenge us to find new ways of constructing meaningful lives.[1] James Martin[10] asks two important questions: What shall we do? and What needs to happen? In relation to these questions he notes that human beings consistently fall short of actualising their full potential. However, he concurs with Csikszentmihalyi[7] in pointing out that to adapt from our current self-destructive habits, we will need to engage our intelligences. Indeed, Martin asserts that the intelligent management of human potential will become central to the creation of meaning in the 21st century.[1] But first we have to ask: what current conceptualisations of meaning exist in the modern world, and how will they help or inspire humanity to transform consciousness?[1] Physicist Amit Goswami[11] believes that it is through engaging our intelligences to address shifts in consciousness and identity we can facilitate meaningful transformation.

The dynamic role of intelligences in the pursuit of a meaningful existence reflects our human capacity to select the right courses of action.[11] It stresses the importance of acknowledging our problem-solving abilities in discovering and making wise choices in the way that we live. The position that I am advocating in this chapter is for the development of a holistic view of intelligence. I am not referring to intelligence as an IQ test, or some other objectified measure. On the contrary, I am suggesting that our natural intelligences can enable us to live close to our deepest nature and connect to all life as a whole, which Deepak Chopra[12] calls a universal intelligence. In light of our need as a species to reconnect with a holistic view of life in this time of global crisis, Goerner[13] sums it up well when she points out that our chances of survival are improved by intelligence. I further propose three discrete aspects of human intelligence that will help to usher in an age of transformation in terms of helping us to engage meaningfully in life and change our consciousness. These intelligences are occupational, spiritual and Akashic.

Occupational intelligence

I developed the concept of occupational intelligence[8,9] after many years of con-templating the deep connections between human occupations and the actualisa-tion[8,9] of our transpersonal potential.[14,15] Human intelligence can go way beyond the traditional ways of measuring IQ through psychometric testing.[16]

Indeed, the uses of human intelligence are reflected in our abilities for learning, acquiring knowledge, reasoning and responding to life circumstances,[17] including the ability to problem solve. The work of Howard Gardner[18,19] has expanded the horizons for understanding the multiple dimensions of human intelligence: linguistic, musical, logical-mathematical, spatial, and bodily-kinaesthetic. Gardner[18] asserts that there are no set numbers of intelligences that exist, and the ones we possess may be used singularly or in combination.[8] From this perspective, intelligence is not just a measure of human ability, it is also meaningful, purposeful, adaptive, occurs in real-world contexts and implies living with creativity and wisdom.[20,21] According to Marcus Anthony, the idea of integrating intelligence into our lives is important, because it can expand our experience of life beyond a limited self-referential view. Anthony[22] quotes Einstein, saying that when our minds have been expanded by new thoughts and ideas, can never return to their previous level of operating. This intimates that navigating our human consciousness requires not only an exploratory attitude, but also the ability to find intelligent responses or solutions to the challenges that arise, as we engage our human potential.[1]

We are fully capable of expanding our lived engagement in life, which has enormous implications for how we are occupied intelligently,[8] both individually and collectively.[23] This also involves engaging our capacities in daily life as we connect to experiences of the transpersonal[9] and numinous mystery.[15] Psychologist Marsha Sinetar[24] has discussed the need for modern culture to put greater emphasis on our spiritual development. She argues that this is about living lives, which is much more than just making do, or adapting ourselves to the needs of others. Sinetar further proposes that intelligence is capable of supporting the integration of new experiences in consciousness,[24] as conveyed in the comments from a research participant in a study carried out by psychologist Jennifer Elam[25] who said that the level of transformation that occurred from a mystical encounter connected to a deep experience of knowing that completely changed their direction in life. Elam's study participant reveals the importance of taking our transpersonal experiences seriously, which reflects a form of intelligent action.[9]

Previously, I have written about human potential from the viewpoints of humanistic and transpersonal psychology, and linked these ideas to the intelligent engagement and expression of our multi-sensory capacities in everyday life.[8] I connected my ideas to the work of Arnold Mindell,[26] who has stated that unless we fully develop our capacities for awareness, we often only use certain multi-sensory channels of human perception and expression, which are *occupied* through familiarity and habit. Mindell notes that the multi-sensory channels that are not used with intent are *unoccupied* in terms of our conscious awareness. Building on the work of Mindell,[26] I pointed out that the intelligent use of our multi-sensory modes of perception and expression offer a greater range of possibilities for how we engage in life and fulfil our transpersonal and occupational potential.[8,9] Thus, occupational intelligence is at the core of the interface between doing and being,[8] which is committed to an embodied (multi-sensory) engaged existence.[27]

One of the complex issues that I tackled in the conceptual development of occupational intelligence was to show how an intelligent (multi-sensory) engagement of human potential,[8,9] cannot avoid engaging the fluid nature of the self.[28] This highlights the importance of understanding the complex reflections and interactions between personal and transpersonal experiences.[29] In my explorations, I found that there are creative tensions within the journey of self-actualisation, which are punctuated by occasional experiences of self-transcendence. I noted how our everyday occupational engagements in life can act as a link to help integrate experiences, between self-actualisation[8] and experiences of self-transcendence.[9] Here, our occupations provide a sense of continuity, whilst we undergo transitions between experiences of the personal-ego and the transpersonal-Self, which intelligently supports or contains new ways of doing and knowing that facilitate moments of Self-realisation.[15] I summarised this process of intelligent integration through occupational engagement in a previous publication, which I've adapted in the vignette below.[9]

Thresholds to the mystery

The role of bringing conscious awareness to our everyday occupations can play a pivotal part in the unfolding experience of mystical encounters. The following life-changing experience was discussed by Boyce Batey.[30] It occurred in the summer of 1954 when he was 21 years old, after he had read *The Prelude* by William Wordsworth. Boyce described reading aloud Wordsworth's dramatic account of ascending a Scottish mountain bathed in moonlight. Having climbed up the mountain to break through the clouds, Wordsworth recounted the ineffable beauty and state of awe that he felt. The climb eventually became a catalyst or a state of awareness in which Wordsworth felt at one with the universe. After reading the poem Boyce re-flected on his life and the nature of consciousness and decided to experiment with his own awareness, using all of his senses. He explored in minute detail his experience of touch, his sense of smell, hearing, and then seeing. Boyce described the event that followed as the most important experience of his life. He stated that the onset was unexpected, was of short duration, but significantly transformed his life.

    The transformational nature of Batey's encounter illustrates how trans-personal experiences can have an impact on ways of doing, knowing and being. In relation to *doing*, he recounted how the experience led him to prioritise spiritual matters in his life. He engaged in occupational behaviours that were new to him, such as prayer, meditation and yoga, which reflected the profound impact of the experience. He spoke about how the encounter was spiritual and resulted in him being connected to life at a soul level. The sense of *knowing* described by Batey occurred through his multi-sensory capacities, which resulted in him functioning at a level of awareness not experienced before. Batey described the experience as a *quality in consciousness* and exultation in dimensions he had not experienced before or since. In terms of *being,* he described a sense of joy, peace and love. He said the experience was one of grace. He puts into words the totality of the transpersonal experience that impacted deeply upon his sense of self. He said that he felt inwardly connected to everything outside of him, and at the same time he felt outwardly connected to everything inside of him. His sense of *being* was momentarily extended, which is typical of this kind of transpersonal experience, where there is no sense of separation between inner and outer.[31] The profundity of this transcendent experience is telling when we discover that he did not write these words until 39 years after the event.

Batey's[30] experience is a powerful example of how an everyday occupational engagement involving exploration of his multi-sensory capacities led to a life-transforming experience. Whilst Batey never had another experience like the one described above, it had such an impact on him that he was spurred into changing his occupational behaviours.[9] He used his occupational intelligence consciously to select activities that would enhance the engagement of his human potential in daily life as a key part of his spiritual development,[9] bringing greater vitality to body, mind and soul.[32] These types of transformational encounters not only expand the boundaries of the self,[33] they also reveal how human beings may participate in a wider field of consciousness.[34,35,36] This also needs to be grounded and expressed in daily life through our occupations. [9,15]

Jack Kornfield[37] has discussed the need for an affirmative multi-sensory engage-ment in life, stating that there is no need for us to find a solution to the mystery of life; rather it is a multi-sensory reality that we experience daily in the ways that we use our vision, hearing and feeling. Transpersonal participation includes our multi-faceted sensory connection to life, which is intelligently expressed and engaged through our daily occupations in the service of our lived potential.[8,9] We need to ensure that the evolution of consciousness is connected to our occupational engagement, as a process of co-creative action. However, at a collective level our participation in the modern world, to a greater or lesser extent, is dominated by production and consumption, and our current relationship to the global situation reveals that we are out of balance in the way we live. It is evident that our consumer-based behaviours are nothing short of collective mindlessness, reflecting our loss of contact with the sacred and divine. Conversely, Agosin[38] suggests that when the sacred is present in our lives it has a profound impact. It raises the question, where do we seek the inspiration for how we can live more holistically?

The importance of reflecting on and integrating transpersonal awareness into our lives has significant implications for our conscious orientation in relation to ways of doing, knowing and being. As noted in chapter one, Edelman and Tonini[39] ask whether we are imprisoned by a life of description, or if we are gaining a sense of mastery in terms of meaning. I would add, that to be masters of meaning, requires intelligence in the way we engage our human potential in co-creative ways. For example, mastering meaning has to include how we consider our relationship to transpersonal experiences, which raises questions about what it means to be fully human and what steps we take to live and actualise our potential. Rosemary Anderson[40] advocates that the discovery of *who we are* involves going to the edge of our lived experiences to explore the possibilities. In that way, she notes that our future is created in all the ways that we live our lives, which hints at a productive link to our occupational potential.[8,9,15,28]

Human beings are fully equipped to engage their capacities in life and live more deeply, beyond the confines of a self-referential ego-based consciousness.[9] Indeed, the notion of living a transformative life and evolving our human potential comes about through our willingness and preparedness to view life from myriad perspectives.[12] As we immerse ourselves in an experiential world of doing, knowing and being, we engage with, and participate in, life as a mystery, where our deepest intelligence resonates with a universal intelligence.[1,15] That is, we connect with a life force, where we are part of the whole. In this way, occupational intelligence[9] is linked to spiritual intelligence,[15] and they function in a reciprocal relationship. From this perspective, our connections to transpersonal experiences require intelligent reflection, as well as intelligent action in our daily lives. Maxwell and Tschundin[41] discuss one person's account of how a transpersonal experience inspired them to live more fully. The person described being enveloped in warmth and love, feeling a sense of oneness connected to all creation. Therefore, if we are to engage our transformative potential we also need to consider the role of spiritual intelligence in the processes of our active participation in life as a unitary whole.

Spiritual intelligence

It is evident that our transpersonal potential cannot be addressed in an isolated way, and this means that we have to consider the integration of physical, psychological, social, cultural and spiritual/transpersonal dimensions in lived experience. In this regard, intelligence has a pivotal part to play in the synthesis and integration of a whole life perspective. Marcus Anthony[42] has discussed how in the modern world our ego-based consciousness has been fragmented and consequently has become alienated from the transpersonal, which has set a course for a limited rational existence that is only capable of maintaining the status quo. Anthony[43] quite rightly points out that integrated intelligence has to happen within a social milieu that leads to collective change. Significantly, Anthony refers to the importance of human actions and work,[43] that coheres with the occupational focus I am advocating. For the reasons emphasised throughout this book, we need to consider deeply the occupational potential of people and populations, and how our deepest intelligence resonates and connects our actions to living as part of a greater cosmological whole.[1,9,15]

The link between transpersonal experiences and our occupational behaviours provides possibilities for a broader understanding of human potential in daily life.[9] This is a point intimated by Richard Tarnas[44] who notes that our lives have many meanings, possibilities and potentials that are latent within us *awaiting enactment*, which suggests the engagement of intelligent reflection and action through our ways of living.[28] It is here that occupational intelligence[9] links to spiritual intelligence,[1] increasing our understanding and integration of the transpersonal within everyday life. Yet, spirituality as intelligence is at present a very tentative concept.[1] Indeed, there is very little agreement about what constitutes a universal definition of spirituality,[45] therefore the suggestion is that it needs to be approached in an exploratory, rather than definitive way.[46] Personality psychologist Robert Emmons[47] has outlined a set of propositions for spiritual intelligence: noting first that we need to have the capacity for transcendence; second, that we possess the ability to experience spiritual states of consciousness; third, that we are capable of infusing everyday activities and relationships with a sense of the sacred or divine; and finally that we draw upon spiritual resources for problem solving. This last point is pertinent, in this era of global crisis.

Whilst theoretical ideas and propositions are important, they can never convey the lived experience of spirituality as intelligence, where for example a transpersonal encounter or a shift in consciousness can facilitate a deeper connection to life as a whole.[1] Zohar and Marshall[48] note that such intelligence extends our sense of self in a wider experience of life. Stanislav Grof[31] further suggests that spiritual intelligence reflects our capacity to engage in life, which can open us up to new questions about the nature of reality or existence, adding depth to what it means to be a human being. Grof[31] views spiritual intelligence as an orientation for engaging our capacities in life that helps to fulfil our transpersonal potential. He links processes of psycho-spiritual development to our intelligent engagement of transpersonal opportunities, directions and transformations. Here, the link to occupational intelligence is clear, for it is through our multi-sensory experiences[8,9] that we find connections between body, mind and soul,[49] and in this way spiritual intelligence is noted by Selman[50] as a problem-solving approach to life from a multi-sensory perspective.

The importance of *doing* for integrating and expressing spirituality as intelligence is explicit in the work of Robert Emmons,[51] who suggests that spiritual intelligence not only *is* something, it *does* something in relation to the demands of daily life. This emphasis on *doing* highlights the potential for intelligent action and integration of our transpersonal experiences for the co-creation of new patterns and new possibilities for living now and in the future.[1] It helps us to contextualise transpersonal phenomena and enable connectedness to a wider field-like experience of consciousness: body, mind and soul.[1] This wider and deeper orientation in life is put into a greater context when we realise that humanity can no longer continue to construct a view of reality that is solely based on self-referential terms, as noted by Zohar and Marshall.[48] They have spoken about the engagement of our spiritual intelligence as a way of connecting meaning and purpose to greater evolutionary processes in the universe. It is here that the ancient Indian concept of Akasha exemplifies this greater cosmological connection for how we understand life as an interconnected whole. It also takes our awareness of participating in life to a new level, in that we have an opportunity to connect our occupational and transpersonal potential to a wider and deeper field of influence.

Akashic intelligence

As discussed previously, physicist David Bohm[52] proposes there is an order in the universe that reflects an underlying wholeness. Bohm has suggested that at a manifest level the world appears to be made of separate parts, which he described as being *explicate* or unfolded; however, at a deeper non-manifest level there is an *implicate* order, which is enfolded. Bohm[52] used the workings of a hologram to illustrate his theory, whereby individual photons of light in a laser beam join to form a coherent whole.[53] The hologram is a useful representation of the underlying wholeness in the universe, and is nicely illustrated by Larry Dossey.[54] He writes about when a beam of coherent light (laser) is directed through a photographic plate, and then produces a three-dimensional image projected into space. The hologram provides us with a vivid illustration of the way that all parts of a system are inextricably connected to a whole. The issue for human beings living today is that we have created, and are still functioning in, a Newtonian world of apparent separateness and parts. One of the central points of realisation that we need to embrace and embody today, which is neatly symbolised by the hologram, is that we are all connected to the *whole*.

The neurophysiologist Karl Pribram found in his research that the human brain is capable of both analytic and holographic functioning,[55] which suggests that our brains are capable of engaging information at a local (physical) and non-local (quantum) level. This quantum view of human functioning has been developed by process-oriented psychologist and physicist Arnold Mindell,[56] who explored the field-like nature of what he has called the *quantum mind*, revealing how our minds are entangled with the deep mystery of life. Mindell[56] has noted that *local events* give rise to a consensus view of reality, whereas *non-local experiences* can reflect *non-consensus experiences* and these are typically associated with transpersonal encounters. In such a quantum reality there is no distance in time or space and everything is interconnected. The physicist John Wheeler[57] has stated that the indeterminate field of quantum physics gives the microscopic world of particle physics a dreamlike quality. That is, within the object we may also see a reflection of the subject. This has led to a perception where, says Talbot,[58] the omni-jective nature of reality (beyond subjective and objective) gives it a dreamlike status. This expanded view of reality means that we can participate in a *local*, concrete and materially-orientated existence, as well as being part of a *non-local* universe, which remains a fluid and indeterminate mystery.

In terms of our potential to live and experience both conventional and mystical realities we could say that we are entangled in a dreamlike world of possibilities. For example, what we do in conventional reality is local, embodied and personal, but the question we need to consider is: how do we interact with the non-local, mystical and the transpersonal, which is ever present in our lives? Indeed, from such a perspective how do we reflect upon 'Who is occupied?'[28] as we engage our everyday actions in an occupationally entangled quantum world? Do we view our actions in ways that understand the interconnected nature of reality, where we fully comprehend: *what I do to the world, I do to myself?* That is, we are not only functioning locally in everyday consensus reality, we also exist in a unified non-local field, where the flow of a universal life force is pulsing through us. From such perspectives how do we consider the question: 'I do, therefore I evolve'. These types of reflections have important implications for how we grapple with our deepest potential, including how we live, work and socialise as co-creators living in a universal whole. Collectively (particularly in the west), we have over-invested in conventional consumer-based lives (consensus reality), which are individualistic and self-referential, not giving any recognition for how we are interconnected and participating in a mystery of life. Chopra[59] explains how the Akashic field connects everything to an integrated and intelligent whole. We could say that this dynamic field is omni-intelligent.

Ervin Laszlo's[60,61] concept of the Akashic field provides a transpersonal perspective for how human beings could transcend their current self-referential outlook on life, which to date has been dominated by selfish and non-cooperative behaviours. This could lead to the development of more actualised and altruistic relationships in terms of self, others and the planet.[15] The current global situation is challenging human beings to recognise that a key variable for evolving a sustainable future is our ability to adapt creatively through intelligence and innovation.[1] The Akashic field provides a universal context for conceptualising a collective transformative process, through a deeper engagement of consciousness. Such a position represents a universal experience of *belonging* at a subtle level.[59] From this Akashic perspective, I am proposing that the integration of transpersonal phenomena, linked to our occupational engagement, could lead to transformations of our worldview and behaviours in everyday life.[15] Laszlo's concept of the Akashic field[60] provides a universal context for exploring the emergence of transpersonal meaning in the 21st century. But, before we explore its usefulness, we need to understand what it means to our life as occupational beings.[15]

The origins of the Akashic field[60] lie in Indian philosophy, where everything that exists is connected and arises out of the same cosmic memory field (Akasha). Ervin Laszlo[61] has drawn on the work of physicist John Wheeler, who explains that in such a field, information is ever-present in time and space, everywhere. These insights are creating a powerful momentum that is radically challenging the Cartesian notions of self-referential existence, and heralding a deeper understanding of an interconnected reality. A breakthrough[62] is gradually occurring in the modern world, linked to the new sciences, which are well represented in the work of Ervin Laszlo.[63,64] Some of the insights expressed in the new sciences, such as quantum field-theory (non-locality) and entanglement, are found in the transformative narratives of people who have experienced deep transpersonal encounters, which reveal the importance of non-local and non-consensus views of reality.[65] However, a *quantum leap* is still needed to change mainstream consensus attitudes, where we can begin to embrace a more fluid representation of reality. We find examples of quantum entanglement in stories about synchronistic events, as the following account reveals. These meaningful coincidences can take people into a deeper relationship to life. Von Franz also notes that synchronicity may also occur following the death of an individual who was close to us in life,[66] as the following story reveals.

The falconer's spirit

A friend of mine once told me a story about Peter, who was very good friends with a man called Robert. They had got to know each other since working together in 1987 and soon became great friends. Peter described Robert as someone who would always see the good in others. In 2002, Robert was diagnosed with terminal cancer, and it was at this point in his life that he decided to fulfil a life ambition to become a falconer. In March 2007, Robert's condition was deteriorating, but Peter and his wife had pre-arranged a trip to Australia to see their son. Five days after saying goodbye to Robert, Peter and his family were in Australia when they received the news that Robert had passed away. Robert's sister spoke the last words to him, saying: "You're free now, Robert, fly away." Two days after the sad news of Robert's passing, Peter and his family had travelled to the Sunshine Coast, staying in an apartment on the 5th floor with a balcony overlooking the beach. Peter awoke at 6.30am and went to the balcony where he found an osprey perched on the balcony rails. He said: "It was aware that I was looking, but showed no fear and didn't flinch as I took photos." The osprey stayed on the balcony for 20 minutes, in very close proximity to Peter, which is highly unusual behaviour for a wild bird. Peter said: "It was Robert's spirit just checking that we were all right." This story is a wonderful example of synchronicity, and the ways that meaningful events in our external world are often entangled with our inner world, and vice versa. This story sits comfortably within the theory of the Akashic field.

The Akashic field explains the importance of transpersonal experiences in light of an understanding of consciousness beyond the brain,[67] but which also includes the brain's capacity to connect and read quantum-physical information.[62] Barbara Marx Hubbard[68] has considered the importance of human beings connecting to such a field-like existence. She notes that we have wonderful opportunities to engage our potential in life, between our *local* sense of self and a greater *non-local* sense of self. From this perspective Marx Hubbard suggests humans are co-creators when we connect to a universal intelligence that flows through us. Furthermore, Stanislav Grof[69] has asserted that the Akashic field provides an understanding of the baffling problems that are often encountered when researching consciousness and transpersonal phenomena, which he illustrates in his book, *When the Impossible Happens*.[69] Whether we like it or not, we are gradually being put into a position where we will be forced to seriously consider the interconnectedness of life and the transpersonal reality that brings us into contact with a wider experience of consciousness[70] and a sense of *oneness with nature*.[63]

Life: an EPIC encounter

Modern consciousness is on the threshold of change, precipitated by a variety of factors, such as the global crisis, new sciences and an emerging transpersonal vision that is becoming a reality for more and more individuals and groups.[71] This ever-growing transpersonal movement is informing the way people understand and engage their psycho-spiritual potential, including their occupational behaviours.[8,9] Because our modern needs, values, thoughts, decisions, behaviours and actions are increasingly based on an unsustainable mode of consciousness,[72] we are fast approaching a tipping point for either destruction or transformation. We need a deep engagement of our transpersonal potential, through our *experience, participation, intelligence* and *consciousness* (EPIC), to facilitate greater coherence between our various ways of doing, knowing and being. This EPIC transpersonal orientation considers the whole person in relation to body, mind, emotions, community, culture and spirit.[73] It includes all of the actions that are carried out in everyday life – eating, washing dishes, socialising and sexual relations – which are potentially sacred or spiritual[74] and can inform new ways of orienting and engaging in life.[75] There is a need for an occupationally grounded existence that brings a transpersonal vision into reality, one that takes into account the importance of the conventional world, as well as a mystical dimension of reality.[9,15] The new worldview that is beginning to emerge, that all life belongs to an interconnected whole, has been described by Hamilton[76] as the *physics of participation*. Indeed, acknowledging that quantum physics has direct meaning in our daily life, via Laszlo's[60] concept of the Akashic field, offers a new understanding of consciousness: where our experiences of freedom are more likely to be connected to fostering awareness of non-locality,[56] which is the very essence of the Akashic field.

There are important questions about how we participate, not only in the routines of the everyday world, but also how we are mindful of the collective field that we share with others and nature as a whole.[1] We have a monumental task ahead of us to re-orientate ourselves to explore new ways of living, almost a revolution, as intimated by Skolimowski[77] who calls for a new myth of cooperation, which is based on an ecological spirituality and is expressed in daily life as co-creative unfolding. Our work is to create and develop this myth in the context of the global challenges we face. We must remember that as a species we are ancient, and the connections to the guiding myths that we used to live by still exist within us. These myths reside in the Akashic field.[12]

In relation to a new mythic engagement of our transpersonal potential, I have formulated an approach to support our reflections and actions that enables transformations in consciousness, connected to new ways of doing, knowing and being. It is interesting to note that the meaning of the word *epic* portrays a heroic and mythical quest. I propose that we can start to prepare for an EPIC journey of transformative living through the following questions:

> *Qualities of Experience:* that is, exploring how we relate to the experiences that happen to us. How do we question our everyday experiences in life, and do we acknowledge and make room for the transpersonal?

> *Qualities of Participation:* where do we direct our resources in terms of the relationships we cultivate with others and life as a whole? How do we participate in relation to social, political, ecological, and transpersonal dimensions?

> *Qualities of Intelligence:* how are we growing in awareness, psychologically, ecologically or spiritually? How are we using our talents for problem solving? What are we doing to actively engage the process of individuation and wholeness?

> *Qualities of Consciousness:* how are we engaging our potential in consciousness – from understanding our personal-ego to creating links to a greater transpersonal-Self? How are we exploring and cultivating our co-creative capabilities?[8,9]

This *epic*, mythic and heroic journey requires individual and collective effort. Essentially, the global crisis is challenging us to die to our old identities, and to our old ways of doing, knowing and being. The current state of the world is calling us forth to live a sacred vocation in the world, where we can live as mystics, without the need to live separately in monasteries.[78] To engage with the issues that have been presented in this book, each of us will have different paths and different challenges, but our journeys of transformation will have collective resonance with others who are seeking to heal themselves and the world. Indeed, Daniel Goleman[79] has suggested that our capacity for collective reflection and action to start using finite resources wisely reveals our ability to develop ecological intelligence. At this time in human evolution, such an awakening is vital, and most importantly we need to believe that we are capable of co-creating the world as we live in it. Caroline Myss[78] has sound advice for taking such a soulful path, suggesting that we find our calling and engage in life as an act of service.

This action-orientated approach to living our potential fully and deeply includes engaging the sacred dimension, where we cultivate a healing connection to life. Our dreams, for example, offer possibilities for signposting our personal difficulties, as well as revealing our potential to transform consciousness in soulful ways. Dreams offer a rich connection to the unconscious, because they may symbolically represent archetypal forces, which often resonate with the numinous. Jean Shinoda Bolen[80] has said that the soul responds to mystical or numinous encounters creatively, and this has to include our dream life. Dreams provide us with a soulful connection to life, they are often highly inspirational, as well as being instrumental in the process of healing. The healing functions of dreams will be explored in the next chapter. However, it is worth noting that it was Jung[81] who said that in a time of social degradation and crisis, dreams are a valuable guide. The revelatory function within dreams at a collective level is put into further context by Andrew Samuels[82] who notes that when an individual citizen dreams about the socio-political context in which they live, those dreams provide us with important information about the state of that socio-collective situation.

Exercise

- The Akashic field represents all life as an interconnected whole.

- In what ways are you engaging a greater ecological and transpersonal awareness?
  - What qualities of Experience are you focusing on?
  - What qualities of Participation are you engaging?
  - What qualities of Intelligence are you aware of?
  - What qualities of Consciousness are evident in the way that you are relating to others and the world?

- Find a thread that weaves through the four EPIC qualities above. What do they tell you about the way you are cultivating your relationship to life as a whole?

- From the above points, can you notice where you are inspired to act, e.g., where in your development are you most inspired and animated?

- How are you actualising your talents and potential in the world to help co-create an improved future?

Dreams are like portals in our conscious life.
Wise are those who welcome these sacred guests.

CHAPTER TWELVE

Dreaming and the mystery of healing

Overview

In this chapter I discuss how, as human beings, we can enter into a healing relationship with ourselves and nature as a whole. I explore the meaning and value of dreams as a direct source of healing potential that can also connect us to a deeper mystery in life. I illustrate the ancient use of dreams for the purposes of healing, and discuss how the archetypal figure of Asklepios reminds us of the sacred function of dreams to human consciousness. In this way I explore the profound and archetypal mystery associated with dreams, indicating that they are not only inspirational, but how they also connect us to a creative spirit, which can deeply inform our ways of doing, knowing and being in the world.

The co-creative mystery of dreams

Psychotherapists have been using dreams for over a century to help people reflect on their difficulties in life, as well as assisting in their search for a meaningful life.[1,2] I have yet to meet a person who is not fascinated, at some level, by their dreams. Yet some scientists try to explore and explain dreams as purely brain-based phenomena, using reductionist methods to investigate sleep patterns and neurobiology.[3] Dreams are more than neural phenomena; they reflect deep layers of knowing, which can have an impact upon our ways of doing and being. The story of Victor Frankl,[4] a psychiatrist who spent three years in a Nazi concentration camp, reveals a remarkable story about the power of dreams. As a doctor, Frankl tried to help as many prisoners as he could, who would often lose the physical, psychological and spiritual will to carry on. One day in the camp Frankl recounted how a fellow inmate confided in him about a strange dream that he had in the month of February that year. The inmate revealed that a voice spoke to him in his dream and said he could ask a question about anything he wanted to know the answer to. The inmate told Frankl that in his dream he wanted to know when the camp would be liberated and the suffering ended: the voice answered his question with the date, 30 March. The dream gave the inmate great hope of freedom; however, on 29 March he suddenly became ill, and by 31 March he had died. It would appear that this person's body 'knew' that it would soon be liberated from the camp (literally). This incredible dream illustrates a level of knowing or intelligence at work, which was beyond the conscious awareness of the prisoner. We could say that such important information is capable of manifesting in dreams, which reveals a greater function in consciousness than we currently imagine.

Perhaps one of the most famous examples of the mystery of dreams is the story of Albert Kekulé's chemical discovery told by Linda Shepherd.[5] Kekulé was a 19th-century chemist who dreamt about a snake biting its own tail, which created the shape of a circle. In mythology this symbol is the Ourobos. Upon waking, as if in a lightning flash, Kekulé understood that the chemical structure of benzene was circular. This problem had been long unsolved in chemistry, yet Kekulé's dream solved this scientific conundrum. Shepherd also tells the story of a relatively uneducated poor boy from India, who was given a mathematical text to read. Soon after reading the book he dreamt of meeting a Hindu goddess – Namagiri – who taught him mathematical formulae in his dream. He went on to develop an impressive body of mathematical work that helped him gain a scholarship at a world leading university, where he found that his work was ahead of the mathematical knowledge of the time. These extraordinary examples show us that dreams are a source of great inspiration and revelation. The thing that intrigues me about dreams is how they create a dynamic relationship to everyday life, because they are tinged with mystery and full of potential meaning.

One dream that I had many years ago is still having a profound effect on my spiritual direction in life. I dreamt that three monks were standing before a baptismal font and they were carrying out some kind of ritual. In the dream the monks cupped their hands together to form a chalice over the font. A young boy appeared and stood on tiptoes to pour sand into the 'chalice' of hands, whereupon the sand started to move clockwise of its own volition. The circulating sand gradually produced a few drops of water, and each drop then seeped slowly through the monk's fingers into the font (fluidity). Each droplet of water that went into the font sent an ecstatic ripple of bliss throughout me. I woke up with an indescribable sense of sacredness pulsating throughout my whole body. It was one of a few, and very rare occasions in my life, where I felt something close to a deep sense of reverence and profound humility. It was an immense experience of grace, filled with numinosity, which affected me for many hours after I awoke, and still inspires my spiritual direction today. A dream is revelatory and often – through a gradual process of reflection – it yields pearls of wisdom, hitherto undetected. Working with dreams is co-creative action, that is, we can enact and evolve the wisdom from the dream into daily life. Dreams are the royal road to transpersonal development.

I have tried to create enough space in my life to let the above dream work on me. It inspired me to recall that the meaning of my dream was about transformation, from one substance to another, e.g., matter (sand and grit) to spirit (water and grace). The beauty of the dream for me was that it was about making a covenant with the spirit (baptism), where we need a sense of innocence (the young boy), as well as strong devotion (three monks). I also thought that the font (sacred vessel) was connected to a sacred space (*temenos*), which represents a sacramental understanding of context. The dream had a quality of devotion to the spirit that I have been attempting to engage throughout my adult life. I called the dream the *numen fontis,* after reading the book: *Healing, Dream and Ritual* by Jungian analyst C.A. Meier.[6] In the book Meier mentions the *healing springs* associated with the ancient Greek god of medicine Asklepios, who used dreams as a vehicle to heal people. My studies in transpersonal psychology included the use of dream work, which provided me with a deep appreciation of the healing potential of dreams. Twelve years after having the dream about the monks, I had an article published that explored the dream-healing methods of Asklepios[7] and I discussed how such an archetypal healing approach could inspire people in the modern world. Indeed, the power of dream work lies in its ability to connect the dreamer to the numinous, archetypal and transpersonal spheres of influence, which can fuel and inspire the ongoing process of psycho-spiritual awakening, or individuation.

Jung[8] had recognised that dreams can open the dreamer to a profound sense of the sacred, and he saw their great value for influencing our ongoing development.[9] In a similar way, Feinstein[10] also suggests that dreams which have a numinous quality can deepen a person's values in life, inspire their creative potential, and expand their perspectives on life. Indeed, dreams are what I call portals of inspiration, which not only help us to encounter the mystery of life, they lead our consciousness to the edge of our co-creative potential for reflection and action. 14th-century Christian mystic Meister Eckhart[11] speaks about having a dream of being pregnant, he describes being filled with *nothingness,* out of which God was born. This mystical statement provides a poetic reflection on the preparation of the soul for giving birth to the spirit in life. Yet, we must also play our part in working with the inspiration that is revealed through our dreams. Indeed, dream work is soul work.

A classical ancient Greek description for the care of the soul is found in the Platonic phrase *techne tou bio*, which means *the craft of life.*[12] The Greek word *psyche* means soul, therefore how we craft our daily lives can be a measure of how much awareness or ability we have to care for the soul. The idea of the soul, which is not easy to conceptualise, becomes less abstract if we consider the words of Edward Tick,[13] who notes that the language of the soul is found in our experiences connected to symbols or metaphors. Moreover, the soul is visceral,[14] which means it is capable of resonating with deep experiences and expressions in life, such as *soul music* (evocative and full of feeling), *soul food* (earthy and full of goodness), a *soul mate* (connected and related through deep love), and so on. In essence, the soul comes forth in our lives when we are connected to something deeply human, and also touched by the numinous (spirit). David Elkins[15] has suggested that we try to imagine what it would be like if we took the soulfulness out of the writings of Homer, Dante, Goethe, Shakespeare, Rilke or Rumi, and then consider what would be left (or felt)? It is through the human soul (*psyche*) that we have a sacred centre, and Meister Eckhart[16] has suggested that there is a spirit that resides in the soul. It is where we connect to the sacred whole in all life.

Living connected, at a soul level, has powerful implications for how we craft (*techne*) our responses to daily life. Such development concerns our ways of doing, knowing and being, as a depth of co-creative expression in life, both inwardly and outwardly. And it is through a greater connection to the soul that we can shift the focus of over-identification with the ego.[17] A significant challenge for human beings in this high-tech age will be to *craft* soulful ways of living; indeed, as stated earlier, modern technology is not the problem per se. The real issue concerns whether humans are capable of using modern technologies in soulful ways (beyond materialism), or whether we will be driven by technologies that create greater distance from the soul. Gary Zukov[18] has said that an important part of our human condition is to ensure the health of our souls. This poignant focus contains a great deal of wisdom that should be at the heart of our endeavours in the world. Yet, the reality for many people today is greater exposure to high levels of stress due to the demands of daily life,[19] and on top of this, the world is slipping into a deeper crisis year on year. As our societies, institutions and working lives are becoming increasingly stressful and soulless, the soul of the world, the *anima mundi*, is increasingly lost from our vocabularies and our visions. Now is the time to reconnect to our transpersonal roots and potential, cultivating a spiritual response in life that is healing for the planet and ourselves.[20] Perhaps a greater interest in dreams (the language of the soul) could help us to regain a healthy connection to the soul in life, healing ourselves and helping to heal the planet. Making deeper and more holistic connections in our understanding of consciousness could be the impetus for change in our actions.[22] The archetypal figure of Asklepios represents the connection between healing and dreaming,[21,22] as discussed in the following section adapted from a previous publication.[7]

— Dreaming, Asklepios, and the archetype of soulful transformation —

I first came across Asklepios in the writings of Carl Jung, who noted how the healing god would visit people in their dreams to heal them. Whilst we do not find many references to the soul in the writings about Asklepios, it is important to note that the Asklepian healing method was holistic. Indeed, in the ancient writings of Aelius Aristedes, *Sacred Tales* (*Hiero Logoi*), we discover the author was a devotee of Asklepios, and recorded his dreams, reflections, as well as his *ailments* and their *alleviation*.[23] Aristedes found meaning in his life through his encounters with the healing god. Kee has stated that Aristedes not only wrote about his physical cures, but also mentioned how his soul was strengthened.[23]

Asklepios is an important figure to consider in any discussions about healing and the soul. He represents an archetypal figure that brings human beings into deep contact with the divine, and especially focuses on health and wellbeing. Asklepios was first mentioned in Homer's *Iliad*, where he was described as an ordinary mortal.[24] Asklepios came to be seen as a divine figure at some point in the late 6th or early 5th century BC, when his rise as a significant healer coincided with the great plagues of Athens (at a time of collective crisis). The importance of Asklepios as healer has been lost today, yet the great physician, Hippocrates, who was also referred to as an Asklepiad, had experienced a vision of Asklepios, where the healing god had held out his hand to him.[23] This image of the mortal physician Hippocrates, connecting to a divine archetypal healer, is not a celebrated part of contemporary medicine, which prefers the high-tech and increasingly soulless practices of healing that many medical staff and patients find objectionable. Archetypal figures such as Asklepios are important in these crisis-ridden times in two ways. First, the fact that humans have such historical reference to the divine, encapsulated in processes of healing, suggests the soul and spirit are essential components of health and wellbeing. Second, when human beings reconnect to their lives at a soul level (for example, when inspired by dreams) it creates greater resonances and recognition of the soul in other people, animals and the natural world.

Sanctuaries, known as Asklepieia,[25] were found throughout the ancient Greek empire, and the temple complexes were built on sacred land. These healing sanctuaries provided dedicated areas for votive offerings, baths for purification and an inner sanctuary (*abaton*) where people would eventually sleep overnight and await a healing dream (*enkoimesis*). Asklepios would appear to people in either his human form or as a dog or snake,[13] and would either cure the person or give medical advice.[26] The healing process at Asklepian sanctuaries involved personal preparation, which included the shedding of thoughts and feelings relating to envy, anger, dissatisfaction and insecurity, as well as developing a pre-conditioned mood for a successful outcome.[27] These preparations all contributed towards what Kerényi[28] has described as a numinous encounter with the healing god.

The meaning of divine, heroic and archetypal figures like Asklepios could be inspirational for the troubling times we are living in, because they remind us about what it is to be a soul-centred human and how we relate to the sacred and archetypal. Remember, we flourish when we are connected to myths that remind us of the depth of engagement we are capable of living in this life. The ancient Greeks had *faith* in Asklepios, in that they believed he was healing them, but the most important point about Asklepios is that he personifies the deep archetypal potential of endogenous healing, which means that people could connect to healing processes as active participants, through their dreams.[22] Kirmayer has linked the Asklepian method with an archetype of healing,[29] and Tick[30] has explicated this further, suggesting that Asklepios, as the divine healer, has qualities of kindness, compassion and devotion, which we can also evoke. The reality of Asklepios reveals how the archetypes were active in the ancient world, whereas today they still operate within us all, but we are mostly asleep to the wisdom they embody. Maxwell and Tschundin[31] have reported the extraordinary dream of a young girl who had tuberculosis, who dreamt that she could walk. The girl spoke about feeling a power within her as she dreamt. In the morning she was determined to try and walk and was motivated to connect with the power she experienced within herself, during the dream. The dream is a powerful affirmation of the inspiration that can come when we are connected to the spirit in our dreams, which is revealed in the way that the young girl was helped to pursue her ambition to walk again. Anyone who doubts the healing power of dreams in antiquity can visit the Asklepian temple at Epidaurus, Greece, where you can still see the inscriptions (in stone) of healing cures.

Inspiration, dreaming and deep occupations

The word spirit across many languages means breath. In Hebrew it is *Ruah*, in Sanskrit it is *Prana*, in Greek it is *Pneuma*, and in Latin it is *Spiritus*. If we think about the root meaning of the word inspire ('to breathe in'),[32] it then follows that inspiration through the breath (spirit) leads to an *animation* in body, mind, and soul, through the experience of being alive (the word *anima* in Latin means soul). The thing that we have to ask ourselves is, how are we being inspired, and how are we animated in this life in our ways of doing, knowing and being? What sources of inspiration are we drawing into our lives? Amy Mindell[33] says of dreams that they connect us to an unknown, living creation that is sacred and mystical. Mindell[33] approaches the world of dreaming as a creative process, and she includes night-time dreams, as well as dreaming while awake, which is akin to Aboriginal cultures' experiences of *Dreamtime*. I am suggesting here that our dreaming mind has an integral connection to the Akashic field, which can inspire us to live more fluidly and intelligently. Dreams can act as transition points, between the experiences of our personal-ego and the transpersonal-Self. They are a prime source of inspiration for our emergent potential.

Working with dreams means that we must be prepared to step into the unknown and often mysterious realms of life with a spirit of curiosity and receptivity.[34] It is during such times that working with dreams becomes a co-creative act. However, whilst dreams can provide a sense of revelatory knowing for the dreamer, they can also be confounding or confusing and lead to a sense of 'not knowing'. Process-oriented psychologist Lee Spark Jones[35] has written about the value of not-knowing as an ancient mystical approach to life, which offers an inspiring way of staying with the creative tension of the unknown. This means that we can be inspired, open and curious about the connections we are making and co-creating in life as a whole, where our reflections and actions can accommodate both the known and the unknown.

The relationship between knowing and not-knowing affects the ways we can be inspired and creative in life, which can come through our dreams. Dreams bring the whole issue of *doing* and *being* under the spotlight. In her inspirational book on dreams, Connie Kaplan[36] describes them beautifully as letters from the soul. However, her focus on dreaming and spiritual development is predominantly concerned with ways of being. Dream work affords us the chance to connect to our human potential through exploration and encountering new ways of doing, knowing, being, becoming and belonging. These could include reflecting on old patterns in life, or integrating new patterns for living.

Dreams can play a powerful role in revitalising our life force and energy,[34] acting as a bridge between the ego and the unconscious. In this way, dreams can inspire transformations in the way that we make deep connections to life; therefore it follows that the links between dreaming and doing are important in terms of their potential to influence and change behaviours.[37] If we return to the ideas expressed in the previous section, where the tension between the known and the unknown was discussed, we can appreciate that the numinous nature of dreams often confounds the rational ego. Here, the known world of a person is confronted with the mysteriousness of the unknown, as noted by Leon Schlamm.[38] The dream presents new opportunities for working on the polarity between the known and the unknown, but also the polarity between the ideas of 'me' and 'not-me', as observed by Miller.[39] Schlamm[38] puts Jung's concept of the transcendent function into context, saying it reflects the potential for a powerful encounter with the numinous dimension of the unconscious. The power of engaging the transcendent function is put into the context of individuation as an active process, where we are free to co-create and experience the sacred.[39] In the same way dreams provide us with a direct connection to the sacred, across a numinous threshold into the mystery of life, as the following illustration (adapted from a previous publication) reveals.[40]

A dream of facing a dinosaur

The important link between dreaming and human occupations reveals how dream work directly affects and changes occupational behaviours. I worked with a male client who had been severely depressed for 11 years. The man's problems were exacerbated by serious alcohol abuse, and at the time I saw him for therapy he was becoming more and more withdrawn and was developing a social phobia. The client had previously had Cognitive Behaviour Therapy and hypnotherapy to try and help with his difficulties, which had been initially helpful, but his symptoms had become progressively worse. We worked on helping him to recognise his destructive patterns of thought and behaviour. After about six months of therapy he had a dream that we explored together.

The dream took place in a field, where in reality the client had experienced difficult events in adolescence. In the dream, a ferocious dinosaur was heading towards him with the intention of doing him harm. He turned to the dinosaur and said, "Stop, you cannot hurt me, I am from God." The dinosaur vanished into thin air after he said these words. I was very interested in this dream because the dreamer had said he had no relationship with God, religion or spirituality. In fact, when he was recounting the dream, he was so proud that he had stood up to a ferocious dinosaur that he paid no attention to the fact that he had declared that he was from God. I asked him what God meant to him and this proved to be a vital line of exploration, which tapped into a quality of engaging in life that helped him to regain a connection to his creative impulses as a musician, and also opened up a rich seam of inquiry into spiritual matters. I was fortunate that I had a piano in my therapy room, which belonged to music therapists, and at times the man would get up and play the piano spontaneously, putting all of his emotion, depth and creativity into his improvised music.

The man told me one day that he had found a connection to God through music. I recounted in the article that I wrote: "Listening to him play was deeply moving and I always fed back to him how his creativity had touched me." Interestingly not long after having this dream the man started to reduce his alcohol consumption, and after a few relapses, he gave up alcohol altogether. He continued to have a deepening connection to his spiritual life and his creative impulses. This case illustration gives an indication of how the dream linked directly to the client's sense of doing, which created a shift from destructive ways of living, to a more inspired occupational engagement where music playing became an integral part of his life. In this case the creative act of doing was inspired by a dream, which then informed the man's process of renewal. The point about dreaming and occupations is that they act as a prompt to us to engage in life as deep occupational beings. Dreaming provides depth to the journey of individuation, and Feinstein suggest that dreams which have a numinous resonance can lead to greater inspiration that deepen our values and creative ways of living.[10]

Dreaming spirit – co-creative spirit

Creativity, like dreaming, helps humans to connect to deep soulful processes within. For example, Jung [41] was very aware of the importance of vocation, or in Latin, *vocaire*, which refers to hearing a voice within as an expression of the soul. Archetypal psychologist James Hillman[42] has discussed how in the modern world we have been robbed of our true biographies, and as a consequence we go to therapists to help recover it. We hope to recapture our imagination and deep potential for living, which can be caught in the flickers of a daydream or a night-time dream, which are percolations of potential arising from our soul.

As an example of the soul's urge to express a deep sense of vocation, Hillman recounts the story of Ella Fitzgerald, who entered a talent contest in Harlem when she was a young girl. Ella thought that she wanted to do a dance routine, but at the last minute she asked if she could sing instead, and after three standing ovations, the rest is history. Hillman is suggesting that the soul possesses a hidden biography, one that wants to break free from the binds and conditions of external influences. We need to ask ourselves how our *everyday biographies* connect to or obscure the *hidden biographies* in our souls. How are we connected to the unexplored potential in our dreams, aspirations and creative life? Where are our dreams helping us to express our hidden biographies? Moreover, where is our hidden biography seeking to be expressed in our daily occupations?

Hillman[43] has spoken about possibilities for enabling change inspired by the ancient Greek axiom at Delphi, advising people to cultivate wisdom and *know thyself*. Hillman adds a dynamic twist to this ancient quest for self-knowing – *reveal thyself*. I believe we can bring out our hidden selves through our occupational behaviours, between *knowing thyself* and *revealing thyself*, which reflects different facets of our co-creative potential for doing, knowing and being in the world. It is through the quality of our occupational engagement that we gain knowledge and reveal our soul's potential. However, another Delphic proclamation says: *nothing too much*, meaning that it is wise to be moderate in our ways of living. In classical Greece, the twin consequences of 'doing too much' were pride (Hubris) and the resultant harm from our ego-inflated actions (Nemesis). We only need to look at how we are behaving in the world today to see that we are *doing too much* without thinking of the consequences of our actions. Our consumer-based lifestyles are dominating the planet. This is where we need to renew our understanding of doing, so that it is in the service of living a wise and soul-centred existence.

The way that we reveal ourselves, through our everyday ways of doing, knowing and being reflects the extent to which we are able to make choices about what we do, and to exercise our freedom to imagine and act. Engaging our imagination and deepest reflections has transpersonal significance and represents a sacred response to lived experience. Dreaming holds much of our creative potential for transformation,[44] and Hefner[45] has said that when we access our spiritual potential (which can be inclusive of dreams), we can imagine new possibilities. In a similar way, Alan Watts[46] has spoken about spiritual freedom and how the symbols found in dreams are powerful means for growth and liberation. Therefore, dreams play an important part in the process of self-knowing and revelation, connecting us to our deepest aspirations, as we reconcile conventional modes of everyday reality to a transpersonal experience of wholeness. Working with our night-time dreams,[47] or even dreaming whilst awake, as noted by Arnold Mindell, has creative potential that can lead to a mystical level of awareness.[48]

A very touching dream experience is reported by Maxwell and Tschundin.[31] The dreamer is ascending a steep hill carrying their mother (on the back). Struggling to get to the top of the hill to reach a monastery, the dreamer had no strength to finish the climb. Then, suddenly a hand took hold of their arm and they were flooded with compassion and love as they were helped to the top of the hill. The dreamer said it was like being touched by the Holy Spirit. The dream resonates with the archetypal vision of Hippocrates discussed earlier in this chapter, when the healing god Asklepios reached down and held out his hand to Hippocrates. Such archetypal encounters have great power to inspire us. In addition, the archetypes also connect us to a deeper level of engagement in life when we connect our symbolic and dreaming worlds to the process of doing, or archetypal occupations.[49] Tomoyo Nonaka provides an apt description of the relationship between dreaming and doing, suggesting if we are capable of dreaming something, then we are capable of doing it in some way.[50] Indeed, our dreams can inspire us and spur us on to act.

This chapter supports the idea that dreams connect us to the spiritual. Yet, it is our attitude towards dreams that determines how the spirit works in and through our lives. In terms of our co-creative unfolding with life, we can be inspired by dreams, including the ideas and associations we have about them. But, we must also leave some time for the dream to work on us. That is, to let the dream open us up to its intelligence, its meaning and purpose. In doing so, we remain receptive to the numinous layers within the dream, and then we are living with a closer connection to a mystery in life.

Throughout this book I have explored a range of perspectives on life as a mystery, and what it is to be alive as a conscious participant in life's wholeness. I have provided many examples of spiritual emergence and the issues that can arise when we encounter spiritual emergencies. In the next chapter I reveal my own journey through a spiritual emergency. It has taken me decades of inner and outer work to integrate these transpersonal experiences into a journey of transformation. I have tried to convey the sense of calling and vocation that was catalysed by this deep experience. I learnt – rather painfully at times – that the meaning in the work can lead to dissonances in identity and distressing personal experiences of consciousness, and that the work includes facing and working on the personal shadow, as well as the light.[51] However, I have also found that if we are willing to meet the transpersonal dimension of consciousness with humility, to be accepting of non-linearity and paradox in our lives, then we are free to co-create, in the knowledge that we are never the finished product, rather we are always a work in progress, connected to life's unfolding process. The meanings associated with our personal and transpersonal journeys in life reveal how we are discovering and manifesting a process of renewal through engaging new ways of doing, knowing and being. It means we take our spiritual development seriously.

The transformative narratives of first-person accounts of life experiences are significant for understanding consciousness.[52] These stories of transpersonal participation reveal new ways of living and relating to nature, which are important to the collective, particularly in these times of global crisis. For example, Maxwell and Tschundin[31] report one person's account of a mystical encounter, which the individual described as overwhelming, joyful and awesome. Yet, they also spoke about the new knowledge that they gained in the experience, which impacted on their sense of self, and helped them to readjust their vision in life. Such transpersonal encounters can be so profound that it takes effort and adjustment to integrate them into our daily lives. Yet, in doing so, they become a guiding vision for life's unfolding, as my autobiography of a spiritual emergency reveals in the next chapter.

Exercise

- Consider your current 'ways of doing' and if they reflect the authentic life you would like to live.

- How do you *know* yourself? How do you *reveal* yourself?

- What night-time dreams or daytime musings do you have that may be leading the way for the changes that you would like to make in your life that would benefit the collective? You might be inspired by any of the following:

  o A dream figure or mythical spirit that connects with your journey?
  o A person you connect with in your daily life that embodies or acts in ways that inspires you?
  o An activity you currently do that reflects a deeper calling of transition in your life?

- Try to connect to a message that this figure, spirit, person or activity has for your life.

- What advice can you take from this message that helps you to plan your next step?

We cannot have the light without casting a shadow. In our journey of psycho-spiritual transformation we grow in the light and the shade.

CHAPTER THIRTEEN

An autobiography of crisis and transformation

Overview

In this chapter I discuss my own experience of a transpersonal crisis that happened in the mid-1980s, whilst I was living in a Buddhist monastery. This deep, numinous encounter set a whole new course for my life, leading to profound changes, in terms of my doing, knowing and being in all areas of life. I outline how this numinous encounter exposed me to states of consciousness that I was initially ill-prepared to deal with. Through a gradual process of acceptance over many years, I was able to engage with the process of transformation and integrate any insights gained. One of the consequences of my spiritual emergency was to realise directly that opening to the transpersonal often requires us to deal with unprocessed psychological material. Yet, doing so enables a deepening of the journey of self and spiritual renewal.

Conventional life and a mystical encounter

This autobiographic chapter is adapted from a previous publication.[1] I was born in 1956 and my mother was unmarried, which resulted in me being adopted. The new life with my adoptive parents involved frequent moves around the UK and abroad due to my father's work. My experience of growing up can only be described as a very fluid existence. I was an only child in a fairly rootless existence: interestingly, my adoptive parents had no extended family either; my mother's parents died when she was 13 and she went to live with a distant uncle and aunt (she had no brothers and sisters). My father also had adoptive parents, who became my only 'grandparents'. I was physically well cared for by my parents, but the frequent geographical moves led to a disrupted education and social contacts. Moreover, the emotional atmosphere at home could be quite unpredictable and sometimes volatile. Combined with no stable social connections, it had an impact on my inner confidence and emotional development.

After leaving school at 15 in 1972 I worked as a manual labourer for two years. During this time I was regularly getting into trouble with the police and after a few difficult episodes with the law, I decided to join the Military to help gain a new focus in life and change my anti-social behaviours. I spent three and a half years in the infantry, eventually specialising as a combat engineer. In 1977, I left the army and decided to travel abroad. I spent six years on the road, travelling across the world, living and working in interesting places. At the time I was young, wild and free spirited, but underneath I was also seeking something more fulfilling in the way that I was living my life. My years of travelling became a major life transition, a rite of passage, where I gradually opened up to bigger questions about life. I started to read thought-provoking literature, particularly Herman Hesse, and books on eastern philosophy. Living in communal settings, I met inspirational people who helped me reflect on life in new ways. Over time I gradually understood that for me, travelling was the equivalent of an education, where the world was an open campus with an abundance of 'life professors'.

During one of my long excursions in East Asia, I started to take an interest in culture and religion. I became interested in Buddhism and started to read books, particularly from the Zen and Tibetan traditions. I continued on my travels and through a network of contacts, I heard that a dear friend of mine, Russ Thornton, from New Zealand (whom I had previously met on a kibbutz), was living in a community in the north of England. In the early 1980s I returned to the UK with the intention of visiting Russ for a few days (I later discovered that he was actually living in a Tibetan Buddhist Monastic College). It was a windy November evening as I walked down the long dark lane towards the community and I could see distant silhouettes of gothic spires. The place looked bleak and eerie, making me wonder if I had made the right decision to visit Russ. I also thought to myself: "What on earth is he doing in a place like this?" When I entered the building I was struck by its grandeur. It was a huge old mansion that was being renovated and it housed a community of resident Tibetan teachers, monks, nuns and lay people. The community was short of people with construction skills, so I was invited to stay. I worked as a layperson on the building restoration team in exchange for teachings from the resident Geshes (Tibetan Buddhist teachers) as well as three meals a day, lodgings, and a small financial allowance (£12 per month). I took part in a small number of Tantric initiations (as part of my meditation practice) and was engaged in study and contemplation as part of community life. I went for a two-day visit and ended up staying for just under three years.

I immersed myself in the manual work, teachings and community life. I started to contemplate Buddhist philosophy and the teachings that I was receiving, with its emphasis on compassion and impermanence, especially the belief that there is no self-supporting, substantially existent self, or 'I'. The Buddhist doctrine of two truths[2] interested me enormously: that we live in a *conventional existence* of everyday life, and yet we are part of an *ultimate existence* in which we are all enfolded. At this time I started contemplating the various attachments and aversions in my 'conventional' existence, and also began reflecting on the significance of what a more 'ultimate' perspective could mean to the way I lived my life. I began to observe and question how duality was embedded in my thoughts and behaviours, including the distinctions I frequently made between what I thought was good and bad. At the same time I was also trying to consider what is meant by the Buddhist notions of a non-duality and emptiness: where we are at one with all life, and all phenomena are empty of any substantive existence. The contemplative atmosphere of the community was very helpful in generating a steady focus for living in the world, without getting too caught up in it, and being mindful that ultimately, life is a mystery. I was fascinated by this sense of mystery that underpins our lives, particularly in the way it intrudes upon our conventional understanding of reality, such as the Buddhist Heart Sutra, which notes the mysterious interplay between form and emptiness as outlined by Thich Nhat Hanh,[3] where emptiness is form and form is emptiness.

The essence of the Buddhist teachings helped me to realise the impermanence of the conventional world of appearances that we have labelled with our conceptual minds. I was excited by the idea that reality is in constant flow of flux and change. In the Diamond Sutra (*prajñaparamita* – the perfection of wisdom) the teachings are based on the cultivation and application of awareness that helps us cut through our dualistic ways of looking within, and at the world around us. Thich Nhat Hanh[4] has illustrated the way that mind training can operate in our lives by developing our capacities for non-attachment. For example, when looking beyond the appearance of a rose, we know that a rose has no ultimate existence. But this realisation does not stop us from enjoying the temporal beauty and fragrance of the flower. The Buddhist teachings on emptiness[5] are designed to help us realise that we cannot cling to the world of form, and that investing time and energy in trying to make anything more permanent is futile. The teachings helped me to get a new perspective about the meaning of form and emptiness in life. For example, a good gardener knows that roses are transient, yet the same gardener continues to grow flowers with great care, in the knowledge and understanding that their pride and glory will soon be wilting. Similarly, our life is a short duration, in which we have to wake up and see the conventional world for what it is – impermanent – in all of its transience. Ken Wilber[6] suggests that we exist as emptiness whilst embracing all form. However, it is easier to appreciate and acknowledge the emptiness and impermanence in the short life of a rose bud and flower, but so much harder to do with our own lives, as I found out.

Who am I – What am I doing?

My studies in Buddhist philosophy inspired new ways of looking at life, for example, the tensions that arise when attempting to live a conventional life, tempered by the knowledge that all life is connected to a greater ultimate existence, in which we, and all that we cherish, will eventually turn to dust. The tension between our conventional life and ultimate existence gives us deeper opportunities for engaging meaning in our ways of doing, knowing and being. Lao Tsu[7] wrote in the *Tao Te Ching* that there is such a thing as non-action, where we engage in activities and work without doing. This assertion may appear paradoxical and confusing, but it reveals how the mystery of life can be present in the qualities of our doing, knowing and being if we cultivate awareness that is not driven by the ego. The Taoist concept of *wu-wei* (non-doing) is more accurately concerned with not-forcing, or not-striving, and Alan Watts[8] has suggested, for example, that when our awareness is trained, *through the act of doing*, the idea of doing disappears. Watts[8] tells a story about a Zen monk who asked his teacher how we can be free from mundane tasks, such as dressing and eating. The teacher replied with a very occupation-focused response, suggesting to the adept that he just *do* the tasks. The teacher then said if he did not comprehend his instructions, the best way to gain an understanding is to actually put the clothes on and eat the food. This simple story illustrates how non-doing is not a literal interpretation of the words. Indeed, it reveals subtleties for engaging ways of doing and knowing in conventional existence, which can awaken consciousness through mindfulness and non-attachment in action (*wu-wei*).

I have held the view for many years that our quality of experience in the way that we are occupied[9] can empower the present moment, here and now. But of course how we are occupied depends upon how we view life, whether we are bound to a conventional view of material existence, or able to appreciate that an ultimate, mystical reality permeates all life in both form and emptiness. In turn, this highlights questions about our self-awareness and ability to reflect fluidly. Buddhist psychology states that consciousness is an interaction of the five aggregates: 1) form – the senses; 2) feelings/sensations – pleasant, unpleasant or neutral; 3) perceptions/impulses – recognition and discernment towards events/objects; 4) dispositional factors – habits of thought, feeling, perception and action; 5) consciousness – all the above. The Buddhist view of consciousness is that there is no fixed sense of self, and this philosophical position underpinned an article I wrote, titled: *Who is occupied?*[10] Indeed, when we bring this idea of fluidity into our understanding of identity and our daily actions we hold great potential for engaging a creative approach to living.

Our daily occupations may have conventional meaning on one level, but they are also incredible sources of creativity and purpose, which provide opportunities to appreciate the mystery of our daily lives. Our ability to be occupied in the conventional world of form, whilst also recognising the inherent emptiness and formlessness of existence, gives us the potential to adapt fluidly in the doings of our everyday lives.[10] When we awaken to the all-encompassing nature of non-dual reality, we awaken to a freedom, which Alan Watts[8] has described as transforming our most insignificant acts, whereby activities in everyday life can become a sacrament. Hence our occupational orientation in life is revelatory, because so much of *what we do* reflects *who we are, what we may become* and the worldviews that permeate our sense of *belonging* as well as our experiences of *emptiness.*

In the Buddhist community where I lived, the Tibetan Geshes would often tell stories as part of the daily teachings. I remember hearing the story about the great Tibetan yogi, Milarepa, and how early in his life he had killed people and practised sorcery. Then he met the revered Buddhist teacher, Marpa, who began to help him change his ways. The Geshes would tell us stories about how Marpa would make Milarepa build a house, and upon completion would tell him to tear the house down and move to another location, only to build the house again, and so on. On the surface it looks as though Marpa is punishing Milarepa, but if we think about the teachings of form and emptiness, it is quite apparent that Milarepa would have been cultivating great detachment through the *doing* and *not-doing* connected to the building work. Of course, Milarepa experienced deep remorse for his previous negative actions and would have understood that the repetitive task of futile building work was intended to be meaningful for his spiritual development and transformation. In his determination to change his ways, Milarepa captures his devotional relationship to his beloved teacher Marpa in one of the 60 songs he composed. He stayed with Marpa for six years and eight months. He tells us in one of the songs that he built many houses before Marpa agreed to accept him as a student.[11]

The story of Milarepa is an exemplar for reminding us that everything is impermanent. It highlights an approach to life that is fluid and interdependent, yet the story is infused with great devotion and commitment. These are qualities that all human beings share; when used they can bring about great changes in our thoughts and actions, as noted by Sogyal Rinpoche.[12] From an occupational perspective, we can engage in the conventional world, bringing forth our talents, making a livelihood and contributing to the co-creation of an improved world. However, we can also be mindful of not investing too much importance and attachment to temporal and material existence, which is capable of clouding the sensitivity required to be with life's mystery and unfolding grace.

It takes a deep sense of *occupational congruence* between the inner and outer reaches of our everyday actions to engage in life's forms and functions, whilst recognising that we are also embedded in a formless mystery that is empty of inherent existence. For example, if we engage our contemplative vocation seriously, we need to constantly remind ourselves that all forms have an underlying emptiness. The mystical perspective that results is based on the deep reality that nothing is fixed or enduring, even our own bodies are fluid and ever changing, as explained in chapter one. From this perspective, our multi-sensory modes of perception and expression are *thresholds to the mystery*. Psychologist Jennifer Elam[13] describes the numinous encounter of one research participant who reported that their mystical encounter impacted on all their senses, bringing forth a highly charged awareness, which felt as though every cell in the body was affected. Our senses bring us into contact with the numinous, which presents us with opportunities to engage our awareness and actions fluidly, as part of our psycho-spiritual development.

Spiritual emergence and crisis

My time living in the Buddhist monastery gave me the impetus to contemplate life deeply and also to carry on with the usual reference points for daily living, such as working on the building restoration programme, although (thankfully) not with the same intensity as Milarepa. I did not travel much during my stay in the Buddhist community. However, one time I made a long train journey to visit some friends in the west of England. On the train I spent my time either reading Buddhist literature or reciting mantra (meditative repetition of syllables). It was whilst reciting mantra that I experienced a heightened sense of compassion for the people sitting on the train. As I looked around the carriage this feeling of compassion grew and developed into a profound experience of love. The experience was extraordinarily beautiful and blissful. Yet, I remembered my Buddhist teacher's advice not to dwell on such states, but rather, detach from them and let them pass naturally. Despite my attempts not to dwell on this heightened state of consciousness, the experience continued to grow stronger. By the time I got off the train I was immersed in an experience of love and reverence for all forms of life, both animate and inanimate, even discarded rubbish on the street appeared as though it was sacred, and ordinary colours were luminal. In addition, my body was experiencing intense and pulsating waves of bliss. I had never experienced anything like this in my life, and the effects of this experience radiated through my whole being for just over two days. Yet, as the intensity of the experience slowly faded away I started to slip into a diametrically opposed state. I felt very unsettled and unsure of what was happening to me. If I had not been prepared for the experience that I have just described above, I could never have anticipated what was to follow.

By the time I returned to the Buddhist community I was experiencing episodes of intense heat around my navel and a corresponding coldness in the lower part of the legs. I experienced a low-level vibration throughout my whole body and a pressure around my forehead, which are characteristic signs of a Kundalini experience.[14,15,16,17] I also experienced paranormal phenomena. For example, on one occasion I was having a cup of tea in a cafe when my cup suddenly shot off the table without any human involvement. I was both staggered and distressed by this event, which was compounded by my inability to explain what had happened to the waitress (who also witnessed the event and looked shocked). The phenomenon of psycho-kinesis is recognised as the involvement of mind being able to affect or move matter, without direct physical involvement from people.[18,19] Moreover, Braud[20] has discussed how experiences of psycho-kinesis reflect extreme cases of human ability, and gives some indication for how consciousness may function in the physical world. I did not have then, nor now, any real interest in exploring this type of mind-matter interface. At the time I was in a very disturbed state, and this was just one of the surprising events that happened to me during this period, which only compounded my confusion and distress.

I became quite disorientated by the powerful nature of the experiences that I was encountering, a phenomenon noted by Grof and Grof.[21] Numinous experiences are recognised as a potentially important variable in the ongoing development of a sense of 'I',[22] and Jung[23] acknowledged that such powerful encounters can make a person feel like they are in the grip of a force far greater than them. These deep transpersonal experiences can have a profound impact on identity through the processes that Washburn[24,25] has described as an ego-eclipsing dynamic reality. In short, these type of mystical encounters have the potential to take human beings to the limits of their conscious experience, otherwise known as a growing edge.[26] However, whilst the edge between the personal and the transpersonal spheres of experience may be seen as a border crossing that can reveal new knowledge,[27] spiritual emergencies can also push individuals 'over the edge'. Christopher Bache[28] stresses the importance of an autobiographical element in transpersonal philosophy, based on the notion that each person has to take their own transformational journey.

My experience included strong feelings of anxiety and agitation, and I made an appointment to see the resident Geshe at the monastery to explain what I was experiencing, and get some help. He recommended that I should not focus too much on the content of what was happening. Whilst my teacher's advice was true to the Buddhist spiritual teachings (detachment), the explanation lacked any psychological understanding of such experiences. On reflection I do not think he understood the complexity of spiritual crises, or indeed, knew what to do. I was frightened by the experience, confused, and at times angry. I had no prior knowledge of what Jung called the shadow; yet, this unconscious process was now fully manifest in my consciousness. I was flooded with intense emotions, I had no idea what was happening, nor any effective way of meta-communicating with the experience.[29] That is, I did not have the knowledge or the capacity (at the time) to work with my reactions to the inner and outer events that were taking place. In addition to the anxiety, agitation, physical symptoms and strange experiences that were happening to me, I started to feel revulsion at the iconography in the monastery, and became distressed at these reactions; more worryingly, I was psychologically and spiritually stuck and did not know what to do and how to be. I was in a mess, and any attempt at meditation or mindfulness just amplified my disturbance.

John Weir Perry[30] has said that when the human psyche encounters such powerful experiences, where the self is in a deep process of reorganisation, it is quite common for a negative self-image to be experienced. Furthermore, it is recognised that people can feel caught in a 'cosmic conflict', experienced as a battle of light and darkness, or chaos and order. This was certainly true for me. I often felt as if I were caught in a conflict between good and evil, where I experienced violent thoughts and projections. These extreme impulses, turmoil and panic would flood into me, and due to the profound nature of the experience I was not able to focus productively on my usual routines and interests in daily life. Eventually, I decided to leave the community and seek refuge in a less spiritually stimulating environment, away from the powerful mystical iconography, and away from people. I had been trying to carry on as usual, but the totality of the experiences I have outlined above became too much to manage. Grof and Grof[21] have asserted that in the acute phase of a spiritual emergency, all forms of dynamic inner exploration and spiritual practice should be ceased. The Grof's book was not published at this time, but thankfully I had done what they recommended. A friend of mine had a quiet house by the coast in North Wales, where I stayed during the most extreme part of the process. It was a time when I came quite close to contemplating suicide, due to the power of the experience being overwhelming and relentless. I could barely cope with this extreme state of consciousness, but somehow I managed to find a way through.

Encountering the numinous

It has been noted by Edinger[31] that mystical and numinous encounters can have a pulverising effect on people, and this was true of my experience. My confusion about the situation was compounded by feelings of fear and terror. I learnt an important lesson, that transcendent experiences are integral for catalysing meaningful transformation,[32] but I was totally unprepared for the chaos that was unleashed. Everything that I was experiencing appeared to be the antithesis of the mind training and study of spirituality that I had recently engaged in, and I had no idea what was going on. One of my saving graces was having made friends with an older psychologist from India, Arvind Patel, who had visited the Buddhist community. He had previously been in a very long and close working relationship with Krishnamurti, and he suggested that I try and let the process unfold naturally and to develop *choice-less awareness*, a term used by Krishnamurti,[33] which is explained by Wilber[34] as an action that is not driven by egocentric concerns. My friend's kindness, understanding, patience, warmth and caring attitude reassured me that what I was experiencing was a natural process, which needed to unfold in its own time. I am indebted to the compassion that he showed me. It was his attitude and insight that gave me the motivation and strength to work through the process. During this time I had very little contact with people, and save for a few trusted friends, told nobody about what I was experiencing. I found going through the process as best I could, alone, a highly complex ordeal. It must be pointed out that there was very little recognition of spiritual emergency in mainstream society in the early to mid-1980s. A participant in a study carried out by Caroline Brett[35] describes going through a transformative crisis, noting that the experience only gets worse if you try to resist it. Indeed, the process of integrating such profound shifts in consciousness reflects both a deep unfolding and a deep renewal of new modes of doing, knowing and being. Christina Grof[36] speaks about the journey of no return once a transformational journey has started. She suggests that this process is like taking a shirt out of its cellophane wrapping, which is impossible to put back in the same way, once it is out of the wrapper. Grof notes that our psycho-spiritual development is similar.

I was fortunate that in the UK in the 1980s it was possible to claim social security and also receive an accommodation allowance, with no pressure to get a job. It took me well over two years to work through the worst of the spiritual emergency and the aftermath of the psychological disturbance it had triggered in me, which I later understood was also connected to my early life experiences. During this period I led a very quiet life and I engaged in daily occupations that were quite therapeutic. For example, I took up watercolour painting, learnt to play a musical instrument, and did regular conservation work in nature, as well as cooking simple meals and self-care (doing). I kept any social relations to an absolute minimum, and especially avoided intimate relationships, preferring to concentrate my efforts on recovery, to try and integrate the experience into my daily life. I attempted to *do* something simple (and if possible meaningful) on a daily basis in order to help restore and renew my sense of *being*. At this time I had no theoretical training or understanding of how to manage such subtle processes of transformation. Rather, I lived intuitively and in hope that *all shall be well*, as the famous Norwich mystic from the Middle Ages, Mother Julian, often said. Yet, it remained a very difficult period, because I was taking a deep journey into the unknown, without a map. The only person who I spoke to about the experience in any depth was Arvind Patel. I felt blessed that I had the great good fortune to meet such a wise man. When I think about that period of my life I believe that he saved my life. We only met three times, but he gave me the strength to trust that I could get through the process.

The spiritual emergency had brought to the fore the fragility of my early ego development and attachments, as well as emotional disturbances experienced in childhood. This constellation of deep personal complexes needed working with. Much of my recovery and self-renewal involved understanding and re-evaluating strong emotions connected to my early life experiences. Clements[37] has commented on how spiritual growth often requires revisiting and working with unfinished psychological issues of earlier ego-developing levels, and this is certainly true in my experience. Indeed, dealing with psychological complexes can be a core part of the transformative process.[38] A part of what I was experiencing was a direct encounter with the personal shadow,[39] which reveals our disavowed or repressed experiences. Yet, the shadow also helps us to wake up to these unconscious processes in the psyche, and can be productive for developing authentic psycho-spiritual awareness.[40] Eventually, my experience and recovery through the spiritual emergency led me to want to use my personal experience and knowledge to benefit others, which became part of my interest in finding a vocation.

The process of renewal

In 1989 I studied for a diploma in health science, which then led to studying for a degree in occupational therapy. I worked in a variety of health contexts and eventually specialised in mental health work in an acute admissions unit, and also in an outpatient psychological therapy team. I was a formal student of process-oriented psychology from 1996 to 2005, which provided me with an extensive training for working with psycho-spiritual processes and interventions. This transpersonal training enabled me to work with the individuation process that arose from my numinous encounter with a spiritual emergency. In my experience, Jung[41] was correct when he said that it is pointless trying to get the upper hand when the numinous is encountered; we cannot conquer it. He goes on to say that our task is to open ourselves to the numinous, letting it overpower us and to trust the meaning that it brings into our lives. Indeed, it is through encounters with the numinous that we find our place in the cosmos.[42]

Since 1986 I have engaged in a life-changing journey of discovery and meaning. My long journey of self-renewal, from spiritual emergency to a transformative life path, has included becoming acclimatised to more subtle levels of consciousness, which have required attention and care, as noted by Bragdon.[43] Moreover, my autobiography illustrates how spiritual emergencies can directly lead to a deep search for meaning in life, and this coheres with my long-standing interest in spiritual development, which I incorporated into my professional life as a therapist. My own encounter with a spiritual emergency inspired me to find a meaningful vocation. Indeed, the experience has given me a more sophisticated understanding of the dynamic interplay between *doing* and *being*, which I have explored deeply both personally and professionally. I have seen how doing and being are complementary functions in the process of transformation from crisis to renewal.

My experience of a spiritual emergency has inspired and informed the core development of this book, which is focused on the transformative effects of engaging spiritual potential, and particularly the value of occupational engagement in life. It is through complex transitions such as spiritual emergencies that our orientation in life is challenged and changed. Spiritual emergencies are threshold experiences, particularly in the way that they challenge our ways of doing, knowing and being. However, the human potential contained in such encounters – from crisis to renewal – may not only be significant for individual transformation of consciousness, but also at a collective level. My own transformative journey through a spiritual emergency challenged my pre-existing habitual patterns of doing, knowing and being, as well as catalysing new ways of becoming and deepening my sense of belonging in the world, which set me on a course for new ways of engaging in life. The last three decades have been a healing journey for me. I have had to heal my own traumas from the past, I've contributed to the healing journeys of others and I've taken an interest in the environmental healing of the planet. In the last chapter I hope to share the deeper meaning of our collective healing path and how we are entering a global process of convergence, through spiritual emergence.

Exercise

- Look at all the various crises that you have gone through in your life.

- Be kind to yourself in the way that you recall these events and reflect on them. Try to take the view that you did the best you could to manage in these trying circumstances.

- Notice if there is a quality in your reflections, such as understanding that – whilst you may not have thought it at the time – you are strong, resilient, humble, wise or free, etc.

- Try and notice what has been your greatest learning from these crises.

To be a warrior of the soul is to be committed to a journey that is open to grace, endowed with humility, focused on living a full life and serving the whole.

CHAPTER FOURTEEN

We do, therefore we evolve

Overview

In this chapter I explore the personal and transpersonal meanings of transformation. I link to aspects of my own process of renewal through spiritual emergency, highlighting how significant breakthroughs in consciousness can lead to further engagement of our human potential. I discuss how the meaning found in such encounters touches into experiences of life as a mystery, which can open us up to a co-creative edge. Such creative encounters allow us to explore deeply our occupational potential. The chapter reveals the interface between creativity and occupational intelligence, and how the process of living our full potential to co-create a better world is a heroic act.

Individuation and collective transformation

The philosopher Mircea Eliade[1,2] said that one of the key problems of the modern era is the lack of myth and imagination, which has been accompanied by a diminishing interest in rites of passage that have deeper meaning.[3] I agree with Eliade, as my own experience of a spiritual crisis was a profound rite of passage and individuation, which I was ill-prepared to face. However, three decades on, and the process continues to unfold through the writing of this book. Indeed, it has become an integral part of my transformational journey. I published my first article on spirituality in 1998, but at that time I feared talking openly about my encounter, due mainly to the powerful nature of the experience and the possibility that the whole process could be misinterpreted as pathological (at the time I was working in acute psychiatry), or worse, trivialised altogether. It has taken me many years to put my spiritual crisis into context, and my position on this subject today is that the more people share their deep transformative experiences, the more we can be collectively inspired to work with shifts in consciousness and behaviours. I believe that spiritual emergencies are meaningful for both the individual and the collective.

James Hollis has spoken about the discovery of finding new perspectives in dismal places, and has noted that *going through* transformative processes provides new opportunities for how we view ourselves, with a new sense of imagination.[4] In addition Emma Bragdon[5] has considered the implications of psycho-spiritual development and notes that it includes dealing with our unprocessed personal psychology. By publishing an autobiographical account of my spiritual emergency in 2008, I was taking (in my view) a social activist position, which gave me the courage to *speak out*, as Dawn Menken[6] advocates. I believe the autobiography represented a significant step in my individuation process, which conveyed my authentic experiences and reflected the trust I had in my humanistic and transpersonal therapy trainings.

After the publication of my autobiography,[7] I gradually experienced a renewed sense of vocation. It freed my thinking about what spiritual emergencies mean in light of engaging human potential at a collective level. From this perspective, I developed an outlook that viewed spiritual emergencies as having a prospective function in the service of realising and expressing our transpersonal potential (individuation). In the afterword to her book on spiritual crisis Fransje de Waard[8] states that spiritual emergencies may result in a revolution in the way that we connect to new ideas for the way that we live.

In this book I have taken the view that a significant challenge for humanity is to recognise the transformative narratives of people who have already experienced and integrated encounters with spiritual emergencies. Thus, collective representations of spiritual emergencies could start to catalyse a deeper appreciation of the transformative value of spiritual crises in human experiences and consciousness. However, it is also my view that the collective response to changing our conscious outlook and behaviours will include a range of reactions, including denial, avoidance and unwillingness to face our global predicament. My own experience has taught me that any transition in consciousness is complex. Collective change may not happen in a uniform and linear way (indeed, collective transformation may not happen at all if we do not act). Yet, in the face of great challenges, humanity's recognition of the need for deep change could itself be the catalyst for an increase in spiritual emergencies. The key point, as mentioned by de Waard,[8] is that spiritual emergencies are powerful experiences in consciousness that strip us of our assumptions and challenge us to live differently.

This book has explored how sustainable transformations of consciousness and behaviours rely on the complementary functions of doing and being, in order to effect a deep transition collectively, which is focused on the creation of an improved future. I have witnessed the value of new ways of doing and being in my own transformational journey and with clients I have worked with as a therapist. I contend that new ways of doing, knowing and being will be pivotal in the transformation of consciousness, as we encounter the worst effects of the current global state of emergency. Roberto Assagioli[9] sums up the spirit of deep engagement in life when he suggests that transpersonal experiences can inspire humanitarian and social actions that are directed towards the greater good. This book reflects the view that the catalyst for social action may only come about when we are prepared to embrace the responsibility of engaging our full human potential, inclusive of spiritual emergence and spiritual emergency. Indeed, Skolimowski[10] informs us that our levels of social functioning (now and in the future) must first and foremost be cooperative and he notes that in order to be fully human we must connect with the spiritual.

Such a transformative undertaking is not an easy proposition, and spiritual emergencies are only the beginning of a deep process of change. It is through the journey of transformation that the actual work is done – in daily life – where we undertake the task of integration, which is linked to the complementary functions of reflection and action. There is no prescribed formula for integrating spiritual experiences into daily life as transformative phenomena; indeed, the journey is itself *a path that is made by walking*.[11] Yet, it has been my experience that the transpersonal nature of this unfolding journey in consciousness defies the usual milestones of worldly achievement, as succinctly expressed by Jiddu Krishnamurti,[12] who speaks about being a guest in this world of transience, where we are all interconnected, living in a reality that has no boundaries.

Living with mystery

My studies in mysticism, depth psychology and the science of human occupation continue to pose questions for me about how the act of doing creates tension between two aspects of reality. It contrasts conventional modes of existence, which favour an over-reliance on egocentric actions, versus mystical experiences, which reflect greater possibilities for connecting to processes of Self-realisation. From this perspective, the interface between the conventional world and mystical experience is akin to a *quantum conundrum* (where particles and waves are derived from one essence). In essence, the conventional world and mystical experience can co-exist, we do not have to invest in an either/or reality. If we accept this fluid representation of life, we are confronted with questions about the known world and the unknown; between I and the not-I; between doing and not-doing. When we awaken to the reality that we exist in a mystical flux of form and emptiness, it is comparable to the realisations of mystics, who know at a conventional level they exist, whilst recognising that at an ultimate level, they have no substantial existence at all.[13] If we ever need a more pertinent illustration of how emptiness works in our lives, just think about the phenomena of apoptosis, as discussed in chapter one. In about a decade from now there will be nothing left of you or me as we are today, as the cellular infrastructure underpinning our existence continues its dynamic unfolding through ongoing cell death and creation. Such is the reality of biological decay and regeneration within us, for the short time that we are alive in this world.

We are living representations of form and emptiness at a cellular level. There is nothing permanent about us, even though our modern one-sided view of the world may resist this notion. Since training as an occupational therapist, my interest has been to study how human occupations can lead to a deeper engagement and integration of our human potential, through everyday forms and functions, whilst remaining sensitive to the formlessness and fluidity in life as a sacred mystery. Here, doing mediates and grounds any shifts in consciousness, through the continuity of our occupational engagement, providing opportunities for cultivating greater awareness between the inner and outer spheres of life. Ram Dass[14] has discussed the dynamic creativity of human occupations, especially when they are linked to our conscious awareness and freedom from attachments. He says that whatever activities human beings do, they simply reveal how evolved our consciousness is.

The above words of Ram Dass are essentially a lifetime's work that involves cultivating awareness, between our ways of doing, knowing and being, which is the grist for the mill of our human potential. As I draw this book to a close, I am reminded of all the encouragement, help and inspiration I have received from others directly and indirectly. In this grateful moment of reflection I realise how much I have profited from the wise words in the transformative stories of other people, as well as my own experiences. Barbara Marx Hubbard[15] has discussed the conditions needed to encounter and sustain a journey of transformation, where we commit to change through regular practice of reflection and action. Yet, we must not forget the reason for engaging with and developing greater connection to the transpersonal and mystical path, which is summed up by Gilbert[13] as a way of serving in the world.

In the coming years it will take great courage for us all to engage in a journey of change and transformation to co-create an improved future, but such a transition can start today with the smallest acts in our everyday lives and routines. It does not matter whether we have a direct life-changing mystical encounter, or not. What is really important is that we trust, and have faith that at the deepest level we are connected to the world and all life, inseparably. We are stronger together, in the knowledge that we are capable of changing our values, attitudes and behaviours. And it is on this point that people's mystical encounters are testimonies to the closeness of the sacred dimension to our everyday lives, through which we can see intimations of an interconnected and indeterminate mystery. Maxwell and Tschundin[16] discuss a person in their study who found that their mystical experience led them to feel great empathy for all people. The person said that we are all in this life together.

The ongoing unfolding and expression of our transpersonal potential is much needed in the world today, not only for you and me, our families, other species and the planet as a whole, but also for future generations. Our commitment to transform our consciousness today and to be pioneers for new ways of doing, knowing and being is our legacy to this incredible world, which – it must be remembered – we are already *at one* with. It reminds us that we are only caretakers, not the owners of the earth. We need to consider carefully and collectively the qualities of the new myth we are going to create, one that is hopefully underpinned by the deep truth that *we are the world, and the world is us*. However, we must also remember that any new myth that we create requires that the vision is put into action.[17] Such an occupation-focused approach has been the hallmark of human innovation since the earliest of times: 'I do, therefore I evolve'.

Love and the co-creative edge

Our human ancestors evolved because our larger brains gave us the ability to analyse and associate, and develop social connectivity.[18] Human evolution also occurred through our abilities for innovation and creativity, as occupational beings. This enabled us to engage meaningfully and purposefully in life.[19] How we embrace a co-creative imperative for living at this crucial time in history is paramount. We are adept at adaptation. But the transformation required at this time is different from any previous epoch. This era will be defined by how well we make an inner adaptation, and change outwardly, in our relationship to ourselves, others and the planet as a whole. This will also depend on creating a new myth and vision for life.

Physicist David Bohm[20] speaks about the role of consciousness in helping human beings shift from living with the appearance of separateness (explicate order) to the realisation of an interconnected reality of life as a whole (implicate order). Collectively, we are heading towards the end of a materialist (and overly consumer-based) philosophy for determining meaning-in-life. We could view this changing orientation in worldview as problematic, particularly as the worst effects of climate change take hold, but in reality we are simply being forced to consider how our modern existence is unsustainable. If we reframe the crisis in the world as indicating an ecological challenge that requires a co-creative response, then we are in a better position to act in positive ways to support such a transition and transformation. Matthew Fox[21] believes that in their current forms, none of our modern institutions or professions are capable of helping, as they lack any real sense of creative understanding of our place in the cosmos. So what shall we do?

I believe that real change and transformation in the world will be connected to grassroots and bottom-up processes of social and spiritual activism. The real work will happen if each of us takes personal responsibility and joins with like-minded people to engage our transpersonal potential. Perhaps the most underrated, but also greatest, expression of our creative potential is reflected in how we engage in transforming our day-to-day existence in all the simple and complex ways in which we are occupied. The spirit of Rosa Parks springs to mind and how she took a stand against entrenched racism at a time of struggle for civil rights in the USA. She refused to give up her seat to a white man on a bus. Her peaceful defiance catalysed the US civil rights movement in new ways, inspiring Martin Luther King and others to be bolder in calling for change. The challenge for us at this time is to wake up to the unique gifts and capacities we possess as human beings and do something that inspires change. Sir Ken Robinson[22] says this includes using our imaginations, intuitions and intelligences. Yet, it will also take courage to bring to the fore our latent qualities and talents for creative living that expresses our human potential in terms of new awareness linked to our actions.[23] We also need to consider the place of love in our relationships and actions. Sam Mickey and Kimberly Carefore[24] identify love as a force for transforming contact between people, as well as inspiring people's contact with other species and nature as a whole. They suggest that our task is to love the planet and all who inhabit it.

When we look at this incredible world and indeed our own awesome potential, we realise that every day and every moment we have the opportunity to connect with something vibrant, sacred and creative in the pulse of life. Matthew Fox[21] asks what life would be like if we co-created with spirit. For me, this question is at the very heart of what it means to orientate ourselves to our deepest potential. Amy Mindell[25] puts it another way, she considers that we are living creations, and that there is an unknown force in life *dreaming us into being*. The question that is pertinent for all of us today is: how will we respond to the call of creative action in these troubled times? Will we respond to the state of the world as a nightmare that we want to avoid? Or, will we dare to dream of co-existing with others and nature in ways that enable deeper expression of our co-creative potential? Like our innovative ancestors, will we face the challenges before us and use them to transform our relationship to life as part of our evolutionary development? Or, will we deny what is happening and arrange another holiday, or go shopping with our friends? The game is up, and it is time for us – as a species – to front-up and do the right thing to make a better world. More than that, we need to consider our transformative potential to initiate deep change: 'I do, therefore I evolve'.

Throughout this book I have provided examples of creative change in people's lives, including my own. These illustrations reveal how people shifted their consciousness, and were inspired by spiritual experiences, dreams, encounters with the natural world and human relationships. I am suggesting that we are more than capable of meeting the challenge of change and transformation to co-create an improved future collectively. I have no doubt in our ability, but I am not so sure about what will catalyse our motivation to get started. Something needs to touch us deeply to make us effect such change, especially when on a day-to-day basis everything looks fine on the surface. But it isn't, and we need to be honest with each other about the global state of affairs, as well as inspiring each other to begin to reflect and act differently. The challenge of living creatively today is also to find ways to live more consciously and cooperatively. Sir Ken Robinson[22] says we have to imagine and develop a new focus for creating a greater purpose for humanity.

Such a creative purpose is to live our collective potential as an expression of wisdom, gratitude and compassion. Robert Sternberg[26] has considered how wisdom is not only about thought; it is also a way of doing things with creativity and intelligence. Most importantly this wisdom is an expression of a love for life. Psychologist Mihalyi Csikszentmihalyi[27] suggests that a creative life involves finding out about what we love to do in life, and then to make sure we go and do it. Our highest purpose is also activated when we view such creative endeavours from a collective vantage point, as intimated by Matthew Fox[21] who believes that our co-creative efforts enable us to express our love of life on a greater scale than previously imagined. And so, our co-creative task involves living a myth that envisions an interconnected whole, which enables us to enact our full potential, where we are empowered to support a journey of emancipation in connection with life's unfolding: it is a myth that guides us to a greater sense of wholeness.

To live authentically connects us with not only *what* we do, but also *how* we do the things we do.[28] In this way our doing has the potential to express love through what we are bringing forth in our lives. David Haberman[29] says without joy, love and care we will lack the motivation to do the right thing. The very scale of the task ahead is epic and heroic, but it was Joseph Campbell[30] who noted that to be heroic, one also has to be a warrior. To really make a difference at this time of global crisis, we have to shift from being *worriers* about the world that we have destroyed, and become *warriors* for the co-creation of a new world. Such an endeavour is the very essence of our occupational intelligence, that is, our ability to act to fulfil our deepest potential in life.[31] David Haberman[29] further reminds us about the need for love in action. The Greek word *agape* encapsulates the idea of communal love, where we seek to overcome differences and embrace diversity, whilst working together in a spirit of cooperation for the wellbeing of all. It is with such respect and consideration that we can tackle the challenges that lie ahead.

Warriors of the soul

To tackle the worst of the world's problems, we will need to dig deeper into what it means to be fully human. There are many examples of people who have taken a stand in times of adversity and acted as beacons for others. I would like to share three short examples of individuals who exemplified the courage and spirit that we are all capable of discovering in ourselves.

The first story is about Etty Hillesum, a young bright woman in her late twenties who lived in Amsterdam during World War II. Etty's life took a transformative turn when she entered into therapy with a Jungian analyst, with whom she had a deep positive connection, coupled with powerful erotic transferences. Through her psychotherapy sessions Etty gradually worked on issues connected to her family, her anxieties and depression, as well as her budding self-awareness, yet she also started to discover a connection to her spiritual life when her therapist introduced her to religious texts. Although Etty was Jewish, she had never formally engaged in Judaism within her family or in the Synagogue. This new discovery of her psycho-spiritual potential was amplified in the heat of Nazi oppression, which escalated in intensity during the years 1941-2, when Jewish people (and other groups) experienced increasingly degrading and brutal treatment. Etty refused to hate the Nazis, despite knowing that deportation to death camps was already happening. She found it within herself not to stoop to the same depths of hatred as her persecutors. Her inspirational psycho-spiritual journey is recorded in her published journals, revealing how she actively worked to retain a spiritual focus in daily life and refused to live dominated by fear. Patrick Woodhouse[32] has written an inspirational book about her and says that her disciplined inner life was based on her openness and vulnerability to the sacred, which helped her in her determination not to hate the Nazi oppressors.

Etty worked with her fears activated by what she experienced in the concentration camp and she continually transformed her reactions as part of her spiritual practice. She reflected on the many aspects of human suffering in her diary. She writes about how the causes of suffering can come through tyrants like Hitler and Stalin, or other persecutors. Or, she mentions that suffering can come through ecological disasters. Etty realised that in such circumstances it is important to cope with the pain and also to preserve the soul.[32] She reminds us of the importance of doing our inner work, for Etty does not only anticipate pain coming from the hands of human oppressors, but also acknowledges that environmental catastrophe requires the same inner preparation and fortitude if we are to be transformed through our actions in the face of such challenges. Her words are a timely reminder of the need for such psycho-spiritual development at this time of ecological degradation. Etty's inspirational soul journey embodies a central theme outlined in this book, particularly because she furthered her spiritual development and awareness through doing and being. She was not consumed with fear or trivial thoughts, despite the turmoil wrought by the Nazis. Indeed, she connected her spiritual journey to her actions and in doing so she lived her short life to the full.[33]

Woodhouse notes that Etty's spiritual direction revealed to her a secret, that good or bad, all life is interconnected. However, it is clear that Etty was deeply impacted by all the suffering she witnessed, meted out by Nazis on weakened and defenceless people, but she never lost connection to a spiritual core that enabled her to put the needs of others before herself, nor did she ever lose sight of nature's beauty, often marvelling at the colour of the lupins just outside the barbed wired perimeter of the concentration camp. Three months before her own death, Etty wrote about the many miracles to be discovered in a human life, yet it is in her diaries that we find the depth of her spiritual strength. She wrote down her reflections about whether she would survive the concentration camp, or not. Yet, even in this despicable situation Etty found a source of inspirational strength when she wrote that if she should find herself facing death, she would observe how she meets her last moments, and this will reveal who she really is.[32] Etty died in Auschwitz on 30 November 1943 at the hands of the Nazis.[32] Every time I reflect on this young woman's words I am deeply moved. This is not only sadness for the terror we are capable of inflicting on one another, but also feelings of gratitude. This humble and feisty woman was truly a warrior of the soul and her sacred actions continue to reverberate throughout time, revealing a great truth about spiritual practice, that is, it continues to grow the more we put it into action.

Another deeply inspiring story occurred in 1992 in the midst of the war in Bosnia. One day Vedran Smailovic, a cellist who played in the Sarajevo Opera Theatre, was looking out of his apartment window, and he noticed a queue of hungry people lined up outside a bakery in the hope of getting bread. This particular bakery was the only place in the city that had enough flour to bake bread. Vedran then witnessed 22 people being blown to pieces by shell fire. Joan Chittister[34] tells us that the next day Vedran dressed up in his black suit and tie, and took his cello and a chair down to the bakery. Amidst the carnage of war and despite the risk to his own life, Vedran played Albinoni's *Adagio* every day for 21 days. His music conveyed a profound message of hope and beauty in a world of carnage and misery. It also resonated with a powerful sense of defiance, not to surrender to those who were intent on committing barbarous acts.[34]

Etty and Vedran reveal the courage to enact a deeply graceful response to life, despite the most desperate circumstances. They show us what is possible if we hold tight to the spirit. Joan Chittister[34] reminds us that human beings are magnificent and possess a spirit that is irrepressible. Indeed, when we connect with that spirit of vitality our actions are indomitable, and they reveal more about human potential than can be formulated in words or ideas. Who cannot be moved by the memory of a brave young Chinese man obstructing tanks in Tiananmen Square, Beijing? It is up to us to be inspired and cultivate spirit into action if we are to bring about new ways of living in the world, based on respect for all life. Yet, it takes courage to break out of the status quo and do differently. Woodhouse[32] points out that spiritual development emerges through practice and effort, as in the case of Etty Hillesum who aimed to live artistically, making creativity her spirituality and her prayer.[32]

Not only is it through doing that we are transformed, but our deepening journey of awareness connects us to myths of renewal, as noted by Etty when she wrote about the archetypes of the Titans, who she imagined were working inside of her, bringing forth a new outlook in the world. [32] And so, to be a warrior of the soul at this time in human history is also to live mythically and this means that we can become warriors of the *anima mundi*, the soul of the world, for there is no separation at a soul level between the individual and the whole. It means that the shift from ego self-identification to eco-Self relations is an all-encompassing perspective of honouring unity within diversity. Joanna Macy[35] says that our expanded sense of ecological self has to include all life on Earth. This means that we must begin to enhance greater possibilities in our human purpose through tackling occupational deprivation,[36,37] thereby liberating people from oppression, so that we are all able to contribute our talents and passions to co-create a just and fair world for all.[38] If we care about the future of the planet and all its inhabitants, we need to reframe our ideas about what we are capable of doing in terms of harnessing our human and transformational potential. This is based on a deep understanding: 'I do, therefore I evolve', which is actually a precursor for a greater shift in human evolution. It is through our collective ability to re-align our human purpose towards the co-creation of an improved future – together – that we discover the true gift of our ancestral human heritage: *we do, therefore we evolve.*

Exercise

- In order to co-create an improved future we will need to shift from being worriers about the state of the world, to becoming warriors for deep change and transformation.

- Consider the journey of your life to date and think about it from the perspective of being a warrior. What kind of warrior have you been, or are becoming?

  - o Social activist
  - o Spiritual warrior
  - o Warrior of the heart
  - o Political activist
  - o Mystical warrior
  - o Eco warrior
  - o Or use your own description

- Notice where you feel that sense of the warrior in your daily life – notice the quality of its lived engagement, and its energy.

- Notice where in your body you experience this warrior energy, then consider the following:

  - o Is it outwardly expressed and dynamic?
  - o Is it inwardly contained and concentrated?
  - o Is it cool and detached?
  - o Is it hot and engaged?

- Now, let this warrior energy radiate throughout your whole body.

- Once you feel this warrior energy throughout your whole body, imagine that energy moving out, beyond your body, and see how it connects to the world.

- Imagine this warrior energy as a force in nature. What is it co-creating? How is it connected in the service of creating an improved future?

- How could this warrior energy connect with other activists to make a difference in the world?

Reflection and action are the seeds of emancipation,
how much more so if we join together with others
to co-create an improved future.

AFTERWORD

Doing the work –
being transformed

Throughout this book I have argued the case for a change in consciousness, but the shift that I have proposed is not an adjustment within the existing boundaries of our one-dimensional, consumer-based existence. On the contrary, I have drawn on the work of Carl Jung, Stanislav and Christina Grof, as well as other transpersonal practitioners such as Arnold and Amy Mindell, who have recognised the need for a greater alignment between the ego and the Self, where the ego functions in the service of a wider and deeper transpersonal reality. However, I have also pointed out that such an undertaking will be a complex process, particularly as our modern industrialised consciousness and our material, consumer-based societies have resulted in a form of arrested development, giving us a skewed understanding of our place in the cosmos.

Our one-dimensional, ego-orientated and technologically-driven worldview has obscured the extent to which we have collectively dissociated from the natural world, which is our *one and only* life support system. This denial and lack of respect for the earth as a spiritual home for ourselves and countless other species will be reflected back to us, through worsening ecological conditions as well as impacting on our health and wellbeing. The forces of nature, revealed through increasing patterns of ecological destruction, open us up to the numinous mystery and power in life, over which we have little control. Yet, we can work with nature, and adapt to deal with the ecological mess that threatens us. Arnold Mindell[1] reminds us that the numinous is at the core of a community, and this highly significant observation should not only awaken us to our collective potential, but also inspire us to realise our mystical connection with all life. From this perspective we can work through our differences, and start to believe in a unifying vision for how we are all interconnected, and how we can live together more harmoniously, whilst also caring for the world.

I have outlined in this book how the act of co-creation is also a mystical path, a path we are creating as we walk it. There is no map or blueprint that will show us how to collectively create an improved future. Indeed, the only thing that we can rely on is our rich human heritage of wisdom, intelligence and creativity to take the next evolutionary step. We can begin by just simply knowing that we are connected to the world in innumerable ways. Then, as a species, we can do what we are good at: draw upon our evolutionary human heritage and begin to adapt and co-create a better world for all. If we truly believe that we can grow through the global crisis we are facing, then like the epic myths throughout all cultures in human history, not only will we be rediscovering our fullest potential, we will be living closer to the transformative nature that makes up this universe of which we are a part. Then, our ways of doing, knowing, being, becoming and belonging are in tune with the flow of life's wholeness.

In the world today it is up to all of us to reflect and act in ways that transcend the limitations of our current destructive behaviours collectively. We will be heading into uncharted territory, yet we have an opportunity to discover new expressions of our magnificent connection to life. I believe we can do it. We have enormous, unmet potential as human beings, which must be recognised, if we are to change and transform. Sir Ken Robinson[2] has noted that we need to inspire ourselves and others to use our talents and abilities beyond our usual and habitual ways of engaging in life. We will also need to tap our deepest reserves of motivation to act and make sustainable changes. I am reminded of the words of Martin Luther King, when he spoke for equality and liberty during the American civil rights marches: *I have a dream*. These words continue to echo throughout time because they resonate with the possibility of connecting to a new vision for a better world. It is now time we shared our dreams and worked together to co-create an improved future.

In the Preface of this book, Professor Tim O'Riordan writes about *preparing humanity for a damaged planet*. We have to steel ourselves to face the consequences of the ecological changes brought about by our collective actions. However, a central message in this book focuses on how humanity can prepare for an improved future. It suggests that we are capable of adapting and working for the greater good. We can start engaging a process of transformation as follows:

- Believing in our full human potential.
- Connecting with other agents of transformation.
- Listening to, and working with, our dreams.
- Being inspired by the natural world.
- Making a difference in the ways we live in our homes and communities.
- Engaging our talents and passions to co-create a better world.

The process of transformation is about making a commitment to reflect, act and transform. I would like to draw this book to a close with an inspiring story about the mother of Rachel Remen,[3] a medical doctor, who asked her mother what she would like to do for her 80th birthday. Her mother, who had lived most of her life in New York, replied that she would like to go to the top of the Statue of Liberty, something she had never done. She then announced her wish to take the stairs to the top. Despite her mother's heart condition and the 342 steps to the top of the statue, Rachel agreed to support her mother's wish, albeit she did reflect on how she had got into this situation. But she also knew her mother's will of iron. It is interesting to note that the Statue of Liberty is a symbol of freedom. Remen reflects on her mother's six hour, step-by-step climb to the top of the statue, and considers the symbolic value of such a feat, to the journeys we can all take in life. She notes that we are all capable of accomplishing great things in unique and achievable ways. She speaks about the symbolic meaning of her mother's climb, which includes having the freedom to break from limitations or expectations (imposed by self or other), even if it takes a few steps at a time. What an inspiration. It shows the power of motivation and determination when we are moved to act, to do something meaningful in our lives.

In this book I have outlined how the next frontier for human purpose is the emancipation of the human imagination, which reflects and acts in accord with the wisdom, compassion and intelligence of our full potential. If we all take small steps to make a better world, helping one another in our areas of influence, at home, in our local communities and at work, we are then able to live closer to our true nature, where we are more intimately connected to life as a whole. The central question at this pivotal point in history is *will we do it?* At this moment in time no one knows. Yet, for all those who are willing to begin this transformative journey, we need to hold on to the truth of our human heritage, that is, what we do in this world together for the greater good can contribute to the evolution of an improved future. This process of collective awakening is the very future of spiritual practice in the world. Indeed, the following idea expressed by Mahatma Gandhi is a fitting conclusion to the idea expressed in this book: that through action and doing we could address the majority of problems experienced in the world.[4]

Exercise

- Recall a time when you had a deep sense or experience of the mystery in life.

- What were you doing at the time?

- What part of that experience do you remember most?

- How did you reflect on the experience?

  o Has the experience enabled you to connect more deeply to life?
  o Have you considered that daily life could be a sacrament?
  o Has anything changed in your ways of doing or being as a result of that experience?

- If this experience has taught you one thing to appreciate about life beyond consensus reality and material existence, what is it?

- How does this experience inform the way you relate to others and nature?

Glossary

Archetypes (Jungian): The archetypes manifest through images and symbols (as in dreams and fantasies), which are intuitions or intimations of a greater archetypal reality that cannot be experienced in its entirety, but can be found (symbolically) across cultures, for example in myths that have heroic or wise figures. Jungian archetypes are viewed as original patterns or behaviours, as represented in the example of a bird building a nest, which remains structurally consistent with the techniques used by the same species of birds, without ever having been shown how to construct such a nest.

Archetypal occupations: The individuating human being will inevitably have to encounter what Jung described as the transcendent function, where the ego bears the tensions of meeting unconscious material. Archetypal occupations reflect deep levels of human reflection and action, where the meaning found in unconscious material (e.g. symbols, dreams, symptoms) is able to be expressed and integrated in everyday activities or projects. These deep actions (doing) provide a transitional function in relation to new ways of being in daily life with transpersonal significance.

Enantiodromia: An ancient Greek term (from Heraclitus) that reflects a natural flow to an opposite position, especially when a situation has become too one-sided.

Individuation: A term used by Jung to capture the psycho-spiritual growth and development of individuals who are working with and integrating material from the unconscious (via dreams, symbols, symptoms, conflicts, and relationships).

Kundalini: An experience that can occur as a result of regular meditation practice (and sometimes spontaneously). Within Indo-Buddhist philosophy Kundalini is referred to as the 'serpent power', which is a process that occurs when meditation practice results in a rising of energy from the base of the spine to the crown of the head. The raising of Kundalini reflects an awakening of the feminine energy; Shakti, which unites with the masculine energy; Shiva for the purposes of enlightenment. Physical signs of Kundalini include subtle vibrations throughout the body, disorientated thoughts and bodily sensations of heat and cold.

Meta-communication: A person's ability to track and process a range of experiences, such as thoughts, feelings and intuitions, without becoming lost, unbalanced or fixated on one part of the process. Meta-communication could be regarded as a well-developed level of reflexive awareness, e.g., having awareness of awareness.

Numinous: The word numinous is derived from the Latin *numen*, which refers to the sacred and divine. The numinous was used by theologian Rudolph Otto in his landmark book *The Idea of the Holy*, which proposed a more holistic view of the sacred as being both beatific and wrathful. Carl Jung integrated the numinous into his psychology of individuation.

Occupational intelligence: The engagement of multi-channelled capacities in human beings (visual, auditory, kinesthetic, feeling/emotional, olfactory, gustatory and relational), which are directed towards life goals. Occupational intelligence reflects the full potential and expression of people's psycho-spiritual potential (self-actualisation or individuation) through doing.

Occupational science: An academic discipline (social science) that is focused on exploring the purpose and value of occupations (doing) in relation to human potential (being, becoming and belonging). Occupational science considers the diverse ways that people live across different cultures, taking account of occupational form (and performance), function and meaning.

Occupational therapy: A profession that uses occupations (doing) as a therapeutic medium. Occupational therapists consider human beings from a holistic perspective, taking account of physical, psychological, social, cultural, political and spiritual considerations in therapeutic practice. Occupations encompass three broad areas: (1) productivity, such as paid employment (or voluntary work) and education; (2) self-care, which can include personal hygiene, grooming and dress, or lifestyle choices that impact upon wellbeing, for example in relation to diet and exercise; (3) leisure pursuits can include hobbies, interests, social events and so on. Occupational therapy encourages and supports people to express themselves in terms of engaging and maintaining their independent functioning, whilst meeting challenges and making adaptations.

Self: The self with a lower case 's' reflects *personal* experiences that are connected to ego, identity and personality. The Self with an upper case 'S' reflects a more *transpersonal* level of experience (as noted by Jung), where a person (through the process of individuation) connects to a wider experience of consciousness, life and the cosmos.

Temenos: Where a context or experience becomes invested with a sense of the sacred. The spiritual atmosphere of a *temenos* can influence the attitudes of people within it.

Transcendence: The interpretation used in this book suggests that the process is connected to a movement beyond ego-consciousness. That is, our transcendent potential leads to greater connections with the cosmos, and a transpersonal reality.

Transpersonal: Humanistic psychology's interest in human potential (inclusive of spirituality) resulted in the emergence of transpersonal psychology, which aimed to study those experiences that are encountered through or beyond (trans) the individual ego. Classically, the transpersonal position embraces experiences of non-ordinary states of consciousness and does not consider them anomalous.

References

Preface

1. Lenton, T., & Watson, A. (2011). *Revolutions that made the Earth*. Oxford: Oxford University Press.
2. Rockstrom, J., & Klum, M. (2012). *The human quest: Prospering within planetary boundaries*. Stockholm: Langenskiolds.
3. Federation of Red Cross and Red Crescent Societies (2013). *Think differently: Humanitarian impacts of the economic crisis in Europe*. Geneva.
4. Organisation for Economic Cooperation and Development (2013). *Survey of adult skills*. Paris.

Foreword by the Author

1. Harvey, F. (2013). Just 30 years to calamity if we carry on blowing the carbon budget, says IPCC. *The Guardian*, Saturday 28th September, 17.
2. Harland, M., & Keepin, W. (2012). Introduction. In *Song of the earth: A synthesis of the scientific and spiritual worldviews*, eds M. Harland & W. Keepin, xi-xiv. East Meon, Hants: Permanent Publications.
3. Emmott, S. (2013). It took 200,000 years for the population to reach one billion. Now our numbers increase by a billion every decade. *The Observer*, Sunday 30th June, 8-11.
4. Vidal, J. (2013). Global threat to food supply as water wells dry up, warns top environmental expert. *The Observer*, Sunday 7th July, 23.
5. Brooks, M. (2013). Frack to the future. *New Scientist, 219*(2929), 36-41.
6. Goldenberg, S. (2013). 'Dear God help us...' How drought and fracking left Texas town without water. *The Guardian*, Monday 12th August, 3.
7. Bradley, I. (2012). *Water: A spiritual history*. London: Bloomsbury.
8. DEFRA, (2013). *The National adaptation programme: Making the country resilient to a changing climate*. Retrieved 21st August 2013, from www.gov.uk/defra.
9. Helm, T. (2013). Osbourne's cuts shape the economy – and the role of the state too. *The Observer*, Sunday 23rd June, 22.
10. Tacey, D. (2011). *Gods and diseases: Making sense of our physical and mental well-being*. London: Routledge.
11. McKie, R. (2014). Global warming 'to hit Asia hardest'. *The Observer*, Sunday 23rd March, I & 9.
12. Goldenberg, S. (2014). Vision of the future: Poor and marginalized are least to blame but will suffer the most. *The Guardian*, Monday 31st March, 7.
13. Monbiot, G. (2014). So which bit of the world are you prepared to lose? *The Guardian*, Tuesday 1st April, 29.
14. Iwama, M. (2006). *The Kawa model: Culturally relevant occupational therapy*. Edinburgh: Churchill Livingstone.
15. Whittaker, B. (2012). Sustainable global wellbeing: A proposed expansion of the occupational therapy paradigm. *British Journal of Occupational Therapy, 75*(9), 436-9.
16. Wagman, P. (2014). The model of human occupation's usefulness in relation to sustainable development. *British Journal of Occupational Therapy, 77*(3), 165-7.
17. Hollick, M. (2006). *The science of oneness: A worldview for the twenty-first century*. Winchester: O Books.
18. West, W. (2011). Practice around therapy, spirituality and healing. In *Exploring therapy, spirituality and healing*, ed W. West, 214-23. Basingstoke, Hants: Palgrave Macmillan.

Introduction

1. Cox, B., & Cohen, A. (2013). *Wonders of life*. London: Harper Collins.
2. Darwin, C. (2010). *Evolutionary writings*. Oxford: Oxford University Press.
3. Loye, D. (2004). Darwin, Maslow, and the fully human theory of evolution. In *The great adventure: Toward a fully human theory of evolution*, ed D. Loye, 20-36. Albany,NY: State University of New York Press.
4. Loye, D. (2004). Introduction. In *The great adventure: Toward a fully human theory of evolution*, ed D. Loye, 1-17. Albany, NY. State University of New York Press.
5. Loye, D. (2010). *Darwin's lost theory: Bridge to a better world*. Carmel, CA: Benjamin Franklin Press.
6. Berry, T. (1995). The viable human. In *Deep ecology for the 21st century*, ed G. Sessions, 8-18. Boston, MA: Shambhala.
7. May, R.M. (1991). *Cosmic consciousness revisited: The modern origins and development of a western spiritual psychology*. Rockport, MA: Element.
8. James, W. (1902/1982). *Varieties of religious experience*. New York: The Modern Library.
9. Brunton, P. (1952/1970). *The spiritual crisis of man*. London: Rider and Company.
10. Swimme, B. (1996). *The hidden heart of the cosmos: Humanity and the new story*. Maryknoll, NY: Orbis Books.
11. Penrose, R. (1994). *Shadows of the mind: A search for the missing science of consciousness*. London: Vintage.
12. Globus, G. (1995). *The postmodern brain*. Amsterdam: John Benjamins Publishing Company

13. Van Lommel, P. (2013). Non-local consciousness: A concept based on scientific research on near-death experiences during cardiac arrest. *Journal of Consciousness Studies, 20*(1/2), 7-48.

14. Combs, A., & Krippner, S. (2008). Collective consciousness and the social brain. *Journal of Consciousness Studies, 15*(10/11), 264-76.

15. Blackmore, S. (2005). *Conversations on consciousness*. Oxford: Oxford University Press.

16. Macy, J., & Johnstone, C. (2012). The great turning. In *Song of the earth: A synthesis of the scientific and spiritual worldviews*, eds M. Harland & W. Keepin, 93-8. East Meon, Hants: Permanent Publications.

17. Brunton, P. (1937/1972). *The quest for the overself*. London: Rider and Company.

18. Berry, T. (1999). *The great work: Our way into the future*. New York: Random House.

19. Lenton, T., & Watson, A. (2011). *Revolutions that made the earth*. Oxford: Oxford University Press.

20. Lukoff, D. (2010). Foreword. In F. de Waard. *Spiritual crisis: Varieties and perspectives of a transpersonal phenomenon*. Exeter: Academic Imprint.

Chapter one

1. Gewies, A. (2003). *Introduction to apoptosis*. Retrieved 25th September 2012, from www.celldeath.de/encyclo/aporev.htm.

2. Chopra, D. (2004). *The book of secrets*. London: Rider.

3. Levine, S. (1997). *A year to live: How to live this year as if it were your last*. London: Thorsons.

4. Lipton, B. (2005). *The biology of belief*. Santa Rosa, CA: Elite Books.

5. Chopra, D. (2009). *Reinventing the body, rediscovering the soul*. London: Rider.

6. Maturana, H., & Poerksen, B. (2004). *From being to doing: The origins of the biology of cognition*.Trans, Koeck, W., Koeck A. Heidelberg: Carl-Auer Verlag.

7. Maturana, H., & Varela, F. (1980). *Autopoiesis and cognition: The realization of the living*. Trans, Cohen, R., Wartofsky, M. Dordrecht, Holland: Kluwer Academic Publishers Group. 74-5.

8. Capra, F. (1996). *The web of life: A new synthesis of mind and matter*. London: Harper Collins.

9. Capra, F. (2002). *The hidden connections: A science for sustainable living*. London: Harper Collins.

10. Niesser, A. (2004). Neuroscience and Jung's model of the psyche: A close fit. IAAP Congress, Barcelona. Retrieved March 25th 2013, from http://iaap.org/Congress/Barcelona-2004/neuroscience-and-jung's-model-of-the-psyche.

11. Dobbs, D. (2006). A revealing reflection. *Scientific American Mind, 17*(2), 22-7.

12. Maturana, H., & Varela, F. (1998). *The tree of knowledge: The biological roots of human understanding*. Boston: Shambhala.

13. Rose, S. (1997). *Lifelines: Biology, freedom, determinism*. London: Penguin Books.

14. Bronowski, J. (1973). *The ascent of man*. London: British Broadcasting Corporation.

15. Yerxa, E. J. (2000). Occupational science: A renaissance of service to humankind through knowledge. *Occupational Therapy International, 7*(2), 87-98.

16. Roberts, A. (2011). *Evolution: The human story*. London: Dorling Kindersley.

17. Oubré, A. (1997). *Instinct and revelation: Reflections on the origins of numinous perception*. London: Taylor and Francis.

18. Winkelman, M. (1993). The evolution of consciousness? Transpersonal theories in light of cultural relativism. *Anthropology of Consciousness, 4*(3), 3-9.

19. McKie, R. (2012). When Homo sapiens hit upon the power of art. *The Observer*. Sunday 9th December, 22-3.

20. Tallis, R. (2004). *I AM: A philosophical inquiry into first-person being*. Edinburgh: Edinburgh University Press.

21. Bateson, G. (1991). *Sacred unity: Further steps to an ecology of mind*. New York: Harper Collins.

22. Mickey, S., & Carefore, K. (2012). Planetary love: Ecofeminist perspectives on globalization. *World Futures, 68*(2), 122-31.

23. Zemke, R. (1996). Bain, mind, and meaning. In *Occupational science: The evolving discipline*, eds R, Zemke., F. Clark, 163-70. Philadelphia: F.A. Davis Company.

24. Blackmore, S. (2005). *Conversations on consciousness*. Oxford: Oxford University Press.

25. Westerhoff, J. (2013). What are you? *New Scientist, 2905*, 34-7.

26. Blackmore, S. (2009). *Zen and the art of consciousness*. Oxford: Oneworld.

27. Edelman, G.M., & Tononi, G. (2000). *Consciousness: How matter becomes imagination*. London: Penguin Books.

28. Nicol, M. (1952) *Living time*. London: Vincent Stuart.

29. Vaughan-Lee, L. (2012). *Prayer of the heart in Christian and Sufi mysticism*. Point Reyes, CA: The Golden Sufi Centre.

30. Griffiths, B. (2003). *Return to the centre*. Tuscon, AZ: Medio Media.

31. Kidder, A.M.S. (2009). *Etty Hillesum: Essential writings*. MaryKnoll, NY: Orbis Books.

Chapter two

1. Lipton, B. (2005). *The biology of belief*. Santa Rosa, CA: Elite Books.

2. Washburn, M. (2012). Rethinking the notion of ego. *Journal of Consciousness Studies, 19*(3/4), 194-222.

3. Erikson, E.H. (1959/1980). *Identity and the life cycle*. New York: W.W. Norton & Company.

4. Marcia, J.E. (1966). Development and validation of ego-identity status. *Journal of Personality and Social Psychology, 3*(5), 551-58.

5. Sollod, R. N., Wilson, J.P., & Monte, C.F. (2009). *Beneath the mask: An introduction to the theories of personality*. Hoboken, NJ: John Wiley & Sons, Inc, 8th edition.

6. Erikson, E.H., & Erikson, J.M. (1997). *The life cycle completed*. New York: W.W. Norton & Company.

7. Glover, J. (1988). *I: The philosophy and psychology of personal identity*. London: Penguin Books.

8. Lancaster, B. L. (1991*). Mind, brain, and human potential: The quest for an understanding of self*. Shaftesbury: Element.

9. Klein, J. (1988). *Who am I?: The sacred quest*. Shaftesbury: Element Books.

10. Cox, L.M., & Lyddon, W.J. (1997). Constructivist conceptions of self: A discussion of emerging identity constructs. *Journal of Constructivist Psychology, 10*, 201-19.

11. Kiesling, C., Sorell, G.T., Montgomery, MJ., & Colwell, R.K. (2006). Identity and spirituality: A psychosocial exploration of the sense of spiritual self. *Developmental Psychology, 42*(6), 1269-77.

12. Mautner, T. (1997). *Dictionary of philosophy*. London: Penguin Books.

13. Combs, A., & Krippner, S. (2003). Process, structure, and form: An evolutionary transpersonal psychology of consciousness. *International Journal of Transpersonal Studies, 22*, 47-60.

14. Walsh, R., & Vaughan, F. (2005). On transpersonal definitions. In *Transpersonal psychology: Meaning and development*s, eds D. Fontana, I. Slack & M. Treacy, 51-6. Transpersonal Psychology Review: Special Edition: The British Psychological Society.

15. Palmer, G., & Braud, W. (2002). Exceptional human experiences, disclosure, and a more inclusive view of physical, psychological, and spiritual well-being. *Journal of Transpersonal Psychology, 34*(1), 29-61.

16. Vaughan, F. (1985). Discovering transpersonal identity. *Journal of Humanistic Psychology, 25*(3), 13-38.

17. Jung, C.G. (1954/1993). *The practice of psychotherapy*. London: Routledge.

18. Le Grice, K. (2010). *The archetypal cosmos: Rediscovering the gods in myth, science and astrology*. Edinburgh: Floris Books.

19. Corbett, L (2007). *Psyche and the sacred: Spirituality beyond religion*. New Orleans: Spring Journal Books.

20. Assagioli, R. (1991). *Transpersonal development: The dimension beyond psychosynthesis*. London: Crucible.

21. Ferrer, J.N. (2008). Spiritual knowing as participatory enaction: An answer to the question of religious pluralism. In *The participatory turn: Spirituality, mysticism, religious studies*, eds J.N. Ferrer & J.H. Sherman, 135-169. Albany, NY: State University of New York Press.

22. Sherman, J.H. (2008). A genealogy of participation. In *The participatory turn: Spirituality, mysticism, religious studies*, eds J.N. Ferrer & J.H. Sherman, 81-112. Albany, NY: State University of New York Press.

23. Frosh, S. (1991). *Identity crisis: Modernity, psychoanalysis and the self*. Basingstoke: Macmillan.

24. Johnson, R.A. (1991). *Transformation*. New York: Harper Collins.

25. Perry, J.W. (1953/1987). *The self in psychotic process: Its symbolism in schizophrenia*. Dallas, TEX: Spring Publications.

26. Kelly, S. (1993). *Individuation and the absolute: Hegel, Jung and the path toward wholeness*. New York: Paulist Press.

27. Maslow, A.H. (1970). *Religions, values and peak experiences*. New York: Viking Press.

28. Maslow, A.H. (1971). *The farther reaches of human nature*. Harmondsworth: Penguin.

29. Scharfstein, B.A. (1973). *Mystical experience*. Oxford: Basil Blackwell.

30. Grof, S., & Grof, C. (1989). *Spiritual emergency: When personal transformation becomes a crisis*. Los Angeles: Jeremy P. Tarcher.

31. Collins, M. (2008). Spiritual emergency: Transpersonal, personal, and political dimensions. *Psychotherapy and Politics International, 6*(1), 3-16.

32. Pawle, R. (2009). The ego in the psychology of Zen: Understanding reports of Japanese Zen masters on the experience of no-self. In *Self and no-self: Continuing the dialogue between Buddhism and psychotherapy*, eds D. Mathers, M.E. Miller & O. Ando, 45-55. London: Routledge.

33. Gunn, R.J. (2000). *Journeys into emptiness: Dogen, Merton, Jung and the quest for transformation*. New York: Paulist Press.

34. Wallace, G. (2009). Dying to be born: Transformative surrender within analytical psychology from a clinician's perspective. In *Self and no-self: Continuing the dialogue between Buddhism and psychotherapy*, eds D. Mathers, M.E. Miller & O. Ando, 143-52. London: Routledge.

35. Burnham, S. (1997). *The ecstatic journey: The transforming power of mystical experience*. New York: Ballentine Books.

36. Wilber, K. (1981). *No boundary: Eastern and western approaches to personal growth*. Boulder, CO: Shambhala.

37. Wilber, K. (1998). *The essential Ken Wilber: An introductory reader*. Boston: Shambhala.

38. Bache, C.M. (2000). *Dark night, early dawn: Steps to a deep ecology of mind*. Albany, NY: State University of New York Press.

39. Bulkley, K. (1991). The quest for transformative experience: Dreams and environmental ethics. *Environmental Ethics, 13*, 151-63.

40. Korton, D.C. (2007). Two stories – conflicting visions of the human possible. In *Mind before matter: Visions of a new science of consciousness*, eds T. Pfieffer, J.E. Mack & P. Devereux, 128-39. Winchester: O Books.

41. do Rozario, L. (1997). Shifting paradigms:

The transpersonal dimensions of ecology and occupation. *Journal of Occupational Science, 4*(3): 112-18.

42. Sinetar, M. (1986). *Ordinary people as monks and mystics: Lifestyles for self-discovery.* New York: Paulist Press.

43. Laszlo, E. (1999). Consciousness, creativity, responsibility. In *Wider horizons: Explorations in science and human experience,* eds D. Lorimer, C. Clarke, J. Cosh, M. Payne & A. Mayne, 323-7. Leven, Fife: The Scientific and Medical Network.

44. Sutich, A. (1976). The emergence of the transpersonal orientation: A personal account. *Journal of Transpersonal Psychology, 8*(1), 5-19.

45. Arons, M. (1999). Abraham Maslow: Yesterday, tomorrow, and yesteryear. In *Humanistic and transpersonal psychology: A historical and biographical source book,* ed D. Moss, 334-46. Westport, CO: Greenwood Press.

46. Papadopoulos, R.K. (1991a). Introduction. In *Jung in modern perspective: The master and his legacy,* eds R.K. Papadopoulos & G.S. Saayman, 1-3. Bridport: Prism Press.

47. Halling, S., & Carroll, A. (1999). Existential–phenomenological psychology. In *Humanistic and transpersonal psychology: A historical and biographical source book,* ed D. Moss, 93-124. Westport, CO: Greenwood Press.

48. Westland, G. (1978). *Current crises of psychology.* London: Heinemann.

49. Hamilton, V. (1973). Psychology in society: End or ends? *Bulletin of the British Psychological Society,* 25, 93-100.

50. Fromm, E. (1968). *The revolution of hope: Toward a humanized technology.* New York: Harper and Row.

51. Metzner, R. (2008). *The expansion of consciousness.* Berkeley, CA: Green Earth Foundation/Regent Books.

52. Frankl, V. (1978). *The unheard cry for meaning: Psychotherapy and humanism.* London: Hodder and Stoughton.

53. Frankl, V. (1962). *Man's search for meaning: An introduction to logotherapy.* London: Hodder and Stoughton.

54. Graham, H. (1986). *The human face of psychology: Humanistic psychology in its historical, social, and cultural context.* Milton Keynes: Open University Press.

55. Moss, D. (1999). Abraham Maslow and the emergence of humanistic psychology. In *Humanistic and transpersonal psychology: A historical and biographical source book,* ed D. Moss, 24-35. Westport, CO: Greenwood Press.

56. Moss, D. (1999). The historical and cultural context of humanistic psychology: Ike, Annette, and Elvis. In *Humanistic and transpersonal psychology: A historical and biographical source book,* ed D. Moss, 7-11. Westport, CO: Greenwood Press.

57. Marcuse, H. (1964/1991). *One-dimensional man.* London: Routledge, 2nd edition.

58. Tillich, P. (1952). *The courage to be.* London: The Fontana Library.

59. Watts, A. (1966). *The book on the taboo against knowing who you are.* London: Abacus.

60. Rogers, C.R. (1961). *On becoming a person: A therapist's view of psychotherapy.* London: Constable & Company.

61. Thorne, B. (1996). Person centred therapy. In *Handbook of individual therapy,* ed W. Dryden, 121-46. London: Sage Books.

62. Rice, D. (1999) Carl Rogers: Client heal thyself. In *Humanistic and transpersonal psychology: A historical and biographical source book,* ed D. Moss, 385-93. Westport, CO: Greenwood Press.

63. Reason, P., & Rowan, J. (1981). *Human inquiry: A source book of new paradigm research.* Chichester. John Wiley and Sons.

64. Rowan, J. (1981). The psychology of science by Abraham Maslow: An appreciation. In *Human inquiry: A source book of new paradigm research,* eds P. Reason & J. Rowan, 83-91. Chichester. John Wiley and Sons.

65. Taylor, E. (2009). *The mystery of personality: A history of psychodynamic theories.* Dordrecht, Heidelberg: Springer.

66. May, R.M. (1991). *Cosmic consciousness revisited: The modern origins and development of a western spiritual psychology.* Rockport, MA: Element.

67. Frankl, V. (1967). *Psychotherapy and existentialism: Selected papers on logotherapy.* Harmondsworth: Penguin Books.

68. Maslow, A.H. (1968/1999). *Toward a psychology of being.* New York: John Wiley and Sons, 3rd edition.

69. Battista, J.R. (1996). Abraham Maslow and Robert Assagioli: Pioneers of transpersonal psychology. In *Textbook of transpersonal psychiatry and psychology,* eds B.W. Scotton, A.B. Chinen & J.R. Battista, 52-61. New York: Basic Books.

70. Fromm, E. (1968). *The revolution of hope: Toward a humanized technology.* New York: Harper and Row.

71. Burston, D. (1999). Erich Fromm: Humanistic psychoanalysis. In *Humanistic and transpersonal psychology: A historical and biographical source book,* ed D. Moss, 276-86. Westport, CO: Greenwood Press.

72. Rogers, C.R. (1980). *A way of being.* Boston: Houghton Mifflin.

73. Yerxa, E. J. (1998). Health and the human spirit for occupation. *American Journal of Occupational Therapy, 52*(6), 412-18.

74. Collins, M. (2006). Unfolding spirituality: Working with and beyond definitions. *International Journal of Therapy and Rehabilitation, 13*(6), 254-8.

75. Loye, D. (2004). Darwin, Maslow, and the fully human theory of evolution. In *The great adventure: Toward a fully human theory of evolution,* ed D. Loye, 20-36. Albany, NY: State University of New York Press.

76. Taylor, S. (2011). *Out of the darkness: From turmoil to transformation.* London: Hay House.

77. Mack, J.E. (2007). Why worldviews matter. In *Mind before matter: Visions of a new science of consciousness*, eds T. Pfieffer, J.E. Mack & P. Devereux, 1-2. Winchester: O Books.

78. Brenner, M. (2011). 3rd wave: Discovering the nature of me. In *Conscious connectivity: Creating dignity in conversation*, ed M. Brenner, 65-92. Charleston, SC: Pan American.

79. Wilcock, A.A. (1998). Reflections on doing, being and becoming. *Canadian Journal of Occupational Therapy, 65*(5), 248-56.

80. Moss, D. (1999). The continuing need for a humanistic and transpersonal psychology. In *Humanistic and transpersonal psychology: A historical and biographical source book*, ed D. Moss, 211-26. Westport, CO: Greenwood Press.

81. Collins, M. (2001). Who is occupied? Consciousness, self-awareness and the process of human adaptation. *Journal of Occupational Science, 8*(1), 25-32.

82. Clarke, I. (2001/2010). Psychosis and spirituality: The discontinuity model. In *Psychosis and spirituality: Consolidating the new paradigm*, ed I. Clarke, 101-14. Chichester: Wiley-Blackwell, 2nd edition.

83. Bragdon, E. (1990). *The call of spiritual emergency: From personal crisis to personal transformation*. San Francisco: Harper Row Publishers.

84. Webster, R. (2005). Personal identity: Moving beyond essence. *International Journal of Children's Spirituality, 10*(1), 5-16.

85. Perry, J.W. (1999). *Trials of a visionary mind: Spiritual emergency and the renewal process*. Albany, NY: State University of New York.

86. Kasprow, C. M., & Scotton, W. B. (1999). A review of transpersonal theory and its application to the practice of psychotherapy. *The Journal of Psychotherapy Practice and Research, 8*(1), 12-23.

87. Washburn, M. (1990). Two patterns of transcendence. *Journal of Humanistic Psychology, 30*(3), 84-112.

88. Grof, S. (1987). Psychodynamic factors in depression and psychosis: Observations from modern consciousness research. In *Pathologies of the modern self*, ed D. M. Levin, 439-78. New York: New York University Press.

89. Reich, K.H. (2001). Spiritual development: Han De Wit's and Stanislav Grof's differing approaches. *Zygon, 36*(3), 509-20.

90. Fahlberg, L.L., Wolfer, J., & Fahlberg L.A. (1992). Personal crisis: Growth or pathology. *American Journal of Health Promotion, 7*(1), 45-52.

91. Laszlo, E (2010). The world's health problem: An integral diagnosis. In *A new renaissance: Transforming science, spirit and society*, eds D. Lorimer & O. Robinson, 17-33. Edinburgh: Floris Books.

92. Kason, Y. (1994/2008). *Farther shores: Exploring how near-death, Kundalini and mystical experiences can transform ordinary lives*. Bloomington, IN: iUniverse.

93. Laszlo, E., Grof, S., & Russell, P. (2003). *The consciousness revolution*. London: Elf Rock.

94. Griffiths, B. (2003). *Return to the centre*. Tuscon, AZ: Medio Media.

95. Tacey, D. (2012). *The Jung reader*. London: Routledge.

96. Neumann, E. (1954). *The origins and history of consciousness*. New York: Bollingen Foundation and Pantheon Books.

97. Skolimowski, H. (1993). *A sacred place to dwell: Living with reverence upon the earth*. Rockport, MA: Element.

98. Chopra, D. (2004). *The book of secrets*. London: Rider.

Chapter three

1. Neumann, E. (1954). *The origins and history of consciousness*. New York: Bollingen Foundation and Pantheon Books.

2. Marcuse, H. (1964/1991). *One-dimensional man*. London: Routledge, 2nd edition.

3. Marx-Hubbard, B. (2012). *Emergence: The shift from ego to essence*. San Francisco, CA: Hampton Roads.

4. Chopra, D. (2004). *The book of secrets*. London: Rider.

5. Griffiths, B. (2003). *Return to the centre*. Tuscon, AZ: Medio Media.

6. East, M. (2012). The dual origin of the universe. In *Song of the earth: A synthesis of the scientific and spiritual worldviews*, eds M. Harland & W. Keepin, 36-40. East Meon, Hants: Permanent Publications.

7. Myss, C. (2007). *Entering the castle: An inner path to god and your soul*. New York: Free Press.

8. Kihlstrom, J.F., Barnhardt, T.M., & Tataryn, D.J. (1992). The psychological unconscious: Found, lost, and regained. *American Psychologist, 47*(6), 788-91.

9. Frey-Rohn, L. (1974). *From Freud to Jung: A comparative study of the psychology of the unconscious*. New York: C.G. Jung Foundation for Analytical Psychology.

10. McGuire, W. (1974). *The Freud/Jung letters*. Translated R. Manheim and R.F.C. Hull. London: Picador.

11. Rosen, D. (1996). *The tao of Jung: The way of integrity*. New York: Arkana.

12. Jung, C.G. (2009). *The red book: Liber novus*, ed S. Shamdasani. New York: W.W. Norton & Company.

13. Haule, J.R. (2011). *Jung in the 21st century: Volume 1. Evolution and archetype*. Hove: Routledge.

14. Hollis, J. (2009). *What matters most: Living a more considered life*. New York: Gotham Books.

15. Progoff, I. (1973). *Jung's psychology and its social meaning*. New York: Anchor books.

16. Gunn, R.J. (2000). *Journeys into emptiness: Dogen, Merton, Jung and the quest for transformation*. New York: Paulist Press.

17. Hannah, B. (1981/2001). *Encounters with the soul: Active imagination as developed by C.G. Jung*. Wilmette, IL: Chiron Publications.

18. Drury, N. (2004). *The new age: Searching for the spiritual self*. London: Thames and Hudson.

19. Le Grice, K. (2009). The birth of a new discipline: Archetypal cosmology in historical perspective. *Archai: The Journal of Archetypal Cosmology, 1*(1), 2-22.

20. Greenwood, S. (1990). Émile Durkheim and C.G. Jung: Structuring a transpersonal sociology of religion. *Journal for the Scientific Study of Religion, 29*(4), 482-95.

21. Bache, C.M. (2000). *Dark night, early dawn: Steps to a deep ecology of mind*. Albany, NY: State University of New York Press.

22. Lukoff, D. (2010). Foreword. In F. de Waard. *Spiritual crisis: Varieties and perspectives of a transpersonal phenomenon*. Exeter: Academic Imprint.

23. Von Franz, M.L. (1976). Foreword. In *Jung and politics: The political and social ideas of C.G. Jung*, ed V.W. Odajynk, ix-xii. New York: New York University Press.

24. Tarnas, R. (2009). Archetypal principles. *Archai: The Journal of Archetypal Cosmology, 1*(1), 23-35.

25. Main, R. (2007). *Revelations of chance: Synchronicity as spiritual experience*. Albany, NY: State University of New York Press.

26. White, V. (1960). *God and the unconscious: An encounter between psychology and religion*. London: Fontana Books.

27. Campbell, J. (1991). *Primitive mythology: The masks of god*. London: Arkana.

28. Campbell, J. (1991). *Creative mythology: The masks of god*. London: Arkana.

29. Taylor, E. (2009). *The mystery of personality: A history of psychodynamic theories*. Dordrecht, Heidelberg: Springer.

30. Saunders, P., & Skar, P. (2001). Archetypes, complexes and self-organization. *Journal of Analytical Psychology, 46*, 305-23.

31. Stevens, A., & Price, J. (2000). *Evolutionary psychiatry: A new beginning*. London: Routledge.

32. Mindell, A. (1990). *Dreambody: The body's role in revealing the self*. London: Arkana.

33. Pietikainen, P. (1998). Archetypes as symbolic forms. *Journal of Analytical Psychology, 43*, 325-45.

34. Rosen, D.H., Smith, S.M., Huston, H.L., & Gonzalez, G. (1991). Empirical study of associations between symbols and their meanings: Evidence of collective unconscious (archetypal) memory. *Journal of Analytical Psychology, 36*(2), 211-28.

35. Sharp, D. (1991), *C.G. Jung lexicon: A primer of terms and concepts*. Toronto: Inner City Books.

36. Jung, C. G. (1964). *Man and his symbols*. London: Aldus Books Ltd.

37. Progoff, I. (1987). *Jung, synchronicity and human destiny: C G Jung's theory of meaningful coincidence*. New York: Julian Press.

38. Haule, J.R. (2011). *Jung in the 21ˢᵗ century: Volume 2. Synchronicity and science*. Hove: Routledge.

39. Corbett, L (2007). *Psyche and the sacred: Spirituality beyond religion*. New Orleans: Spring Journal Books.

40. Grof, S. (2001). Non-ordinary states of consciousness: Healing and heuristic potential. In *Thinking beyond the brain: A wider science of consciousness*, ed D. Lorimer, 151-68. Edinburgh: Floris Books.

41. Mindell, A. (1987). *The dreambody in relationships*. London: Arkana.

42. Mindell, A. (2001). *The dreammaker's apprentice: Using heightened states of consciousness to interpret dreams*. Charlottesville, VA. Hampton Roads Publishing Company.

43. Tacey, D. (2012). *The Jung reader*. London: Routledge.

44. Tarnas, R. (2006). Understanding the modern disenchantment of the cosmos In *Sky and Psyche: The relationship between cosmos and consciousness*, eds N. Campion & P. Curry, 183-99. Edinburgh: Floris Books.

45. Storr, A. (1983). *The essential Jung: Selected writings*. London: Fontana Press.

46. Robertson, R. (1995). *Jungian archetypes: Jung, Godel, and the history of archetypes*. York Beach, ME: Nicolas-Hays.

47. Samuels, A., Shorter, B., & Plaut, F. (1986). *A critical dictionary of Jungian analysis*. London: Routledge & Kegan Paul.

48. Campbell, J. (1948). *The hero with a thousand faces*. New York: Bollingen Fondation/ Pantheon Books.

49. Holloway, R. (2013). The word to grasp here is myth. *New Statesman*, 22-28ᵗʰ March, 31.

50. Rebillot, P. (1989). The hero's journey: Ritualizing the mystery. In *Spiritual emergency: When personal transformation becomes a crisis*, eds S. Grof & C. Grof, 211-24. Los Angeles: Jeremy P. Tarcher.

51. Feinstein, D. (1997). Personal mythology and psychotherapy: Myth making in psychotherapy and spiritual development. *American Journal of Orthopsychiatry, 64*(4), 508-21.

52. Larsen, S. (1990/1996). *The mythic imagination: The quest for meaning through personal mythology*. Rochester, VER: Inner Traditions International.

53. de Bus, D. (1991). The self is a moving target: The archetype of individuation. In *Mirrors of the self: Archetypal images that shape your life*, ed C. Downing, 53-62. Los Angeles: Jeremy P. Tarcher.

54. Grof, S. (2009). Evidence for the Akashic field from modern consciousness research. In *The Akashic experience: Science and the cosmic memory field*, ed E. Laszlo,193-211. Rochester, VER: Inner Traditions.

55. Skolimowski, H. (1993). *A sacred place to dwell: Living with reverence upon the earth*. Rockport, MA: Element.

56. Vickers, G. (1983). *Human systems are different*. London: Harper Row.

57. Jung, C.G. (1945). *Modern man in search of a soul*, translated W.S. Dell., and C.F. Baynes. London: Kegan Paul, Trench, Trubner & Co.

58. Grof, S (2012). Science and spirituality: Observations from modern consciousness research. In *The new science and spirituality reader*, eds E. Laszlo & K.L. Dennis, 48-51. Rochester, VER: Inner Traditions.

59. Collins, M. (2006). Unfolding spirituality: Working with and beyond definitions. *International Journal of Therapy and Rehabilitation, 13*(6), 254-8.

60. Le Guin, U. Cited in, Bellamy, J. (1998). Spiritual values in a secular age. In *The spiritual challenge of healthcare*, eds M. Cobb & V. Robshaw, 183-198. Edinburgh: Churchill Livingstone.

Chapter four

1. Casement, A., & Tacey, D. (2006). Preface. In *The idea of the numinous: Contemporary and psychoanalytic perspectives*, eds A. Casement & D. Tacey, xvi-xvii. London: Routledge.

2. Otto, R. (1923/1958). *The idea of the holy: An inquiry into the non-rational factor in the idea of the divine and its relation to the rational*. Oxford: Oxford University Press.

3. Coxhead, N. (1985). *The relevance of bliss: A contemporary exploration of mystical experience*. London: Wildwood House.

4. Hardy, A. (1979). *The spiritual nature of man: A study of contemporary religious experience*. Oxford: Clarendon Press.

5. Hick, J. (2004). *The fifth dimension: An exploration of the spiritual realm*. Oxford: Oneworld Publications.

6. Stein, M. (2006). On the importance of numinous experience in the alchemy of individuation. In *The idea of the numinous: Contemporary and psychoanalytic perspectives*, eds A. Casement & D. Tacey, 34-52. London: Routledge.

7. Hardy, A. (1966). *The divine flame: Natural history and religion*. London: Collins.

8. Smart, N. (1996). *Dimensions of the sacred: An anatomy of the world's beliefs*. London: Harper Collins Publishers.

9. Jung, C.G. (1972). Letter to P. W. Martin. Letters, Volume 1. Princeton University Press. Cited in C. Dunne, *Carl Jung: Wounded healer of the soul*. London: Continuum (2000).

10. Pratt, V. (1970). *Religion and secularisation*. London: Macmillan.

11. Collins, M. (2008). Spiritual emergency: Transpersonal, personal, and political dimensions. *Psychotherapy and Politics International, 6*(1), 3-16.

12. Dunne, C. (2000). *Carl Jung: Wounded healer of the soul*. London: Continuum.

13. Hollis, J. (2003). *In this journey we call life: Living the questions*. Toronto: Inner City Books.

14. Elkins, D.N. (1998). *Beyond religion: A personal program for building a spiritual life outside the walls of traditional religion*. Wheaton, IL: Quest Books, The Theosophical Publishing House.

15. Elam, J. (2005). Soul's sanctuary: Mystical experiences as a way of knowing. In *Ways of knowing: Science and mysticism today*, ed C. Clarke, 50-66. Exeter: Imprint Academic.

16. Collins, M. (2008). Politics and the numinous: Evolution, spiritual emergency, and the re-emergence of transpersonal consciousness. *Psychotherapy and Politics International, 6*(3), 198-211.

17. Collins, M. (2010). Engaging transcendent actualisation through occupational intelligence. *Journal of Occupational Science 17*(3),177-86.

18. Moore, T. (1996). *The re-enchantment of everyday life*. New York: Harper Collins.

19. Jung, C.G. (1961). Cited in, E. Edinger (1986). *Encounter with the self*. Toronto: Inner City Books.

20. Schoen, D. (1998). *Divine tempest: The hurricane as a psychic phenomenon*. Toronto: Inner City Books.

21. Hexham, I., & Poewe, K. (1997). *New religions as global cultures: Making the human sacred*. Oxford: Westview Press.

22. Watts, A. (1966). *The book on the taboo against knowing who you are*. London: Abacus.

23. Erikson, E.H. (1996). The Galilean sayings and the sense of I. *Psychoanalysis and Contemporary Thought, 19*(2), 291-337.

24. Larsen, S. (1990/1996). *The mythic imagination: The quest for meaning through personal mythology*. Rochester, VER: Inner Traditions International.

25. Monick, E. (1987). *Phallos: Sacred image of the masculine*. Toronto: Inner City Books.

26. Maslow, A.H. (1968/1999). *Toward a psychology of being*. New York: John Wiley and Sons, 3rd edition.

27. Allen, M., & Sabini, M. Renewal of the Sacred Tree. (1997). In *The sacred heritage: The influence of shamanism on analytical psychology*, eds D. Sander & S. Wong, 215-25. London: Routledge.

28. Jäger, W. 1995. *Search for the meaning of life. Essays and reflections on the mystical experience*. Ligouri, Missouri: Triumph Books.

29. Bancroft, A. (1991). *The spiritual journey*. Rockport, MA: Element Books.

30. Moore, T. (2004). *Dark nights of the soul*. London: Piatkus.

31. Merkur, D. (1999). *Mystical moments and unitive thinking*. Albany, NY: State University of New York Press.

32. Collins, M. (2010). Global crisis and transformation; From spiritual emergency to spiritual intelligence. *Network Review: Journal of the Scientific and Medical Network*, 103, 17-20.

33. Oubré, A. (1997). *Instinct and revelation: Reflections on the origins of numinous perception*. London: Taylor and Francis.

34. Von Essen, C. (2007). *The hunter's trance: Nature, spirit and ecology*. Great Barrington, MA: Lindisfarne Books.

35. Burkert, W. (1996). *Creation of the sacred: Tracks of biology in early religions*. Cambridge, MA: Harvard University Press.

36. Nelson, K. (2011). *The god impulse: Is religion hard wired into the brain?* London: Simon & Schuster.

37. Beauregard, M., & O'Leary, D. (2007). *The spiritual brain: A neuroscientist's case for the existence of the soul.* New York: Harper Collins.

38. d'Aquili, E., & Newberg, A.B. (1999). *The mystical mind: probing the biology of religious experience.* Minneapolis: Fortress press.

39. Foster, C. (1989). *Wired for God?: The biology of spiritual experience.* London: Hodder and Stoughton.

40. Palmer, J.A., & Palmer, K.L. (2002). *Evolutionary psychology: The ultimate origins of human behaviour.* Boston, MA: Allyn & Bacon.

41. Hardy, A. (1965). *The living stream: Evolution and man.* London: Collins.

42. Walsh, R. (2001). Shamanic experiences: A developmental analysis. *Journal of Humanistic Psychology, 41*(3), 31-52.

43. Eliade, M. (1964/1989). *Shamanism: Archaic techniques of ecstasy.* London: Arkana.

44. Walsh, R. (2007). *The World of shamanism: New views of an ancient tradition.* Woodbury, MIN: Llewellyn Publications.

45. Joseph, R. (2001). The limbic system and the soul: Evolution and the neuroanatomy of religious experience. *Zygon, 36*(1), 105-36.

46. Lancaster, B.L. (2004). *Approaches to consciousness: The marriage of science and mysticism.* Basingstoke: Palgrave MacMillan.

47. Newberg, A.B. (2001). Putting the mystical mind together. *Zygon, 36*(3), 501-7.

48. Holmes, R. (1996). Homo religiousus and its brain: Reality, imagination, and the future of nature. *Zygon, 31*(3), 441-55.

49. Ashbrook, B. (1997). "Mind" as humanizing the brain: Toward a neurotheology of meaning. *Zygon, 32*(3), 301-320.

50. Claxton, G. (1999). Neurotheology: Buddhism, cognitive science and mystical experience. In *The psychology of awakening: Buddhism, science and our day-to-day lives,* eds G. Watson, S. Batchelor & G. Claxton, 90-111. London: Rider.

51. Newberg, A.B. (2001). Putting the mystical mind together. *Zygon, 36*(3), 501-7.

52. Myss, C. (2007). *Entering the castle: An inner path to god and your soul.* New York: Free Press.

53. Austin, J.H. (1998). *Zen and the brain.* Cambridge, MA: The MIT Press.

54. Teske, J. (2006). Neuromythology: Brains and stories. *Zygon, 41*(4), 169-196.

55. Campbell, J. (1991). *Primitive mythology: The masks of god.* London: Arkana.

56. Winkelman, M. (1993). The evolution of consciousness? Transpersonal theories in light of cultural relativism. *Anthropology of Consciousness, 4*(3), 3-9.

57. Winkelman, M. (2002). Shamanism as neurotheology and evolutionary psychology. *American Behaviour Scientist, 14*(12), 1875-87.

58. Winkelman, M. (2004). Shamanism as the original neurotheology. *Zygon, 39*(10, 193-217.

59. Neumann, E. (1954). *The origins and history of consciousness.* New York: Bollingen Foundation and Pantheon Books.

60. Haule, J.R. (2011). *Jung in the 21ˢᵗ century: Volume 2. Synchronicity and science.* Hove: Routledge.

61. De Gruchy, J.W. (1991). Jung and religion: A theological assessment. In *Jung in modern perspective: The master and his legacy,* eds R.K. Papadopoulos & G.S. Saayman, 193-203. Bridport: Prism Press.

62. Yandell, K.E. (1993). *The epistemology of religious experience.* Cambridge: Cambridge University Press.

63. Corbett, L (2007). *Psyche and the sacred: Spirituality beyond religion.* New Orleans: Spring Journal Books.

64. Groesbeck, C.J. (1997). C.G.Jung and the shaman's vision. In *The sacred heritage: The influence of shamanism on analytical psychology,* eds D.F. Sander & S.H. Wong, 29-43. New York: Routledge.

65. Ryan, R.E. (2002). *Shamanism and the psychology of C.G. Jung.* London: Vega.

66. Grof, S. (2000). *Psychology of the future: Lessons from modern consciousness research.* Albany, NY: State University of New York Press.

67. Mindell, A. (2000). *Dreaming while awake.* Charlottesville, VA: Hampton Roads Publishing.

68. Hollenback, J.R. (1996). *Mysticism: Experience, response, and empowerment.* Pennsylvania: The Pennsylvania State University.

69. Mindell, A. (2000). *Quantum mind: The edge between physics and psychology.* Portland, OR: Lao Tse Press.

70. Samuels, A. (1993). *The political psyche.* London: Routledge.

71. Bache, C.M. (2000). *Dark night, early dawn: Steps to a deep ecology of mind.* Albany, NY: State University of New York Press.

72. Main, R. (2006). Numinosity and terror: Jung's psychological revision of Otto as an aid to engaging religious fundamentalism. In *The idea of the numinous: Contemporary and psychoanalytic perspectives,* eds A. Casement & D. Tacey, 153-70. London: Routledge.

73. Huskinson, L. (2006). Holy, holy, holy: The misappropriation of the numinous in Jung. In *The idea of the numinous: Contemporary and psychoanalytic perspectives,* eds A. Casement & D. Tacey, 200-12. London: Routledge.

74. Shamdasani, S. (2012). *C.G. Jung: A biography in books.* New York: WW Norton & Company.

75. Tacey, D. (2006). The role of the numinous in the reception of Jung. In *The idea of the numinous: Contemporary and psychoanalytic perspectives,* eds A. Casement & D. Tacey, 213-28. London: Routledge.

76. Eliade, M. (1959). *The sacred and the profane: The nature of religion.* San Diego: Harcourt Brace Jovanovich.

77. Collins, M. (2007). Spiritual emergency and occupational identity: A transpersonal perspective. *British Journal of Occupational Therapy, 70*(12), 504-12.

78. Whitney, E. (1998). Mania as spiritual emergency. *Psychiatric Services, 49*(12): 1547-8.
79. Tacey, D. (2011). *Gods and diseases: Making sense of our physical and mental well-being*. London: Routledge.

Chapter five

1. Eliade, M. (1978). *A history of religious ideas: From the stone age to the Eleusinian mysteries, volume 1*, translated by W.R. Trask. Chicago: University of Chicago Press.
2. Eliade, M. (1982). *A history of religious ideas: From Gautama Buddha to the triumph of Christianity, volume 2*, translated by W.R. Trask. Chicago: University of Chicago Press.
3. Eliade, M. (1985). *A history of religious ideas: From Muhammad to the age of reforms, volume 3*, translated by W.R. Trask. Chicago: University of Chicago Press.
4. Eliade, M. (1959). *The sacred and the profane: The nature of religion*. San Diego: Harcourt Brace Jovanovich
5. Armstrong, K. (2006). *The great transformation*. London: Atlantic Books.
6. Vaughan, F., & Walsh, R. (1998). Technology of transcendence. In *Inner knowing: Consciousness, creativity, insight, intuition*, ed H. Palmer, 24-30. New York: Jeremy P. Tarcher/Putnam.
7. Eliade, M. (1964/1989). *Shamanism: Archaic techniques of ecstasy*. London: Arkana.
8. Hopkins, J. (1984). *The tantric distinction*. Boston: Wisdom.
9. Yeshe, L. (1987). *Introduction to tantra: A vision of totality*. Boston: Wisdom.
10. Schimmel, A. (2007). The ritual of rebirth in the inner journey. In *The inner journey: Views from the Islamic tradition*, ed W.C. Chittick, 287-90. Standpoint, ID: Morning Light Press.
11. Burckhardt, T. (2008). *Introduction to Sufi doctrine*. Bloomington, IND: World Wisdom.
12. Keating, T. (2001). *The divine indwelling: Centering prayer and its development*. New York: Lantern Books.
13. Freeman, L. (2000). *Jesus: The teacher within*. London: Continuum.
14. Jäger, W. 1995. *Search for the meaning of life. Essays and reflections on the mystical experience*. Ligouri, Missouri: Triumph Books.
15. Fox, M. (2002). *Creativity: Where the divine and the human meet*. New York: Jeremy P. Tarcher.
16. Otto, R. (1923/1958). *The idea of the holy: An inquiry into the non-rational factor in the idea of the divine and its relation to the rational*. Oxford: Oxford University Press.
17. Starr, M. (2002). *Dark night of the soul: Saint John of the cross*. New York: Riverhead Books.
18. Moore, T. (2004). *Dark nights of the soul*. Piatkus. London.
19. Storr, A. (1997). Commentary on "spiritual experience and psychopathology." *Philosophy, Psychiatry, Psychology, 41*(1), 83-5.
20. Jones, K. (1993). *The poems of Saint John of the cross*. Tunbridge Wells: Burns and Oates.
21. Dourley, J. (1987). *Love celibacy and the inner marriage*. Inner City Books. Toronto.
22. Jung, C. G. (1954/2002). *Answer to Job*. London: Routledge & Kegan Paul.
23. Laszlo, E. (1999). Consciousness, creativity, responsibility. In *Wider horizons: Explorations in science and human experience*, eds D. Lorimer, C. Clarke, J. Cosh, M. Payne & A. Mayne, 323-7. Leven, Fife: The Scientific and Medical Network.
24. Vallejo-Nágera, M. (2003). *Un mensajero en la noche*. Barcelona: Belacqva.
25. Jung, C. G. (1964). *Man and his symbols*. London: Aldus Books Ltd.
26. Elam, J. (2005). Soul's sanctuary: Mystical experiences as a way of knowing. In *Ways of knowing: Science and mysticism today*, ed C. Clarke, 50-66. Exeter: Imprint Academic.
27. De Gruchy, J.W. (1991). Jung and religion: A theological assessment. In *Jung in modern perspective: The master and his legacy*, eds R.K. Papadopoulos & G.S. Saayman, 193-203. Bridport: Prism Press.
28. Tacey, D. (2012). *The Jung reader*. London: Routledge.
29. Kelsey, M.T. (1991). Jung as philosopher and theologian. In *Jung in modern perspective: The master and his legacy*, eds R.K. Papadopoulos & G.S. Saayman, 182-92. Bridport: Prism Press.
30. De Voogd, S. (1991). Fantasy versus fiction: Jung's Kantianism appraised. In *Jung in modern perspective: The master and his legacy*, eds R.K. Papadopoulos & G.S. Saayman, 204-28. Bridport: Prism Press.
31. Mc Gilchrist, I. (2009). *The master and his emissary: The divided brain and the making of the western world*. New Haven: Yale University Press.
32. Appleyard, B. (2011). *The brain is wider than the sky*. London: Weidenfeld & Nicolson.
33. Chopra, D. (2009). *Reinventing the body, rediscovering the soul*. London: Rider.
34. Collins, M., Hughes, W., & Samuels, A. (2010). The politics of transformation in the global crisis: How spiritual emergencies may be reflecting an enantiodromia in modern consciousness. *Psychotherapy and Politics International, 8*(2), 162-176.
35. Marcuse, H. (1964/1991). *One-dimensional man*. London: Routledge, 2nd edition.
36. Herman, E.S. & Chomsky, N. (1994). *Manufacturing consent: The political economy of mass media*. London: Vintage.
37. Skolimowski, H. (1993). *A sacred place to dwell: Living with reverence upon the earth*. Rockport, MA: Element.
38. Sheets-Johnstone, M. (2008). On the hazards of being a stranger to oneself. *Psychotherapy and Politics International, 6*(1): 17-29.
39. Hollis, J. (1995). *Tracking the gods: The place of myth in modern life*. Inner City Books. Toronto.
40. Vesey, G., & Foulkes, P. (1990). *Unwin Hyman dictionary of philosophy*. Harper Collins: Glasgow.

41. Mindell, A. (2001). *The dreammaker's apprentice: Using heightened states of consciousness to interpret dreams.* Charlottesville, VA. Hampton Roads Publishing Company.

42. Mindell, A. (2000). *Dreaming while awake.* Charlottesville, VA: Hampton Roads Publishing.

43. Larsen, S. (1976/1988). *The shaman's doorway: Opening imagination to power and myth.* New York: Station Hill Press.

44. Hardy, A. (1966). *The divine flame: Natural history and religion.* London: Collins.

45. Hayman, R. (2002). *A life in Jung.* London: Bloomsbury.

46. Smith, C. (1990). Religion and crisis in Jungian analysis. *Counselling and values, 34,* 177-86.

47. Tacey, D. (2001). *Jung and the new age.* Hove. East Sussex: Brunner-Routledge.

48. Buber, M. (1937/1999). *I and thou.* Edinburgh: T&T Clark.

49. Kelsey, M.T. (1981). *Transcend: A guide to the perennial spiritual quest.* Element: Rockport.

50. Fontana, D. (2003). *Psychology, religion and spirituality.* BPS Blackwell Books: Leicester.

51. Griffiths, B. (2003). *Return to the centre.* Tuscon, AZ: Medio Media.

52. Goswami, A. (2012). The real secret of how we create our own reality. In *The new science and spirituality reader,* eds E. Laszlo & K.L. Dennis, 95-100. Rochester, VER: Inner Traditions.

53. Marx Hubbard, B. (2012). *Emergence: The shift from ego to essence.* San Francisco, CA: Hampton Roads.

54. Huffington Post. (2013). Spiritual quotes of Nelson Mandela, champion of the human spirit. Retrieved March 23rd 2014, from www.huffingtonpost.com/2013/12/05/spiritual-quotes-nelson-mandela.

Chapter six

1. Griffiths, B. (2003). *Return to the centre.* Tuscon, AZ: Medio Media.

2. Skolimowski, H. (1993). *A sacred place to dwell: Living with reverence upon the earth.* Rockport, MA: Element.

3. Kang, C. (2003). A psychospiritual integration frame of reference for occupational therapy part 1: Conceptual foundations. *Australian Occupational Therapy Journal, 50,* 92-103.

4. Collins, M. (1998). Occupational therapy and spirituality: Reflecting on quality of experience in therapeutic interventions. *British Journal of Occupational Therapy, 61*(6), 280-4.

5. Myss, C. (2007). *Entering the castle: An inner path to god and your soul.* New York: Free Press.

6. Maslow, A.H. (1971). *The farther reaches of human nature.* Harmondsworth: Penguin.

7. Graham, H. (1986). *The human face of psychology: Humanistic psychology in its historical, social, and cultural context.* Milton Keynes: Open University Press.

8. Maslow, A.H. (1968/1999). *Toward a psychology of being.* New York: John Wiley and Sons, 3rd edition.

9. Fidler, G.S., & Fidler, J.W. (1978). Doing and becoming: Purposeful action and self-actualization. *American Journal of Occupational Therapy, 32*(5), 305-10.

10. Egan, M., & Delaat, M. (1994). Considering spirituality in occupational therapy practice. *Canadian Journal of Occupational Therapy, 61*(2), 95-101.

11. Egan, M., & Delaat, M. (1997). The implicit spirituality of occupational therapy practice. *Canadian Journal of Occupational Therapy, 64*(3), 115-21.

12. Howard, B., & Howard, J. (1997). Occupation as spiritual activity. *American Journal of Occupational Therapy, 51*(3), 181-85.

13. Christiansen, C. (1997). Acknowledging the spiritual dimension in occupational therapy practice. *American Journal of Occupational Therapy, 51*(3), 169-72.

14. Unruh, A. (1997). Spirituality and occupational therapy: Garden musings and the Himalayan blue poppy. *Canadian Journal of Occupational Therapy, 64*(3), 156-60.

15. Vargo, J., & Urbanowski, R. (1994). Spirituality, daily practice and the occupational performance model. *Canadian Journal of Occupational Therapy, 61*(2), 88-94.

16. do Rozario, L. (1994). Ritual meaning and transcendence: The role of occupation in modern life. *Journal of Occupational Science, 1*(3), 46-53.

17. McColl, M.A. (2000). Muriel Driver lecture: Spirit, occupation and disability. *Canadian Journal of Occupational Therapy, 67*(4), 217-28.

18. Schulz, E.K. (2005). The meaning of spirituality for individuals with disabilities. *Disability and rehabilitation, 27*(21), 1283-95.

19. Unruh, A., Versnel, J., & Kerr, N. (2002). Spirituality unplugged: A review of commonalities and contentions, and a resolution. *Canadian Journal of Occupational Therapy, 69*(1), 5-19.

20. Yerxa, E. J. (2000). Occupational science: A renaissance of service to humankind through knowledge. *Occupational Therapy International, 7*(2), 87-98.

21. Wilcock, A.A. (1998/2006). *An occupational perspective of health.* Thorofare, NJ: Slack, 2nd edition.

22. Townsend, E. (1997). Occupation: Potential for personal and social transformation. *Journal of Occupational Science, 4*(1), 18-26.

23. Asaba, E., & Wicks, A. (2010). Occupational terminology: Occupational potential. *Journal of Occupational Science, 17*(2), 120-24.

24. Wicks, A. (2001). Occupational potential: A topic worthy of exploration. *Journal of Occupational Science, 8*(3), 32-5.

25. Wicks, A. (2005). Understanding occupational potential. *Journal of Occupational Science, 12*(3), 130-9.

26. Collins, M. (2001). Who is occupied? Consciousness, self-awareness and the process of human adaptation. *Journal of Occupational Science, 8*(1), 25-32.

27. do Rozario, L. (1997). Shifting paradigms: The transpersonal dimensions of ecology and occupation. *Journal of Occupational Science,* 4(3): 112-18.

28. Collins, M. (2006). *Who is occupied? Multi-dimensional functioning, quality of consciousness, and the fluid I.* Canadian Society of Occupational Science. Vancouver, 5-6 May.

29. Walsh, R., & Shapiro, D.H. (1983). Epilogue. In *Beyond health and normality: Explorations of exceptional psychological well-being,* eds R.Walsh & D. H. Shapiro, 494-495. New York: Van Nostrand Reinhold Company.

30. Taylor, E. (1997). *A psychology of spiritual healing.* West Chester, PA: Chrysalis Books. The Swedenborg Foundation.

31. Clark, F.A., Parham, D., Carlson, M., Frank, G., Wolfe, R., & Zemke, R. (1991). Occupational science: Academic innovation in the service of occupational therapy's future. *American Journal of Occupational Therapy,* 45(4), 300-10.

32. Mindell, A. (1988). *City shadows: Psychological interventions in psychiatry.* London: Arkana.

33. Mindell, A. (1990). *Working on yourself alone: Inner dreambody work.* London: Arkana.

34. Walsh, R., & Vaughan, F. (1983). Towards an integrative psychology of well-being. In *Beyond health and normality: Explorations of exceptional psychological well-being,* eds R.Walsh & D. H. Shapiro, 399-431. New York: Van Nostrand Reinhold Company.

35. Armor, T. (1969). A note on the peak experience and transpersonal psychology. *Journal of Transpersonal Psychology,* 1(1), 47-50.

36. Maslow, A.H. (1969). The farther reaches of human nature. *Journal of Transpersonal Psychology,* 1(1), 1-9.

37. Maslow, A.H. (1969). Various meanings of transcendence. *Journal of Transpersonal Psychology,* 1(1), 56-66.

38. Moustakas, C. (1985). Humanistic or humanism? *Journal of Humanistic Psychology,* 25(3), 5-11.

39. Vaughan, F. (1995). *Shadows of the sacred: Seeing through spiritual illusions.* Wheaton, IL: Quest Books, The Theosophical Publishing House.

40. Wilber, K. (1977). *The spectrum of consciousness.* Wheaton, IL: Quest Books, The Theosophical Publishing House.

41. Sutich, A. (1976). The emergence of the transpersonal orientation: A personal account. *Journal of Transpersonal Psychology,* 8(1), 5-19.

42. Collins, M. (2010). Engaging transcendent actualisation through occupational intelligence. *Journal of Occupational Science* 17(3),177-86.

43. Csikszentmihalyi, M. (1990). *Flow: The psychology of optimal experience.* New York: Harper Perennial.

44. Collins, M. (2007). Engaging self-actualisation through occupational intelligence. *Journal of Occupational Science,* 14(2), 92-9.

45. Chopra, D. (2011). *The seven laws of super heroes.* London: Transworld Publishers

46. Fadiman, J. (2005). Transpersonal transitions: The higher reaches of psyche and psychology. In *Higher wisdom,* eds R. Walsh & C.S. Grob, 25-45. Albany, NY: State University of New York Press.

47. Woodman, M. (1985). *The pregnant virgin: A process of psychological transformation.* Toronto: Inner City Books.

48. Welwood, J. (1992). *Ordinary magic: Everyday life as a spiritual path.* Boston: Shambhala.

49. Russell, P. (1982). *The awakening earth: The global brain.* London: Ark.

50. Almaas, A.H. (2004). *The inner journey home: Soul's realization of the unity of reality.* Boston: Shambhala.

51. Hartelius, G., Caplan, M., & Rardin, M.A. (2007). Transpersonal psychology: Defining the past, divining the future. *The Humanistic Psychologist,* 35(2), 135-60.

52. Blair, S.E.E. (2000). The centrality of occupation during life transitions. *British Journal of Occupational Therapy,* 63(5), 231-7.

53. Collins, M. (2008). Transpersonal identity and human occupation. *British Journal of Occupational Therapy,* 71(12), 549-52.

54. Vaughan, F. (2003). Contribution in: Caplan M, Hartelius G, Rardin MA. Contemporary viewpoints on transpersonal psychology. *Journal of Transpersonal Psychology,* 35(2): 143-162.

55. Taylor, S. (2005). The sources of higher states of consciousness. *International Journal of Transpersonal Studies,* 24, 48-60.

56. Braud, W. (1998). Can research be transpersonal? *Transpersonal Psychology Review,* 2(2), 9-17.

57. Ferrer, J.N. (2001). Toward a participatory vision of human spirituality. *ReVision,* 24(2), 15-26.

58. Ferrer, J.N. (2002). *Revisioning transpersonal theory: A participatory vision of human spirituality.* Albany, NY: State University of New York Press.

59. Howard, A. (2005). *Counselling and identity: Self-realisation in a therapy culture.* Basingstoke: Palgrave Macmillan.

60. Daniels, M. (2005). *Shadow, self, spirit: Essays in transpersonal psychology.* Exeter: Imprint Academic.

61. Vaughan, F. (1985). Discovering transpersonal identity. *Journal of Humanistic Psychology,* 25(3) 13-38.

62. Collins, M. (2004). Dreaming and occupation. *British Journal of Occupational Therapy,* 67(2), 96-8.

63. Collins, M. (2007). Spiritual emergency and occupational identity: A transpersonal perspective. *British Journal of Occupational Therapy,* 70(12), 504-12.

64. Powell, A (2001). Beyond space and time: The unbounded psyche. In *Thinking beyond the brain: A wider science of consciousness,* ed D. Lorimer, 169-186. Edinburgh: Floris Books.

65. Schlamm, L. (2007). C.G. Jung and numinous experience: Between the known and the

unknown. *European Journal of Psychotherapy and Counselling, 9*(4), 403-14.

66. Miller, J. (2004). *The transcendent function: Jung's model of psychological growth through dialogue with the unconscious.* Albany, NY: State University of New York Press.

67. Van Zyl, D. (2009). Polarity processing: Self/no-self, the transcendent function, and wholeness. In *Self and no-self: Continuing the dialogue between Buddhism and psychotherapy,* eds D. Mathers M.E. Miller & O. Ando, 109-20. London: Routledge.

68. Schlitz, M.M., Vieten, C., & Amorok, T. (2007). *Living deeply: The art and science of transformation in everyday life.* Oakland, CA: New Harbinger Publications.

69. Oubré, A. (1997). *Instinct and revelation: Reflections on the origins of numinous perception.* London: Taylor and Francis.

70. Collins, M. (2008). Politics and the numinous: Evolution, spiritual emergency, and the re-emergence of transpersonal consciousness. *Psychotherapy and Politics International, 6*(3), 198-211.

71. Winkelman, M. (1993). The evolution of consciousness? Transpersonal theories in light of cultural relativism. *Anthropology of Consciousness, 4*(3), 3-9.

72. Winkelman, M. (2002). Shamanism as neurotheology and evolutionary psychology. *American Behaviour Scientist, 14*(12), 1875-87.

73. Winkelman, M. (2004). Shamanism as the original neurotheology. *Zygon, 39*(10, 193-217.

74. Mindell, A. (2001). *The dreammaker's apprentice: Using heightened states of consciousness to interpret dreams.* Charlottesville, VA. Hampton Roads Publishing Company.

75. Collins, M. (2011). The akashic field and archetypal occupations: Transforming human potential through doing and being. *World Futures, 67*(7), 453-79.

76. Tacey, D. (2012). *The Jung reader.* London: Routledge.

77. Maxwell, M., & Tschundin, V. (1990). *Seeing the invisible: Modern religious and other transcendent experiences.* London: Arkana.

78. Shinoda Bolen, J. (2007). *Close to the bone: Life threatening illness as a soul journey.* San Francisco, CA: Conari Press.

Chapter seven

1. White, R.A. (1993). *Exceptional human experiences as vehicles of grace: Parapsychology, faith, and the outlier mentality.* The Academy of Religion and Psychical Research: Annual Conference Proceedings, 46-55.

2. Assagioli, R. (1965). *Psychosynthesis: A collection of basic writings.* New York: Viking Press.

3. Grof, S., & Grof, C. (1986). Spiritual emergency: The understanding and treatment of transpersonal crises. *Re-Vision,* 8, 7-20.

4. Grof, S., & Grof, C. (1989). *Spiritual emergency: When personal transformation becomes a crisis.* Los Angeles: Jeremy P. Tarcher.

5. Lukoff, D. (2006). Spirituality and recovery. www.cimh.networkofcare.org Date accessed: 18th December.

6. Lukoff, D., Lu, F., & Turner, R. (1992). Toward a more culturally sensitive DSM-IV: Psychoreligious and psychospiritual problems. *The Journal of Nervous and Mental Disease, 180*(11), 673-82.

7. Lukoff, D., Lu, F., & Turner, R. (1998). From spiritual emergency to spiritual problem: The transpersonal roots of the new DSM-IV category. *Journal of Humanistic Psychology, 3*(2), 21-50.

8. Laszlo, E., Grof, S., & Russell, P. (2003). *The consciousness revolution.* London: Elf Rock.

9. Collins, M. (1998). Occupational therapy and spirituality: Reflecting on quality of experience in therapeutic interventions. *British Journal of Occupational Therapy, 61*(6), 280-4.

10. Collins, M. (2006). Unfolding spirituality: Working with and beyond definitions. *International Journal of Therapy and Rehabilitation, 13*(6), 254-8.

11. Collins, M., & Wells, H. (2006).The politics of consciousness: Illness or individuation? *Psychotherapy and Politics International, 4*(2), 131-41.

12. Collins, M. (2009). *Spiritual emergency and the politics of transformation within mainstream mental health practice.* The 11th EUROTAS Conference – Beyond the mind: Towards a consciousness of unity, 15-18th October, Milan: Official conference for the European Transpersonal Association.

13. Maxwell, M., & Tschundin, V. (1990). *Seeing the invisible: Modern religious and other transcendent experiences.* London: Arkana.

14. Grof, S., & Grof, C. (1991). *The stormy search for the self: Understanding and living with spiritual emergency.* London: Mandala.

15. Collins, M. (2008). Spiritual emergency: Transpersonal, personal, and political dimensions. *Psychotherapy and Politics International, 6*(1), 3-16.

16. de Waard, F. (2010). *Spiritual crisis: Varieties and perspectives of a transpersonal phenomenon.* Exeter: Academic Imprint.

17. Guiley, R.E. (1991). *Encyclopedia of mystical and paranormal experience.* Edison, NJ: Castle Books.

18. Ankrah, L. (2002). Spiritual emergency and counselling: An exploratory study. *Counselling and Psychotherapy Research, 2*(1), 55-60.

19. Davis, J., Lockwood, L., & Wright, C. (1991). Reasons for not reporting peak experiences. *Journal of Humanistic Psychology, 31*(1), 86-94.

20. Collins, M. (2007). Spiritual emergency and occupational identity: A transpersonal perspective. *British Journal of Occupational Therapy, 70*(12), 504-12.

21. Collins, M. (1999). Quantum questions: The uncertainty principle in psychiatric practice, part 1. *The Journal of Holistic Health, 61*, 21-3.

22. Collins, M. (1999). Quantum questions: The uncertainty principle in psychiatric practice, part 2. *The Journal of Holistic Health, 62*, 21-3.

23. Collins, M. (1999). Paradigms in transition: The dilemma of evidence in the quantum era. Symposium on Evidence Based Practice. *British Journal of Therapy and Rehabilitation, 6*(6), 281.

24. Wain, A. (2005). Myth, archetype and the neutral mask: Actor training and transformation in light of the work of Joseph Campbell and Stanislav Grof. *International Journal of Transpersonal Studies, 24*, 37-47.

25. Douglas-Klotz, N. (2010). Missing stories: Psychosis, spirituality and the development of western religious hermeneutics. In *Psychosis and spirituality: Consolidating the new paradigm*, ed I. Clarke, 49-61. Chichester: Wiley-Blackwell, 2nd edition.

26. Clarke, I. (2001/2010). Psychosis and spirituality: The discontinuity model. In *Psychosis and spirituality: Consolidating the new paradigm*, ed I. Clarke, 101-14. Chichester: Wiley-Blackwell, 2nd edition.

27. Johnson, C., & Friedman, H. (2008). Enlightened or delusional?: Differentiating religious, spiritual, and transpersonal experience from psychopathology. *Journal of Humanistic Psychology, 48*(4), 505-27.

28. Marzanowski, M., & Bratton, M. (2002). Psychopathological symptoms and religious experience: A critique of Jackson and Fulford. *Philosophy, Psychiatry, and Psychology. 9*(4), 359-71.

29. Nelson, J. E. (1994). *Healing the split: Integrating spirit into our understanding of the mentally ill*. Albany, NY: State University of New York Press.

30. Skolimowski, H. (1993). A *sacred place to dwell: Living with reverence upon the earth*. Rockport, MA: Element.

31. Gilbert, R.A. (1991). *Mysticism*. Shaftesbury: Element.

32. Grof, S. (2006). When the impossible happens: Adventures in non-ordinary realities. Boulder, CO: Sounds True.

33. Collins, M. (2010). Global crisis and transformation: From spiritual emergency to spiritual intelligence. *Network Review: Journal of the Scientific and Medical Network, 103*, 17-20.

34. Marx Hubbard, B. (2012). Conscious evolution as a context for the integration of science and spirituality. In *The new science and spirituality reader*, eds E. Laszlo & K.L. Dennis, 56-9. Rochester, VER: Inner Traditions.

35. Metzner, R. (1986). *The unfolding self: Varieties of transformative experience*. Novato, CA: Origin Press.

36. Collins, M. (2008). Transpersonal identity and human occupation. *British Journal of Occupational Therapy, 71*(12), 549-52.

37. Howlett, J. (1999). Beyond physical rehabilitation: The power of inner healing after spinal cord injury. *Topics in Spinal Cord Injury Rehabilitation, 5*(2), 91-4.

38. Brett, C. (2010). Transformative crises. In *Psychosis and spirituality: Consolidating the new paradigm*, ed I. Clarke, 155-74. Chichester: Wiley-Blackwell, 2nd edition.

39. Urbanowski, R. (2003). Spirituality in changed occupational lives. In *Spirituality and Occupational Therapy*, ed M.A. McColl, 93-114. Ottawa, ON: CAOT Publications ACE.

40. Grof, S. (2000). *Psychology of the future: Lessons from modern consciousness research*. Albany, NY: State University of New York Press.

41. Collins, M. (2008). Politics and the numinous: Evolution, spiritual emergency, and the re-emergence of transpersonal consciousness. *Psychotherapy and Politics International, 6*(3), 198-211.

42. Leary, M. (2004). *The curse of the self: Self-awareness, egotism, and the quality of human life*. Oxford: Oxford University Press.

43. Gilbert, P. (2007). The spiritual foundation: Awareness and context for people's lives today. In, *Spirituality, values and mental health: Jewels for the journey*, eds M. E. Coyte, P. Gilbert & V. Nicholls, 19-44. London: Jessica Kingsley Publishers.

44. House, R. (2010). *In, against and beyond therapy: Critical essays towards a post-professional era*. Ross-on-Wye: PCCS Books.

45. Assagioli, R. (1969). Symbols of transpersonal experience. *Journal of transpersonal psychology, 1*(1), 33-45.

46. Grof, S. (1987). Psychodynamic factors in depression and psychosis: Observations from modern consciousness research. In *Pathologies of the modern self*, ed D. M. Levin, 439-78. New York: New York University Press.

47. Grof, S., & Grof, C. (2010). *Holotropic breathwork: A new approach to self-exploration and therapy*. Albany, NY: State University of New York Press.

48. Swinton, J. (2001). *Spirituality and mental health care: Rediscovering a forgotten dimension*. London: Jessica Kingsley Publishers.

49. Cook, C., Powell, A., & Sims, A. (2009). *Spirituality and psychiatry*. London: Royal College of Psychiatrists.

50. Lukoff, D. (2010). Foreword. In F. de Waard. *Spiritual crisis: Varieties and perspectives of a transpersonal phenomenon*. Exeter: Academic Imprint.

51. Perry, J.W. (1999). *Trials of a visionary mind: Spiritual emergency and the renewal process*. Albany, NY: State University of New York.

52. Sperry, L. (2003). Integrating spiritual direction functions in the practice of psychotherapy. *Journal of Psychology and Theology, 31*(1), 3-13.

53. Nelson, P.L. (2000). Mystical experience and radical deconstruction: Through the ontological looking glass. In *Transpersonal knowing: Experiencing the horizon of consciousness*, eds T. Hart, P.L. Nelson & K. Puhakka, 55-84. Albany, NY: State University of New York Press.

54. Collins, M. (2001). Who is occupied? Consciousness, self-awareness and the process of human adaptation. *Journal of Occupational Science, 8*(1), 25-32.

55. Lucas, C (2011). *In case of spiritual emergency: Moving successfully through your awakening.* Forres: Findhorn Press.

56. Lucas, C. (2006). When spiritual emergence becomes an emergency. *Caduceus, 68,* 28-30.

57. Unruh, A.M., Versnel, J., & Kerr. (2004). Spirituality in the context of occupation: A theory to practice application. In *Occupation for occupational therapists,* ed M. Molineux, 32-45. Oxford: Blackwell Publishing.

58. Kang, C. (2003). A psychospiritual integration frame of reference for occupational therapy part 1: Conceptual foundations. *Australian Occupational Therapy Journal, 50,* 92-103.

59. Bateson, M.C. (1989). *Composing a life.* New York: Grove Press.

60. Christiansen, C. (1999). The 1999 Eleanor Clark Slagle lecture – Defining lives: Occupation as identity: An essay on competence, coherence, and the creation of meaning. *American Journal of Occupational Therapy, 53,* 547-58.

61. Christiansen, C. (2000). Identity, personal projects and happiness: Self-construction in everyday action. *Journal of Occupational Science, 7*(3), 98-107.

62. Collins, M. (2011). The global crisis and holistic consciousness: How assertive action could lead to the creation of an improved future. In *Conscious connectivity: Creating dignity in conversation,* ed M. Brenner, 214-23. Charleston, SC: Pan American.

63. Hamel, S., Leclerc, G., & Lefrancois, R. (2003). A psychological outlook on the concept of transcendent actualisation. *International Journal for the Psychology of Religion, 13*(1), 3-15.

64. Collins, M. (2010). Engaging transcendent actualisation through occupational intelligence. *Journal of Occupational Science 17*(3),177-86.

65. Ferrer, J.N. (2001). Toward a participatory vision of human spirituality. *ReVision, 24*(2), 15-26.

66. Tarnas, R. (2003). Contribution in, Caplan, M., Hartelius, G., & Rardin, M. Contemporary viewpoints on transpersonal psychology. *Journal of Transpersonal Psychology, 35*(2), 143-62.

67. Tarnas, R. (2006). *Cosmos and psyche: Intimations of a new world view.* New York: Viking.

68. Tarnas, R. (2002). Foreword. In *Revisioning transpersonal theory: A participatory vision of human spirituality,* ed J. Ferrer, vii-xvi. Albany, NY: State University of New York Press.

69. Puhakka, K. (2000). An invitation to authentic knowing. In *Transpersonal knowing: Exploring the horizon of consciousness,* ed T. Hart, P.L. Nelson & K. Puhakka, 11-30. Albany, NY: State University of New York Press.

70. Collins, M. (2010). *Global crisis and opportunity: From spiritual emergency to spiritual intelligence.* The Scientific and Medical Network Conference – A New Renaissance: Transforming Science, Spirit and Society. 6th November, University of London.

71. Laing, R.D. (1987). Hatred of health. *Journal of Contemplative Psychotherapy, 4,* 77-86.

72. Jung, C.G. (1972). Letter to P. W. Martin. Letters, Volume 1. Princeton University Press. Cited in C. Dunne, *Carl Jung: Wounded healer of the soul.* London: Continuum (2000).

73. Freeman, A. (2006). A Daniel come to judgement? Dennett and the revisioning of transpersonal theory. *Journal of Consciousness Studies, 13*(3), 95-109.

74. Scotton, B. (1996). The contribution of C.G. Jung to transpersonal psychiatry. In *Textbook of transpersonal psychiatry and psychology,* eds B.W Scotton, A.B. Chinen & J.R. Battista, 39-51. New York: Basic Books.

75. Yunt, J.D. (2001). Jung's contribution to an ecological psychology. *Journal of Humanistic Psychology, 41*(2), 96-121.

76. Schoen, D. (1998). *Divine tempest: The hurricane as a psychic phenomenon.* Toronto: Inner City Books.

77. Washburn, M. (1994). *Transpersonal psychology in psychoanalytic perspective.* Albany, NY. State University of New York Press.

78. Washburn, M. (1995). *The ego and the dynamic ground: A transpersonal theory of human development.* Albany, NY. State University of New York Press.

79. Frey-Rohn, L. (1974). *From Freud to Jung: A comparative study of the psychology of the unconscious.* New York: C.G. Jung Foundation for Analytical Psychology.

80. Larsen, S. (1990/1996). *The mythic imagination: The quest for meaning through personal mythology.* Rochester, VER: Inner Traditions International.

81. Theoi. (2014). Kybele. Retrieved March 26th 2014, from www.theoi.com/Phrygios/Kybele.html.

82. Theoi. (2014). Rhea. Retrieved March 26th 2014, from www.theoi.com/Titan/TitanisRhea.html.

83. Theoi. (2014). Rhea-Kybele. Retrieved March 26th 2014, from www.theoi.com/Tita/TitanisRheaTreasures.html#Chariot.

84. Patterson, R. (2014). Lion and lamb as metaphors of divine-human relationships. Retrieved March 26th 2014, from www.//bible.org/article/lion-and-lamb-metaphors-divine-human-relationships.

85. Baring, A. (2013). *The dream of the cosmos: A quest for the soul.* Blandford Forum, DOR: Archive Publishing.

Chapter eight

1. Otto, R. (1923/1958). *The idea of the holy: An inquiry into the non-rational factor in the idea of the divine and its relation to the rational.* Oxford: Oxford University Press.

2. Campbell, J. (1991). *Creative mythology: The masks of god.* London: Arkana.

3. Campbell, J. (2001). On waking up. In *Gathering sparks,* eds D. Appelbaum and J. Kulin, 12-17. New York: Parabola Press.

4. Campbell, J. (1972/1992). *Myths to live by: Mythology for our time.* London: Souvenir Press.

5. Edinger, E. (1984). *The creation of consciousness: Jung's myth for modern man.* Toronto: Inner City Books.

6. Le Grice, K. (2010). *The archetypal cosmos: Rediscovering the gods in myth, science and astrology.* Edinburgh: Floris Books.

7. Neumann, E. (1954). *The origins and history of consciousness.* New York: Bollingen Foundation and Pantheon Books.

8. Skolimowski, H. (1993). A *sacred place to dwell: Living with reverence upon the earth.* Rockport, MA: Element.

9. Mc Gilchrist, I. (2009). *The master and his emissary: The divided brain and the making of the western world.* New Haven: Yale University Press.

10. Chopra, D. (2011). *The seven laws of super heroes.* London: Transworld Publishers.

11. Griffiths, B. (2003). *Return to the centre.* Tuscon, AZ: Medio Media.

12. Feinstein, D., & Krippner, S. (1997). *The mythic path.* New York. Jeremy P. Tarcher.

13. Jung C. G. (1998). In R. Segal, ed. *Jung on mythology.* London: Routledge.

14. Corbett, L. (1996). *The religious function of the psyche.* London: Routledge.

15. Freeman, A. (2006). A Daniel come to judgment? Dennett and the revisioning of transpersonal theory. *Journal of Consciousness studies, 13*(3), 95-109.

16. Laszlo, E. (2007). Elements of the new concept of consciousness. In *Mind before matter: Visions of a new science of consciousness,* eds T. Pfeiffer, J.E. Mack & P. Devereux, 70-82. Winchester; O Books.

17. Sannella, L. (1992). *The Kundalini experience: Psychosis or transcendence?* Lower Lake, CA: Integral Publishing.

18. Marcuse, H. (1964/1991). *One-dimensional man.* London: Routledge, 2nd edition.

19. Yunt, J.D. (2001). Jung's contribution to an ecological psychology. *Journal of Humanistic Psychology, 41*(2), 96-121.

20. Suzuki, D., & Knudtson, P. (1992). *Wisdom of the elders: Sacred native stories of nature.* New York: Bantam Books.

21. Progoff, I. (1987). *Jung, synchronicity and human destiny: C G Jung's theory of meaningful coincidence.* New York: Julian Press.

22. Collins, M. (2008). Politics and the numinous: Evolution, spiritual emergency, and the re-emergence of transpersonal consciousness. *Psychotherapy and Politics International, 6*(3), 198-211.

23. Jung, C.G. (1940). *The integration of the personality,* translated S.M. Dell. London: Kegan Paul, Trench, Trubner & Co.

24. Jung, C.G. (1954/1993). *The practice of psychotherapy.* London: Routledge.

25. Collins, M., Hughes, W., & Samuels, A. (2010). The politics of transformation in the global crisis: How spiritual emergencies may be reflecting an enantiodromia in modern consciousness. *Psychotherapy and Politics International, 8*(2), 162-176.

26. Glenn, J.C., Gordon, T.J., & Florescu, E. (2008). *State of the future: Executive summary.* World Federation of United Nations Associations. Retrieved August 1st 2008, from www.millennium-project.org/millennium/issues.html.

27. Glenn, J.C., Gordon, T.J., & Florescu, E. (2011). *State of the future: Executive summary.* The Millennium Project: Global Futures Studies and Research. Retrieved August 2nd 2011, from www.millennium-project.org/millennium/2011SOF.html.

28. Collins, M. (2010). Spiritual intelligence: Evolving transpersonal potential towards ecological actualization for a sustainable future. *World Futures* 66: 320-34.

29. Collins, M. (2010). Global crisis and transformation: From spiritual emergency to spiritual intelligence. *Network Review: Journal of the Scientific and Medical Network, 103,* 17-20.

30. Samuels, A. (1993). *The political psyche.* London: Routledge.

31. Collins, M. (2011). The global crisis and holistic consciousness: How assertive action could lead to the creation of an improved future. In *Conscious connectivity: Creating dignity in conversation,* ed M. Brenner, 214-23. Charleston, SC: Pan American.

32. Collins, M. (2008). Spiritual emergency: Transpersonal, personal, and political dimensions. *Psychotherapy and Politics International, 6*(1), 3-16.

33. Schoen, D. (1998). *Divine tempest: The hurricane as a psychic phenomenon.* Toronto: Inner City Books.

34. Stewart, H., & Elliot, L. (2013). Nicholas Stern: "I got it wrong on climate change – it's far, far worse." *The Observer,* 27th January, 3.

35. Jung, C.G. (1959). *Collected works, vol 9, part 1: The archetypes and the collective unconscious,* translated R.F.C. Hull. London: Routledge and Kegan Paul Ltd.

36. Jacobi, J. (1980). *The psychology of C.G.Jung.* London: Routledge & Kegan Paul.

37. Tarnas, R. (2002). Is the modern psyche undergoing a rite of passage? *ReVision, 24*(3), 2-8.

38. Laszlo, E., Grof, S., & Russell, P. (2003). *The consciousness revolution.* London: Elf Rock.

39. Read, T., & Crowley, N. (2009). The transpersonal perspective. In *Spirituality and psychiatry,* eds C. Cook, A. Powell and A. Sims, 212-32. London: Royal College of Psychiatrists.

40. Myss, C. (2007). *Entering the castle: An inner path to god and your soul.* New York: Free Press.

41. May, R. (1976). *The courage to create.* London: Collins.

42. Jarvis, M. (2005). *The psychology of effective learning and teaching.* Cheltenham: Nelson Thornes.

43. Moon. J. (2000). *Reflection in learning and professional development.* London: Kegan Page

44. Kolb, D. (1984). *Experiential learning.* Hemel Hempstead: Prentice Hall.

45. Wyld, H. C. (1961). *Universal English dictionary*. London: The Waverley Book Company Limited.

46. Knapper, C., & Cropley, A. (1985). *Lifelong learning and higher education*. London: Croom Holm.

47. Clarke, P.B. (1996). *Deep citizenship*. London: Pluto Press.

48. Samuels, A. (2001). *Politics on the couch: Citizenship and the internal life*. London: Karnac Books.

49. Mindell, A. (2000). *Quantum mind: The edge between physics and psychology*. Portland, OR: Lao Tse Press.

50. Jung, C.G. (1994). The fight with the Shadow. In *The awakened warrior: Living with courage, compassion and discipline*, ed R. Fields, 234-36. New York: Jeremy P. Tarcher/Putnam Books.

51. Mindell, A. (2002). *The deep democracy of open forums: Practical steps to conflict prevention and resolution for the family, workplace, and world*. Charlottesville, VA: Hampton Roads.

52. Mindell, A. (2008). Bringing deep democracy to life: An awareness paradigm for deepening political dialogue, personal relationships, and community interactions. *Psychotherapy and Politics International, 6*(3): 212-225.

53. Shaules, J. (2007). *Deep culture: The hidden challenges of global living*. Clevedon: Multi Lingual Matters Ltd.

54. Ho, D.Y.F. (1995). Internalized culture, culturocentrism, and transcendence. *Counselling Psychologist, 23*(1), 4-24.

55. Naess, A. (1986). The deep ecological movement: Some philosophical aspects. *Philosophical Inquiry, 8*, 10-31.

56. Fox, W. (1990). Transpersonal ecology: "Psychologising" ecophilosophy. *Journal of Transpersonal Psychology, 22*(1): 59-96.

57. Reser, J.P. (1995). Whither environmental psychology? The transpersonal ecopsychology crossroads. *Journal of Environmental Psychology, 15*, 235-257.

58. Reason, P. (2002). Justice, sustainability, and participation. *Concepts and Transformation, 7*(1): 7-29.

59. Collins, M. (2001). Who is occupied? Consciousness, self-awareness and the process of human adaptation. *Journal of Occupational Science, 8*(1), 25-32.

60. Collins, M. (2007). Engaging self-actualisation through occupational intelligence. *Journal of Occupational Science, 14*(2), 92-9.

61. Collins, M. (2007). Spirituality and the shadow: Reflection and the therapeutic use of self. *British Journal of Occupational Therapy, 70*(2), 88-90.

62. Collins, M. (2010). Engaging transcendent actualisation through occupational intelligence. *Journal of Occupational Science 17*(3),177-86.

63. Collins, M. (2008). Transpersonal identity and human occupation. *British Journal of Occupational Therapy, 71*(12), 549-52.

64. do Rozario, L. (1997). Shifting paradigms: The transpersonal dimensions of ecology and occupation. *Journal of Occupational Science, 4*(3): 112-18.

65. Collins, M. (2004). Dreaming and occupation. *British Journal of Occupational Therapy, 67*(2), 96-8.

66. Nicholls, L. (2007). A psychodynamic discourse in occupational therapy. In *Contemporary issues in occupational therapy: Reasoning and reflection*, ed J. Creek, 55-86. Chichester: Wiley.

67. Collins, M. (2011). The akashic field and archetypal occupations: Transforming human potential through doing and being. *World Futures,67*(7), 453-79.

68. Roszak, T. (2001). *The voice of the earth: An exploration of eco-psychology*. Grand Rapids, MI: Phanes Press, 2nd edition.

69. Le Grice, K. (2010). *The archetypal cosmos: Rediscovering the gods in myth, science and astrology*. Edinburgh: Floris Books.

70. Liotta, E. (2009). On Carl Gustav Jung's "mind and earth". In *On soul and earth: The psychic value of place*, ed E. Liotta, 22-40. London: Routledge.

71. Schön, D. (1987). *Educating the reflective practitioner: Toward a new design for teaching and learning in the professions*. San Francisco, CA: Jossey Bass.

72. Pillow, W. (2003). Confession, catharsis, or cure? Rethinking the uses of reflexivity as methodological power in qualitative research. *Qualitative Studies in Education, 16*(2), 175-96.

73. Bleakley, A. (2000). Writing with invisible ink: Narrative, confessionalism and reflective practice. *Reflective Practice, 1*(1), 4-11.

74. Bolton, G. (2006). Narrative writing: Reflective enquiry into professional practice. *Educational Action Research, 14*(2), 203-18.

75. Wellington, B,. & Austin, P. (1996). Orientations to reflective practice. *Educational Research, 38*(3), 307-16.

76. Humphreys, M. (2005). Getting personal: Reflexivity and autoethnographic vignettes. *Qualitative Inquiry, 11*(6), 840-60.

77. White, R.A. (1998). Becoming more human as we work: The reflexive role of exceptional human experience. In *Transpersonal research methods for the social sciences: Honouring human experience*, eds W. Braud & R. Anderson, 128-45. Thousand Oaks, CA: Sage Publications.

78. House, R. (2010). *In, against and beyond therapy: Critical essays towards a post-professional era*. Ross-on-Wye: PCCS Books.

79. Grof, S. (2000). *Psychology of the future: Lessons from modern consciousness research*. Albany, NY: State University of New York Press.

80. Segaller, S., & Berger, M. (1989). *The wisdom of the dream: The world of C.G. Jung*. Boston: Shambhala.

81. Hannah, B. (1981/2001). *Encounters with the soul: Active imagination as developed by C.G. Jung*. Wilmette, IL: Chiron Publications.

82. Leary, T. (1999). *Turn on, tune in, drop out*. Oakland, CA: Ronin Publishing.

83. Coxhead, N. (1985). *The relevance of bliss: A contemporary exploration of mystical experience*. London: Wildwood House.
84. Slattery, D. (2004). The myth of nature and the nature of myth: Becoming transparent to transcendence. *The International Journal of Transpersonal Studies, 24*, 29-36.
85. Stein, M. (2007). On modern initiation into the spiritual. In *Initiation: The living reality of an archetype*, eds T, Kirsch, V. Beanne-Rutter & T, Singer, 85-102. London: Routledge.
86. Jung, C.G. (1983). *Memories, dreams, reflections*. London: Flamingo.
87. Jung, C.G. (2009). *The red book: Liber novus*, ed S. Shamdasani. New York: W.W. Norton & Company.
88. Kelly, S. (1993). *Individuation and the absolute: Hegel, Jung and the path toward wholeness*. New York: Paulist Press.
89. Corbett, L (2007). *Psyche and the sacred: Spirituality beyond religion*. New Orleans: Spring Journal Books.
90. Edinger, E. (1992). *Ego and archetype: Individuation and the religious function of the psyche*. Boston: Shambhala.
91. Scarpelli, M. (2009). The earth, the song, the symbol. In *On soul and earth: The psychic value of place*, ed E. Liotta, 268-76. London: Routledge.
92. Marx Hubbard, B. (2012). *Emergence: The shift from ego to essence*. San Francisco, CA: Hampton Roads.
93. Vaughan-Lee, L. (2012). *Prayer of the heart in Christian and Sufi mysticism*. Point Reyes, CA: The Golden Sufi Centre.
94. Karpf, A. (2012). You can't ignore this. *The Guardian*, Saturday 1st December, 52-3.
95. Larsen, S. (1976/1988). *The shaman's doorway: Opening imagination to power and myth*. New York: Station Hill Press.

Chapter nine
1. Vaughan-Lee, L. (2012). *Prayer of the heart in Christian and Sufi mysticism*. Point Reyes, CA: The Golden Sufi Centre.
2. Griffiths, B. (2003). *Return to the centre*. Tuscon, AZ: Medio Media.
3. Perry, J.W. (1953/1987). *The self in psychotic process: Its symbolism in schizophrenia*. Dallas, TEX: Spring Publications.
4. Marx Hubbard, B. (2012). *Emergence: The shift from ego to essence*. San Francisco, CA: Hampton Roads.
5. Saionji, M. (2012). Guiding our inner evolution. In *The new science and spirituality reader*, eds E. Laszlo & K.L. Dennis, 116-9. Rochester, VER: Inner Traditions.
6. Larsen, S. (1976/1988). *The shaman's doorway: Opening imagination to power and myth*. New York: Station Hill Press.
7. Law, M. (2002). Participation in the occupations of everyday life. *American Journal of Occupational Therapy, 56*(6), 640-8.
8. Whiteford, G. (2000). Occupational deprivation: Global challenge in the new millennium. *British Journal of Occupational Therapy, 63*(5): 200-4.
9. do Rozario, L. (1994). Ritual meaning and transcendence: The role of occupation in modern life. *Journal of Occupational Science, 1*(3), 46-53.
10. Collins, M. (2010). Spiritual intelligence: Evolving transpersonal potential towards ecological actualization for a sustainable future. *World Futures* 66: 320-34.
11. Collins, M. (2001). Who is occupied? Consciousness, self-awareness and the process of human adaptation. *Journal of Occupational Science, 8*(1), 25-32.
12. Ferrer, J.N. (2002). *Revisioning transpersonal theory: A participatory vision of human spirituality*. Albany, NY: State University of New York Press.
13. Lahood, G. (2007). The participatory turn and the transpersonal movement: A brief introduction. *ReVision, 29*(3), 2-6.
14. Lahood, G. (2007). One hundred years of sacred science: Participation and hybridity in transpersonal anthropology. *ReVision, 29*(3): 37-48.
15. Ferrer, J.N. (2001). Toward a participatory vision of human spirituality. *ReVision, 24*(2), 15-26.
16. Ferrer, J.N. (2001). New horizons in contemporary spirituality. *ReVision, 24*(2): 24.
17. Ferrer, J.N. (2008). Spiritual knowing as participatory enaction: An answer to the question of religious pluralism. In *The participatory turn: Spirituality, mysticism, religious studies*, eds J.N. Ferrer & J.H. Sherman, 135-169. Albany, NY: State University of New York Press.
18. Chopra, D. (2011). *The seven laws of super heroes*. London: Transworld Publishers
19. Heron, J. (2001). Spiritual inquiry as divine becoming. *ReVision, 24*(2): 32-41.
20. Collins, M. (2006). *Who is occupied? Multi-dimensional functioning, quality of consciousness, and the fluid I*. Canadian Society of Occupational Science: Conference. Vancouver, 5th-6th May.
21. Collins, M. (2006). *Occupational intelligence: Consciousness, identity and the process of individuation*. College of Occupational Therapists: National conference. Cardiff, 20th-23rd June.
22. Collins, M. (2007). Engaging self-actualisation through occupational intelligence. *Journal of Occupational Science, 14*(2), 92-9.
23. Collins, M. (2010). Engaging transcendent actualisation through occupational intelligence. *Journal of Occupational Science 17*(3),177-86.
24. Heron, J. (1998). *Sacred science: Person-centred inquiry into the spiritual and the subtle*. Ross-on-Wye: PCCS Books.
25. Tarnas, R. (2003). Contribution in, Caplan, M., Hartelius, G., & Rardin, M. Contemporary viewpoints on transpersonal psychology. *Journal of Transpersonal Psychology, 35*(2), 143-62.

26. Marshall, P. (2005). *Mystical encounters with the natural world: Experiences and explorations.* Oxford: Oxford University Press.

27. Drury, N. (1989). *The elements of human potential.* Shaftesbury, Dorset: Element Books.

28. Jung, C.G. (1989). *Psychological reflections.* London: Ark-Routledge.

29. Metzner, R. (2008). *The expansion of consciousness.* Berkeley, CA: Green Earth Foundation/Regent Books.

30. Boucouvalas, M. (1999). Following the movement: From transpersonal psychology to a multi-disciplinary transpersonal orientation. *Journal of Transpersonal Psychology, 31*(3), 27-39.

31. Ferrer, J.N. (2003). Participatory spirituality: An introduction. *Network Review: The Journal of the Scientific and Medical Network, 83,* 3-7.

32. Tarnas, R. (1991/2010). *The passion of the western mind: Understanding the ideas that have shaped our world view.* London: Pimlico.

33. Loy, D.R., & Stanley, J. (2009). The buddhadharma and the planetary crisis. In *A Buddhist response to the climate emergency,* eds J. Stanley, D.R. Loy & G. Dorje, 3-13. Boston: Wisdom Publications.

34. Hunt, H.T. (1995). *On the nature of consciousness: Cognitive, phenomenological, and transpersonal perspectives.* New Haven: Yale University Press.

35. Anderson, S. (2011). What holistic means to me. In *Conscious connectivity: Creating dignity in conversation,* ed M. Brenner, 233-54. Charleston, SC: Pan American.

36. Collins, M. (2011). The global crisis and holistic consciousness: How assertive action could lead to the creation of an improved future. In *Conscious connectivity: Creating dignity in conversation,* ed M. Brenner, 214-23. Charleston, SC: Pan American.

37. Murphy, S. (2009). The untellable nonstory of global warming: Can we really be allowing our planet to die? In *A Buddhist response to the climate emergency,* eds J. Stanley, D.R. Loy & G. Dorje, 195-201. Boston: Wisdom Publications.

38. Walsh, R. (1996). Toward a psychology of human and ecological survival: Psychological approaches to contemporary global threats. In *Textbook of transpersonal psychiatry and psychology,* eds B.W Scotton, A.B. Chinen and J.R. Battista, 396-405. New York: Basic Books.

39. Gore, A. (1992). *Earth in the balance: Ecology and the human spirit.* New York: Rodale.

40. Berry, T. (1999). *The great work: Our way into the future.* New York: Random House.

41. Tarnas, R. (2002). Is the modern psyche undergoing a rite of passage? *ReVision, 24*(3), 2-8.

42. Collins, M., Hughes, W., & Samuels, A. (2012). The politics of transformation in the global crisis. In *Vital signs: Psychological responses to ecological crisis,* eds M.J. Rust & N. Totton, 163-74. London: Karnac Books.

43. Barbalet, J. (2005). Weeping and transformations of self. *Journal for the Theory of Social Behaviour, 35*(2), 125-41.

44. Tarnas, R. (1996). The western world view: Past, present and future. In *Towards a new world view: Conversations at the leading edge,* ed R.E. Di Carlo, 33-47. Edinburgh: Floris Books.

45. Macy, J. (2009). On being with our world. In *A Buddhist response to the climate emergency,* eds J. Stanley, D.R. Loy & G. Dorje, 177-79. Boston: Wisdom Publications.

46. Baring, A. (2007). A metaphysical revolution? Reflections on the idea of primacy of consciousness. In *Mind before matter: Visions of a new science of consciousness,* eds T. Pfeiffer, J.E. Mack & P. Devereux, 233-50. Winchester; O Books.

47. Collins, M. (2008). Politics and the numinous: Evolution, spiritual emergency, and the re-emergence of transpersonal consciousness. *Psychotherapy and Politics International, 6*(3), 198-211.

48. Lucas, C (2011). *In case of spiritual emergency: Moving successfully through your awakening.* Forres: Findhorn Press.

49. Myss, C. (2007). *Entering the castle: An inner path to god and your soul.* New York: Free Press.

50. Berman, M. (1981). *The re-enchantment of the world.* Ithaca: Cornell University Press.

51. Van Der Post, L. (1976). *Jung and the story of our time.* London: The Hogarth Press.

52. Laszlo, E., Grof, S., & Russell, P. (2003). *The consciousness revolution.* London: Elf Rock.

53. Le Grice, K. (2010). *The archetypal cosmos: Rediscovering the gods in myth, science and astrology.* Edinburgh: Floris Books.

54. Wilcock, A.A. (1998/2006). *An occupational perspective of health.* Thorofare, NJ: Slack, 2nd edition.

55. do Rozario, L. (1997). Shifting paradigms: The transpersonal dimensions of ecology and occupation. *Journal of Occupational Science, 4*(3): 112-18.

56. Collins, M. (2007c). Spiritual emergency and occupational identity: A transpersonal perspective. *British Journal of Occupational Therapy, 70*(12), 504-12.

57. Marcuse, H. (1964/1991). *One-dimensional man.* London: Routledge, 2nd edition.

58. Collins, M. (2009). *Spiritual emergency and the politics of transformation within mainstream mental health practice.* The 11th EUROTAS Conference – Beyond the mind: Towards a consciousness of unity, 15-18th October, Milan: Official conference for the European Transpersonal Association.

59. Collins, M., & Wells, H. (2006). The politics of consciousness: Illness or individuation? *Psychotherapy and Politics International, 4*(2), 131-41.

60. Grof, S., & Grof, C. (1989). *Spiritual emergency: When personal transformation becomes a crisis.* Los Angeles: Jeremy P. Tarcher.

61. Nelson, J. E. (1994). *Healing the split: Integrating spirit into our understanding of the mentally ill.* Albany, NY: State University of New York Press.

62. Bragdon, E. (1990). *The call of spiritual emergency: From personal crisis to personal transformation*. San Francisco: Harper Row Publishers.
63. Rust, M.J. (2008). Climate on the couch: Unconscious processes in relation to our environmental crisis. *Psychotherapy and Politics International, 6*(3), 157-70.
64. Laszlo, E. (2004a). *Science and the Akashic field. An integral theory of everything*. Rochester, VER: Inner Traditions.

Chapter ten
1. Taylor, S. (2011). *Out of the darkness: From turmoil to transformation*. London: Hay House.
2. Kumar, S. (2010). The spiritual imperative: Elegant simplicity is the way to discover spirituality. In *A new renaissance: Transforming science, spirit and society*, eds D. Lorimer & O. Robinson, 177-187. Edinburgh: Floris Books.
3. Duncan, M., & Watson, R. (2004). Transformation through occupation: Towards a prototype. In *Transformation through occupation*, eds R. Watson & L, Swartz, 301-318. London: Whurr Publishers.
4. Dass, R. (1970). *Doing your own being*. London: Neville Spearman.
5. Collins, M. (2007). Engaging self-actualisation through occupational intelligence. *Journal of Occupational Science, 14*(2), 92-9.
6. Krishnamurti, J. (1970). *The only revolution*. London: Victor Gollancz Ltd.
7. Krishnamurti, J. (1973). *The impossible question*. London: Victor Gollancz Ltd.
8. Berry, T. (2001). Belonging. In *Gathering sparks*, eds D. Appelbaum and J. Kulin, 64-9. New York: Parabola Press.
9. McGrath, A. (2002). *The reenchantment of nature: The denial of religion and the ecological crisis*. New York: Doubleday.
10. Collins, M. (2011). The Akashic field and archetypal occupations: Transforming human potential through doing and being. *World Futures,67*(7), 453-79.
11. Johnson, R.A., & Ruhl, J.M. (2007). *Living your unlived life*. New York: Jeremy P. Tarcher/Penguin.
12. Hollis, J. (2009). *What matters most: Living a more considered life*. New York: Gotham Books.
13. Moore, T. (1996). *The re-enchantment of everyday life*. New York: Harper Collins.
14. Fox, M. (1994). *The reinvention of work: A new vision of livelihood for our time*. New York: Harper Collins.
15. Pearson, N. (2006). Where the heavens meet the earth: Inspirations from the lives of Carl Jung, Jalal-U-Din Rumi and Mahatma Ghandi. In *Sky and psyche: The relationship between cosmos and consciousness,* eds N. Campion & P. Curry, 169-81. Edinburgh: Floris Books.
16. Moore, T. (2008). *A life at work: The joy of discovering what you were born to do*. London: Piatkus Books.
17. Jung, C.G. (1983). *Memories, dreams, reflections*. London: Flamingo.
18. Churton, T. (2002). The *golden builders: Alchemists, Rosicrucian's, and the first free Masons*. Boston, MA: Weiser Books.
19. Eliade, M. (1962). *The forge and the crucible: The origins and structures of alchemy*. Chicago: University of Chicago Press.
20. Jung, C.G. (1959). *Collected works, vol 9, part 1: The archetypes and the collective unconscious*, translated R.F.C. Hull. London: Routledge and Kegan Paul Ltd.
21. Jung C. G. (1998). In R. Segal, ed. *Jung on mythology*. London: Routledge.
22. Le Grice, K. (2010). *The archetypal cosmos: Rediscovering the gods in myth, science and astrology*. Edinburgh: Floris Books.
23. Marx Hubbard, B. (1998). *Conscious evolution: Awakening the power of our social potential*. Novato, CA: New World Library.
24. Laszlo, E (2009). *Worldshift 2012: Making green business, new politics & higher consciousness work together*. Rochester, VER: Inner Traditions.
25. Daniels, M. (2005). *Shadow, self, spirit: Essays in transpersonal psychology*. Exeter: Imprint Academic.
26. Skolimowski, H. (1993). A *sacred place to dwell: Living with reverence upon the earth*. Rockport, MA: Element.
27. Reich, K.H. (2001). Spiritual development: Han De Wit's and Stanislav Grof's differing approaches. *Zygon, 36*(3), 509-20.
28. Schlitz, M.M. (2009). A path forward: Embracing our creative imagination. In *The new science and spirituality reader*, ed E. Laszlo & K.L Dennis,160-74. Rochester, VER: Inner Traditions.
29. Ricard, M (2009). The future doesn't hurt...yet. In *A Buddhist response to the climate emergency*, eds J. Stanley, D.R. Loy & G. Dorje, 203-7. Boston: Wisdom Publications.
30. Wesselman, H. (2007). The transformational perspective: An emerging world view. In *Mind before matter: Visions of a new science of consciousness*, eds T. Pfeiffer, J.E. Mack & P. Devereux, 192-209. Winchester; O Books.
31. Marx Hubbard, B. (2012). Conscious evolution as a context for the integration of science and spirituality. In *The new science and spirituality reader*, eds E. Laszlo & K.L. Dennis, 56-9. Rochester, VER: Inner Traditions.
32. Lucas, C (2011). *In case of spiritual emergency: Moving successfully through your awakening*. Forres: Findhorn Press.
33. Lajoie, D., & Shapiro, S. (1992). Definitions of transpersonal psychology: The first 23 years. *Journal of Transpersonal Psychology, 24*(1), 79-98.
34. Wilber, K. (1985). *The holographic paradigm and other paradoxes: Exploring the leading edge of science*. Boston: Shambhala.
35. Wilber, K. (1996). *Eye to eye: The quest for the new paradigm*. Boston: Shambhala.
36. Bohm, D. (1980). *Wholeness and the implicate order*. London: Ark.

37. Capra, F. (1975). *The tao of physics: An exploration of the parallels between modern physics and eastern mysticism.* London: Flamingo.

38. Talbot, M. (1991). *The holographic universe.* New York: Harper Collins.

39. Zukav, G. (1979). *The dancing Wu Li masters: An overview of the new physics.* New York: William Morrow & Company.

40. Goswami, A. (2007). From information to transformation. In *Mind before matter: Visions of a new science of consciousness*, eds T. Pfeiffer, J.E. Mack & P. Devereux, 21-37. Winchester; O Books.

41. Mindell, A. (2010). *Process mind: A user's guide to connecting with the mind of god.* Wheaton, IL: Quest Books, The Theosophical Publishing House.

42. Wolf, F.A. (1999). *The spiritual universe: One physicist's vision of spirit, soul, matter, and self.* Portsmouth, NH: Moment Point Press.

43. Casement, A. (2006). Witchcraft: The numinous power in humans. In *The idea of the numinous: Contemporary and psychoanalytic perspectives*, eds A. Casement & D. Tacey, 20-33. London: Routledge.

44. Grof, S. (2006). Ervin Laszlo's akashic field and the dilemmas of modern consciousness research. *World Futures, 62*, 86-102.

45. Mindell, A. (1996). Discovering the world in the individual and the world channel in psychotherapy. *Journal of Humanistic Psychology, 36*(3), 67-84.

46. Laszlo, E. (2006). *The chaos point: The world at a crossroads.* London: Piatkus.

47. Laszlo, E. (2008). *Quantum shift in the global brain: How the new scientific reality can change our world.* Rochester, VER: Inner Traditions.

48. Wilber, K. (2000). *Sex, ecology, spirituality: The spirit of evolution.* Boston: Shambhala.

49. Zimmerman, M.E. (1998). A transpersonal diagnosis of the ecological crisis. In *Ken Wilber in dialogue: Conversations with leading transpersonal thinkers*, eds D. Rothberg & S. Kelly, 180-206. Wheaton, Illinois: Quest Books, The Theosophical Publishing House.

50. Zohar, D., & Marshall, I. (1991). *The quantum self.* London: Flamingo.

51. Zohar, D., & Marshall, I. (1994). *The quantum society: Mind, physics and a new social vision.* London: Flamingo.

52. Chopra, D. (2011). *The seven laws of super heroes.* London: Transworld Publishers.

53. Light, A. (2000). What is an ecological identity? *Environmental Politics, 9*(4), 59-81.

54. Collins, M. (2010). Engaging transcendent actualisation through occupational intelligence. *Journal of Occupational Science 17*(3),177-86.

55. Fickeison, D. (1993). Skills for living together. In *In the company of others: Making community in the modern world*, ed C. Whitmyer, 46-55. New York: Jeremy P. Tarcher.

56. Morgan, A.E. (1993). Homo sapiens: The community animal. In *In the company of others: Making community in the modern world*, ed C. Whitmyer, 12-15. New York: Jeremy P. Tarcher.

57. Dass, R., & Gorman, P. (1993). Service: The soul of community. In *In the company of others: Making community in the modern world*, ed C. Whitmyer, 89-92. New York: Jeremy P. Tarcher.

58. Whitmyer, C. (1993). Epilogue. In *In the company of others: Making community in the modern world*, ed C. Whitmyer, 251-56. New York: Jeremy P. Tarcher.

59. Okoro, K.N. (2011) Towards a new world and new humanity: Rabindranath Tagore's model. In *Conscious connectivity: Creating dignity in conversation*, ed M. Brenner, 255-77. Charleston, SC: Pan American.

60. Diessner, R. (2011). Beauty and the moral education. In *Conscious connectivity: Creating dignity in conversation*, ed M. Brenner, 278-316. Charleston, SC: Pan American.

61. Rust, M.J. (2008). Climate on the couch: Unconscious processes in relation to our environmental crisis. *Psychotherapy and Politics International, 6*(3), 157-70.

62. Gandhi, M. (2014). Quote. Retrieved March 24th 2014, from www.goodreads.com/quotes/24799.

63. Gandhi, M. (2014). Biography. Retrieved March 24th, from www.wikipedia.org/wiki/mahatma-gandhi.

64. Jacobs, A. (1997). *The element book of mystical verse.* Element: Shaftesbury.

65. Corbett, L. (1996). *The religious function of the psyche.* London: Routledge.

66. Collins, M. (2011). The Akashic field and archetypal occupations: Transforming human potential through doing and being. *World Futures,67*(7), 453-79.

67. Washburn, M. (2003). *Embodied spirituality in a sacred world.* Albany, NY: State University of New York Press.

68. Reardson, B. (2005). Cited in C, Partridge. *The re-enchantment of the west: Alternative spiritualities, sacralisation, popular culture, and occulture, volume 2.* London: T&T Clark International.

69. Elkins, D. (1996). I went in search for the meaning of life. *Journal of Humanistic Psychology, 36*(3), 103.

70. Schlitz, M.M. (2012). A path forward: Embracing our creative imagination. In *The new science and spirituality reader*, ed E. Laszlo & K.L Dennis,160-74. Rochester, VER: Inner Traditions.

71. Tacey, D. (2001). *Jung and the new age.* Hove. East Sussex: Brunner-Routledge.

72. Mindell, A. (2010). *Process mind: A users guide to connecting with the mind of god.* Wheaton, IL: Quest Books.

73. Zohar, D., & Marshall, I. (2000). *Spiritual intelligence: The ultimate intelligence,* London: Bloomsbury.

74. Kidder, A.M.S. (2009). *Etty Hillesum: Essential writings.* Maryknoll, NY: Orbis Books.

Chapter eleven

1. Collins, M. (2010). Spiritual intelligence: Evolving transpersonal potential towards ecological actualization for a sustainable future. *World Futures, 66,* 320-34.

2. Glenn, J.C., Gordon, T.J., & Florescu, E. (2008). *State of the future: Executive summary.* World Federation of United Nations Associations. Retrieved August 1st 2008, from www.millennium-project.org/millennium/issues.html.

3. Glenn, J.C., Gordon, T.J., & Florescu, E. (2011). *State of the future: Executive summary.* The millennium project: Global futures studies and research. Retrieved August 2nd 2011, from www.millennium-project.org/millennium/2011SOF.html.

4. Lean, G., & Owen, J. (2008). We've seen the future…and we may not be doomed. Independent on Sunday Investigation: The World View. *Independent on Sunday,* 13th July: 8-9.

5. Meadows, D.H., Meadows, D.L., & Randers, J. (1992). *Beyond the limits: Confronting global collapse – envisioning a sustainable future.* Postmills, VER: Chelsea Green Publishing Company.

6. Diamond, J. (2005). *Collapse: How societies choose to fail or survive.* London: Penguin Press.

7. Csikszentmihalyi, M. (1993). Activity and happiness: Toward a science of occupation. *Journal of Occupational Science, 1*(1), 38-42.

8. Collins, M. (2007). Engaging self-actualisation through occupational intelligence. *Journal of Occupational Science, 14*(2), 92-9.

9. Collins, M. (2010). Engaging transcendent actualisation through occupational intelligence. *Journal of Occupational Science 17*(3), 177-86.

10. Martin, J. (2006). *The meaning of the 21st century: A blueprint for ensuring our future.* Eden Project Books.

11. Goswami, A. (2000). *The visionary window: A quantum physicist's guide to enlightenment.* Wheation, IL: Quest Books, The Theosophical Publishing house.

12. Chopra, D. (2011). *The seven laws of super heroes.* London: Transworld Publishers.

13. Goerner, S. 2004. Creativity, consciousness, and the building of an integral world. In *The great adventure. Toward a fully human theory of evolution,* ed D. Loye, 153-180. Albany, NY: State University of New York Press.

14. Collins, M. (2011). The global crisis and holistic consciousness: How assertive action could lead to the creation of an improved future. In *Conscious connectivity: Creating dignity in conversation,* ed M. Brenner, 214-23. Charleston, SC: Pan American.

15. Collins, M. (2011). The Akashic field and archetypal occupations: Transforming human potential through doing and being. *World Futures,67*(7), 453-79.

16. MacPhail, E. (1998). *The evolution of consciousness.* Oxford: Oxford University Press.

17. Cattell, R (1973). *Abilities: Their structure, growth and action.* Boston: Haughton Mifflin.

18. Gardner, H. (1993). *Frames of mind.* London: Fontana Press, 2nd edition.

19. Gardner, H. (1999). *Intelligence reframed: Multiple intelligences for the 21st century.* New York: Basic Books.

20. Sternberg, R. (1985). *Beyond IQ: A triarchic theory of human intelligence.* London: Bloomsbury.

21. Sternberg, R. (2003). *Wisdom, intelligence, and creativity synthesized.* Cambridge: Cambridge University Press.

22. Anthony, M. (2003). Integrated intelligence: The future of intelligence? *Journal of Future Studies, 8*(2), 39-54.

23. Collins, M., & Linqvist, S. (2013). Interprofessional practice and rank dynamics: Evolving effective team collaboration through emotional, social, occupational, and spiritual intelligences. In *The changing roles of doctors,* eds P. Cavenagh, S.J. Leinster & S. Miles, 89-97. London: Radcliffe.

24. Sinetar, M. (1986). *Ordinary people as monks and mystics: Lifestyles for self-discovery.* New York: Paulist Press.

25. Elam, J. (2005). Soul's sanctuary: Mystical experiences as a way of knowing. In *Ways of knowing: Science and mysticism today,* ed C. Clarke, 50-66. Exeter: Imprint Academic.

26. Mindell, A. (1990). *Working on yourself alone: Inner dreambody work.* London: Arkana.

27. Clocksin, W. (1998). Artificial intelligence and human identity. In *Consciousness and human identity,* ed J. Cornwell, 101-21. Oxford: Oxford University Press.

28. Collins, M. (2001). Who is occupied? Consciousness, self-awareness and the process of human adaptation. *Journal of Occupational Science, 8*(1), 25-32.

29. Amlani, A. (1998). Internal events and archetypes. In *Transpersonal research methods for the social sciences: Honouring human experience,* eds W. Braud & R. Anderson, 179-84. Thousand Oaks, CA: Sage Publications.

30. Batey, B. (1993). My personal experience of the transcendent and its integration into my life. *The Academy of Religion and Psychical Research. Annual Conference Proceedings,* 16-18.

31. Grof, S. (2000). *Psychology of the future: Lessons from modern consciousness research.* Albany, NY: State University of New York Press.

32. Redfield, J., Murphy., & Timbers, S. (2002). *God and the evolving universe: The next step in personal evolution.* London: Bantam Books.

33. Daniels, M. (2005). *Shadow, self, spirit: Essays in transpersonal psychology.* Exeter: Imprint Academic.

34. Corbett, L (2007). *Psyche and the sacred: Spirituality beyond religion.* New Orleans: Spring Journal Books.

35. Mindell, A. (1996). Discovering the world in the individual and the world channel in psychotherapy. *Journal of Humanistic Psychology, 36*(3), 67-84.

36. Nelson, J. E. (1994). *Healing the split: Integrating spirit into our understanding of the mentally ill.* Albany, NY: State University of New York Press.

37. Kornfield, J. (1984). The smile of the Buddha: Paradigms in perspective. In *Ancient wisdom and modern science,* ed S. Grof, 94-109. Albany, NY: State University of New York Press.

38. Agosin, R., (1992). Cited in, R. Halligan. Dreamwork in ministry: Catching the numinous in a silver net. *Journal of Psychology and Christianity, 12*(2), 131-40.

39. Edelman, G.M., & Tononi, G. (2000). *Consciousness: How matter becomes imagination.* London: Penguin Books.

40. Anderson, R. (1998). Introduction. In *Transpersonal research methods for the social sciences: Honouring human experience,* eds W. Braud & R. Anderson, xix-xxxi. Thousand Oaks, CA: Sage Publications.

41. Maxwell, M., & Tschundin, V. (1990). *Seeing the invisible: Modern religious and other transcendent experiences.* London: Arkana.

42. Anthony, M. (2008). A personal view of the integrated society. *Journal of Future Studies, 13*(1), 87-112.

43. Anthony, M. (2008). The case for integrated intelligence. *World Futures, 64*(4), 233-57.

44. Tarnas, R. (2006). *Cosmos and psyche: Intimations of a new world view.* New York: Viking.

45. Collins, M. (2006). Unfolding spirituality: Working with and beyond definitions. *International Journal of Therapy and Rehabilitation, 13*(6), 254-8.

46. Vaughan, F. (2002). What is spiritual intelligence? *Journal of Humanistic Psychology, 42*(2): 16-33.

47. Emmons, R. (2000). Spirituality and intelligence: Problems and prospects. *International Journal for the Psychology of Religion, 10*(1), 57-64.

48. Zohar, D., & Marshall, I. (2000). *Spiritual intelligence: The ultimate intelligence,* London: Bloomsbury.

49. Sommer, F.S. 2003. Contribution in: Caplan M., Hartelius. G., Rardin. M. Contemporary viewpoints on transpersonal psychology. *Journal of Transpersonal Psychology 35*(2): 143-162.

50. Selman, V., Selman, R.C., Selman, J., Selman, S. 2005. Spiritual intelligence quotient. *College Teaching Methods & Styles Journal, 1*(3): 23-30.

51. Emmons, R. (2000). Is spirituality an intelligence? Motivation, cognition, and the psychology of ultimate concern. *International Journal for the Psychology of Religion, 10*(1), 3-26.

52. Bohm, D. (1980). *Wholeness and the implicate order.* London: Ark.

53. Zohar, D., & Marshall, I. (1994). *The quantum society: Mind, physics and a new social vision.* London: Flamingo.

54. Dossey, L. (1982). *Space, time and medicine.* Boston: Shambhala.

55. Battista, J.R. (1995). The holographic model, holistic paradigm, information theory and consciousness. In *The holographic paradigm*, ed K. Wilber, 143-52. Boston: Shambhala.

56. Mindell, A. (2000). *Quantum mind: The edge between physics and psychology.* Portland, OR: Lao Tse Press.

57. Wheeler, J. (1991). Cited in P, Davis., & J, Brown. *The ghost in the machine.* Cambridge: Cambridge University Press.

58. Talbot, M. (1991). *The holographic universe.* New York: Harper Collins.

59. Chopra, D. (2004). *The book of secrets.* London: Rider.

60. Laszlo, E. (2004). *Science and the Akashic field. An integral theory of everything.* Rochester, VER: Inner Traditions.

61. Laszlo, E (2009). *The Akashic experience: Science and the cosmic memory field.* Rochester, VER: Inner Traditions.

62. Laszlo, E. (2006). *The chaos point: The world at a crossroads.* London: Piatkus.

63. Laszlo, E. (2008). *Quantum shift in the global brain: How the new scientific reality can change our world.* Rochester, VER: Inner Traditions.

64. Laszlo, E. (2012). *The Akasha paradigm: Revolution in science, evolution in consciousness.* Printed in USA: Waterfront Press.

65. Collins, M. (2008). Spiritual emergency: Transpersonal, personal, and political dimensions. *Psychotherapy and Politics International, 6*(1), 3-16.

66. Von Franz, M.L. (1964). Science and the unconscious. In *Man and his symbols*, ed C.G. Jung, 304-10. London: Aldus Books.

67. Grof, S. (1985). *Beyond the brain: Birth, death and transcendence in psychotherapy.* Albany, NY: State University of New York Press.

68. Marx Hubbard, B. (2012). *Emergence: The shift from ego to essence.* San Francisco, CA: Hampton Roads.

69. Grof, S. (2006). *When the impossible happens: Adventures in non-ordinary realities.* Boulder, CO: Sounds True.

70. Grof, S. (2006). Ervin Laszlo's Akashic field and the dilemmas of modern consciousness research. *World Futures, 62*, 86-102.

71. Boucouvalas, M. (1999). Following the movement: From transpersonal psychology to a multi-disciplinary transpersonal orientation. *Journal of Transpersonal Psychology, 31*(3), 27-39.

72. Russell, P. (2009). *Waking up in time: Our future evolution and the meaning of now.* San Rafael, CA: Origin Press.

73. Vaughan, F. (2003). Contribution in: Caplan M, Hartelius G, Rardin MA. Contemporary viewpoints on transpersonal psychology. *Journal of Transpersonal Psychology, 35*(2): 143-162.

74. Taylor, S. (2005). The sources of higher states of consciousness. *International Journal of Transpersonal Studies, 24*, 48-60.

75. Collins, M. (2008). Transpersonal identity and human occupation. *British Journal of Occupational Therapy, 71*(12), 549-52.

76. Hamilton, R. (1990). *Earthdream: The marriage of reason and intuition.* Bideford: Green Books.

77. Skolimowski, H. (1993). *A sacred place to dwell: Living with reverence upon the earth.* Rockport, MA: Element.

78. Myss, C. (2007). *Entering the castle: An inner path to god and your soul.* New York: Free Press.
79. Goleman, D. (2009). *Ecological intelligence: How knowing the hidden impacts of what we buy can change everything.* New York: Broadway Books.
80. Shinoda Bolen, J. (2007). *Close to the bone: Life-threatening illness as a soul journey.* San Francisco, CA: Conari Press.
81. Tacey, D. (2012). *The Jung reader.* London: Routledge.
82. Samuels, A. (1998). 'And if not now, when?' Spirituality, psychotherapy, politics. *Psychodynamic Practice, 4*(30, 349-63.

Chapter twelve

1. Freud, S. (1997). *The interpretation of dreams.* Ware, Herts: Wordsworth Classics.
2. Jung, C.G. (1959). *Collected works, vol 9, part 1: The archetypes and the collective unconscious,* translated R.F.C. Hull. London: Routledge and Kegan Paul Ltd.
3. Hobson, J.A. (2002). *Dreaming: an introduction to the science of sleep.* Oxford: Oxford University Press.
4. Frankl, V. (1962). *Man's search for meaning: An introduction to logotherapy.* London: Hodder and Stoughton.
5. Shepherd, L.J. (1993). *Lifting the veil: The feminine face of science.* Boston: Shambhala.
6. Meier, C.A. (1989). *Healing dream and ritual: Ancient incubation and modern psychotherapy.* Einsiedeln, Switzerland: Daimon Verlag.
7. Collins, M. (2013). Asklepian dreaming and the spirit of transformational healing: Linking the placebo response to therapeutic uses of self. *Journal of Religion and Health, 52,* 32-45.
8. Jung, C.G. (1991). *Dreams.* London: Ark.
9. Jung, C.G. (1983). *Memories, dreams, reflections.* London: Flamingo.
10. Feinstein, D. (1997). Personal mythology and psychotherapy: Myth making in psychotherapy and spiritual development. *American Journal of Orthopsychiatry, 64*(4), 508-21.
11. Fox, M. (1983). *Meditations with Meister Eckhart.* Santa Fe, New Mexico: Bear & Company.
12. Moore, T. (1996). *The re-enchantment of everyday life.* New York: Harper Collins.
13. Tick, E. (2001). *The practice of dream healing: Bringing ancient Greek mysteries in modern medicine.* Wheaton, IL: Quest Books.
14. Benson, H., & Stark, M. (1996). *Timeless healing: The power and biology of belief.* New York: Scribner.
15. Elkins, D.N. (1998). *Beyond religion: A personal program for building a spiritual life outside the walls of traditional religion.* Wheaton, IL: Quest Books, The Theosophical Publishing House.
16. Huxley, A. (1969). *The perennial philosophy.* London: Chatto & Windus.
17. Tacey, D. (2012). *The Jung reader.* London: Routledge.
18. Zukov, G. (2000). *Soul stories.* London: Simon & Schuster.
19. Collins, M. (2006). Taking a lead on stress: Rank and relationship awareness in the NHS. *Journal of Nursing Management, 14,* 310-17.
20. Skolimowski, H. (1993). A *sacred place to dwell: Living with reverence upon the earth.* Rockport, MA: Element.
21. Collins, M. (2007) Healing and the soul: Finding the future in the past. *Spirituality and Health International, 8*(1), 301-12.
22. Collins, M. (2011). The global crisis and holistic consciousness: How assertive action could lead to the creation of an improved future. In *Conscious connectivity: Creating dignity in conversation,* ed M. Brenner, 214-23. Charleston, SC: Pan American.
23. Kee, H.C. (1982). Self-definition in the Asclepius cult: In *Jewish and Christian self-definition: Self-definition in the Graeco-Roman world, volume 3,* eds B.F. Meyer & E.P. Sanders, 118-36. London: SCM Press.
24. Wickkiser, B.L. (2008). *Asklepios, medicine and the politics of healing in fifth-century Greece: Between craft and art.* Baltimore, ML: The John Hopkins University Press.
25. Askitopoulou, H., Konsolaki, E., Ramoutsaki, I.A., & Anastassaki, M. (2002). Surgical cures under sleep inductions in the Asclepieion of Epidauros. *International Congress Series, 242,* 11-17.
26. Horstmanshoff, H.F.G. (2004). Asclepius and temple medicine in Aelius Aristides' sacred tales. In *Magic and rationality in ancient near eastern and Graeco-Roman medicine,* ed's H.F.G Horstmanshoff & M.Stol, 325-41. Leiden: Brill.
27. Hart, G.D. (2000). *Asclepius: The god of medicine.* London: The Royal Society of Medicine Press.
28. Kerényi, K. (1956). *Asklepios: Archetypal existence of the physician's existence,* translated R. Manheim. New York: Pantheon Books.
29. Kirmayer, L.T. (2003). Asklepian dreams: The ethos of the wounded healer in the clinical encounter. *Transcultural Psychiatry, 40*(2), 248-77.
30. Tick, E. (2004). On Asklepios, dream healing, and talking with the dead. *Alternative Therapies, 10*(1), 65-72.
31. Maxwell, M., & Tschundin, V. (1990). *Seeing the invisible: Modern religious and other transcendent experiences.* London: Arkana.
32. Wyld, H. C. (1961). *Universal English dictionary.* London: The Waverley Book Company Limited.
33. Mindell, A. (2005). *The dreaming source of creativity.* Portland, OR: Lao Tse Press.
34. Jaenke, K. (2004). Ode to the intelligence of dreams. *ReVision, 27*(1): 2-9.
35. Spark Jones, L. (2001). Not knowing: Ancient mystical approach, postmodern psychotherapeutic practice. *Journal of Process Oriented Psychology 8*(1),17-26.
36. Kaplan, C. (2002). *Dreams are letters from the soul: Discover the connections between your dreams and your spiritual life.* New York: Harmony Books.

37. Dossey, L. (1999). *Dreams and healing: Reclaiming a lost tradition.* Alternative Therapies, 5(6): 12-17.

38. Schlamm, L. (2007). C.G. Jung and numinous experience: Between the known and the unknown. *European Journal of Psychotherapy and Counselling, 9*(4), 403-14.

39. Miller, J. (2004). *The transcendent function: Jung's model of psychological growth through dialogue with the unconscious.* Albany, NY: State University of New York Press.

40. Collins, M. (2004). Dreaming and occupation. *British Journal of Occupational Therapy, 67*(2), 96-8.

41. Jung, C.G. (1940). *The integration of the personality,* translated S.M. Dell. London: Kegan Paul, Trench, Trubner & Co.

42. Hillman, J. (1996). *The soul's code: In search of character and calling.* London: Bantam Books.

43. Hillman, J. (1989). *A blue fire.* New York: Harper Collins Publishers.

44. Bussey, M. (2006). Critical spirituality: Towards a revitalised humanity. *Journal of Future Studies,10*(4), 39-44.

45. Hefner, P. (2002). Technology and human becoming. *Zygon, 37*(3): 655-665.

46. Watts, A. (1995). *The meaning of happiness: The quest for freedom of the spirit in modern psychology and the wisdom of the east.* London: Ryder & Company.

47. Bulkley, K. (1991). The quest for transformative experience: Dreams and environmental ethics. *Environmental Ethics, 13,* 151-63.

48. Mindell, A. (2000). *Quantum mind: The edge between physics and psychology.* Portland, OR: Lao Tse Press.

49. Collins, M. (2011). The Akashic field and archetypal occupations: Transforming human potential through doing and being. *World Futures,67*(7), 453-79.

50. Nonaka, T. (2013). If you can dream it, you can do it. In *Dawn of the Akashic age: New consciousness, quantum resonance, and the future of the world,* eds E. Laszlo & K.L. Dennis, 191-94Rochester, VER: Inner Traditions.

51. Collins, M. (2007). Spirituality and the shadow: Reflection and the therapeutic use of self. *British Journal of Occupational Therapy, 70*(2), 88-90.

52. Varela, F.J., & Shear, J. (1999). First person methodologies: What, why, how? In *The view from within,* eds F.J. Varela & J. Shear, 1-4. Exeter: Imprint Academic.

Chapter thirteen

1. Collins, M. (2008). Spiritual emergency: Transpersonal, personal, and political dimensions. *Psychotherapy and Politics International, 6*(1), 3-16.

2. Gyatso, T. (1985). *Opening the eye of new awareness.* Boston, MA: Wisdom Publications.

3. Hanh, T. N. (1988). *The heart of understanding: Commentaries on the pranaparamita heart sutra.* Berkley, CA: Parallax Press.

4. Hanh, T. N. (1992). *The diamond that cuts through illusion: Commentaries on the pranaparamita diamond sutra.* Berkley, CA: Parallax Press.

5. Hopkins, J. (1987). *Emptiness yoga: The middle way consequence school.* Ithaca, NY: Snow Lion publications.

6. Wilber, K. (2000). *Sex, ecology, spirituality: The spirit of evolution.* Boston: Shambhala.

7. Feng, G.F., & English, J. (1973). *Lao Tsu: Tao Te Ching.* London: Wildwood Press.

8. Watts, A. (1995/2003). *Become what you are.* Boston: Shambhala.

9. Collins, M. (1998). Occupational therapy and spirituality: Reflecting on quality of experience in therapeutic interventions. *British Journal of Occupational Therapy, 61*(6), 280-4.

10. Collins, M. (2001). Who is occupied? Consciousness, self-awareness and the process of human adaptation. *Journal of Occupational Science, 8*(1), 25-32.

11. Khantipalo, B. (1960). *Sixty songs of Milarepa,* translated, Garma C.C. Chang. New York: University Books.

12. Rinpoche, S. (1992). *The Tibetan book of living and dying.* London: Random House.

13. Elam, J. (2005). Soul's sanctuary: Mystical experiences as a way of knowing. In *Ways of knowing: Science and mysticism today,* ed C. Clarke, 50-66. Exeter: Imprint Academic.

14. Eliade, M. (1960). *Myths, dreams and mysteries.* London: The Fontana Library of Theology and Philosophy.

15. Sannella, L. (1989). Kundalini: Classical and clinical. In *Spiritual emergency: When personal transformation becomes a crisis,* eds S. Grof & C. Grof, 99-108. Los Angeles: Jeremy P. Tarcher.

16. Sannella, L. (1992). *The Kundalini experience: Psychosis or transcendence?* Lower Lake, CA: Integral Publishing.

17. Scotton, B. (1996b). The phenomenology and treatment of Kundalini. In *Textbook of transpersonal psychiatry and psychology,* eds B.W Scotton, A.B. Chinen & J.R. Battista, 261-70. New York: Basic Books.

18. Tart, C. (1997). Editor's introduction. In *Body, mind, spirit: Exploring the parapsychology of spirituality,* ed C. Tart, 21-31. Charlottesville, VA: Hampton Roads Publishing Company.

19. Tart, C. (2009). *The end of materialism: How evidence of the paranormal is bringing science and spirit together.* Oakland, CA: New Harbinger Publications.

20. Braud, W. (2001). *Non-ordinary and transcendent experiences: Transpersonal aspects of consciousness.* Retrieved July 2nd 2007, from www.integral-inquiry.com/docs/649/nonordinary.pdf.

21. Grof, S., & Grof, C. (1989). *Spiritual emergency: When personal transformation becomes a crisis.* Los Angeles: Jeremy P. Tarcher.

22. Erikson, E.H. (1996). The Galilean sayings and the sense of I. *Psychoanalysis and Contemporary Thought, 19*(2), 291-337.

23. Jung, C. G. (1987). Cited in A. Samuels., B. Shorter., & F. Plaut. *A critical dictionary of Jungian analysis*. London: Routledge, Kegan and Paul.
24. Washburn, M. (1994). *Transpersonal psychology in psychoanalytic perspective*. Albany, NY. State University of New York Press.
25. Washburn, M. (1995). *The ego and the dynamic ground: A transpersonal theory of human development*. Albany, NY. State University of New York Press.
26. Mindell, A. (1990). *Working on yourself alone: Inner dreambody work*. London: Arkana.
27. Williams, D.E. (1981). *Border crossings: A psychological perspective on Carlos Castaneda's path of knowledge*. Toronto: Inner City Books.
28. Bache, C.M. (2000). *Dark night, early dawn: Steps to a deep ecology of mind*. Albany, NY: State University of New York Press.
29. Mindell, A. (1988). *City shadows: Psychological interventions in psychiatry*. London: Arkana.
30. Perry, J.W. (1974). *The far side of madness*. Dallas, TEX: Spring Publications.
31. Edinger, E. (1984). *The creation of consciousness: Jung's myth for modern man*. Toronto: Inner City Books.
32. Lancaster, B.L. (2002). In defence of the transcendent. *Transpersonal Psychology Review*, 6(1), 42-51.
33. Krishnamurti, J. (1969). *Freedom from the known*. London: Victor Gollancz Ltd.
34. Wilber, K. (2004). *The simple feeling of being: Embracing your true nature*. Boston: Shambhala.
35. Brett, C. (2010). Transformative crises. In *Psychosis and spirituality: Consolidating the new paradigm*, ed I. Clarke, 155-74. Chichester: Wiley-Blackwell, 2nd edition.
36. Grof, C. (1993). *The thirst for wholeness: Attachment, addiction, and the spiritual path*. New York: Harper Collins.
37. Clements, J. (2004). Organic inquiry: Toward research in partnership with spirit. *Journal of Transpersonal Psychology, 36*(1), 26-49.
38. Shalit, E. (2002). *The complex: Path of transformation from ego to archetype*. Toronto: Inner City Books.
39. Hendrix, H. (1991). Creating the false self. In *Meeting the shadow: The hidden power of the dark side of human nature*, eds C. Zweig & J. Abrams, 49-52. New York: Jeremy P. Tarcher/Perigee Books.
40. Collins, M. (2007). Spirituality and the shadow: Reflection and the therapeutic use of self. *British Journal of Occupational Therapy, 70*(2), 88-90.
41. Jung, C. G. (1995). In M. Stein, ed. *Jung on evil*. London: Routledge.
42. Hollis, J. (2003). *In this journey we call life: Living the questions*. Toronto: Inner City Books.
43. Bragdon, E. (1990). *The call of spiritual emergency: From personal crisis to personal transformation*. San Francisco: Harper Row Publishers.

Chapter fourteen
1. Eliade, M. (1954). *The Myth of the eternal return*, translated W.R. Trask. New York: Bollingen Foundation/Pantheon Books.
2. Eliade, M. (1958). *Rites and symbols of initiation: The mysteries of birth and rebirth*, translated W.R. Trask. New York: Harper Torchbooks.
3. Hollis, J. (2001). *Creating a life: Finding your individual path*. Toronto: Inner City Books.
4. Hollis, J (1996). *Swamplands of the soul: New life in dismal places*. Toronto: Inner City Books.
5. Bragdon, E. (1990). *The call of spiritual emergency: From personal crisis to personal transformation*. San Francisco: Harper Row Publishers.
6. Menken, D. (2001). *Speak out: Talking about love, sex and eternity*. Tempe, AR: New Falcon Publications.
7. Collins, M. (2008). Spiritual emergency: Transpersonal, personal, and political dimensions. *Psychotherapy and Politics International, 6*(1), 3-16.
8. de Waard, F. (2010). *Spiritual crisis: Varieties and perspectives of a transpersonal phenomenon*. Exeter: Academic Imprint.
9. Assagioli, R. (1973). *The act of will: A guide to self-actualization and self-realization*. Wellingborough: Turnstone Press.
10. Skolimowski, H. (1993). *A sacred place to dwell: Living with reverence upon the earth*. Rockport, MA: Element.
11. Diamond, J., & Spark Jones, L. (2004). *A path made by walking: Process work in practice*. Portland, OR: Lao Tse Press.
12. Blau, E. (1995). *Krishnamurti: 100 years*. New York: Stewart, Tabori & Chang.
13. Gilbert, R.A. (1991). *Mysticism*. Shaftesbury: Element.
14. Dass, R. (1970). *Doing your own being*. London: Neville Spearman.
15. Marx Hubbard, B. (2012). *Emergence: The shift from ego to essence*. San Francisco, CA: Hampton Roads.
16. Maxwell, M., & Tschundin, V. (1990). *Seeing the invisible: Modern religious and other transcendent experiences*. London: Arkana.
17. Larsen, S. (1976/1988). *The shaman's doorway: Opening imagination to power and myth*. New York: Station Hill Press.
18. Pringle, H. (2013). The origins of creativity. *Scientific American, 308*(3), 22-9.
19. Collins, M., Harrison, D., Mason, R., & Lowden, A. (2011). Innovation and creativity: Exploring human occupation and professional development in student education. *British Journal of Occupational Therapy, 74*(6), 304-8.
20. Bohm, D. (1996). *On creativity*. London: Routledge.
21. Fox, M. (2002). *Creativity: Where the divine and the human meet*. New York: Jeremy P. Tarcher.
22. Robinson, K. (2009). *The element: How finding your passion changes everything*. London: Penguin.

23. May, R. (1976). *The courage to create*. London: Collins.
24. Mickey, S., & Carefore, K. (2012). Planetary love: Ecofeminist perspectives on globalization. *World Futures, 68*(2), 122-31.
25. Mindell, A. (2005). *The dreaming source of creativity*. Portland, OR: Lao Tse Press.
26. Sternberg, R. (2003). *Wisdom, intelligence, and creativity synthesized*. Cambridge: Cambridge University Press.
27. Csikszentmihalyi, M. (1996). *Creativity: Flow and the psychology of discovery and invention*. New York: Harper Collins.
28. Zukov, G. (2000). *Soul stories*. London: Simon & Schuster.
29. Haberman, D. (2012). Tears in the forest. *World Futures, 68*(2), 132-43.
30. Campbell, J. (1994). The hero as warrior. In *The awakened warrior: Living with courage, compassion and discipline*, ed R. Fields, 64-9. New York: Jeremy P. Tarcher/Putnam Books.
31. Collins, M. (2010). Engaging transcendent actualisation through occupational intelligence. *Journal of Occupational Science 17*(3), 177-86.
32. Woodhouse, P. (2009). *Etty Hillesum: A life transformed*. London: Continuum.
33. Kidder, A.M.S. (2009). *Etty Hillesum: Essential writings*. Maryknoll, NY: Orbis Books.
34. Chittister, J.D. (2003). *Scarred by struggle, transformed by hope*. Grand Rapids, MICH: William B. Eerdmans Publishing Company.
35. Macy, J. (2013). The greening of the self. In *Spiritual ecology: The cry of the earth*, ed L. Vaughan-Lee, 145-56.Point Reyes, CA: The Golden Sufi Center.
36. Whiteford, G. (2000). Occupational deprivation: Global challenges in the new millennium. *British Journal of Occupational Therapy, 63*(5), 200-4.
37. Whiteford, G. (2011). From occupational deprivation to social inclusion: Retrospective insights. *British Journal of Occupational Therapy, 74*(12), 545.
38. Townsend, E., & Wilcock, A. (2004). Occupational justice and client-centred practice: A dialogue in progress. *Canadian Journal of Occupational Therapy, 63*(5), 200-4.

Afterword

1. Mindell, A (1989). *The year 1: Global process work*. London: Arkana.
2. Robinson, K. (2009). *The element: How finding your passion changes everything*. London: Penguin.
3. Remen, R. (1996). *Kitchen table wisdom: Stories that heal*. New York: Riverhead Books.
4. Gandhi, M. (2014). Quote. Retrieved March 24th 2014, from www.brainyquote.com

Permissions

Every effort has been made to correctly attribute sources used from my previous publications. I am very thankful to the publishers below for allowing me to adapt the work from my previous publications. Also, many thanks for permission from publishers for allowing me to use the quotes that are listed below. In the case of any errors or omissions the author and publisher will make any corrections in future editions if notified.

Foreword by the Author: The dream quotation. Published with kind permission from Permanent Publications. The dream was published originally in Harland, M., & Keepin, W. (2012). Introduction. In *Song of the Earth: A synthesis of the scientific and spiritual worldviews*, eds M. Harland & W. Keepin, xi-xiv. East Meon, Hants: Permanent Publications.

Chapter two: "Life crisis and a dream of winning the lottery." Published with kind permission from the College of Occupational Therapists: Collins, M. (2004). Dreaming and occupation. *British Journal of Occupational Therapy, 67*(2), 96-8.

Chapter three: "The hidden healer." Published with kind permission from the *International Journal of Therapy and Rehabilitation*. Collins, M. (2006). Unfolding spirituality: Working with and beyond definitions. *International Journal of Therapy and Rehabilitation, 13*(6), 254-8.

Chapter four: "The numinous and human potential." Published with kind permission from Psychotherapy and Politics International. John Wiley & Sons Ltd, publishers. Collins, M. (2008). Politics and the numinous: Evolution, spiritual emergency, and the re-emergence of transpersonal consciousness. *Psychotherapy and Politics International, 6*(3), 198-211.

Chapter four: "Opening to the universe." Published with kind permission from the College of Occupational Therapists: Collins, M. (2007). Spiritual emergency and occupational identity: A transpersonal perspective. *British Journal of Occupational Therapy, 70*(12), 504-12.

Chapter six: "Thoughts of death, doing and transformation." Published with kind permission from the College of Occupational Therapists: Collins, M. (1998). Occupational therapy and spirituality: Reflecting on quality of experience in therapeutic interventions. *British Journal of Occupational Therapy, 61*(6), 280-4.

Chapter six: "Four propositions for transpersonal occupations." Published with kind permission from the College of Occupational Therapists: Collins, M. (2008). Transpersonal identity and human occupation. *British Journal of Occupational Therapy, 71*(12), 549-52.

Chapter seven: "Crisis and the spirit of transformation." Published with kind permission from the College of Occupational Therapists: Collins, M. (2008). Transpersonal identity and human occupation. *British Journal of Occupational Therapy*, *71*(12), 549-52.

Chapter seven: "Trauma, transitions and transformations." Reflections on Stanislav Grof's work with 'Karen'. Published with kind permission from the College of Occupational Therapists: Collins, M. (2007). Spiritual emergency and occupational identity: A transpersonal perspective. *British Journal of Occupational Therapy*, *70*(12), 504-12.

Chapter eight: "Six dimensions for collective transformation." Published with kind permission from *Psychotherapy and Politics International*. John Wiley & Sons Ltd, publishers. Collins, M., Hughes, W., & Samuels, A. (2010). The politics of transformation in the global crisis: How spiritual emergencies may be reflecting an enantiodromia in modern consciousness. *Psychotherapy and Politics International*, *8*(2), 162-176.

Chapter eight: "Archetypal occupations and the alchemy of transformation." Published with kind permission from *World Futures: The Journal of General Evolution*. Taylor & Francis publishers. Collins, M. (2011). The Akashic Field and Archetypal Occupations: Transforming Human Potential through Doing and Being. *World Futures, 67*(7), 453-79.

Chapter eleven: "The evolution of 21st-century intelligences." Published with kind permission from *World Futures: The Journal of General Evolution*. Taylor & Francis publishers. Collins, M. (2010). Spiritual intelligence: Evolving transpersonal potential towards ecological actualization for a sustainable future. *World Futures, 66*, 320-34.

Chapter eleven: "Thresholds to the mystery." Published with kind permission from the *Journal of Occupational Science*. Taylor & Francis publishers. Collins, M. (2010). Engaging transcendent actualization through occupational intelligence. *Journal of Occupational Science*, *17*(3), 177-86.

Chapter twelve: "Dreaming, Asklepios and the archetype of soulful transformation." Published with kind permission from the *Journal of Religion and Health*. Springer Science+Business Media B.V. Collins, M. (2013). Asklepian dreaming and the spirit of transformational healing: Linking the placebo response to therapeutic uses of self. *Journal of Religion and Health, 52*, 32-45.

Chapter twelve: "A dream of facing a dinosaur." Published with kind permission from the College of Occupational Therapists: Collins, M. (2004). Dreaming and occupation. *British Journal of Occupational Therapy, 67*(2), 96-8.

Chapter thirteen: "An autobiography of crisis and transformation." Published with kind permission from *Psychotherapy and Politics International*. John Wiley & Sons Ltd, publishers. Collins, M. (2008). Spiritual emergency: Transpersonal, personal, and political dimensions. *Psychotherapy and Politics International, 6*(1), 3-16.

Useful websites

As well as the extensive reading list in the reference section, these websites may be helpful.

www.spiritualcrisisnetwork.org.uk A very helpful UK-based website that provides important information about spiritual emergency. See also www.in-case-of-spiritual-emergency.blogspot.com

www.iapop.com A very useful list of international practitioners of process-oriented psychology as formulated by Arnold Mindell and his colleagues (process work). The process work paradigm is an excellent approach that uses creative ways of promoting awareness and integrating the wisdom found in altered and extreme states of consciousness, as well as body symptoms and conflicts.

www.epiczoetic.co.uk The author's website, which offers services (transpersonal coaching) for individuals, groups and organisations seeking to engage their transformative potential.

www.rcpsych.ac.uk/spirit The Royal College of Psychiatrists' interest group on spirituality and psychiatry. The website includes information about spiritual emergency.

www.eurotas.org A website representing a wide range of European transpersonal practitioners.

www.zangmoalexander.co.uk Connecting to the work of Zangmo Alexander whose transformative journey is represented in chapter 10.

Index

Enjoyed this book?

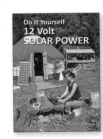

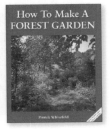

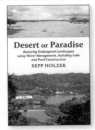

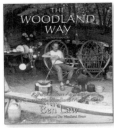

SIGN UP TO THE PERMANENT PUBLICATIONS ENEWSLETTER
TO RECEIVE NEWS OF NEW TITLES AND SPECIAL OFFERS:

www.permanentpublications.co.uk